Advance Praise for

Return to the Heart of God

"Robert Perry beautifully illuminates the principles of *A Course in Miracles*. I highly recommend it."
— MARIANNE WILLIAMSON, AUTHOR OF *A RETURN TO LOVE*

"Holy Scriptures tell us that in all our getting we should get wisdom. *Return to the Heart of God* is a phenomenal source of wisdom. Robert Perry has done a masterful job of presenting the true essence, the heart and soul, of *A Course in Miracles* in a way that offers hope and healing. And, he has done it with compassionate wisdom. This book is a service to the planet. Whether you are a student of the Course or someone who has never read it, if wisdom is what you seek, you are guaranteed to find it in the heart of God."
— IYANLA VANZANT, FOUNDER OF INNER VISIONS INSTITUTE FOR SPIRITUAL DEVELOPMENT, AUTHOR OF *LIVING THROUGH THE MEANTIME: LEARNING TO BREAK THE PATTERNS OF THE PAST AND BEGIN THE HEALING PROCESS*

"*Return to the Heart of God* is a profound meditation on *A Course in Miracles*, probably the greatest revealed Scripture of the twentieth century and, as I see it, an updating of Jesus' message in contemporary terms. Perry, who has studied and prayed over the Course for twenty-five years, leads us through many of the Course's key teachings with intelligence, deep understanding, and great compassion for the profound spiritual confusion that afflicts most of the world in the first decade of the twenty-first century. I recommend the book to all who truly desire to return to the heart of God."
— JIM MARION, AUTHOR OF *PUTTING ON THE MIND OF CHRIST*

D1383201

"Imagine taking all the brilliant and complex wisdom of *A Course in Miracles* and making it easy to read, understand, and even apply to your spouse—that's what Robert Perry offers us. In *Return to the Heart of God*, he is so clear, I found myself hungry to read as fast as I could and understand even more of *A Course in Miracles*. Next time you're in the desert of not understanding how to love, forgive, or experience a miracle, pick up this book and drink from the glass of pure water that Robert Perry provides."
— TAMA J. KIEVES, *A COURSE IN MIRACLES* TEACHER AND COACH,
    FOUNDER OF AWAKENING ARTISTRY, AND BESTSELLING AUTHOR OF
    THIS TIME I DANCE! CREATING THE WORK YOU LOVE

"I think of Robert Perry not only as a teacher, but as a teacher of teachers as well. In reading his words in *Return to the Heart of God*, you too will breathe in the inner peace which is the goal *A Course in Miracles* leads us to. It has softened my heart and calmed my mind once again by making the sometimes seemingly complex concepts of the Course simple and easy to access for the beginning and the advanced student alike. And if you've thought the Course is too daunting for you to understand, this book will gently walk you beyond those thoughts."
— JACOB GLASS, AUTHOR OF *INVOCATIONS: CALLING FORTH THE LIGHT THAT HEALS*

"Robert Perry is a gifted scholar and teacher who has dedicated himself to making the teachings of *A Course in Miracles* not only accessible but, more importantly, practical and applicable to daily life. Both those who are new to the Course and those who have worked with it for years can benefit greatly from his insights and perspectives."
— DIANE BERKE, AUTHOR OF *LOVE ALWAYS ANSWERS: WALKING THE PATH OF 'A COURSE IN MIRACLES'*

Return to the Heart of God

Other Books by Robert Perry:

Path of Light: Stepping into Peace with *A Course in Miracles*
An Introduction to *A Course in Miracles*
Relationships as a Spiritual Journey: From Specialness to Holiness
Guidance: Living the Inspired Life
Glossary of Terms from *A Course in Miracles*: Nearly 200 Definitions
    to Help You Take an Active Role in Your Study of the Course
Reality and Illusion: An Overview of Course Metaphysics
The Elder Brother: Jesus in *A Course in Miracles*
Seeing the Face of Christ in all our Brothers
The Workbook as a Spiritual Practice
Shrouded Vaults of the Mind

By Robert Perry and Allen Watson:

How to Bring *A Course in Miracles* to Life: A Complete, Easy-to-use
    Guide to Discovering the Meaning of the Course for Yourself
Let Me Remember You: God in *A Course in Miracles*
The Answer Is a Miracle
The Certainty of Salvation
A Workbook Companion Volumes I and II

By Robert Perry, Allen Watson & Greg Mackie:

One Course, Two Visions: A Comparison of the Teachings of the
    Circle of Atonement and Ken Wapnick on *A Course in Miracles*

Return to the Heart of God

The Practical Philosophy of
A Course in Miracles

Robert Perry

CIRCLE PUBLISHING

Published by Circle Publishing
A division of The Circle of Atonement Teaching and Healing Center
P.O. Box 4238 • West Sedona, AZ 86340
(928) 282-0790 • Fax: (928) 282-0523
E-mail: info@circleofa.org • Website: www.circleofa.org

Cover design by George Foster; www.fostercovers.com
Design and layout by Phillips Associates UK Ltd
Printed in the USA

ISBN-13: 978-1-886602-27-4
ISBN-10: 1-886602-27-1

Library of Congress Cataloging-in-Publication Data

Perry, Robert, 1960-
   Return to the heart of God : the practical philosophy of A course in miracles / Robert Perry.
      p. cm.
   Includes bibliographical references and index.
   ISBN-13: 978-1-886602-27-4
   ISBN-10: 1-886602-27-1
   1. Course in miracles. I. Title.

   BP605.C68P48 2006
   299'.93--dc22

2006021837

Return to the Heart of God

We bring glad tidings to the Son of God,

who thought he suffered.

Now is he redeemed.

And as he sees the gate of Heaven

stand open before him,

he will enter in and

disappear into the Heart of God.

Workbook Part II, Section 14: "What am I?"

Contents

Contents

Contents

Contents

Contents

Contents

Introduction

In 1976 a unique book appeared on the contemporary spiritual scene. "Appeared" is an apt word in view of the unusual way it came into being. Its words, along with the idea to write it, came from an inner voice, which dictated the material to a reluctant "scribe." Its original thought system has the appearance not of depending on prior traditions and discoveries, but of appearing fully formed out of nowhere. Even the publishing of it came not from any plan to widely disseminate it, but from the serendipitous pressure of events. The "guilty secret" of two academic psychologists, it finally came out of their closet in photocopied form. Once out, it generated a wave of enthusiasm and demand that made publishing it the natural thing to do.

When this book finally landed on the public stage, its strange journey continued. Large numbers of people spontaneously embraced it. Groups formed to study it. Centers came into being to serve its students. Additional books came out based on it. Some became bestsellers, enabling its principles to reach millions of people. At this time, thirty years later, there are over a million and a half copies in print, with a dozen translations currently available and more in process. Over two thousand study groups meet worldwide. And thousands of people, perhaps tens of thousands, consider it their path to God. According to a book on its history, it has become "one of the most popular and perplexing phenomena of contemporary spirituality."[1]

I first discovered *A Course in Miracles* in the fall of 1980. I learned about it from an article in *Psychology Today* mockingly titled "The Gospel According to Helen." From it, I learned that a psychologist at Columbia University named Helen Schucman had taken dictation from an inner voice, resulting in a three-volume book called *A Course in Miracles*. The article referred to the Course as a kind of Christian Vedanta, blending elements from Christianity with Eastern mysticism, as well as modern psychology.

I thought that this sounded right up my alley, given that I was into mysticism as well as channeled teachings. And when I finally got the Course, some months later, that thought was confirmed. It slowly earned a place as one of my many treasured spiritual teachings. Initially, I was taken in by the beauty of the language. Certain passages lifted and transported me. I eventually gathered these together for an audio tape produced by Miracle Distribution Center in 1985 entitled *The Forgotten Song*. I was also struck by the Course's practical efficacy. When I experienced an interpersonal conflict, I would turn to the Course to help me see things differently, something at which it was very good.

It was not long before I could also tell there was an intellectual system embedded in its words. *A Course in Miracles* wasn't a loose stream of inspirational ideas that meandered here and there. Rather, the ideas were connected in very definite ways, as definite as the parts of a machine, and both the ideas and connections between them remained consistent throughout. The more I read, the more I could sense a vast network of ideas looming behind the Course's poetic presentation. Having an innate love for systems of ideas, this really hooked me. At this point in my life, my ambition was to be a professional philosopher and I was actively engaged in building my own system. I couldn't resist trying to tease out the system that I sensed in the Course.

In 1985, I was asked to begin teaching at Miracle Distribution Center, and I spent months in preparation, poring through the Course, compiling notes, all in the hopes of grasping this system. However, I could never quite arrive at a final understanding. The same thing happened about a year later. I was asked to write an introductory booklet for Miracle Distribution Center, entitled *An Introduction to 'A Course in Miracles.'* I spent a year studying the Course further, testing out different ways of summarizing its teaching. A prominent teacher who read the end result asked why I was presenting the Course in a new way—why reinvent the wheel? My whole conviction, however, was that this wheel had not yet been invented.

This search for the Course's system developed into an urge that could not be satisfied. Each time I was called on to present an overview of the Course, I would try out a different way to present the overall system. Each time, I came away dissatisfied. In the meantime, I was writing up research papers in my attempt to crack this nut, as well as sharing new insights with the weekly classes I was conducting.

This was an intellectual issue for me, but also a very practical one. The practice of the Course primarily amounts to applying its teaching to specific persons, situations, and events. Thus, the more deeply one understands the teaching, the more powerful the practice becomes. This contributes to an understandable need to settle on a simple account of what the Course is saying. With this simple account in hand, we could quickly apply the Course to everything that crosses our path. However, when I went to access my understanding of the teaching, instead of some neat catchphrase what I found was a garage full of parts, some assembled, some lying by themselves. Further, these parts were spontaneously organizing and reorganizing themselves into ever-new shapes. This was not exactly the simple basis for practice that I was looking for.

The need I was feeling for that simple, concise account of the Course's teaching is the need that every Course student feels. The Course does not present itself in a systematic way. You never get the fundamentals explained to you in a clear, step-by-step fashion. The terms are never defined; they are simply used, leaving you to figure out their meaning based on context. Consequently, when you begin reading at page 1, you feel as if you have started halfway through the book. You can't help but suspect you have missed some foundational explanation that would make it all clear. You can easily feel that you are groping about in a half-lit room, a feeling which often persists for twelve hundred pages. You can tell that themes are repeating. What you probably don't realize is that there are hundreds of themes whizzing by that you aren't even noticing, and these too are repeating and interweaving at the periphery of your vision. Our reading of the Course is very much like a five-year-old listening to a Wagner opera—the child may notice some beautiful melodies, but will have no concept of all that is happening in that music, no idea of all the leitmotifs that are flowing by unnoticed.

The net effect is that the Course's teaching is extremely unwieldy. This leaves all of its students scrambling to get a handle on it. Most do so by trying to distill it down to a few key themes or capture its essence with some simple formula. The problem with these attempts, however, is that they single out a few themes while ignoring countless others. The Course is not formulaic, and this is clearly on purpose. It doesn't want us to just focus on a few strands. It wants us to grasp how its multiple strands interweave and fuse together. At one point it says, "We are now emphasizing the relationships among the first fifty of the ideas we have covered, and the cohesiveness of the thought system to which they are leading you."[2] Seeing how fifty ideas come together into a cohesive whole is surely different than selecting one idea and throwing the rest away. Consequently, what I was seeking was a way of summarizing the Course that, though relatively simple, honored the real breadth and complexity of the Course's thought system.

Finally, in the mid-nineties, I felt that I hit on that way. The summary I came up with has several advantages. It doesn't cover all of the Course's themes, not by a long way, but what it does is organize everything around the Course's central teaching of forgiveness. Thus, everything in the summary, from start to finish, is designed to make the concept of forgiveness make sense. In doing so, the summary quite naturally follows the chronology of our own journey. It therefore begins in Heaven before the separation, then descends down into the separation, then travels the long trek upward as we learn the art of forgiveness, and finally ends back in Heaven, where we started. Each point along this journey is specifically designed to contribute to the logic of forgiveness. Thus, the first half of it describes the problem that forgiveness solves, in such a way as to reveal forgiveness as *the* logical solution, as the only key that really fits this lock. The second half then describes forgiveness itself: what it is and what its effects are. It shows forgiveness undoing, one by one, all of the awful symptoms of the separation, until the separation is itself undone, and we return to the Heart of God.

In order to make this summary truly effective, I did three things. First, I fleshed it out into sixteen points that captured its essence. These points, read serially, constitute a mini-summary of the Course. Second,

I expanded those sixteen points into ninety-six key ideas. These key ideas were worded as complete statements, so that, if you read them all in order, you would have an expanded version of the sixteen-point summary. Third, I drew a diagram that was my attempt to illustrate the sixteen points as they trace our journey away from Heaven and then back to Heaven. All three of these are meant to enhance one's ability to grasp the Course's teaching as a whole, as a unified system.

One advantage of this summary was that, even though it was organized around the single theme of forgiveness, it still hit most of the bases that I considered important. It was a genuine attempt to reflect the real breadth of the Course, rather than a reduction of the Course down to a few favorite ideas. It therefore contained a number of themes that typically get left out of summaries of the Course, or go unmentioned by Course students altogether.

That summary, as you may have guessed, became the basis for this book. The sixteen points became sixteen chapters and the key ideas became sections within the chapters. Having at last a solid summary in hand, I poured myself into the writing of this book, which I intended to be my major statement about the Course. When I finished, in the late nineties, a high-profile literary agent became enthused about it and felt that he could sell it to a major publisher. At that point, I approached the Foundation for Inner Peace, who owned the copyright at that time, for permission to use the Course quotes that were in the book. However, over a year passed before they were able to get me a decision. I finally received the news that the Course's copyright had been transferred to Ken Wapnick, and he would be the one to decide about permission to quote in my book. This was not welcome news, for Ken is a fellow teacher of the Course, whose interpretation is significantly different from mine, a fact that was discussed in a number of footnotes in the book. A short while later I received a letter from him denying me permission to quote in the book, saying that it would compromise the integrity of the Course.

I was not alone in my copyright difficulties. At this time, many Course centers, churches, and Internet discussion groups received letters about their supposed violations of the copyright. The Course community erupted in controversy. At one point, there were four lawsuits underway. It was finally over in the spring of 2004, when a judge in New York dismissed the copyright on the First Edition of the

Course. Now authors such as myself were free to use quotations from the Course however they wished.

To prepare this book for publication, I have significantly revised my earlier manuscript. While I have kept the basic structure intact, I have rewritten a number of sections. In some cases, this was simply because I thought of a more effective way to make my point. In other cases, it was because my grasp of the Course had grown in the intervening time. I wanted this book to reflect, at time of publication, my latest understanding of the Course's teaching.

As useful as I think this summary is, it is not *the* way to summarize the Course. No summary of the Course can really do it justice, simply because, unlike my string of sixteen points, the Course's thought system is not a linear string of concepts. Rather, it is much more like a web. An even more apt image would be a three-dimensional web. Imagine trying to describe an intricate, three-dimensional spider web by following just one thread at a time. This is why I believe that the best way to learn the Course is to carefully study the Course itself, because every section is filled with the interweaving of its ideas, thus giving the reader a constant sense of the web-like nature of the teaching. On the other hand, even when we study the Course itself, we bring to that study certain orienting concepts about the system as a whole, and these, for good or ill, shape everything we read. If they are accurate, these orienting concepts can illumine what we are reading, both revealing and clarifying truths that we would have otherwise failed to grasp. In that spirit, I offer this overview of the Course's teaching to you, not as a substitute for studying the Course, but as a way to enter into or enrich your own encounter with the endless treasure house that is *A Course in Miracles*.

Return to the Heart of God

One

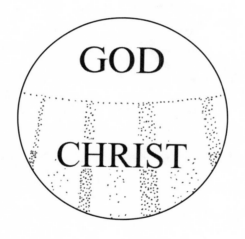

Our home is reality, Heaven, the Kingdom of God, a spiritual realm of pure oneness and boundless joy which can never be threatened.

One

1.1. Since nothing real can be threatened, the world is not real.

> *Nothing real can be threatened.*
> *Nothing unreal exists.*
> *Herein lies the peace of God.*

This is how *A Course in Miracles* begins. It makes a fundamental distinction between the real and the unreal.[1]

The Course begins on this very lofty philosophical note—the question of what is truly real. Such a question seems very far from our day-to-day concerns. Yet is it really? Are we not dealing with this question all the time? Are we not constantly trying to distinguish appearance from reality? We run into someone who looks so glad to see us, but we wonder how she really feels. An advertisement shows us people who are incredibly happy because they have used the advertised product, but we figure they are just acting. We see a pool of water on the hot pavement in front of us while driving, and we quickly try to discern if it is real water or just a mirage.

We carry out this process constantly because the stakes are extremely high. If we decide that something is real when it isn't, we are in danger of living in a fantasy. If we decide that something is not real when it *is*, we are in danger of getting broadsided by the very thing we dismissed. Consequently, most of us put a lot of energy into separating out reality from mere appearance.

Yet strangely, that energy is largely limited to the details. We use all our intelligence and experience to decide what is real in particular cases, while we leave largely unasked the question of what is real in general. Why this strange contradiction? I suspect there are many reasons for it, but one of them must certainly be that what is real on a general level seems so patently obvious. What is real is what we can see with our eyes and hear with our ears and touch with our fingers. What is real, we assume, is the physical world as disclosed by our physical senses. We may believe in things that can't be seen or touched, but surely our account of reality *begins* with the visible and the tangible. That is the bottom line. That is what cannot be doubted.

Yet why can't it be? People have been doubting the reality of the physical world for ages. The philosopher René Descartes pointed out in his famous "dream problem" that it is impossible to distinguish our waking experience from our most vivid dreams. Therefore, the possibility exists that the world we see while awake is just as imaginary as the worlds we see in our dreams. Descartes ultimately put his doubts to rest by deciding that God wouldn't do such a thing to us, but for most of us that argument is probably not very convincing. Given the unsatisfying nature of Descartes' solution, we are still stuck with his problem: How in fact do we know the world we see right now isn't a dream?

It is hard to believe that our senses could lie to us so consistently. Would my eyes tell me that something is there if in fact nothing were there? Would my fingers stop at a wall if there were no wall? Yet consider this: Our senses are part of our body, and our body is part of the larger collection of bodies that we call the world. Thus, when we believe in the reality of the physical world, we are really saying this: When *my* body tells me that *other* bodies are real, the investigation is over. Doesn't this strike you as odd? It is like asking the defendant if he is innocent, and when he says yes, considering the case closed. The Course makes the same basic point:

> It [the body] gives the eyes with which you look on it, the hands that feel it, and the ears with which you listen to the sounds it makes. It proves its own reality to you.
>
> Thus is the body made a theory of yourself, with no provisions made for evidence beyond itself.[2]

There is a story about the eighteenth-century writer Samuel Johnson discussing with some friends the ideas of the idealist philosopher George Berkeley, particularly Berkeley's claim that physical objects are merely ideas. Johnson clearly didn't take this theory seriously, and when asked how he would refute Berkeley, he answered, "I refute him thus!" and rammed his foot against a large stone, apparently "proving" how real the stone was. Yet *of course* a physical foot is going to tell you that a physical stone is real. The question is whether you can believe the foot's testimony, whether the *foot* is real.

As this story shows, it is hard to seriously question what our senses tell us. The Course is fully aware of this, yet says that our seemingly unshakable conviction is actually a cover for something else. It sets up its point by talking about those people who display total conviction on the flimsiest of evidence. It says that their "conviction" is really "but a cloak for the uncertainty it would conceal."[3] It says they defend their views irrationally and that this defense "seems strong, convincing, and without a doubt because of all the doubting underneath."[4] This is a familiar image, is it not? It calls to mind a long list of narrow-minded, bigoted people shrilly defending their views, as if the louder they defend them the more they will silence their own secret doubts. Then the Course takes this familiar image and applies it in a shocking way:

> You do not seem to doubt the world you see. You do not really question what is shown you through the body's eyes. Nor do you ask why you believe it, even though you learned a long while since your senses do deceive. That you believe them to the last detail which they report is even stranger, when you pause to recollect how frequently they have been faulty witnesses indeed! Why would you trust them so implicitly? Why but because of underlying doubt, which you would hide with show of certainty?[5]

In other words, when it comes to the question of the world's reality, *we* are those narrow-minded people who seem absolutely certain based on paltry evidence. This means that our supposed certainty about the reality of the world is really a *show of certainty* that we use to mask our underlying doubt. Could this be true? Our senses, after all, have lied to us again and again. Somewhere inside we must be wondering how far the lie can go. Is it possible that deep within we are harboring profound doubts about the reality of what our senses report, and that we are trying to cover up these disturbing doubts with a surface display of certainty? Maybe Descartes was speaking for all of us when he voiced his doubt about the world's reality and then tried to silence that doubt with a false surety.

Perhaps we can muster the intellectual courage that Descartes may have been lacking, and that Samuel Johnson was clearly lacking. Perhaps we can let whatever underlying doubt we have about the world's reality come out into the open and have its voice. Perhaps we can acknowledge the fact that our senses have deceived us, that our minds do play tricks on us, and use these observations to help us face the one question that almost no one wants to face: Is it possible that this world is unreal?

As we dive into the Course's view of reality, we will need this open-mindedness. For its view of reality could not be more different than our conventional view. We can see this right in the quote with which we opened this section: "Nothing real can be threatened." There is something about this statement that appeals to our logical mind. If something is truly real, how could its reality be threatened? How could its reality suddenly turn into the opposite, into unreality? Yet however logical this statement may seem, it flies in the face of our entire experience of life. For what in this world does not live under threat? All living things are under a more or less constant threat, until the day when the inevitable threat of death catches up with them. The earth itself is under threat. It could be, and some day will be, destroyed by some cosmic cataclysm. Finally, the entire universe can be threatened. It might eventually just wind down into what physicists call "heat death."

Everything in this world can be threatened. Thus, if the Course is right, and nothing *real* can be threatened, think of the ramifications. It means that *everything we think is real is actually unreal*. This radical notion is the starting point of *A Course in Miracles*. Everything we have ever seen with our eyes, heard with our ears, touched with our fingers, everything we have valued, coveted, and sought after—all of it is *unreal*. This initially can seem to be a very bizarre notion. I am not asking you to swallow it whole, but just to consider the possibility.

What, then, is real? If everything we thought was real is not, then reality itself must be something *completely unfamiliar*. And this is precisely what the Course claims in the following two passages:

> You cannot understand how much your Father loves you, for there is no parallel in your experience of the world to help you understand it. There is nothing on earth with

which it can compare, and nothing you have ever felt apart from Him resembles it ever so faintly.[6]

God's peace is recognized at first by just one thing; in every way it is totally unlike all previous experiences. It calls to mind nothing that went before. It brings with it no past associations. It is a new thing entirely.[7]

Could it be that what is real is so totally unfamiliar, as these passages say, that it calls to mind nothing that has gone before, that it has no parallel in this world, and that nothing we have experienced here can even faintly compare? If this is so, how can we understand this reality? Quite simply, we cannot. We have no reference point for it, no analog in our experience. Words will not describe it, for words only refer to experiences we have already had. They simply point to something already seen, felt, heard, tasted. When you say that some new kind of meat tastes like chicken, everyone knows what you mean. But what if it tasted completely unlike anything else? How would you describe it then?

So we have before us a paradoxical task. We cannot really describe this reality the Course is speaking of. Yet we must say something about it. We must venture into this unfamiliar territory. For the entire foundation of the Course lies here. As our earlier quote said, "This is how *A Course in Miracles* begins." Everything in the Course follows from this starting point. Therefore we must use words as best we can to convey something about this reality. We must use them to obtain some dim sense of what this reality is. Yet even while using them, we must never forget that they do no more than vaguely point in the direction of it. As the old Zen saying goes, they are merely fingers pointing at the moon.

1.2. Reality is formless, spaceless, timeless oneness, beyond all limitation, opposition, and distinctions.

What would a reality be like that was fundamentally different from this world? Perhaps we imagine a celestial realm with scintillating colors unlike any we have seen before, with translucent trees, mountains, streams, and temples of such beauty they could not be described, with bodies that radiate light, that could travel at the speed of thought and that would last forever, and with everything constantly suffused with a gentle celestial light.

Would such a realm be *fundamentally* different from our world? No, it would not. Why? Because it still has mountains, trees, colors, buildings, and bodies. It still has *space* to move through and *time* to move in. You cannot say there is no space if you still have a tree over *here* and a stream over *there*. And you cannot say there is no time if you still have one happening followed by another. Therefore, the celestial landscape I just described is merely a kinder, gentler variation of the basic pattern on which our world is built.

What is this pattern? What are the fundamental structures that comprise our world? First, there is *space*, an immense expanse in which things are located and are separated by distance. Inhabiting this space are innumerable *forms*—galaxies, stars, planets, mountains, rocks, plants, etc. These forms are constantly passing through *time*, an ever moving stream of happenings that flows from past to present to future. As the forms are carried along this stream, they themselves are in constant flux, undergoing continual *change*.

Some of these forms contain bits of consciousness. These are *separate selves*, locked inside fleshy containers called bodies. From within these bodies, they peer out at their world through the windows of their senses. They never look on their world directly, only through the middleman of the senses. For this reason, they are never quite sure what is out there, and so their understandings are constantly shifting and being revised. They are in a state of *perception*, in which subjects try to know objects beyond themselves and thus beyond the range of certainty.

Space, form, time, change, separate selves, perception—these are the basic structures that make up our world. What is not immediately apparent about this list is that all of these things are variations on a single theme. That theme is the idea of *separateness*: separate locations, separate forms, separate moments, separate minds. Reality as we experience it is the single idea of separateness played out in manifold ways.

Therefore, if we are looking for a reality that is fundamentally different, then we have to imagine a reality that is completely without separateness: no separate locations, no separate forms, no separate moments, and no separate selves. There couldn't be any space, which means there would be no distance to keep things apart from each other. There couldn't be any forms, any finite things marked off by a boundary, and thus there would be nothing bounded, nothing finite. There couldn't be any time, and so there would be no river which flowed from past to future, in which things constantly morphed from one state into another. Most importantly, there couldn't be separate selves locked away inside fleshy containers, trying to know a world that must remain forever beyond their grasp.

This is precisely how *A Course in Miracles* describes reality, as void of all these things. Yet this makes one wonder: What is there instead? In place of these familiar elements, based on separateness, the Course says, there is only *perfect oneness*:

> Heaven is not a place nor a condition. It is merely an awareness of perfect oneness, and the knowledge that there is nothing else; nothing outside this oneness, and nothing else within.[8]

This oneness is composed of what might be called *pure spirit*, spirit without form or boundary, so that it has no limitation, no end, and nothing outside of it. And it is composed of *eternity*, which is not an endless crawl of moments, but a single, all-encompassing moment which the Course calls "always." It does not flow like a river from past to future because, as the Course says in a play on words, "Always has no direction."[9] In eternity, there is no perception, but only what the Course calls *knowledge*. This refers not to the knowing of mundane facts and information, but to the direct, unshakable certainty that comes from being one with the very essence of what is known.

Thus, while our world is made, from top to bottom, of the fabric of separateness, the Course teaches that true reality is composed of the fabric of oneness. "It is merely an awareness of perfect oneness." If this is so, then such a realm is clearly beyond our current comprehension. "For while you think that part of you is separate, the concept of a oneness joined as one is meaningless."[10] We can only approximate an understanding of it using crude symbols and metaphors. Perhaps a visual metaphor can help. In one beautiful passage, the Course builds, one step at a time, the metaphor of a vast field of radiant light, without gaps or shadows and without end. It will help if you try to visualize each step as it unfolds:

> Beyond the body, beyond the sun and stars, past everything you see and yet somehow familiar, is an arc of golden light that stretches as you look into a great and shining

circle. And all the circle fills with light before your eyes. The edges of the circle disappear, and what is in it is no longer contained at all. The light expands and covers everything, extending to infinity forever shining and with no break or limit anywhere. Within it everything is joined in perfect continuity. Nor is it possible to imagine that anything could be outside, for there is nowhere that this light is not.[11]

1.3. God is a Being of limitless, changeless Love Who is incapable of anger or vengeance.

The Course rarely uses the kind of impersonal language we have just employed to talk about reality. In fact, it says that the experience of reality is "intensely personal."[12] The Course usually describes reality in traditional Christian language, calling it Heaven or the Kingdom of God, and depicting it as an eternal love relationship between God the Father and His perfect Son.

The question of God is one of the biggest issues we will ever face. The issue is not just whether we believe in God, it is also the *kind* of God we believe in. How we answer these questions will inevitably color our entire outlook on life.

We are all familiar with the popular Western image, in which God is a kind of giant person. Like a person, God is thought of as a separate being of some sort, distinct from other beings. He has some kind of form, for there must be a boundary that marks where He ends and where what is not Him begins. He is thought of as male, possessing predominantly male characteristics. And He has a personality, with distinctly human traits and emotions. He creates. He plans. He acts. He has relationships. He loves and cares, yet also grows angry and vengeful.

The conventional God's personality, in fact, is seemingly split down the middle. One the one hand, He is loving and forgiving. He cares about His children—all of them, not just the wealthy and powerful. He wants to free them from suffering and bondage, as we see in the story of the Exodus. On the other hand, He is aware of sin in them and responds with anger and punishment. He sends illnesses, wars, and earthquakes. And if these wake-up calls do not suffice to turn the sinners around, He tosses them into hell for eternity. I often hear this split expressed as the tension between God's Love and His justice. To remain just He *must* punish sin, even if, perhaps, His Love would incline otherwise. As a result, His justice sets a natural boundary on His Love, creating at least a friction, at most a war, between these two aspects of Himself.

Most of you reading this book have probably left this image of God behind. Our reasons for becoming disenchanted with this view are obvious. God comes off looking like an overblown monarch—human, male, jealous, and punitive. As such, He looks suspiciously like a mere projection of our minds. The real God, we assume, must be more grand, more ineffable, more all-encompassing, and more *loving*. It is hard to imagine any decent person sending someone to hell forever. Yet this God sends most people there, without any hope of reprieve. How can we worship a God with a less-developed morality than the people around us?

The Course, like many of us, sees the conventional God as a mere projection of the human ego (which, oddly enough, is how the Course sees the devil, too). The true God, it teaches, is something altogether different. He is not a separate person, like a large human being, for there is nowhere He ends and something else begins. Thus, He has no form of any sort, no body, no boundary. He is not a male, even though the Course retains the traditional usage and refers to God as "He." Yet His characteristics are as motherly as they are fatherly, and at one point He is likened to a mother, a brother, and even a lover, in addition to a father.[13] Clearly, these human roles are merely symbols that send our minds in the direction of That which lies beyond all earthly symbols.

Yet the Course freely employs such human symbols, for they convey something crucial about God. They say that a person is a better symbol for God than is an impersonal force or energy field. Often, when we realize that God is not a giant human like the gods of Olympus, our minds start conceiving of God as some kind of impersonal energy, like the Force of *Star Wars*. Yet this seems to make God *less* than a person. Shouldn't we go in the opposite direction? If we are to believe the Course, we should view God as having the same faculties as a person—awareness, intelligence, will, emotion—yet simply see these expanded to an infinite degree. In other words, we should see God as the basic stuff of personhood shot into infinity.

This God still thinks, but His Thoughts are limitless realities that neither arise nor pass away. He still wills, but His Will is not one force among many, striving to surmount the obstacles that stand in its way.

Rather, it is the only Force there is, so that nothing stands in its way. He still feels, but His Love and peace and joy are like the vastness of interstellar space—infinite and unchanging. And He still responds to our needs here in this world, yet His Mind is too immense to deal on the level of specifics. He makes one response that answers all needs in all beings throughout all time. "God answers only for eternity. But still all little answers are contained in this."[14] In Chapter 9 we will discuss how this one answer translates into the little answers that meet our everyday needs.

One way to approach a concept of this God would be to take the traditional Western God, strip away His vengeful side and leave only His loving side. Then expand that loving side to an infinite degree, until all of reality was filled with nothing but His Spirit and His Love. This gives us some sense of the God of the Course. He is loving beyond our ability to comprehend. Think of our earlier quote: "You cannot understand how much your Father loves you, for there is no parallel in your experience of the world to help you understand it." This means that the greatest love we have experienced in our earthly relationships is not a true parallel of God's Love, just as a firefly is not a true parallel of the sun.

Therefore, we need to carefully distinguish this Love from love as we know it. Human love always engages in favoritism. Yet according to the Course, "God gives no special favors."[15] He does not reserve greater amounts of affection for certain special children, withholding it from others. "God is not partial. All His children have His total Love, and all His gifts are freely given to everyone alike."[16] In our experience, love is always partial. We always love some more than others. But God's Love is not like that.

We also see love as entailing demands. The more someone loves us, the more pressure we expect that person's needs to exert on us. Yet again, says the Course, God's Love is not like that. "God...demands nothing, for He does not will to take away. He does not require obedience, for obedience implies submission."[17] Imagine that—a God Who does not demand our obedience or submission.

We also believe that the loved one naturally requires a certain amount of ego-stroking. In the religious sphere, this translates into the popular belief that God needs lots of praise and worship. The Course teaches that this is a concept so alien to God's Mind that He does not even understand it:

[Praising God] hardly means that you should tell Him how wonderful He is. He has no ego with which to accept such praise, and no perception with which to judge it.[18]

The meeting of demands and the stroking of egos is all about earning someone's love. We all know that the number of assigned hoops we jump through is directly proportional to the love we will receive. We know, in other words, that love is conditional, that love is a bargain which says, "I will love you *if* you meet my needs." Yet God has no needs. Therefore, He is free to just love, to just give, without any strings attached. As the Course says, "Giving Himself is all He knows."[19]

Finally, for all of the above reasons, we are accustomed to a love that changes, as the amount of demand-meeting, ego-stroking, and hoop-jumping rises and falls. How, then, can we understand a Love that will never change, no matter what we do, no matter what we think we have become? According to the Course, it is impossible that God's Love could waver even in a minute degree. It is impossible that "His Love could harbor just a hint of hate, His gentleness turn sometimes to attack, and His eternal patience sometimes fail."[20]

There is something deep in the human spirit that yearns for a God Who is perfection itself. We want a God Who combines in Himself the noblest of all qualities in infinite measure. We want a God Who is pure Love, pure goodness, so that it would be worth eons of struggle just to stand in His Presence. To feel His Love for just one instant would be a joy surpassing any treasure this world has to offer. And uniting with Him would be eternal bliss, a bliss of which we would never grow tired. We want a God to Whom we can give every ounce of our being without reservation. We want a God Who deserves the title of "God."

We find such a God in the pages of *A Course in Miracles*. Its words speak of a God Who satisfies every unexpressed longing of our hearts. Words, however, can only vaguely hint at His true reality. As the following passage says, when we truly know God, there are no words to use, no lips to speak with and no separate self to entertain a concept of a God distinct from ourselves:

We say "God is," and then we cease to speak, for in that knowledge words are meaningless. There are no lips to speak them, and no part of mind sufficiently distinct to feel that it is now aware of something not itself. It has united with its Source. And like its Source Itself, it merely is.[21]

1.4. God extended Himself to create His Son, the Christ, Who is one with God and is the single Self of the Sonship.

God is not alone. He creates. But in a radical departure from traditional Western beliefs, the God of the Course does not create humans, animals, and plants, nor even planets and stars.[22] He does not create any kind of form at all, anything involving time or space. When He creates, He merely extends His Spirit. *What* He creates, then, is simply more of Himself, "for He makes no distinctions in what is Himself and what is still Himself [His creation]. What He creates is not apart from Him."[23]

God does not have many creations, only one. All of His Love, all of His Will, all of Himself, He poured into His one Son, the Christ. This Son is exactly like the Father: a Self of unimaginable magnitude, a bodiless Spirit Whose vastness stretches to infinity. The Son's qualities—his power, holiness, perfection, and love—are every bit the equal of God's, because they *are* God's. The Course never tires of singing the praises of this infinite Being, as in the following passage:

> For Christ is the Son of God, Who lives in His Creator and shines with His glory. Christ is the extension of the Love and the Loveliness of God, as perfect as His Creator and at peace with Him.[24]

By using such anthropomorphic terms as Father and Son the Course is not implying that Heaven is just a big human household. It is saying that the relationship between God and His creation is less like the interface of cold abstractions and more like the warmth, affection, and deep, unspoken closeness of the perfect father-son relationship. The father-son relationship is one of the richest cultural images that we have, and that richness allows it to carry truths about God and His Son deep into our minds.

An ideal father regards his son as a part of him, a continuation of his line, an extension of his very identity. He looks upon his son as his joy and treasure. He therefore lavishes on his son all that he has to give. All he wants is his son's happiness. And so he protects his son and keeps him safe. He provides for all of his son's needs, making sure he lacks nothing. The father eventually passes onto his son all that he has, including his name, his station in life, and his estate. As a result, all that the son possesses, including his very life, he has received from his father, who loves him with every ounce of his being.

This image of human love can help give us a vague idea of the all-encompassing divine Love of the Father for the Son. All of the elements above have a counterpart in the heavenly Father-Son relationship as portrayed by the Course. And this presents us with a paradox: Even though the Son is absolutely continuous with the Father, at one with the Father, even though "nowhere does the Father end, the Son begin as something separate from Him,"[25] still there is a *relationship*, a love relationship. You could say, in fact, that the story of God and Christ is the ultimate celestial love story. Theirs is a "love that is not of this world,"[26] of which human love is only the most distant and dim reflection. Their love is what Heaven is. All that They do for all eternity is sing to each other, sing of Their everlasting Love. They sing an "ancient hymn,"[27] "a song of gratitude and love and praise,"[28]

> the song the Son sings to the Father, Who returns the thanks it offers Him unto the Son. Endless the harmony, and endless, too, the joyous concord of the love they give forever to each other.[29]

This may seem only distantly relevant, at best, but in fact it is the most relevant thing there is. For, according to the Course, the Son is our real nature, underneath the disguise of this human form. He is our true Self. He is our forgotten Identity. As the Course plainly states, "The Son of God is you."[30] This single Fact means everything. If our deepest desire is to be somebody, to be important, to be good, to be loved, this means that in reality this desire is already satisfied—infinitely. The Course tells us what mystics have also told us for thousands of years, that nothing can compare with the inexpressible joy of discovering who we really are. The teaching that we in truth are God's perfect Son is central to the Course and we will revisit it again and again as we traverse the Course's thought system.

There is one more paradox. The Son of God is one Self, yet He contains within Himself countless God-created *parts*, "in number infinite."[31] These are what the Course calls the Sons of God, the children of God, or the creations of God. This plurality is why the Course frequently uses the term "Sonship," a term like "readership" that indicates a body of members. Yet even though these members are called parts, they

17

are completely unlike parts as we know them. A car is a good example of how parts operate in this world. To make a car, you take separate parts, which are different in size, shape, and function, and assemble them together into a larger whole. The parts of God's Son, however, are nothing like that. They are not separate from each other; they are all *one*. They are not different in size, shape, and function; they are exactly the *same* in every way. And they are not smaller pieces of a larger whole. Every part *contains* the whole; each part has the entire whole inside of it. Indeed, "every aspect *is* the whole."[32] Thus, the whole is not made up of smaller parts. Rather, *each part is literally made of the whole.* Though we cannot truly imagine this state, a useful analogy in our world is the hologram, every part of which contains the same three-dimensional image; each part contains the whole.

We are these parts. "We are creation; we the Sons of God."[33] We appear to be separate parts, "broken pieces"[34] of the whole, different from each other in gender, age, race, status, and ability. Yet all of us, every person and every living thing, share a single Self, the Christ. This contrasts sharply with our conventional view. In that view, we interface with others only at the periphery, where we may join our activities and even our bodies, while deep inside we remain solitary. There at the center lies that unique identity that we alone possess. At the core of us there is only ourself. The Course, however, turns this picture around, saying that only at the periphery do we appear separate and unique. When one day we reach the core of our being and gaze directly on our identity, we will find it is a *collective* Self, the exact same Self that everyone else has at their core. While at the periphery we appear alone, here at the center lies not our uniqueness but our oneness.

In summary, a conceptual picture of Heaven must include the following three elements: God, His Son, and the parts of the Son—the Sons of God. Though Heaven cannot literally be pictured, a helpful image is that of radiating light. We can picture God as the central Source of light, with rays of light emanating from Him. The act of light shining out from Him is creation (or extension, which we will discuss in the next section). The resulting field of light is His Son, the Christ. And we can view the individual rays in this field of light as the *Sons* of God. The overall result is a realm in which there is no time, no space, no change, no form, no separate selves, and no perception—only shining.

1.5. Extension is the dynamic of reality, in which reality timelessly extends itself and eternally increases.

This Heaven can sound extremely listless, as if everyone is floating around like cosmic jellyfish. And it is true that Heaven is characterized by receptive stillness, by pure contemplation. What we do there is simply know God. Yet there is another dimension, a dynamic one. According to the Course, everyone in Heaven (God and all His Sons) has a *function*, a function which they are carrying out continually, without pause, and with everything that they are. In Heaven everyone is engaged in the mighty task of increasing the Kingdom, of "extend[ing] the Allness and the Unity of God."[35] This function is creation, which is also called *extension*. Extension is all that goes on in Heaven. God extends Himself to create the Son, and all the members of the Son unite in creating new parts of the Sonship (our creations, which we will discuss below).

Extending the Allness and Unity of God sounds very foreign to our ears, yet the dynamic of extension is inherent to our minds. We all have within us an innate impulse to take what is inside us and express it outward, and then look upon that expression. That is what we do on earth and that is what we do in Heaven. Extension is a central idea in the Course which we will see in many different forms in the chapters to come. So we will try to get an initial handle on it here.

Think of what an artist does. He takes an impulse that is born deep within him, an impulse that reflects some essential part of who he is, and then he expresses it outward and gives birth to something new. Or think of someone in love. It is not enough for the lover just to feel the love inwardly; it must be expressed outwardly. Only then can that love be fully experienced. Only then can the impulse be satiated.

The self-expression of an artist or a lover is an earthly shadow of extension as it occurs in Heaven. There, however, extension is much more total. It involves our whole being and it actually produces other eternal beings—our creations. In heavenly extension, rather than expressing an idea or feeling that is close to our heart, we extend the essence of what we are. Our very being overflows in an ecstatic act of creation. And as it does, it brings into being "new" creations, "new" limitless, eternal spirits.

These creations stand in relation to us in the same way that we stand in relation to God. Just as we love God for giving us life, so our creations love us for the same reason. "Your creations love you as you love your Father for the gift of creation."[36] Just as we are simply the extension of God's Being and therefore possess His Nature and attributes, so our creations are simply the extension of our being, possessing our nature and attributes. Thus, like everything else in Heaven, they possess the traits of personhood—awareness, intelligence, will, emotion—without the limits and fallibilities we associate with personhood. Like everything else in Heaven, they are pure spirit, formless, timeless, bodiless, immortal. According to the Course, each one is:

> A perfect being, all-encompassing and all-encompassed, nothing to add and nothing taken from; not born of size nor place nor time, nor held to limits or uncertainties of any kind.[37]

All of this, however, is an attempt to describe in words what stands beyond our comprehension. To picture new spirit being added onto pre-existing spirit may be a helpful concept, yet the Course is quick to remind us that this is not what really happens. Creation, it clarifies, "adds to all that is complete already, not in simple terms of adding more, for that implies that it was less before."[38] To appreciate the paradox here, let me rephrase this quote: Creation does not add more; it adds to what is already so complete that it can't be added to. Another problem with the idea of more spirit being added onto existing spirit is that it implies an actual change. Again, the Course says this is not so: "[Spirit] does not change by increase, because it was forever created to increase."[39] Again we face a paradox: In order for spirit to stay the same, it must increase.

Even though we cannot understand heavenly extension in this world, the Course says that we deeply, profoundly *miss* it. For it was a state of infinite joy. Though we do not consciously remember our function, something in us dimly realizes that we are not fulfilling it. As a result we feel vaguely purposeless and guilty—and know not why.

> In this depressing state the Holy Spirit reminds you gently that you are sad because you are not fulfilling your function as co-creator with God.[40]

> In the end, whatever form it takes, your guilt arises from your failure to fulfill your function in God's Mind with all of yours.[41]

1.6. Reality is maximal; it is the supreme joy.

A realm of no form, no action, and no personal identity can sound terribly boring, like an eternity of watching snow on your TV set. Yet if we assume that formless oneness is boring it is only because we have not *experienced* it. The mystics of all times and cultures have reported that formless oneness is unspeakable happiness. To help us obtain some dim appreciation of the joy of reality, the Course at one point gives us the following thought experiment,[42] which I have separated into four parts:

1. "Try to remember when there was a time,—perhaps a minute, maybe even less—when nothing came to interrupt your peace; when you were certain you were loved and safe."
2. "Then try to picture what it would be like to have that moment be extended to the end of time and to eternity."
3. "Then let the sense of quiet that you felt be multiplied a hundred times...."
4. "...and then be multiplied another hundred more."

This is a powerful thought experiment. You are taking the most happy and serene moment of your life and imagine it being multiplied ten thousand times and lasting forever. Yet all this yields, according to the Course, is this:

> And now you have a hint, not more than just the faintest intimation of the state your mind will rest in when the truth has come.[43]

Would you consider this boring?

So rather than imagining reality as the absence of anything remotely interesting, we might better imagine it as all happy states magnified to an infinite degree, so that all barriers fall away and we pass into a happiness that is without limit. One of the best words for describing reality, then, is *maximal*. This means that reality is the utmost. It is the supreme happiness. Nothing could possibly exceed it. It is characterized by maximal peace, maximal joy, and maximal love. In the presence of reality, words fail, for all words refer to experiences within our tiny conventional state of mind, a state that reality exceeds as the ocean exceeds a drop of water.

Yet hopefully the preceding words can give us just the "faintest intimation" about the Kingdom that God created. A happier, more blessed, more exalted condition could not possibly exist. The Kingdom is pervaded by the unlimited Love of the Creator, "Whose love shines out and in and in-between...to embrace all living things within its golden peace."[44] This Love plays no favorites. It wraps all minds in "the sweet embrace of everlasting Love."[45] And rather than coming to an end, it only increases. The joy of the Kingdom is ever ascending as the circle of its light continually expands, from the Father to the Son to the Son's creations, like concentric waves of divine radiance rolling ever outward, "extending to infinity forever shining."[46]

1.7. Reality is home, the longing of our hearts, the object of all our desires.

"Home" is one of the most rich and meaningful concepts available to us. Think for a moment about the idea of "home." Home is an environment that fits you. It fits your needs, your comfort, your happiness. It is a place of safety, where you go to find shelter, where you retreat when things get hard. It is where you can relax and let your guard down. It is your origin, where your roots are, the place that defines you. It is where your family lives, your kind, those who are like you. It is where you are loved and cared for, and where you love in return. When you are home, you feel that you are no longer out of place, that you fit, that you *belong*.

We generally think of this world as home. Yet does our world really fit the description? Do we really feel *at home* here? If we did, why would we put so much energy into setting up our own private homes, which are designed to keep the rest of the world out? Yet once these homes are set up, how at home do we feel in *them*? The Course talks about two people living "under a common roof which shelters neither."[47] Who of us can't relate to that? Unfortunately, most of us have no place on earth where we feel completely at home. Along with our chronic feeling of being out of place comes a sense that there is *somewhere* we fit perfectly, as well as a longing to be in that place. See if the following passage describes your experience:

> This world you seem to live in is not home to you. And somewhere in your mind you know that this is true. A memory of home keeps haunting you, as if there were a place that called you to return, although you do not recog-

nize the voice, nor what it is the voice reminds you of. Yet still you feel an alien here, from somewhere all unknown. Nothing so definite that you could say with certainty you are an exile here. Just a persistent feeling, sometimes not more than a tiny throb, at other times hardly remembered, actively dismissed, but surely to return to mind again.[48]

It is this vague memory that sets us to seeking. Why, one wonders, do all creatures here seek so restlessly? Why, even in our moments of greatest triumph and achievement, do we look ahead to some greater utopia, some brighter paradise? The Course's answer is plain and direct: "You *will* undertake a journey because you are not at home in this world. And you *will* search for your home whether you realize where it is or not."[49]

At the core of all our seeking lies what seems to be a universal nostalgia for a golden age, a time when everything was as it should be, a time that fulfilled the true conditions of home. Depending on who we are, we locate this golden age in our childhood, in Bible times, in Goddess-based cultures, in Atlantis—the list could go on and on. We grope to situate this memory somewhere within historical time, but it is not there. We do not realize that when we feel that wistful nostalgia, we are dimly remembering a state that predates time entirely. We are recalling "a little wisp of melody" from "the forgotten song."[50]

> Listen,—perhaps you catch a hint of an ancient state not quite forgotten; dim, perhaps, and yet not altogether unfamiliar, like a song whose name is long forgotten, and the circumstances in which you heard completely unremembered. Not the whole song has stayed with you, but just a little wisp of melody, attached not to a person or a place or anything particular. But you remember, from just this little part, how lovely was the song, how wonderful the setting where you heard it, and how you loved those who were there and listened with you.
>
> ....Listen, and see if you remember an ancient song you knew so long ago and held more dear than any melody you taught yourself to cherish since.[51]

Could it be that we are not really from here at all? Could it be that Heaven actually exists and that Heaven is where we belong? If not, where does this memory that haunts us, this voice that calls to us, come from? Why do we feel so out of place here?

Yet if Heaven is our home, someone has a lot of explaining to do. Someone needs to explain what we are doing here in this world, how we got here, and why we do not experience ourselves in Heaven.

Two

We tried to attack reality, to separate
from it, thus making a separate
identity—the ego—and the world
of space and time.

Two

2.1. We tried to separate, motivated by a desire to elevate ourselves above our brothers and above God.

> Into eternity, where all is one, there crept a tiny, mad idea,
> at which the Son of God remembered not to laugh.[1]

With these ominous words, *A Course in Miracles* describes the event in which we broke with the rapturous experience of Heaven, the event which gave birth to time, space, and the physical universe. Nearly every spiritual thought system has its account of what went wrong, of our disruption of the primordial harmony. Christianity calls it the Fall. The Course calls its version *the separation.*

Let's look at the above passage. "Into eternity, where all is one..." In the last chapter we examined eternity, a state of perfect, timeless oneness. In this state, our passage says, an idea snuck into our minds. This idea was two things. First, it was "tiny," meaning that it was trivial, powerless. Second, it was "mad"; it was insane, crazy, out of touch with reality.

We have all had crazy, trivial ideas cross our minds. And we know the normal response to such ideas: laughter. Isn't that what laughter is, the natural response to harmless craziness, to "tiny madness"? It is only when madness becomes serious and destructive that it no longer evokes laughter. So when we, the Son of God, "remembered not [i.e., forgot] to laugh," that is exactly what we implied—that this idea was anything but trivial and powerless. The next line makes this same point: "In his forgetting did the thought become a serious idea, and possible of both accomplishment and real effects."[2]

The mind as God created it is an extremely powerful thing. When we believed this tiny, mad idea was a genuine, potent reality, that idea became our experience. We suddenly seemed to be living *inside* the tiny, mad idea and its apparent colossal effects. It appeared to have mushroomed into the totality of existence, blocking out the light of Heaven. With one single thought, then, "Heaven seemed to disappear,"[3] and "the time of terror took the place of love."[4] Before this, there was no time or space. This is how it all began. All that we have been doing since then, says the Course, is reliving that primordial event, reviewing that tiny idea.[5]

How could this possibly occur? This is a question that every Course student raises at one time or another, usually right off the bat. While one could tease many answers out of the Course, it has only a few direct things to say in answer to the question "How could the separation occur?":

1. The question is not a true question

"How did the separation occur?" implies that it really did. The question is thus a statement to that effect. It is actually a covert attempt to establish that the separation did in fact occur. To answer such a question would only play right into the questioner's attempt to make the separation real, as this passage implies:

> Who asks you to define the ego and explain how it arose
> can be but he who thinks it real, and seeks by definition to
> ensure that its illusive nature is concealed behind the words
> that seem to make it so.[6]

2. It is more helpful to give a concrete example *from the* present[7] *than to give an abstract answer about the past*

Here is such an example: A person in this world can experience Heaven in moments of mystical union, yet can then recoil from the experience, in effect throwing that state away. This is exactly the same as what happened in the beginning. The Course then asks, "If this occurs in the present, why is it surprising that it occurred in the past?"[8]

The reason that this concrete, present example is more helpful is twofold. First, the mind (in its current state) relates more meaningfully to concretes. Second, change can only occur in the present, not the past. Only in the present can we stop repeating the original mistake. And if we did, there would no longer be a past to ask about.[9]

3. True correction of the error is more valuable than a theological explanation

In an important passage, the Course says, "Yet there is no answer; only an experience [the experience of Heaven]. Seek only this, and do not let theology delay you."[10] This is part of a discussion in which the Course teaches that theological explanation of the error does not lead to correction of the error.[11] Rather, it entangles one in endless controversy and thus delays correction—which is precisely its underlying intent. The Course's only aim is to correct the error, and so it steers clear of purely theological issues.[12] Instead, the Course simply helps us make a different choice in the present. This undoes our error and brings us to the ultimate experience which is the *true* answer to our condition. The answer to the separation is not an explanation, it is Heaven.

All three of these points agree: The search to find out exactly how the separation occurred is *part* of the separation system, not a way *out* of it. The Course, therefore, does not aid and abet this search. It only helps us to stop opting for separation in the present. It helps us undo the error now. This ushers us into the experience in which all our questions evaporate because perfect certainty has dawned. The Course urges us to answer the separation itself, not to answer how it occurred.

The Course does, however, explain *why* the separation *seemed* to happen. It does explain the motivations behind it. For those motivations are still in force, and understanding them *can* help us make a different choice in the present.

According to the Course, the separation was motivated by two things. The first was the desire to be special in God's eyes. "You were at peace until you asked for special favor [from God]."[13] We might imagine ourselves entertaining thoughts like these: "Maybe Heaven can get even better. Since God's Love for me is my whole happiness, what if I were His very favorite Son?" We can certainly relate to the secret wish to be the favorite. It was in this wish that the separation was born— "born of the hidden wish for special love from God."[14]

One may wonder how the thought "Maybe Heaven can get better" could even arise. Wouldn't such a thought only make sense if there were a pre-existing lack in Heaven? If Heaven truly is perfect and maximal, how could such a thought appear? Though the Course does not directly provide an answer, an answer does suggest itself.[15] As we saw in Chapter 1, the idea of increase is already a part of Heaven. Heaven is constantly increasing in some inscrutable way. So our minds already had the thought that Heaven could increase. Perhaps, then, we simply sought this increase through inappropriate means, through the seizing of specialness rather than the extension of love.

The second motivation behind the separation was the desire to replace God Himself. "He [the Son of God] would not accept the fact that, although he was a creator, he had been created."[16] We simply could not abide the fact that we had been caused by a prior Cause. We wanted to be the supreme Cause, not a mere effect. To accomplish this, we imagined ourselves detached from God, floating free from Him, as if we had appeared from nowhere. "This leaves you in a position where it sounds meaningful to believe that you created yourself."[17] At this point we just convinced ourselves that we had in fact created ourselves. The Course calls our problem with having a Creator "the authority problem."[18] This problem may sound crazy, yet it is simply a transcendental version of our everyday authority problems. Is not any authority problem a case in which someone else has power over us yet we want to be self-determining?

In both of these motivations we see the same essence. We wanted to be elevated above our brothers and above God. We wanted to steal their status and lay claim to the supreme status. We wanted to be the ultimate power in Heaven. We wanted to stand alone and victorious at the summit of reality, with our brothers and our Father cowering worshipfully at our feet.

It may be difficult for us to imagine such a motivation arising in a transcendental mind that was truly perfect and pure. However, we do not remember the state of Heaven. How, then, can we know what kinds of thoughts were possible in that state? Rather than trying to speculate about a state that is utterly foreign to our conscious experience, I think we should follow the Course's advice: Stick to the present. In the *present* we possess the motivations to be self-made and special. And these motivations arise in minds that *right now* are transcendental, perfect, and pure. That, at least, is the Course's teaching. You could even say that realizing that these minds are perfect and pure, *even though* such motivations arise in them, is the entire goal of *A Course in Miracles*.

There is one more point that must be mentioned. Although I am going tell the story of the separation as if it happened in a matter of hours, that is not actually the case. The Course says that, in our experience of time, the process of disconnecting our awareness from God took eons. "The separation [the initial process of separating] occurred over millions of years."[19] It took so long simply because it was so unnatural to us. At first, we probably entertained the subtlest trace of a thought of separation. Then, in a process that was so slow as to be imperceptible, our minds were drawn further and further into this alien way of thinking. As a result, our awareness gradually descended away from the light. We sank further into the experience of hard edges and concrete forms, and finally into the form of a completely separated self with truly vicious motivations.

2.2. The *ego* is the belief behind the separation; it is our core self-concept which says we are separate, autonomous beings.

What was the tiny, mad idea? Very simply, it was the idea of being *separate*. As we saw in Chapter 1, Heaven is composed of the fabric of oneness. There is no such thing as a separate entity. The tiny, mad idea was the bizarre and novel notion that we could tear ourselves away from this oneness, that we could "break away a part of God Himself."[20] It was the thought that we could disconnect ourselves and stand "beyond the Everywhere, apart from All, in separation from the Infinite."[21] In short, it was "the tiny, mad desire to be separate, different and special."[22]

This thought is what the Course calls the *ego*. What is the ego? As *A Course in Miracles* uses the term, the ego is not our self, nor even some real part of us. Nor is it some separate thing residing in us or force possessing us. It is merely an *idea*, a concept in our minds. It is the deep-seated self-concept which says that I am a separate entity, a "limited and separated self."[23] It claims that I have my own separate mind, my own private thoughts, my own independent will, my own personal history, my own individual goals, my own unique make-up. It says that at the core of my being I am utterly alone; not just alone, *on* my own; I am my own creator, master, protector, and provider. The Course gives this excellent brief definition: "The ego is the mind's belief that it is completely on its own."[24]

What, we ask, could be more unquestionable than the idea that we are separate individuals? Our bodies seem to prove to us that we are genuinely separate. While we live in these bodies it seems that we are walled off from the rest of the world in our own private cell. "You see yourself locked in a separate prison, removed and unreachable, incapable of reaching out as being reached."[25] Yet from the Course's point of view, the body does not establish the ego's existence. Rather, the ego established the body. The ego is the belief that there is a boundary, a membrane, around our minds, and the body arose as a concrete reflection of this belief. "This [belief] produces what seems to be a wall of flesh around the mind."[26] But we are getting ahead of ourselves. Let us return to the story of the separation.

2.3. When we tried to separate, we seemed to shatter reality into countless separate fragments.

What would happen if a being, in the state of pure oneness, imagined itself to be separate? Would it still see the rest of reality as unified? No, the mind naturally projects its self-concept onto the entire field of its experience. So when we conceived the notion of being a separate self, our minds automatically projected this idea onto Heaven itself. The effect was horrific. The thought of separateness seemed to fan out from our minds like a shock wave roaring across a frozen lake, breaking up the seamless whiteness into billions of splintered fragments. We seemed to see Heaven itself shattering like a pane of glass into countless disconnected pieces.

> What is the world except a little gap perceived to tear eternity apart, and break it into days and months and years? And what are you who live within the world except a picture of the Son of God in broken pieces, each concealed within a separate and uncertain bit of clay?[27]

After this shattering, we can imagine ourselves adrift in the dark void of space, amidst the chaotic rubble of what had been Heaven—a vast asteroid field of rolling, tumbling fragments, some large, some small, and all of them different. The Sons of God, each one equal in beauty, identical in nature, and one with the All, now appeared to float scattered about "in broken pieces," each one unique and each one alone.

These "separate" parts are the exact same parts we discussed in key idea 1.4, the parts of God's Son. Yet now that they seem to be *separate* parts, we must carefully clarify their nature. Each part has two aspects. 1) It *appears* to be a separate form, a "bit of clay," a physical body. This appearance, however, is an illusion that has been projected onto it by the mind. 2) In reality this part is exactly as it was before the separation; it is still pure, boundless spirit, at one with all that is. Thus, when we look at another person, we are seeing an illusion of a separate form superimposed onto a seamless part of infinity. A good analogy would be a movie on a screen. The movie screen is an unbroken expanse of whiteness. Yet onto this screen are projected various separate images. To apply this analogy to the Course, to see a person as that body moving about on the screen is incorrect; that is the illusion. It is the screen that represents who that person really is.

Back to our story of the separation. We did not know that the Son of God remained intact; we thought the shattering had really occurred. And so imagine our experience at this point. It was as if a child who had dearly loved and deeply cherished his home spoke one unkind word to his parents and watched it all—his parents, his house, his whole world—immediately explode into a cloud of jagged fragments. What do you think the child would be feeling at this point? What do you think *we* were feeling at this point?

2.4. We made the world by selecting and organizing the fragments.

The following important passage both summarizes what we have covered and carries it another step forward:

> But nothing you have seen begins to show you the enormity of the original error, which seemed to cast you out of Heaven, to shatter knowledge into meaningless bits of disunited perceptions, and to force you to make further substitutions.
>
> That was the first projection of error outward. The world arose to hide it, and became the screen on which it was projected and drawn between you and the truth.[28]

We have seen that "the original error," the idea of being separate entities, seemed to expel us from Heaven, and to shatter our unified awareness into tiny bits of perception. This seeming expulsion and shattering "was the first projection of the error outward."

Now we come to the next step: "The world arose." The *purpose* for which it arose we will discuss in 2.8. For now we will simply focus on its arising.

After the apparent shattering of Heaven, the next step was quite logical. Like a scavenger in a junkyard, we started sifting through the rubble, selecting the parts that suited our fancy. We looked for the ones that looked special and made us feel special, the parts that shined and glittered, that had the right curves and gave us what we wanted. Then, with these parts, we started arranging and organizing, adding a part here, taking away a part there. Out of this "continual process of accepting and rejecting, organizing and reorganizing, shifting and changing,"[29] we built our own world, our own kingdom. The entire process is summarized, point by point, in the following important passage:

> Obsessed with the conviction that separation is salvation, the ego attacks everything it perceives by breaking it into small, disconnected parts, without meaningful relationships and therefore without meaning....
> ...[It] is left with a series of fragmented perceptions which it unifies on behalf of itself. This, then, becomes the universe it perceives.[30]

And this is the universe that *we* now perceive. It is literally nothing more than our own cosmic junk sculpture. In making it we took "little bits of glass, a piece of wood, a thread or two, perhaps,"[31] "a thread from here, a scrap from there, and wove a picture out of nothing."[32] It is really just a big pile of parts, parts which over time have been carefully organized. Sometimes the parts get thrown into disorder, as when a hurricane or earthquake or some other disaster hits. But gradually they get put back in place again and the world goes on.

2.5. The world we made is the opposite of Heaven in every way.

So what kind of world have we made? There is a lovely song which says, "And I think to myself, what a wonderful world." *Is* it a wonderful world?

We already saw in key idea 1.2 that this world is literally the opposite of reality. Time is the opposite of eternity. Space is the opposite of infinity. Form is the opposite of boundlessness. Change is the opposite of changelessness. All in all, separation is the opposite of oneness, making this world fundamentally alien to what the Course calls reality.

But might not this be a good thing? After all, in this world we have bodies that can enjoy the forms and the changes. Without a body we could never taste a peach. Without distance we could never appreciate closeness. Without change we would have no variety. As the aforementioned song says, "I see trees of green, red roses too. I see them bloom for me and you." Without time and space there would be no green trees or red roses. How good would life be then?

Yet let's be honest here. The reason we are so appreciative of the green trees and red roses, so hungry for them, is that they are tiny islands of joy in a sea of suffering. The world is filled with suffering. This indisputable fact gave rise to the Buddha's First Noble Truth: *Life is suffering.* Let's step back and take an honest look at life on planet Earth.

When we survey the big picture here, what do we see? We see masses and masses of tiny bodies trying to survive and to protect themselves from the savage onslaught of other tiny bodies. Each one is outfitted by nature with an array of ingenious defenses—shells, scales, camouflage, quills. And each one is outfitted with its own *weapons*—teeth, claws, poison, and the best weapons of all: big brains and opposable thumbs. The fighting is so desperate because everybody survives by literally eating the other bodies (plant or animal), which means that each one is an item on someone else's menu. Each body keeps up the fight as long as it can, but in the end, everyone dies and everyone gets eaten, even if only by the worms or microbes—who of course are in the same deadly business as everyone else.

We try to eulogize this death. My two older kids used to love the Disney movie *The Lion King*. At one point the Lion King is training his son in the beauty and wisdom of the natural balance. He says, "Everything you see exists together in a delicate balance." He urges his son to therefore "respect all creatures, from the crawling ant to the leaping antelope." "But Dad," says the son, "don't we eat the antelope?" "Yes, Simba," he replies, "but let me explain. When we die, our bodies

35

become the grass, and the antelope *eat* the grass. And so we are all connected in the great circle of life."

Ah, the great circle of life. This thought is initially quite comforting. We may even feel tinges of spiritual reverence. But why exactly are we comforted? Apparently, if the lions only ate others, that would be unfair, and would make this a cruel world. But if it all gets balanced out, and the lions themselves get eaten in turn—indeed, if *everything* is both eater and eaten—then it is a *wonderful* world, a beautiful circle of life. True, I may eat you, but then you get to turn around and eat me, and thus we are both connected (apparently, by being in each other's stomachs) and the wondrous circle is complete. This brings us to a final, not-so-comforting conclusion: The circle of life is really the circle of *lunch*.

That is what this world is, and *that* is why it is the opposite of Heaven. "The world...is a place of sorrow...a place of war...a place of tears"[33] and "a place of death."[34] Can we really dispute these facts? To some degree we have grown used to them and thus give them little thought. We are from here, we assume, and this is just the way things are. Yet what if we are not from here, and this world is the complete violation of the way things really are? That is the perspective we find in this ironic passage from the Course:

> Here the deathless come to die, the all-encompassing to suffer loss, the timeless to be made the slaves of time. Here does the changeless change; the peace of God, forever given to all living things, give way to chaos. And the Son of God, as perfect, sinless and as loving as his Father, come to hate a little while; to suffer pain and finally to die.[35]

2.6. God did not make the world; we did.

Every believer in God knows that God created the world. Some claim He created it as a thoroughly good thing, as a soaring testament to His power and glory. Some believe He created it as a kind of inner-city classroom for recalcitrant souls. Yet obviously He created it. The world is so much bigger and more complicated than we are. Some colossal force must have created it. That force must have been what we call God.

This is one area where the Course really breaks ranks. It makes the shocking claim that we, not God, made the world. Can *A Course in Miracles* really mean this? It can and it does.[36] Further, by this world the

Course means far more than merely this planet. It means the entire visible cosmos, including the very fabric of time and space, its basic stuff of matter and energy, and all its "laws" of physics, chemistry, and biology; everything from "the stars...and the sun" down to "the smallest leaf" and "blade of grass."[37] By implication, we also made any plane of existence that, though not strictly physical, still contains even a hint of form, such as the astral, etheric, and subtle planes of occult lore. All phenomenal existence is of our making, says *A Course in Miracles*.

Yet how can we ourselves have made all this? This idea produces more problems for Course students than perhaps any other, for at least two major reasons.

First, it seems nothing short of arrogant to believe we made the world. In our eyes, we are not big enough to have made the cosmos, nor old enough to have done something several billion years ago, nor smart enough to have fashioned the intricacies that our science may never completely unravel. This assumes, however, that we know how big, how old, and how smart we are. And is that not arrogance? "Yet the reason for the course is that you do not know what you are."[38] If the Course is right, we *vastly* underestimate our abilities. Not too many centuries ago, we believed that the earth was the center—and pretty much the sum total—of the universe. Now, in similar fashion, we assume that our tiny mind is virtually the sum total of our being. Just as we discovered that the earth is merely a mote in the greater cosmos, perhaps in time we will learn that our current mind is only a tiny speck within our larger Self.

Second, we have been taught for so long, by so many traditions, that God created the world. The very idea of God must have been, at least in part, an attempt to explain how all of this got here. To disconnect God from the creation of the world would not only violate many religious traditions, West and East, ancient and modern, it would seem to violate the very idea of God.

Yet *A Course in Miracles* has a very forceful answer to this idea, an answer which once heard is difficult to discount or forget:

> Is it not strange that you believe to think you made the world you see is arrogance? God made it not. Of this you can be sure. What can He know of the ephemeral, the sinful and the guilty, the afraid, the suffering and lonely, and the mind that lives within a body that must die? You but accuse Him of insanity, to think He made a world where

such things seem to have reality. He is not mad. Yet only madness makes a world like this.[39]

Who of us has not thought, at one time or another, that this world is crazy, that nothing is fair, that nothing makes any sense? Hasn't something in us wanted to say to this crazy system, "I *demand* to talk to your supervisor"? Now, if we think *God* is the Supervisor, aren't we accusing Him of insanity, just as the above passage says? Doesn't logic dictate that only a crazy God would make a crazy world like this?

It is odd to hear a spiritual teaching saying such things, for this is exactly what the unbelievers, atheists, skeptics, and the like have been saying. For centuries people have been leaving the religious fold because they could not square a loving God with the pain and senselessness of this world. *Maybe they were right.* There is something seriously wrong with this place. It *is* a circle of lunch. It *is* a place of death. And that is *why* God could not have created it.

It seems so arrogant to think we made the world, for that so clearly seems to be God's role. The Course turns both of these objections on their head as the passage we quoted above continues:

> To think that God [made the world and so] made chaos, contradicts His Will, invented opposites to truth, and suffers death to triumph over life; all this is arrogance. Humility would see at once these things are not of Him.[40]

It is not arrogant to think we made the world; it is arrogant to think God did.

2.7. The ego has one need: to keep itself going, to confirm itself, to reinforce its reality, to protect itself from God's Love.

Why would we make this world? To answer this question we must backtrack a bit and discuss the ego's fundamental drive. We will see this drive at work in all of our subsequent discussions.

The ego's one and only drive is to keep itself going. Its only need is the "need to confirm itself,"[41] to confirm its reality. It wants to be real, so real that it lasts forever. Yet it fears that it lacks this reality. It senses that reality is not on its side, that there is some grand Presence which seems to be not only ignoring it but threatening to shine it away. "While the ego is...unaware of spirit, it does perceive itself as being rejected by something greater than itself."[42] In short, it is profoundly insecure, not unlike your average human. It lives in fear that it will one day be sucked into the formless void of God's Mind, where it will simply vanish. "And," as the Course says, "on this alone it is correct."[43]

We share this fear of the ego's, for a very simple reason: We believe that we *are* the ego. As long as we identify with the ego, its insecurity becomes our insecurity, and its drive to confirm its existence becomes ours. As we will see in later chapters, this explains a huge amount about human nature. We seem to be so controlled by impulses that in the end are self-destructive. Why do we repeat behaviors over and over that we know from experience will lead to our undoing? The Course's answer is that we are trying to preserve the self we think we are. We are trying to keep its boundaries intact, to keep it from disappearing in the boundlessness of God, for we think that if *it* disappears, so do we.

This places us in a rather bizarre position. It makes us afraid of our own reality, afraid to reunite with the joy of our real Self. As we saw in key idea 1.4, our minds are indissoluble parts of the Christ Mind, like sunbeams shining from the sun, or like ripples on the ocean. Being part of this oceanic Mind is what we are. Yet from the ego's perspective this Mind appears to be a ravenous monster: "The sun becomes the sunbeam's 'enemy' that would devour it, and the ocean terrifies the little ripple and wants to swallow it."[44] As long as we identify with the ego, slipping into the shining sea of our true Mind looks like total annihilation. And so we spend all of our energy trying to solidify the ego's "reality" and trying to stay away from our own reality. This crystallizes the strangeness of our position, for the very thing that we equate with loss of identity is actually the discovery of our real identity.

> Would you...say "no" to Heaven's calling, were you not afraid to find a loss of self in finding God? Yet can your self be lost by being found?[45]

2.8. We made this world of separate places and different moments to confirm the ego. It does so by "proving" that separation is an objective reality.

How does the previous point (2.7) explain why we made the world?

Let me answer that with a story. A homeless man one day was day-dreaming, and a crazy little fantasy crossed his mind. "Wouldn't it be great," he thought, "if I were a king?" This thought felt so good that he basked in it for a long while until, with his mind still absorbed in the fantasy, he fell asleep.

As so often happens when we go to sleep in the grips of a certain thought, his thought provoked a dream. His unconscious mind dished up for him a real extravaganza. Instead of waking up in his usual alley, he found himself in the royal bed, in a room filled with priceless furnishings. Attendants came to him, calling him "Sire," and put his slippers and robe on for him. Ministers reported to him about global decisions to be made. Servants brought him food fit for a king. Literally everything he saw, down to the most insignificant detail, reinforced one single message: You are the king. He was not aware, of course, that his own mind had manufactured all of these images. And so, for the brief space in which the dream lasted, he could only conclude that this message was the truth; he *was* the king. One might even speculate that his mind had produced the dream in response to his yearning; that his dream was a simple product of wish fulfillment.

What is the moral of this story? If you want to hang onto a crazy idea, you need only surround yourself with manufactured evidence for it, and then *forget that you manufactured the evidence*. At that point, you are forced to conclude that what the evidence points to is not your own subjective whim, but is objective reality.

And that is the twisted brilliance behind the making of this world. Everywhere we look, through the telescope or the microscope, all we can see is evidence for the reality of separation. As we saw in Chapter 1, the world is made of the fabric of separateness; separate locations, separate moments, separate minds in separate forms. It is thus a "world in which the proof of separation seems to be everywhere."[46] Who, in such a world, could possibly doubt that we are individual beings? "In a world of form the ego cannot be denied for it alone seems real."[47]

So the world seems to transform separation (and thus the ego) from a tiny, mad idea we made, to an objective reality independent of our making. Not only does it look like we did not make separation; it looks like separation made *us*. The world of separation, in the guise of our parents, gave birth to us. Its laws of nature outfitted us with a body and a brain and stamped onto us a list of genetic predispositions. Its winds of fate shaped us through the childhood environment it dropped us in and the pivotal events it blew our way. It *made* us—at least that is our experience.

And that *is* our experience. Have you ever felt that you were "helpless prey to forces far beyond your own control, and far more powerful than you"?[48] Have you ever felt like you were nothing "but a dancing shadow, leaping up and down according to a senseless plot conceived within the idle dreaming of the world?[49] This is the typical human experience. Yet according to the Course, you yourself put on the entire charade, to give yourself this all-important message: Separation is my cause and I am its effect, and thus I *must* be separate and have no power to change that fundamental fact.[50]

I realize that this teaching sounds outlandish. Yet *if* it is true, if we really did make the world for this reason, then we must admit that *our plan has worked.* The world has had the precise psychological effect on us that we designed it to have. It has convinced us that we are separate egos. It has convinced us that reality is a mass of separate objects moving through space toward their eventual demise. There are countless examples of the world's persuasive power. The body has convinced us that we are individual. Hunger has convinced us that we are lacking. Disease has convinced us that we are vulnerable. Parents have convinced us that we are not responsible. Space has convinced us that we are tiny. Death has convinced us that we are temporary. Onto all of these undeniable facts, *A Course in Miracles* would merely add this question: *What if we made the world for this very purpose?* What if we made it as an ingenious instrument of psychological persuasion? What if we, the Sons of God, manufactured the world solely to persuade ourselves that we are not the Sons of God?

The beauty of this theory is that it links two things that are normally seen as poles apart. It links the original purposes that set the universe in motion with our current experience in this world. It says the world was originally made in order to give ourselves the very experience we are having today, the experience that being a separate entity is no dream, but an objective reality.

This theory also says that the purposes which set the world in motion are ones we can observe in our lives right now. The forces that caused our world billions of years ago are the ones that move our lives today. For we are still making war on each other, just as the Course says we did in the beginning. We still seek to be better than each other, to be special, as if in memory of the tiny, mad idea. We still try to be self-made not God-created, seeking through our own efforts and ingenuity to shape ourselves into a preferred image. We still carve up reality into separate bits by our incessant naming, classifying, and distinguishing. We still build our own little worlds, by selecting the various characters and scenery we prefer and then organizing those preferred elements into our own personal kingdom. And we still do it all to confirm and reinforce the unstable, insecure self we think we are.

The separation and the making of the world, as described by *A Course in Miracles*, was the product of urges that dominate the world to this day. Though we have forgotten the event itself, something inside of us has not forgotten. Something inside of us still lives in that original moment, frozen inside its terrible patterns:

> Each day, and every minute in each day, and every instant that each minute holds, you but relive the single instant when the time of terror took the place of love.[51]

Three

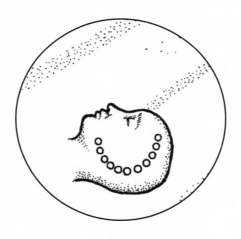

But the separation occurred only in our minds; in reality it never happened.

Three

3.1. The separation had no effect, for nothing can change the Will of God.

When one pauses to reflect on it, the scenario we sketched in the last chapter is a truly horrifying one. This is the Course's story of the origin of the world, and in contrast to the uplifting creation myths of other traditions, this one looks like it came straight out of a horror movie. It is a story in which the most sublime paradise is apparently transformed into a demented nightmare. In this nightmare, "God Himself has lost the Son He loves, with but corruption to complete Himself, His Will forever overcome by death, love slain by hate, and peace to be no more."[1] So much for the glorious Big Bang.

The seeming tragedy of this story is that it appears that God's Will, which lovingly established Heaven as a realm of unspeakable perfection, has been actually defeated and overthrown. The story thus contains the terrifying implication that there is

> a power beyond God's, capable of making another will that
> could attack His Will and overcome it; and give His Son a
> will apart from His, and stronger. And each part of God's
> fragmented creation would have a different will, opposed
> to His, and in eternal opposition to Him and to each other.[2]

Yet does this scenario really sound plausible? Does it make sense to us that God's Will could be overpowered? What kind of God *could* be dethroned? And would such a God really deserve the title of "God"? Let us recall what we said about this in Chapter 1. The God described by the Course is so purely omnipotent that nothing can actually go against His

Will. Not only can nothing *overpower* His Will, nothing can even *challenge* it. Nothing can raise the slightest impediment to His power. In a brilliant passage, the Course says that if power meets with even the slightest opposition, then it must contain some weakness. Otherwise, the opposition would be effortlessly swept aside. And thus this power is actually both power *and* weakness, two completely contradictory things. It is a "weak power," which, of course, is an inherent contradiction, like a "square circle." As such, it makes no sense and cannot be real.

> Power is unopposed, to be itself. No weakness can intrude on it without changing it into something it is not....And by this does it join to the idea [of power] a something it is not [weakness], and make it unintelligible. Who can understand a double concept, such as "weakened-power"?[3]

Because God's power is real power, nothing can oppose it. This single idea carries the most sweeping and fundamental implications conceivable. These implications are summed up in one profound line, one of the most important in the Course: *"the separation never occurred."*[4] Think what this implies. The break with God, the entire universe of time and space, nature's system of tooth and claw, the human condition, and the sad saga of human history, all that we know as real—all of it never happened. Why? Because, in the words of the Course, "God still is Love, and this is not His Will."[5] The separation never occurred because God is *God*.

For this reason, the separation remained merely a tiny, mad, *laughable* idea. The Course calls it a "quaint absurdity....a foolish thought, a silly dream."[6] It even calls the separation a *joke*: "It is a joke to think that time can come to circumvent eternity, which *means* there is no time."[7] To appreciate this admittedly rather dry joke, we might imagine the author of the Course as a stand-up comedian, saying: "So the ego walks up and says that time can actually barge into eternity and replace it, when everyone knows that the very nature of eternity is the *complete absence of time*!" (Imagine loud laughter and a rim shot from the drummer.)

The Course uses several humorous images to capture the comedy of our attempt to change the changeless. It calls our ego "a frightened mouse that would attack the universe,"[8] and then gives us these questions to reflect on:

How likely is it that it will succeed? Can it be difficult to disregard its feeble squeaks that tell of its omnipotence?[9]

In this same vein, the Course likens us to "a child who throws a stick into the ocean" and actually thinks that he is going to "change the coming and the going of the tides, the warming of the water by the sun, the silver of the moon on it by night."[10] Thinking that we could separate ourselves from God, it says, is the same as thinking "the sun could choose to be of ice; the sea elect to be apart from water, or the grass to grow with roots suspended in the air."[11] Though we forgot to laugh at the tiny, mad idea, God did *not*. And in these humorous images we can hear the distant echoes of His "gentle laughter"[12] in response to our foolish thought.

The tragic saga of this world, of course, seems anything but funny, and the Course is fully aware of this. It explains, however, that the world only seems so serious because we are looking upon all the outer effects of the tiny, mad idea. Looking only on those effects, the situation appears to be extremely grave. "It is not easy to perceive the jest when all around you do your eyes behold its heavy consequences, but without their trifling cause."[13] If we could only see beneath the outer forms to "their trifling cause," to the ridiculous idea they came from and rest on, then we would wholeheartedly join in God's "gentle laughter."

3.2. We did not actually separate; we merely withdrew our awareness from reality into a private mental state.

To understand what the separation really was, we will repeatedly call upon a single principle, one that is very simple and familiar to all of us. It is this: *The mind can lose touch with reality and experience its own fantasy world as real*. This is a fundamental fact of life. It is also a source of endless fascination for us. The stories we write are littered with cases of amnesia, with dream sequences, with hypnosis, insanity, and mind control. We are fascinated with the mind's ability to cross the line between reality and illusion, to step into its own manufactured reality and lose sight of the real thing.

In everyday life, we assume that this ability operates within safe boundaries. Yes, people distort the facts and, yes, the occasional person may see actual hallucinations, but the big picture is that we are collectively in touch with a common reality, and this common reality *is* reality. Or so we assume. Yet who of us isn't fascinated with scenarios that stretch these safe boundaries, even break them? We love a story that poses the question: "What if our ability to mistake illusion for reality goes much further than we ever imagined?" This was much of the allure of the 1999 movie *The Matrix*. It made us ponder the unsettling notion that the entire world as we know it is a manufactured illusion.

What if this is not just a science fiction scenario? The Course takes the mind's ability to live in a self-made illusion and removes all the boundaries from it. It sees this ability operating on a grand scale that we can scarcely conceive of. It invites us to consider that the mind can not only make up a world, but can dream up an entire universe, convincing down to the last atom. It asks us to consider the possibility that everything outside the perfect oneness of Heaven, every image, every form, even the very fabric of space and time, is an illusion of the mind.

What does this say about the separation? It says that the separation was the mind's ability to live inside its own fantasy world run amok. This means that it was not a real occurrence, but merely a *psychological* event. It wasn't an objective occurrence that changed reality itself. Rather, it happened only in our *minds* and changed only our *experience* of reality. In light of this interpretation, let us take another, more accurate look at this event called the separation.

When the ego crept into our minds in Heaven, in our experience we *became* the ego. We appeared to tear ourselves away from Heaven and became individual, like a tiny spark detaching from the mother sun and heading off alone. And as we left, we looked back and saw this sun go supernova and explode into a cloud of glowing sparks. This, however, was simply how it appeared to us. What really happened was that our minds went dim. We withdrew our awareness from the bright light of reality into our own private, murky state. In doing so we used a psychological dynamic familiar to us all. We see examples of it in at least three common psychological processes, processes which the Course makes frequent reference to. These are *denial*, *insanity*, and *sleep*.

In *denial* we mentally turn our back on something and act as if it is not there. Think of someone in denial about her terminal cancer. The cancer is still there; it has not gone away. Her mind has simply retreated into its own little corner, its own private alcove, where it hides from the facts.

Insanity is when someone has lost touch with public reality and has withdrawn into his own private, senseless world. The world goes on as before, the rest of us still see it. But for the insane person this world has vanished. He has retreated into a reality that exists only inside his mind.

Sleep, too, though not a mental disorder, fits this basic pattern. When we fall asleep we lose touch with our physical surroundings and withdraw into a dim private state. The room in which we sleep and the world outside it are completely unchanged. But for us they have disappeared.

In all three of these processes we can see the same basic idea: *The mind has the ability to withdraw from reality into a private, separate state.* What would happen if we did this in the formless oneness of Heaven? The answer is not hard to discern. As we withdrew our awareness from Heaven, it would appear to us that we were literally leaving Heaven, and that Heaven was actually disappearing. And as we retreated into our own private state, it would seem to us that we were *becoming* separate individuals with private minds.

This, says the Course, is exactly what happened. We did not really detach ourselves from reality and become separate entities. We did not go anywhere, nor did reality itself shatter and disappear. Reality remained exactly as it was, and we remained an inextricable part of it. We merely went into denial, went insane, fell asleep. If these processes are so widespread and commonplace now, might they not explain what happened in the beginning? As the line quoted in Chapter 2 says, "If this occurs in the present, why is it surprising that it occurred in the past?"[14]

3.3. The world is not an objective reality; it is only a dream, a projection of our belief in separateness.

The first move is to withdraw into the privacy of our minds, away from reality. This inward retreat is then followed by an outward expression. We turn right around and expand our private state into *what looks like* an objective reality. In place of reality itself, we now see the "reality" that we would prefer. We see our wishes blown up onto the screen of reality itself. We are all familiar with this process. It happens with each of the three psychological processes we just discussed. When we deny something that we don't want to be real, we then *project* outward what we *do* want to be real. When we go insane and have a break with reality, we begin to *hallucinate* our own reality. When we fall asleep we begin to *dream*.

The Course discusses our mind's fascinating ability to manufacture its own reality in a section entitled "The Basis of the Dream."[15] In this section, the Course engages us in a penetrating dialogue about the profound implications of the phenomenon of dreaming. Let us, then, turn to this section and allow it to engage us:

> Does not a world that seems quite real arise in dreams?
> Yet think what this world is. It is clearly not the world you
> saw before you slept. Rather it is a distortion of the world,
> planned solely around what you would have preferred.[16]

We can see this last point most clearly in the case of wish-fulfillment dreams. You spend weeks yearning for some woman (or man, as the case may be) you barely know. She won't even give you the time of day. Yet you keep hoping she will see how amazing you really are and end up in your arms. Then you fall asleep and, as if by magic, there she is, in your arms. This is definitely not the world you saw before you slept. It is a distortion of that world, planned around what you want. Yet it *seems* real.

> They [dreams] are the best example you could have of how
> perception can be utilized to substitute illusions for truth.[17]

Who could deny that dreams are a great example of our mind's ability to replace the actual truth with the fantasies we crave?

> You do not take them seriously on awaking because the fact
> that reality [or what we think is reality] is so outrageously
> violated in them becomes apparent. Yet they are a way of
> looking at the world, and changing it to suit the ego better.
> They provide striking examples, both of the ego's inability
> to tolerate reality, and of your willingness to change reali-
> ty on its behalf.[18]

Again, dreams are said to be a great *example*. Of what? Of the fact that our ego cannot stand the way things are (for instance, that we have been rejected by the woman of our dreams) and of our willingness to make up a world in which we get our way. Yet this very violation of reality is why we do not take dreams seriously when we awake.

Let us now skip ahead in the section. In the following sentences, the Course makes some basic observations about dreams. See if each sentence is not true in your experience of dreams:

Dreams show you that you have the power to make a world as you would have it be, and that because you want it you see it. And while you see it you do not doubt that it is real. Yet here is a world, clearly within your mind, that seems to be outside. You do not respond to it as though you made it, nor do you realize that the emotions the dream produces must come from you. It is the figures in the dream and what they do that seem to make the dream [including your emotions in it].[19]

From here the Course moves toward its chilling conclusion about dreams:

You seem to waken, and the dream is gone. Yet what you fail to recognize is that what caused the dream has not gone with it. Your wish to make another world that is not real remains with you.[20]

This last point is indisputable. Even when the alarm clock goes off and the dream of the girl is gone, the thing in you that made the dream is still there. You still want to make an unreal world in place of the real thing. That the dream has ended means nothing, for its cause remains. It is like discovering that someone has stolen your valuables, and taking comfort in the fact that at least the crime is over, not realizing that the burglar is *still in the house.*

We can say, then, that dreams demonstrate three things: 1) that we have the power to make a fantasy world in place of reality, 2) that we have the desire to use this power, and 3) that this desire is with us all the time. In light of these three things, the Course's conclusion, though deeply disturbing, seems difficult indeed to set aside:

And what you seem to waken to is but another form of this same world you see in dreams. All your time is spent in dreaming. Your sleeping and your waking dreams have different forms, and that is all. Their content is the same. They are your protest against reality, and your fixed and insane idea that you can change it.[21]

We conveniently assume that nighttime dreams are this special cubicle, the only place in which our mind's desire to make its own world has free rein. Yet that desire is always there. How do we know it doesn't have free rein all the time? This, of course, is what the Course is claiming. It says that just as our nighttime dreams are our protest against our frustrating daytime "reality," so our daytime "reality" is our ongoing protest against true reality, Heaven.

From these passages we can see that the Course quite literally means that the world is our own dream. It is our projection, our hallucination, our fantasy. Not only did God not make the world; strictly speaking, we did not make a world, either—in the sense of making an *actual* world. We did not splinter Heaven and use the pieces to build a physical universe. We merely projected the illusion of fragmentation onto Heaven. Then we projected the illusion of organization and arrangement onto those perceived fragments.

So the world, like a nighttime dream, is merely a collection of images we are juggling inside of our minds. This brings us to the Course's stunning claim that in truth there is no such thing as this world. If you woke up this morning having dreamt of an imaginary island which contained buried treasure, and you then decided you would get on a plane and fly to that island, your spouse would probably say, "Honey, there is no island. It was just a dream." *A Course in Miracles* is saying the exact same thing. "There is no world! This is the central thought the course attempts to teach."[22] The world is not an actual place, hovering somewhere outside of Heaven. It is just a batch of images in our minds.

If the world is a dream, however, why do we all recognize that our nighttime dreams are unreal, yet remain convinced that our daytime dream is real? One reason, of course, is that every morning we wake up from our nighttime dreams, thus giving us the opportunity to compare them to the daytime world. Likewise, if we had regular experiences of waking up from this world, would it still seem so real? The answer is no mystery, for throughout time there have been mystics who have had experiences of what the Course calls reality. Their testimony is that when you momentarily awaken from this world and experience reality, you know beyond doubt that, by comparison, this world is merely a shadow.

Yet why is our daytime world so much more stable, consistent, intricate, and vast than our nighttime worlds? The explanation is that our nighttime dreams are dreamt from a shallower place in the mind, a place not much deeper than the conscious mind. Our daytime world, on the other hand, is dreamt from a far deeper and broader place in the mind. This deep place is fully equal to the (relative) stability, consistency, intricacy, and vastness of this world. Also, at this deep place our minds are more clearly linked to all other minds. Therefore, whereas our night-time worlds are private, our daytime world is shared. It is a *collective* dream.

3.4. We are not who we think we are; we are the Sons of God with amnesia.

If we dreamt this world, then we are not at all the creatures we seem to be in this world. We are wrong about ourselves. We all know we have a capacity to be wrong about ourselves. Just as the mind can lose touch with reality, so it can lose touch with its own reality and think it is some-thing else.

We see little examples of this all the time. We often decide we have been wrong about ourselves. We even go on searches to find ourselves. And we *know* that everyone around us is wrong about *them*selves. A friend of ours thinks that he is hilariously funny, but we know he is deluding himself. A coworker thinks she is great at her job, but we are sure she is crazy.

This ability can take even more extreme forms. Think, for instance, of a man in a mental ward who believes that he is actually Napoleon, or a woman who has amnesia and has forgotten who she is. Amnesia is a fascinating phenomenon, and highly relevant to our discussion. As we have seen in countless fictional stories, a person can actually forget his or her identity and can even take up a new life in a new environment. This can even happen due to a purely emotional shock; due, in other words, to strictly mental causes.

My favorite example of this general ability is feral children, human children who have been raised apart from human contact, sometimes by animals (wolves, bears, cattle, sheep, dogs, monkeys). These children truly experience themselves as animals. Apparently, if they are caught too late, they can never be trained to act like humans. They will behave like an animal in every way. They may never learn to talk, use a toilet, or walk upright. In their minds, they *are* animals, and will be so for as long as they live.

Here, then, we have an ability which is evident in mild forms in all of us, yet which can take forms of ever increasing extremity. This prompts us to wonder where the limits really are. How far can this ability go? How fundamentally wrong could we be about ourselves? On the most basic level, we think that we are human beings, that we are separate minds encased in physical bodies. We think we are biological creatures, with perhaps a bit of mind or soul stuck inside. Could we even be wrong about this? Could we be something else entirely?

According to *A Course in Miracles*, we *are* wrong and we *are* something else. We are, in fact, still exactly the same as we were in the beginning. What else could we be if the separation never occurred? We, then, are still the Sons of God, vast, limitless spirits, without boundary or defect. We merely dream that we are tiny, flawed *homo sapiens*.

This may sound like the familiar idea that we have two selves, a higher self and a lower self, a divine self and a human one. For the time being we are this human self, yet there is a divine part of us, too, and we remain connected to it. Perhaps our higher self is a divine spark buried deep inside of us. Or perhaps the higher self is a kind of parent self, which has sent forth our human self like a tentacle into time and space.

This theory of two selves, however, is decidedly, emphatically, *not* what the Course is saying. This is extremely important to understand. For the idea of two selves assumes that we are basically right in believing we are this human being. It says, "Yes, we *are* this self, but in *addition* to it we have another self of which we are not aware." This absolutely is not what the Course teaches. "You are not two selves in conflict."[23] "The opposites you see in you will never be compatible. But one exists."[24]

Only one self exists. Think of a man who is convinced he is Elvis. Are there two selves, the man himself and Elvis? Or is there only the man who believes he is someone else? In the exact same way, there is only one "you." You are the Son of God who believes he is this human named so-and-so from such-and-such a place. And you are wrong about yourself. Like the amnesiac, you have forgotten who you are and have even (in your dreams) started a new life in a new environment as someone else. You are delusional. Yet rather than being a John Doe who has delusions of grandeur and believes he is Jesus Christ, Son of God, you are the Son of God who has delusions of littleness and believes he is John Doe. Similar to the case of feral children, you are a Christ Child who has been living among these human animals for so long that you actually believe you are a human. In the words of a popular saying in spiritual circles, you are not a human being having an occasional spiritual experience, you are a spiritual being having a human experience—rather, *dreaming* about a human experience.

The whole matter hinges on the identity of this person we call "you." Who is this "you"? Underneath all the qualities and attributes you ascribe to yourself, there is the essential you about which we know certain basic facts. "You" are the one who is thinking your thoughts, making your choices, feeling your sensations, experiencing your emotions. You are the one who right now feels your body sitting on a chair or couch or bed, who is causing your fingers to hold this book, who is directing your eyes to move across this page. You are not the thoughts, the choices, the sensations, the emotions. You are the thinker, the chooser, the feeler, the experiencer.

Do you know who this "you" is? To put it bluntly, you don't, for even though you *are* this "you," you have never seen yourself. You may see the thoughts, choices, feelings, and emotions, but not the "you" that is right on the other side of them. Rather, you are the one *doing* the seeing. You are what sees, not what is seen. Seeing yourself, the seer, would be like trying to see your eyeballs without a mirror. It can't be done, of course. And just as you can't see your eyeballs, so you have never seen yourself.

Because you cannot see the "you" who is doing the seeing, you have spent your life trying to figure out what this creature is, who *you* are. What question could be more central? You have tried to answer it by observing all kinds of evidence: whether your thoughts are kind or wicked, whether your deeds are intelligent or foolish, whether people like you or ignore you, whether you have earned a place in the world or are a nobody. Each bit of evidence points to certain conclusions about who you are. But what if all this evidence is false evidence? What if none of it tells you who the "you" behind all this activity is.

The teaching of *A Course in Miracles* is that this very you *is* the Son of God. You are the Son of God with amnesia. You are a limitless spirit who has fallen into delusions, who has gone mad. The Son of God is not some buried spark within you, not some higher self, not some hidden part of you. It is this very "you" who thinks your thoughts, who makes your choices, who feels your feelings. The one who is reading this page and pondering these ideas is the one who is the Son of God. "The Son of God is you."[25] This "you" is perfect in nature, yet, paradoxically, is also capable of feeling pain, making mistakes, and forgetting the truth. Perhaps now you can hear in a new way the Course's statements about what you are, and rather than deflect them onto some remote hypothetical higher self, realize they are speaking directly about the very you who reads these words:

> You are a child of God, a priceless part of His Kingdom, which He created as part of Him. Nothing else exists and only this is real. You have chosen a sleep in which you have had bad dreams....Your dreams contain many of the ego's symbols [the external symbols of separation we discussed in Chapter 2] and they have confused you. Yet that was only because you were asleep and did not know. When you wake you will see the truth around you and in you, and you will no longer believe in dreams.[26]

In the same way, try to hear the following passage in a new way, as words that God is speaking directly to the you, the very you that seems so fumbling and confused, yet in truth is perfect:

> You are still My holy Son, forever innocent, forever loving and forever loved, as limitless as your Creator, and completely changeless and forever pure. Therefore awaken and return to Me. I am your Father and you are My Son.[27]

3.5. We are not here in this world or in these bodies. We are in Heaven dreaming that we are here.

So, we are a spiritual being. This means, does it not, that we are a spirit who is not of this world yet who traveled here, who entered this body at birth, will exit this body at death, and can even on occasion leave it temporarily in what are called out-of-body experiences? No, just like the idea of two selves, this is *not* what the Course is teaching. And, as with that idea, it is essential to understand this.

We certainly seem to be here in this world. We appear to know, in fact, exactly where we are located. We are in a particular country, in a certain town, in a specific room or outdoor locale. Moreover, we are obviously inside this particular body. We are inside this head, and, to be precise, right behind these two eyes.

Or are we? For just as the mind can give itself an illusion of being some*one* it is not, so it can also give itself an illusion of being some-*where* it is not. You can experience yourself in a place other than where you are. This may sound strange, but it is truly an everyday occurrence. Each night when you fall asleep you dream of being somewhere else. You might dream of being at work, or back at your childhood home, or on some imaginary landscape. As a child, I used to dream of being chased by Godzilla in Tokyo.

Now when you dream of being back at your childhood home, you really experience yourself as located there. You feel that you are there in that dream house, in that dream body, even behind its dream eyes. But where are you really? You are in bed, of course (at least according to conventional understanding). Your mind has given you a very convincing experience of being in a place you are not.

A high-tech example of this is virtual reality (VR), which allows you to experience yourself inside a computer-generated environment. My colleague Allen Watson tells a great story of his son experiencing virtual reality:

> My son, Ben, is getting his Computer Science Ph.D. at Georgia Tech with a strong emphasis on virtual reality. Not long ago he visited VR laboratories in Japan, where they were experimenting with VR in connection with robots. He put on a VR helmet (so his eyes and ears now beheld and heard what was projected on the screen of the helmet or played through its speakers); he wore a VR sleeve on his arm and hand. These were connected to a robot, which had a camera and microphone on its "head" and whose mechanical arm and hand responded to the movements of Ben's arm and hand. He was seeing what the robot "saw," hearing what it "heard," and picking up objects with its hand.
>
> Then he had a very odd experience. He turned his (the robot's) head, looked across the room, and saw his fleshly body sitting on the other side, wearing all this weird-looking gear. Ben's awareness was inside the robot, although his body was on the other side of the room. He seemed to be separate from his body.[28]

Ben had an illusion of being located somewhere that he was not. It is not hard to see why. His vision and hearing came through the robot's eyes and ears, and his movements moved the robot's arm. Of course he felt like he was inside the robot. You would feel like you were inside *anything* that your sensory and motor functions were hooked up to. Imagine that there were technology that could hook you up to a cricket, so that you saw from the vantage point of its eyes, heard from the vantage point of its ears, and were able to swivel its head and move its legs. Wouldn't you feel like you were inside the cricket?

Right now, your sensory and motor functions are hooked up to this human body. How do you know that this body is any different from the cricket or the robot? How do you know that you are not somewhere else entirely, merely experiencing yourself as being located in this body? How can you be sure that this is not a dream body, fundamentally no different from the imaginary body you have in your dreams?

Furthermore, when you experience yourself in a certain body—whether the robot body, the cricket body, or your human body—you also quite naturally experience yourself as being inside the environment *it* is inside. If the robot that Ben had been hooked up to was not in the same room, but was under the ocean, Ben would have experienced himself as being under the ocean. If, then, you are not in that body, then you may well not be in that environment at all. If you are not inside this human body, then it is quite possible that you are not anywhere in the physical world. You may be outside of time and space altogether.

The Course's radical claim is just that: that we are not here. We are not inside these bodies and never have been. "It must be that you are not within a body."[29] Likewise, we have never set foot in this world, never even visited here. How *could* we come here? There is no *here* to come to. It is just a set of images in our minds. Coming here would be like actually traveling to that nonexistent island you dreamed about.

If this world is a dream, where, then, is the bed in which we sleep? Where are we truly located? According to the Course, we are exactly where we have always been:

You are at home in God, dreaming of exile.[30]

You dwell not here, but in eternity. You travel but in dreams, while safe at home.[31]

Do you see the irony in these lines? We are dreaming that we have been banished from our home and are living a life of exile, a wanderer with no permanent refuge. Yet we are having this dream while safe at home, asleep in our Father's Arms. Just as we can be asleep in bed and experience ourselves in some fantasy locale, so we can be asleep *in God* and experience ourselves in this fantasy world.

The two previous points are closely related: We can be wrong about *who* we think we are and about *where* we think we are. To bring these home, let me relate the story of the weird disease. Imagine, if you will, the following events really happening to you. Try to make them real to you.

You contract a really weird disease, a disease like no other known to humankind. Its first symptom is blindness. You go blind and cannot see a thing. Then you go deaf. You cannot hear even the loudest noise. The sights and sounds of the world have now been shut off. But you still know that the world is there. You can move about in it and feel things with your hands. Yet the weird disease progresses further. Its next step is to paralyze you. You cannot move your arms, your legs, your head, your mouth, even your eyes.

Thankfully, though, you can still feel sensations. You can feel the sun on your skin, the bed beneath your back (for by now you are surely in bed). But the weird disease keeps progressing. Now your body goes entirely numb. You cannot feel your body at all and have no sense of smell or taste. This puts you in a very strange position. How would you know where you are? How would you know if you are at home, in a hospital, or being transported in a car? And how would you know what is happening to you? If you were right in the middle of a car accident, would you know it? If they were amputating your leg without anesthesia right this second, would you have the remotest idea?

All communication with the world has now been severed. Yet at least you still know who you are. You have your memories; millions of memories telling you exactly who you are, who you know, and what your place is in the world. Now imagine that the weird disease goes one step further and gives you a case of absolute amnesia. You don't remember a thing, not your name, not your face, not your parents or children, not your home, nothing. As a result, you no longer know who you are.

And now the weird disease takes its final step. In the total darkness of your mind, you begin to dream. But this is no ordinary dream.

Because of the weird disease, this dream has none of the bizarre irrationalities and inconsistencies of normal dreams. It is totally consistent and completely logical down to the last detail. And it doesn't end after a few minutes. It keeps going and going, for years without letup.

In the dream, you are an intelligent rodent-like creature living on an alien planet. You have a job and a family and a name. You serve a useful function in the rodent society. You have an entire life. You look out at this planet through the rodent eyes. You feel as if you are literally inside the rodent body. Everything you see, hear, touch, smell, and taste tells you that this is *what* you are and this is *where* you are. It all seems completely real.

This dream goes on for ten years. In your mind, it is the only reality you have ever known. Then one day in your dream life, you encounter a dream book. This book finally tells you exactly what the real truth is. It tells you that you are not this rodent creature at all, that you are not contained inside the rodent body, nor do you live on the alien planet. It says that you are really a creature called a human being living on a planet called Earth. You have merely contracted a weird disease, it tells you, one that has shut down your awareness of your real surroundings, given you amnesia, and caused you to dream. Finally, it says that all the things you now experience—your rodent identity, your rodent body, your rodent life, and the entire alien planet—are simply images inside your mind as you lie motionless on a hospital bed. Of all your experiences in this long-running dream, only this book is telling you the real truth.

Would you believe it?

Now, in what we call real life, a book has come to face us with a similar radical idea. *A Course in Miracles* has come to tell us that we are not the human creature we think we are, nor are we located in the world in which we experience ourselves. We are neither *what* nor *where* we think we are. Rather, we are still the Sons of God in Heaven, merely dreaming that we are separate humans in a physical world. With great certainty, this book presents a completely different understanding of what and where we are:

> God created you as part of Him. That is both where you are
> and what you are. It is completely unalterable.[32]

In other words, *what* we are is part of God, and *where* we are is part of God—in God. In one of the Course's prayers, we are given the words that each one of us, deep in our hearts, is aching to say to God, which tell Him that we have never deviated from His original creation of us: "As You created me I have remained. Where You established me I still abide."[33]

Could this glorious idea really be true? Could the news truly be this good? And now that this book, *A Course in Miracles*, is telling us such news, will we believe it?

3.6. The instant the separation seemed to occur, God created the Holy Spirit, Who awakened us that same instant. We are now only reviewing a journey that is over.

Let us now go back to the moment when the separation seemed to begin, so we can complete our telling of the real story of the separation. When our minds entertained the tiny, mad idea and began to fall asleep and dream, God became aware, not of what we were dreaming, but *that* we were sleeping. The Course tells us this quite directly in two important passages:

> His joy is not complete because yours is incomplete. And this He does know. He knows it in His Own Being and its experience of His Son's experience. The constant going out of His Love is blocked when His channels are closed, and He is lonely[34] when the minds He created do not communicate fully with Him.[35]

> What God does know is that His communication channels are not open to Him, so that He cannot impart His joy and know that His children are wholly joyous....So He thought, "My children sleep and must be awakened."[36]

Both passages say the same thing, that God "does know" that "His channels"—His Sons—are closed down to Him, not communicating with Him. He knows they are asleep.

In response to this, God did not get angry; He did not retaliate. He merely called His children to wake up. He breathed out His Voice and gave forth a Call to awaken that echoed through every sleeping mind, that sang in the heart of every dreamer, calling him to simply come home.

This Voice is what the Course calls the Holy Spirit. We will look at the Holy Spirit in greater detail in Chapter 9 (along with the paradox of God's Voice also being a Being, in a sense, in Its Own right). For now it will suffice to say that as soon as the separation seemed to occur, God created the Holy Spirit. And as soon as God created the Holy Spirit, the separation was over. The Father spoke one Word and the Son awoke. How else could it go?

This teaching, however, leaves us with a great many paradoxes and subtleties, which I will attempt to briefly explain in the remainder of this chapter.

According to *A Course in Miracles*, the separation lasted only a microsecond, a "tiny tick of time."[37] This tiny instant contained the single error of the separation: the choice for separateness over oneness, for death over life. And it contained this error fragmented into billions of separate situations and events, as if this one error were seen refracted in a kaleidoscope. Each situation and event was a fractured version of the original error.

Then, into this primordial moment God shone His single Correction for our single error. This Correction (the Holy Spirit), though single, adapted Itself to every variation of that error. It took the specific form needed for each specific situation:

> The tiny tick of time in which the first mistake was made, and all of them within that one mistake, held also the Correction for that one, and all of them that came within the first.[38]

In that tiny tick, these two met, our error (along with its fractured forms) and God's Correction (along with Its specific answers). And out of their meeting there arose a single time line, a script for our entire journey through time and space. Each event in the script is composed of both error and correction, though which one predominates differs from event to event. This script, written by the Holy Spirit,[39] is simply the story of our journey from our error to His correction. The beginning parts of the script are dominated by the dark story material we provide. In these early chapters, His correction is standing off to the side, nearly invisible. Yet as the story proceeds, the Holy Spirit's story ideas come increasingly to the fore, as we choose more and more His answer over our mistake. Finally, we allow Him to write only His story, which thus concludes with a happy ending, a joyous homecoming, as we abandon our error entirely in favor of His correction.

I am talking about this story as if it takes place over time. Yet, as I said earlier, all of it took place simultaneously. It happened all at once, inside the original tiny tick. In that tiny tick (as the old saying goes) our life passed before our eyes. Not just a few decades, though; countless eons were compressed into a single instant. Billions of fractured forms of the original error met with billions of specific forms of the one Correction. And then it was over.

> And in that tiny instant time was gone, for that was all it ever was. What God gave answer to is answered and is gone.[40]

This all happened at the dawn of time, a long, long time ago. Yet, if it is all over, why are you still experiencing it? The Course's answer is that, quite simply, you are trying very hard "to hold it to your heart, as if it were before you still."[41] Like any disturbing (or delightful) incident we can't get over, we began to ruminate on it, retracing in our mind each episode in its progression, "reviewing mentally what has gone by."[42] This process of mental review is what produces what we call real life. In seeing the scene before us, the objects in front of us, the things that are happening, we are not seeing, we are *remembering*. What we are looking on right now, this instant, is a memory. "You keep an ancient memory before your eyes."[43] Like someone gone senile, we are living in our memories.[44]

Our entire lives, then, can be likened to watching an old movie on videotape. We are so absorbed in this movie that we feel like we are actually living inside it. We think that its ending is really up for grabs. Yet, "The script is written."[45] The movie was shot and edited ages ago. None of it can be changed, not the characters, the scenes, or the story line—and especially not the ending. As we will see later (key idea 10.5), there is only one difference we can make: Whenever we want we can hit the fast forward button. This happens by accepting a miracle, which allows us to jump past a batch of scenes and more quickly reach the happy ending.[46]

This theory of time can sound nothing short of bizarre. Yet it is not nearly as implausible as it sounds at first. The Course points to the very nature of time as evidence for its theory.[47]

Time is composed of cycles, rhythms, repetitions; the cycle of the days and nights, the tides, the seasons. When we look closer at these cycles, we see that each one is composed, in essence, of a single repeating pulse of *birth* and *death*. Each cycle springs up with a fresh burst of life, and then sinks down into the deterioration of death. At any given moment our body is undergoing countless such pulses, as old cells die off and new cells are born, as new air is inhaled and old air exhaled. These smaller pulses exist within the larger pulse of the day; each morning we are reborn only to "die" at the end of the day. Each day in turn exists within the larger cycle of the seasons, as nature itself dies and is reborn each year. And for those who believe in reincarnation, these repeating years exist within the larger cycle of repeating lives.

Time, then, is composed of repeating pulses of birth/death, smaller ones within larger ones, larger ones within still larger ones, and all within the single pulse of the birth and death of the universe itself. Time itself, then, is merely the endless repetition of birth/death. Onto this, the Course would merely add: Of course it is, for time is our incessant attempt to repeat that ancient instant of birth/death. Time is a continual repetition of that instant when we tried to replace life with death, when we "chose to die instead of live."[48] It is "a repetition of an instant gone by long ago that cannot be relived."[49]

We keep dying in countless ways through all of time's cycles because we continuously repeat that original choice to die. And we keep being born because we can never really succeed in dying; we can never kill eternal life. Hence, every time we die we find that we are merely born again and faced with the same choice once more: Will we choose death again, or life? "Each instant is the Son of God reborn until he chooses not to die again."[50] The very fact that we never succeed in completing the cycle, that we cannot die once and for all, reflects the Course's claim that we are trying to do the impossible. We are trying to relive an instant that cannot *really* be relived, for it is gone.

Thus what initially looked like an extremely bizarre theory we now see reflected all around us, in every breath, day, and year; in all the little births and deaths that make up time; and in the very nature of time itself. And thus we now can more fully appreciate the line we quoted at the end of Chapter 2:

> Each day, and every minute in each day, and every instant that each minute holds, you but relive the single instant when the time of terror took the place of love.[51]

This theory of time adds a crucial piece into our overall picture of the separation. Not only is the world merely a dream, it is a dream that lasted only an instant and was over a long time ago:

> Only in the past,—an ancient past, too short to make a world in answer to creation,—did this world appear to rise. So very long ago, for such a tiny interval of time, that not one note in Heaven's song was missed.[52]

Hence, in an evocative passage, the Course compares us to someone standing on the beach and fantasizing that he is actually across the ocean, living in a romantic time and place that have long since been swallowed up by history. He starts by merely imagining he is there, yet begins to really believe he is there. Finally, he goes completely mad and becomes utterly convinced that he is not on the beach, but really living a life in that far away, ancient land.

> And who can stand upon a distant shore, and dream himself across an ocean, to a place and time that have long since gone by? How real a hindrance can this dream be to where he really is? For this is fact, and does not change whatever dreams he has. Yet can he still imagine he is elsewhere, and in another time. In the extreme, he can delude himself that this is true, and pass from mere imagining into belief and into madness, quite convinced that where he would prefer to be, he *is*.[53]

We, then, are the Sons of the Most High standing (so to speak) on the formless shore of Heaven. We dream we are across an ocean of nothingness, totally convinced that we are living in this fantasy place called earth, in this fictional time called the twenty-first century, even though this place and time have long since vanished into nothingness, even though all that exists is the Kingdom in which we stand and its present moment of eternity.

This image ties together a chapter in which we have covered some of the most mind-boggling and counterintuitive ideas that we shall touch upon in this book. In sum, we have said that we have the ability to experience ourselves as a *person* we are not, in a *place* we are not, and even in a *time* we are not. Our entire "reality" can be a trick of the mind. And, according to the Course, so it is. In laying out this concept, we have ranged very far beyond the daily concerns of those of us who still tie our shoes and butter our toast, "who count the hours still, and rise and work and go to sleep by them."[54] Why, then, is all this so important? What makes it relevant?

We will be taking the rest of the book to explain that. But for now, suffice it to say that all of us have spent our whole lives looking for Eden. Whatever roads we have chosen we are all searching for that paradise, that pristine home that still glistens in the first dawn, unmarred by all that has happened since. We are looking for our real home, a place of real safety where we know in the depths of our being that we truly belong. And we are all searching for that ideal person we think we could have been, and perhaps at some point were. We all secretly desire to recover the innocence we sense we lost somewhere along the thorny roads we have traveled on. *A Course in Miracles* says,

> It is for this [lost innocence] you yearn. This is your heart's desire. This is the voice you hear, and this the call which cannot be denied.[55]

In short, we are all trying to get back to the Garden.

Would not the following news, then, be the most exhilarating, the most *relevant* that we could possibly hear? One perfect spring day, while still in the innocence of divine youth, we merely fell asleep in the grass there in the Garden. And all that has happened since, all that we think we have become, has just been our idle dream while we napped on the grass. And we are still there on the grass. Only a moment has passed. The gentle breeze blows across our innocent faces, while nearby the Lord God walks in the Garden in the cool of the day. Our home is as peaceful as ever, and we are as immaculate as the moment of our creation. We don't need to find this place. We don't have to make ourselves worthy. We merely need to open our eyes.

Four

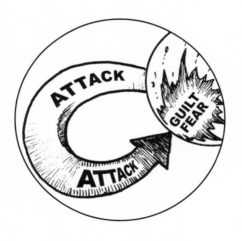

Yet we believed we had really done it. We thought we had sinned and had thereby thrown our happiness away forever.

Four

Listen to the story of the prodigal son....: This son of a loving father left his home and thought he had squandered everything for nothing of any value, although he had not understood its worthlessness at the time. He was ashamed to return to his father, because he thought he had hurt him.[1]

In the last chapter we explored from several angles just how empty of reality, consequence, and duration the separation was. That, however, is how the separation looks from outside of it, from the vantage point of the waking state. While one is inside the dream (as we know from our own nightmares) it can seem hideously real. Its consequences can appear tragic, even cosmic. And it can seem to last forever. In this chapter, then, we will be exploring, not the separation's lack of impact on reality, but its excruciatingly *painful* impact on our *minds*.

The parable of the prodigal son is the only biblical parable retold by the author of the Course, perhaps because its story so closely resembles the Course's own story of our journey. In this chapter we will continue tracing the Son's journey away from home and from his loving Father. At this place in the story, he has traveled to that distant land of opportunity, the "far country," only to find it to be a place of famine and death. As the above quote says, he discovers that he has seemingly "squandered everything for nothing of any value."

4.1. We thought that we had separated ourselves from all that we loved and consequently experienced a state of lack.

If you had a lover who literally was everything to you, and you suddenly felt completely cut off from this person, how would you feel? Now imagine that you shared with this person the loveliest of homes, a place of comfort, safety, and great happiness, and you were cut off from this too. Finally, imagine that the two of you had the most beautiful, happy children, and that they were severed from you as well.

This begins to give us some idea of how utterly lacking and empty we felt as a result of the separation. For God had been everything to us, our Mother, our Lover, our Brother, our Father.[2] In Heaven He had been "my Source of life, the life within, the air I breathe, the food by which I am sustained, the water which renews and cleanses me."[3] Apparently cut off from Him, from our home, and from our creations, our heavenly children, we felt severed from our own being, from our own wholeness. As the Course says, we quite naturally experienced "depression, a sense of worthlessness, and feelings of impermanence and unreality."[4]

> And where, you wonder, does your strange uneasiness,
> your sense of being disconnected, and your haunting fear
> of lack of meaning in yourself arise?[5]

This passage is right. We *do* wonder from whence comes our strange uneasiness, our sense of being a floating leaf, a wandering stranger in an alien land. We wonder where this massive cavity inside us comes from, this gnawing emptiness that feels like a void at the core of our very identity. We may have traced it back to not being breastfed, not being held enough, being the middle child, having the wrong body type, or any number of things. Yet according to *A Course in Miracles*, this sense of lack comes from one place only: our feeling of being separate from God. "A sense of separation from God is the only lack you really need correct."[6]

4.2. We thought that we had sinned against God, that we had launched a real attack which caused real destruction.

The idea of being separate from God, however, is only half the story of our pain. The other half is the idea that we *caused* it. We were responsible. As a result, we believed (and still believe) we mortally sinned and so *deserved* our state of lack.

This belief in sin sets the stage for the entire remainder of the Course's thought system. It is therefore essential for us to understand.

What is sin? A sin, of course, is a violation of the laws of God, a crime against God. In addition to this definition there is a more interpersonal definition which is also important for the Course. From this angle, a sin might be defined as *a real attack*, an attack with real intent and real effects. Let us break this up into two separate points. A sin is:

1. *An attack that attempts to do harm for the sake of selfish gain*
2. *An attack that succeeds, that results in real harm and brings gain to the attacker*

Both of the above points are important. You can hardly blame someone if she had truly no idea that her actions would hurt anyone. And you do not blame her all that much if she tried to do harm but failed, if her attack had no effect. By definition, a sin must cause injury. "To sin would be to violate reality, and to succeed. Sin is the proclamation that attack is real."[7] In other words, someone gets violated, someone gets hurt. It matters not whether the injury is a bruised face, a wrecked car, an empty wallet, or merely a "wounded self-esteem."[8] It is still a sin.

Though sin is a word most of us tend to avoid, the concept this word stands for is one of the most pervasive "realities" in this world. Everywhere we look we see people doing selfish things that cause harm to others. That is what the nightly news is all about, along with the fictional stories we read and watch, and of course the personal stories we tell. The sins we see run the gamut, from a dictator who unleashes genocide, to a mother who abandons her children, to a friend who says an unkind word, to a husband who leaves the toilet seat up. And all of these are not, in our eyes, merely violations of human decency. In some sense, they seem to be crimes against God, against God's notion of the way things ought to be.

Strangely, however, most of us do not see sin very much in ourselves. This is truly odd, if indeed the Course is correct. For according to its teaching, we believe we are criminals of metaphysical proportions. Genocide is nothing compared to what we think we did. As we saw in Chapter 2, we believe we really succeeded in attacking God and demolishing His Kingdom. Strange, then, that we do not walk around feeling like cosmic criminals. We will explore the reasons for this later in this chapter.

There is one thing that the Course emphasizes repeatedly in all its discussions of sin: "*Sin is impossible*."[9] We cannot *really* harm another.

Since that person's reality is part of the fabric of reality, truly harming him would mean damaging reality itself. And, as we saw in the last chapter, this is completely impossible. For the same reason, the idea of committing a crime against God is absurd, for God cannot be injured. Therefore, thinking we have sinned is not a humble thought. It is literally a delusion of grandeur:

> Sin is the grand illusion underlying all the ego's grandiosity. For by it God Himself is [supposedly] changed, and rendered incomplete.[10]

Do we really think we have the power to change God?

4.3. The result of sin was a massive sense of guilt, which we denied and so pushed into the unconscious.

Sin produces guilt. What is guilt? Guilt, very simply, is the emotional experience of the belief that I am a sinner, that I have intentionally injured another. Guilt says that once my sin wounded my victim, it turned around and tainted me, changing me into a bad person, reaching inside and planting some kind of rot or corruption at my core. Isn't that how we feel in the pit of our stomach when we think we have sinned? It feels like there is a stain on our soul which can never be washed away, a black mark on our record that can never be erased. Few feelings are more terrible.

Perhaps you do not consider guilt to be one of the bigger problems in your life. If you are a longtime Course student, this was especially true before you began studying the Course, as it observes in this passage: "Of one thing you were sure: Of all the many causes you perceived as bringing pain and suffering to you, your guilt was not among them."[11] Let's look at the phenomenon of guilt.

We are generally aware of only the most superficial kind of guilt, guilt over very clear and concrete things we have done wrong. The Course makes an astute comment about this:

> You do experience the guilt, but you have no idea why. On the contrary, you associate it with a weird assortment of "ego ideals," which the ego claims you have failed.[12]

In other words, our guilt appears to come from what you might call sins against our pride. We feel guilty for violating our personal code for being a capable, responsible, *exceptional* ego. Consequently, we might feel acute guilt over forgetting a lunch date and yet feel strangely cold about turning our back on someone for good. Such guilt ends up affirming the sanctity of our ego ideals, and ultimately the sanctity of the ego itself. And this strengthens our fundamental guilt, for in the final analysis, guilt does not come from failing our ego ideals, but from failing our divine nature by believing that we *are* an ego.

These bouts of acute guilt over isolated and relatively tame errors are the topmost ice crystal on the tip of the proverbial iceberg. Beneath these, there is a judge we have permanently stationed in the back of our minds. This judge observes our every thought, our every comment, our every deed, and duly notes how self-centered and coldly disconnected each one shows us to be. While our conscious life rolls blithely on, this self-judging goes on without interruption. The Course says that every thought not directly inspired by God "is attended by guilt at its inception, and maintained by guilt in its continuance."[13] The result is a long list of harsh labels that we secretly whisper to ourselves. The Course provides one such list:

> The ego can and does allow you to regard yourself as supercilious [haughtily contemptuous], unbelieving, "light-hearted," distant, emotionally shallow, callous, uninvolved and even desperate.[14]

How many of these labels have you accused yourself of? You are probably lucky if you can find one that you have *not* accused yourself of.

Let's look more closely at this list. Can you see a theme running through the items on it? You should be embracing certain beliefs and engaging with situations, but instead you stand off—you are unbelieving and uninvolved. You should be connecting with the emotional gravity of a situation, but instead you are "light-hearted" and emotionally shallow. When it comes to people, you should feel connected and caring, but instead you are distant, callous, and supercilious. In each of these cases you are standing apart from something you believe you ideally should connect with or commit to. You are separating. And that is what the judge within you condemns you for—for separating.

Yet far, far underneath all of this, "kept still deeper in the mists below"[15] your conscious mind, lies your deepest guilt, what could be called *primordial guilt*, guilt from the dawn of time. This ancient guilt lies buried and supposedly forgotten beneath the very foundations of your personal selfhood. "The darkest of your hidden cornerstones holds your belief in guilt from your awareness."[16]

Let's imagine just for a moment that there is a place in us, beneath some dark, hidden door, in which we harbor our primordial guilt. Imagine, if you will, that you open that door and walk in. There you dimly remember a celestial paradise in which you were a celestial being, as pure as God Himself. Yet there you also remember that you (supposedly) wrecked this paradise. You recall a nightmarish story in which, in an attempt to elevate yourself above all else, you tore yourself out of your Father's Heart, mortally wounded Him and shattered the pristine sky of His Mind. As a result of this (apparent) demonic crime, you believe you transformed your once angelic perfection into pure evil. You nurse the sad, "lingering belief that you have made a devil of God's Son."[17]

Finding such a place in your mind would be the ultimate horror. Can you even conceive of how this would feel? If you sensed this memory was down there, would you not do absolutely everything in your power to avoid such a discovery, to bury it in your mind as deep as you possibly could? We know that children can bury terrifying memories of abuse. Could you not bury this incomparably *more* terrifying memory? According to the Course, this is precisely what you did. "Denial has no power in itself, but you can give it the power of your mind, whose power is without limit."[18] If you could use your limitless power to deny your natural state, why could you not also deny the guilt from that act?

From the Course's standpoint, then, our lives could be likened to that of a war criminal who committed gruesome atrocities during the war, yet who managed after the war to flee to a new country, change his identity and start a new life. Through a virtually superhuman act of denial, he even managed to suppress the memory of his atrocities. Thus, he carries on as if it never happened, except for one thing: Some nameless horror hangs over him like a cloud, dogging his every footstep and lurking behind every corner. As the Course points out in the following passage, no matter how deeply guilt is denied, it does not just go away, and always manages to work its way to the surface:

What form of murder serves to cover the massive guilt and

frantic fear of punishment the murderer must feel? He may deny he is a murderer and justify his savagery with smiles as he attacks. Yet he will suffer, and will look on his intent in nightmares where the smiles are gone, and where the purpose rises to meet his horrified awareness and pursue him still. For no one thinks of murder and escapes the guilt the thought entails.[19]

4.4. Guilt says that we deserve punishment. This belief is the source of all of our suffering.

If human life as we know it is a tiny colony of water striders scurrying about on a sea of guilt, this changes everything. It redefines our lives, our cultures, and our world. I know that this sounds extremely depressing, that it seems to cast an exceedingly dark pall over our lives. Yet please bear with me, for, believe it or not, this actually leads directly to the Course's message of unconditional liberation.

For the moment, we need to face the fact that this primordial guilt is truly pivotal to the Course's account of things. This, in fact, is the Course's single explanation for why we suffer. Remember that quote from the previous section, which said you did not think that guilt even made it onto the list of all the things that cause your pain? The truth, says the Course, is all the way on the other end of the spectrum. The real list is a one-item list: "Guilt is...the sole cause of pain in any form."[20]

How could guilt be the sole cause of all pain? Let's follow the Course's logic. If we sinned, if we truly injured another for our own gain, what do we deserve? The answer is easy: punishment. Punishment is the natural consequence of sin. "If sin is real, then punishment is just and cannot be escaped."[21] If in fact we did attack and did cause real harm then, naturally, we should be harmed in return. We gave pain, so we should receive it. What we sow, we should reap. This seems like simple justice.

We are intimately familiar with this idea. Human culture is held together by this notion of justice. It is the basis for the justice system, it permeates traditional religion, and indeed it governs the whole of human interaction. Nation retaliates against nation, parent scolds child, wife gives tongue-lashing to husband, judge sentences criminal, lover withdraws affection after a perceived slight. No matter how small the sin, the scales of justice must be balanced.

Now imagine once again that you really do carry bottomless guilt in that hidden place in your mind. In that same place, then, you would believe you deserve punishment whose "wrath is boundless, merciless, but wholly just."[22] Imagine further that your mind really does have unlimited power, power to make all its beliefs come true (at least in its experience). Now what do you think would follow from this combination of total power and bottomless guilt? What would be the result of deeply believing that you deserve punishment and having the power to make your beliefs come true?

Would it not perhaps be *your life*, with all of its punishing circumstances, with all the ways it handcuffs you, with all the shackles it puts you in, with its forced labor, and with its cruel guards who seem bent on keeping you in line? Don't we all feel at times like we are in prison? And aren't we all on death row? Has it not ever seemed like we are being constantly punished for something we don't ever remember doing? According to the Course, we *are*; but not by God, by ourselves.

Perhaps now we can see the logic behind the idea that all human suffering is a manifestation of guilt. Guilt says quite simply that we *deserve* to suffer. Therefore, guilt calls on the power of the mind to dream suffering into our existence. This includes all forms of suffering: "All sorrow, loss, anxiety and suffering and pain, even a little sigh of weariness, a slight discomfort or the merest frown."[23] This even includes the most extreme and final "punishment," physical death: "death is...punishment for sin."[24] According to the Course, none of this world's misery is mere random injustice. All of it is self-punishment for imagined guilt. We will expand on this concept in the next chapter.

Before we go on, I want to offer one more reflection on this idea that guilt is the heart of our suffering. This idea has always struck me as out of place because it seemed like I was suffering over a great many other things—for instance, over not having this thing I wanted or that person I loved. I finally realized that whatever my primary pain really is, it must be the flip side of my primary desire. In other words, guilt can only be my core pain if my core desire is for guilt's opposite. By saying that feeling defiled and corrupt and evil—feeling guilty—is my deepest pain, the Course is implying that my deepest yearning is to feel clean, holy, innocent, loving. Personally, I sense that this is true. If I were truly honest with myself, I would see that my desire for the things of this world counts as nothing next to my desire to be pure goodness.

To really accept, then, that guilt is the heart of your suffering, you will also have to accept (in the words of a passage we quoted in Chapter 3) that innocence "is your heart's desire," that "this is the voice you hear, and this the call which cannot be denied."[25] And if you can accept that innocence is your heart's desire, perhaps you can go the next step and accept that innocence is a part of your heart, that holiness is at the core of your nature.

4.5. We project our belief that we deserve punishment onto God and so perceive a punitive, fearful God.

One of the most crucial moves we make with our guilt is to project it onto God. This does not so much mean that we see a guilty God; it means we see a God Who looks on us as we look on ourselves—as guilty. It means believing in a God Who is simply an overblown image of our own guilty conscience. If we think we actually sinned, are truly guilty, and honestly deserve punishment, then we will inevitably believe that God shares those views, for how could God be out of touch with reality?

Therefore, in that same deep place which holds our primordial guilt, we carry a literally terrifying image of God, a God Who thirsts for vengeance on us for what we did. On a conscious level, we see ourselves surrounded by a dangerous world, bristling with all manner of sharp edges, from terrorists to toxic mold to quarrelsome spouses. On an unconscious level, however, we see all of these as God's puppets, mere pawns in His campaign to hunt us down and pay us back. As the Course puts it, we see His "fearful image...at work in all the evils of the world."[26] Hence, in this buried place we live in mortal fear of Him. An important passage in the Manual for Teachers describes this hidden belief of ours:

> Who usurps the place of God and takes it for himself now has a deadly "enemy." And he must stand alone in his protection, and make himself a shield to keep him safe from fury that can never be abated, and vengeance that can never be satisfied.[27]

This is a harrowing image, this picture of our beloved Father turning into our deadly enemy, and of us scurrying to erect our measly defenses, to hold up our tiny shield before the onslaught of His almighty storm. In such a despairing situation, how would one try to cope? How could we possibly win a war against God Himself? The same passage goes on to address how we try to resolve this hopeless dilemma:

> How can this unfair battle be resolved? Its ending is inevitable, for its outcome must be death. How, then, can one believe in one's defenses? Magic...must help. Forget the battle. Accept it as a fact, and then forget it. Do not remember the impossible odds against you. Do not remember the immensity of the "enemy," and do not think about your frailty in comparison. Accept your separation, but do not remember how it came about. Believe that you have won it, but do not retain the slightest memory of Who your great "opponent" really is. Projecting your "forgetting" onto Him, it seems to you He has forgotten, too.[28]

There is no way to win a battle with God. Hence, our defense against Him had to be an imaginary wave of a mental magic wand. Like a child who closes his eyes and thinks that no one can see him, we decided to forget the battle and hope that this made it magically go away. This is the Course's explanation for how we could be filled with such terror yet be unaware of it. Just like our guilt, we buried this terror deep in our minds and then carried on as if it had never been there.

This can look like a rather convenient move on the Course's part. One can hypothesize any kind of emotion in the mind and then, when asked why we do not feel it, say that, well, it is unconscious. Where, then, is the evidence for this unconscious fear of God?

The evidence lies in thousands of years of traditional images of God. We are all familiar with these images, which portray God as both loving and vengeful. For those brought up in the Judeo-Christian tradition, we remember this "loving" God kicking Adam and Eve out of the Garden, wiping out almost the entire earth with a flood, killing His own Son for sins that other people committed, and promising us that we will one day stand before His throne as He critically reviews our every deed and quite possibly sends us into the lake of everlasting fire. For those not brought up in the Judeo-Christian tradition, other gods are no better. One thinks of the Hindu Shiva, who is destroyer as well as creator, or bloody Kali with her necklace of skulls, or the Islamic Allah who is both caring creator and annihilating judge.

These traditional images are reflected in our conflicting personal attitudes toward God. We comfort ourselves by saying He's got the whole world, including our fragile lives, in His hand. But this thought has a disturbing flip side which does not go entirely unnoticed: "He holds your little life in his hand but by a thread, ready to break it off without regret or care, perhaps today."[29] We go on searches to find God and make Him ours, but we also carry this haunting fear that *He* will catch up with *us*, "somewhere, sometime, in some form that evens the account [we] owe to God."[30] We want His guidance, yet we fear what sacrifice it might demand of us, for somewhere inside we "cannot trust Him not to strike [us] dead with lightning bolts torn from the 'fires' of Heaven."[31]

The Course forcefully rejects these fearful images. In a wonderful line, it says, "He does not lead you through a world of misery, waiting to tell you, at the journey's end, why He did this to you."[32] This, of course, pokes fun at a common view. In that view, God hands us a life in this world, and we then spend the duration of that life just trying to figure out why we are here and why on earth it is so damn hard. Then we console ourselves by saying He will reveal it all to us—once it is too late and we are dead. Similarly, we believe God sends gifts into our lives, yet these gifts often show up initially in the form of pain and sacrifice. However, we are supposed to have faith that the gift will someday reveal itself as good, and then be grateful for this goodness in advance. The Course minces no words with this point of view:

> Good in disaster's form is difficult to credit in advance. Nor is there really sense in this idea.
>
> Why should the good appear in evil's form?...There is no reason for an interval in which disaster strikes, to be perceived as "good" some day but now in form of pain.[33]

A Course in Miracles teaches that all of these fearful images have nothing to do with God at all. They are purely projections of our minds. For centuries people have suspected that this God is merely our own projection, a blown-up version of our image of ourselves. There certainly is truth in that, though the Course is making a subtly different point here. It is saying that this God is a *companion image* required by our self-image. If our underlying self-image is that of an evil criminal, we will naturally project a terrible judge that frowns upon and condemns us. Only a *guilty* person would dream up a *punishing* God.

These traditional images, then, are the evidence for our unconscious fear of God. Indeed, from the Course's perspective, we did not really acquire these images from the religion of our parents. Instead, that religion inherited them from deep within the collective psyche, from deep within *us*. Religion, in fact, is only one avenue through which our universal fear of God finds expression. Atheism is another. The faithful believe in a God Who seeks vengeance upon them. The atheists, according to the Course,[34] believe in a God Who abandoned them. Yet is not abandonment one of the most severe forms of punishment?

This projection of our guilt onto God is a truly brilliant move by the ego. Remember key idea 2.7, in which we said that the ego's only need is to confirm itself, to keep itself in business? The ego's root fear is that it will disappear in the formless radiance of God's Love. The ego fears God's Love (which is quite different than fearing His *punishment*). To stay alive, therefore, the ego must do everything it can to keep *us* away from His Love. It must teach us to fear Him just as it does. This guarantees that we will keep away from Him and so keep our ego intact. There is one problem with this plan: There is no good reason to fear Him; He is only Love. The ego must therefore *provide* us with a reason. Projecting our guilt onto God gives us a terrific reason. Now we see a God Who is waiting to barbecue us with lightning bolts. Who wants to unite with a God like that? You may worship Him from afar, but you dare not get too close.

As an analogy, imagine that you met a person in this life who asked you to marry him. This person was flawless. He was perfectly loving. Unfortunately, however, he was a foreigner, and to marry him required that you leave your entire life behind, everything you knew. If you found this frightening, might you not protect yourself by making him look bad in your mind? Might you not make up some story about his flaws so that you had an excuse to not marry him and thus hang onto the life you knew? That is precisely what we have done with God.

Even among those of us who no longer believe (or never believed) in frightening images of God, this fear of His vengeance is still down there in our unconscious. For us, it doesn't show up in the form of intellectual belief in a punitive God. Rather, it shows up in the form of the suspicion that what God asks of us is not really in our best interests. He asks us to love others, but we suspect that this leaves us vulnerable to being taken advantage of. He asks us to meditate, but we think our time is better spent watching TV. He asks us to be generous, but we wonder if He really understands that we have a mortgage to pay. We ask for His guidance, but secretly fear that He will ask us to make some noble sacrifice for the sake of the higher good. These beliefs make us drag our feet on the way to God. They make every step toward Him a slog through deep mud. It's as if we don't trust Him, as if we think we need to protect ourselves from Him. Might it not be that these beliefs are nothing more than the conscious manifestation of our fear of His vengeance?

The fear of God's punishment and the fear of God's Love are two different, but intimately related, things. The fear of His wrath is a mask worn by the underlying fear of His embrace. It is an excuse cooked up to give us reason to stay away from One Who is only Love. And so far it has done an excellent job.

4.6. Guilt, then, gives rise to fear, which really is the expectation of punishment. Fear is the dominant emotion of this world.

We have spent this chapter tracing the logic of sin:

- When I think I have intentionally done real harm, I will believe I have sinned (4.2).
- When I think I have sinned, I will feel guilty (4.3).
- When I feel guilty, I will believe I deserve punishment (4.4).
- And when I think I deserve punishment, I will fear punishment from God (4.5).

Guilt, then, looks back into the past, at the sin I supposedly committed. And it looks forward into the future, at the punishment that I can expect.

This brings us to the final step in the logic of sin, a step which we saw in our last point: *fear*. Webster's Dictionary defines fear as "a distressing emotion aroused by impending pain, danger, evil, etc." The Course makes a critical addition to this: Unconsciously, we see the impending pain, danger, and evil as the comeuppance we deserve for our sins. This means that fear is the distressing emotion aroused by *anticipated punishment for sin*. "Whenever you respond to your ego you will experience guilt, and you will fear punishment."[35] We think we fear the world attacking us unjustly, but we forgot that we hired it to carry out all those attacks as the sentence for our crimes.

According to the Course, fear is the diametric opposite of love. Love is a going out, in which we happily extend ourselves to join with something we love. Fear, in contrast, is a withdrawal, in which we shrink back from a perceived danger. We can see the essential contrast between love and fear in this succinct quote: "Everyone draws nigh unto what he loves, and recoils from what he fears."[36] Love goes out to join, fear shrinks back to separate.

As most Course students know, the Course teaches that fear and love are the only two emotions. Each one contains within itself several other emotions, which may seem separate, but are merely smaller aspects of love or fear. Fear is like a snowball, which gets started with the core of anger (the emotion behind attack), then gathers into itself guilt, and finally becomes a giant ball of fear. Love, on the other hand, includes joy, for love is joyous. "There is no difference between love and joy."[37] Love also contains peace within itself, for real love leaves one feeling totally at peace.

Fear is where the entire system of the ego leads us. We all have jolts of fear now and then. According to the Course, however, fear is not an emotion we intermittently experience; it is the state we live in. Think of the sheer number of things we fear. A workshop I did on the Course yielded this brief list: cancer, AIDS, insults, spiders, public speaking, food past the expiration date, abandonment, traffic police, aging, "my mother," losing your keys, death, calories, mosquitoes, registered letters, a knock at the door, the phrase "I've got something I want to talk to you about," appliance malfunctions, germs, car trouble, pollutants, late charges, loss of job, bugs in your food, insomnia.

These are just a couple dozen of what must amount to untold thousands of things we fear. Now, if we can safely assume that at any given moment we are faced with at least several out of these countless sources of fear, then we can logically conclude that we are almost *always* feeling fear. And we are not just feeling it; we are responding to it. Virtually all of our time is spent trying to head off some impending danger, some unfortunate outcome which will befall us if we sit and do nothing. If we are feeling fear all the time, and continually acting from the basis of this fear, then fear is very far from an occasional emotion. It is the human condition.

This is not a comfortable conclusion, is it? Who of us wants to admit that we are afraid all the time? Here we spent the first decades of our life trying to climb out of being so scared, trying to outgrow the need to run to Dad or hang onto Mom's apron strings, trying to become self-reliant, only to now concede that we are *still* afraid all the time? What an embarrassing admission of weakness and failure! Thus, "afraid" is just about the last thing we want to admit we feel. The Course says so in this passage, which I quoted earlier but left off its last words:

> The ego can and does allow you to regard yourself as supercilious, unbelieving, "light-hearted," distant, emotionally shallow, callous, uninvolved and even desperate, but not really afraid.[38]

In our eyes, it is much better to be coldly separate (which, as we saw, is really the essence of this list) than to be simply scared.

Admitting that we live in a state of fear would represent more than just a failure in becoming autonomous from our parents. It would be a failure in our attempt to gain autonomy from God. If you recall, key idea 2.1 said that the whole promise of the separation was that we could steal power from our brothers and God and thereby gain for ourselves the status of supreme power. Power was the ego's campaign promise. If all the ego has yielded is fear, it has been a complete failure:

> [The ego's] one claim to your allegiance is that it can give power to you....How, then, can its existence continue if you realize that, by accepting it, you are belittling yourself and depriving yourself of power?[39]

Here is yet another way in which we can see how opposite this world is from Heaven. Heaven is summarized in the dynamic of love, in which we joyously extend our hearts to unite with infinity, and in which we extend our will to bring into being eternal creations. It is a state in which we experience unlimited expression and unopposed power. In contrast, this world is captured in the dynamic of fear, in which we cower behind walls, cringing in terror from the danger we see everywhere, in which we feel permeated with weakness and vulnerability.

This state of fear, this cowering behind walls while trying to convince ourselves how strong and autonomous we are, is the final outcome of the separation. We "left" Heaven filled with the promise of a better alternative, but all we got was the opposite of Heaven. As the Course tersely puts it, "All [you] ever made was hell."[40]

The separation, then, was like so many of our current dreams and schemes, which promise paradise yet deliver something painfully different. Instead of the fairy-tale ending we hope for, they "leave the taste of dust and ashes in their wake, in place of aspirations and of dreams."[41] The separation, in fact, was the grand template for them all, the archetype for all those best laid plans that go awry, for all our "senseless journeys, mad careers and artificial values."[42] Just as we saw in the Course's theory of time (see key idea 3.6), they are all just tiny repetitions of the one big senseless journey.

In light of this, perhaps we can look upon the ancient parable of the prodigal son with fresh eyes. For we are that son. The unhappiness we are feeling right now is his pain. We are the ones who squandered our inheritance in the "far country" of this universe, where we sought exotic pleasures, but instead found ourselves among the swine; poor, hungry, and covered with guilt. Yet just as with him, seeing what a failure our senseless journey has been can turn our hearts back to our Father. As the Course teaches, recognizing that separation has brought us nothing but fear is the beginning of the journey home:

> Your recognition that whatever seems to separate you from God is only fear, regardless of the form it takes and quite apart from how the ego wants you to experience it, is therefore the basic ego threat. Its dream of autonomy is shaken to its foundation by this awareness.[43]

Five

We then projected the cause of our
suffering onto the world, producing the
illusion that it had sinned against us
and had robbed us of our happiness.

Five

Having explored the nature of reality, the separation and its illusory nature, and the dynamics of sin, guilt, and fear, we now have a sufficient theoretical foundation and can turn our attention to more concrete matters, to our lives in this world. In the next four chapters, then, we will explore life in this world: the basic problem we are faced with, our attempted solution, the real nature of our solution, and why our solution does not work.

5.1. A law of mind is that mind causes its own experience.

Mind causes its own experience. This sounds simple, but is quite a radical idea. In this chapter we will use this principle to turn upside down virtually everything we experience in this world. We already saw this principle at work in the last chapter, where we saw that our pain in this world is self-caused, stemming from our own choice to throw God away and the guilt that resulted. The self-caused nature of our suffering is part of a larger law of mind, which runs throughout the entire Course: Mind is the cause of its own experience. Mind takes its own *ideas* and expresses them outwardly, and this *expression* is then looked upon, whereby it becomes the mind's *experience*. We go from idea to idea expressed to idea experienced. The Course describes this same process in the following passage:

> What I see reflects a process in my mind, which starts with my idea of what I want. From there, the mind makes up an image of the thing the mind desires, judges valuable, and therefore seeks to find. These images are then

87

projected outward, looked upon, esteemed as real and guarded as one's own.[1]

This passage actually expands my three steps (idea, expression, experience) into five:

1. I have an idea of what I want.
2. I turn this idea into a mental image, a picture of what I want.
3. I project this image outward.
4. I then look upon this projected image, thus taking it back into myself.
5. There I esteem it as real and guard it as my own. It has become my experience.

The mind therefore works like some kind of fanatical painter. A painter has an idea in his mind, he expresses that on canvas, and then he looks at his canvas and lets it fill his eyes. His *idea* has become his *expression* has become his *experience* (to use my three-step version). This painter, however, is not a part-time painter. He cannot stop painting, and so when he is done with his canvas, he begins to paint the walls, the floor and ceiling, the furniture, the TV screen, and even the windows. And if you walk into his studio he will paint you, too. Thus he becomes surrounded by images that began as ideas in his mind. They are literally all he sees.

We first saw this law in key idea 1.5, under the heading of the dynamic of extension in Heaven. In Heaven we are still the painter, but we do not paint our own separate ideas or forms. We paint the Thoughts we receive from God. We extend our own being, which is itself a Thought of God, being made of God's Love. The Course puts the law in this way: "Love creates [more of] itself, and nothing but itself."[2]

This law, however, cannot take its true form in a false world. And so on earth the law becomes translated, adapted to this world. It becomes "perception's law that what you see reflects the state of the perceiver's mind."[3] To further complicate matters, this law of perception is then split up into two opposite versions. One version is what could be called earthly extension, which is a *reflection* of heavenly extension. This will be the topic of Chapter 13. The other version is what the Course calls projection. It is a *distortion* of the mind's true dynamic of extension. It will be our focus in this chapter.

5.2. Projection is the dynamic whereby causation is thrown outward: what our mind has caused now seems thrust upon us from without.

Understanding projection, a concept which comes out of modern psychology, is crucial to understanding the Course's thought system. In fact, the author of the Course hinted that this may have influenced him in selecting two research psychologists to be the scribes of *A Course in Miracles*. In a personal message to them he said, "There are certain advantages in being a psychologist. A major one is the understanding of projection and the extent of its results."4 This last line is really the mission of this chapter. We will attempt to understand both projection *and* the extent of its results.

The problem with trying to understand projection in the Course is that it takes on so many different forms. All of them involve projecting something in your mind onto the outside world, but beyond that, they seem genuinely different. There is the projection we discussed above: seeing an idea in the world that we want to see. There is the classic projection of guilt: blaming others for what we secretly feel guilty of. There is another kind of projection of guilt: projecting the *belief in* our guilt onto others so that we see them as believing in our guilt and wanting to punish us for it. There is the projection of character traits: seeing in others the traits we can't face in ourselves. And there are many others.

I believe that all forms of projection as discussed by the Course can be seen as variations on a single idea, which I will attempt to summarize in this definition:

> Projection throws outward something in the mind that we still want but do not want to acknowledge as inside of us. We therefore see it as external: as existing in, being caused by, or being acted out by the outside world.

In this section, I want to discuss a key element of projection as discussed in the Course. It sounds very different than the standard "I see in you what I don't want to see in myself," yet it too fits the definition I just gave above, and it runs through all of the variations I listed above. The element that I'll describe could be called the *projection of causation*.

Recall first how we said the mind works. It begins with an idea. This idea is then expressed outward, and this outer expression is then experienced within. Projection is an example of this process, with one important qualifier: We don't want to admit that the idea started out inside of us. We want to see it as purely external. Now, the idea seems to come from outside of us. Rather than going from the inside to the outside, it seems to go the other way. It seems thrust on us from without, independent of our wishes. It seems to be externally caused. It's as if that fanatical painter, after painting everything in his studio, turned around and said, "Who did all this?" In projection, then, we are using the power of the mind in two ways simultaneously:

1. We are using the power of our mind to cause our experience (in the way we outlined in the previous section).
2. We are using that same power to throw our own causation outward, where it seems to turn around and exert causation on us. Now it appears that something outside is causing our experience, and that we are powerless to do anything about it. We have used the mind's power to make the mind seem powerless.

Perhaps some examples will serve to clarify this initially difficult concept. We will first look to the familiar example of our dreams. No one would question that our dreams are projections of our own mind. Yet while we are in the dream, it does not seem that way. Rather, the dream seems to have all the power, power to gratify us or terrify us. Here, then, is the power of our own mind masquerading as an outside force that has us in its grip. "In dreams effect and cause are interchanged, for here the maker of the dream believes that what he made is happening to him."[5] Dreams seem to be an innocent example of this, one with biological roots. Yet according to the Course, dreams are motivated by the same desire I sketched in my definition above, the desire to see as external what you don't want to admit is internal. Specifically, you are making the figures in the dream "act out for you." They are acting out impulses that are really yours but you don't want to see as yours:

> You do not respond to it [the dream] as though you made it, nor do you realize that the emotions the dream produces must come from you. It is the figures in the dream and what they do that seem to make the dream. You do not realize that you are making them act out for you, for if you did the

guilt would not be theirs, and the illusion of satisfaction would be gone.[6]

One of the best examples of projecting causation is the whole realm of excuses. When we ask someone, "Why did you do that unkind thing?" or "Why didn't you do what you said you would?" think of all the responses we hear: "Because traffic was really heavy, because something came up, because the devil made me do it, because he said that incredibly rude thing to me, because I had a chemical imbalance, because my parents never told me I was good, because in a past life she boiled me alive, because my dog ate my homework." Does anyone ever say, "You know, I was late because it's just not a real priority to be here with you on time"?

A great example of our excuse making is given in the Workbook. Review III addresses a pervasive phenomenon in doing the Workbook of the Course, in which we miss practice periods simply because we do not want to do them. However, we then attribute our not doing them to unsuitable circumstances. The passage even implies that we might subtly arrange (or "establish") those circumstances in order to give ourselves a good excuse:

> Unwillingness [to practice] can be most carefully concealed behind a cloak of situations you [supposedly] cannot control. Learn to distinguish situations that are poorly suited to your practicing from those that you establish to uphold a camouflage for your unwillingness.[7]

In our excuse making, then, we cause something (being late, lashing out at someone, not doing our Workbook lesson), but then we attribute its causation to some outside power over which we have no control. This outside power becomes a "cloak" or "camouflage" which hides the true cause within us. This is a perfect example of projection of causation.

Another example is the Course's claim that physical illness is generated by projection. This example goes beyond what is normally accepted in our culture, but is nevertheless an instructive one. In Lesson 136, the Course teaches that in a flash of a second we intentionally decide to get sick. We decide to project sickness onto the body. Then in that same flash we immediately forget our decision. This forgetting makes sickness appear to strike us from outside our intent:

But afterwards, your plan requires that you must forget you made it, so it seems to be external to your own intent; a happening beyond your state of mind, an outcome with a real effect on you, instead of one effected by yourself.[8]

The above lines deserve review, for they so perfectly express what the Course is saying. Projection—in our dreams, in our excuse making, in our physical illnesses, and in countless other examples—gives the illusion of producing "an outcome with a real effect on you, instead of one effected by yourself."

The most important area in which projection operates, and the area to which all this has been leading, is that of our emotions. We universally attribute our emotions to outside events: I was overjoyed because she said she loved me. I was dejected because I lost my job. I was excited because I got this huge check in the mail. I was afraid because that car was coming right at me.

If, on the other hand, it is projection at work here, think what that implies. Why am I upset? Because I chose to be upset; I caused my own upset. This, however, is something I do not want to own. Hence, I projected this inner cause onto my outer world. This made it seem that the cause of my feelings lay not within, but in the world outside of me. The implications of this idea are clearly enormous, and central to the Course. We will be discussing these implications over the rest of the chapter, and throughout the rest of the book.

For now, though, I simply want to clarify how projection of causation operates in the case of our emotions, for this is an area in which standard concepts of projection will steer us wrong. Again, what we project is the *cause* of our emotions, not the emotions themselves. This makes the cause, which is really inside of us, appear to be external. If you want to test your understanding of this idea, try to answer this question: If you projected your own fear, your own terror, onto another person, how would that person now seem to you? Standard notions of projection would tell you that this person would seem afraid, scared, or frightened, yet that is incorrect. The following passage from the Course tells us exactly what happens when we project our fear onto another:

Who sees a brother as a body sees him as fear's symbol. And he [the one who does this] will attack, because what he beholds is his own fear external to himself, poised to attack, and howling to unite with him again. Mistake not the intensity of rage projected fear must spawn. It shrieks in wrath, and claws the air in frantic hope it can reach to its maker and devour him.[9]

This, says the Course, is how we see our brother when we project our fear onto him. Do we see a quivering, terrified brother? No, we see a powerful wild beast, howling in rage and pawing the air as it prepares to tear us limb from limb. Though an extreme image, this is not far from how we often see people. Many have ex-husbands and wives whom they would swear fit this description exactly. The point is that what we see in the other is not fear, but the *cause* of *our* fear.

How does this fit the definition of projection I gave above? There is within us an impulse to feel fear, because, although unpleasant, fear is a great reinforcer of the ego. Yet at the same time, we don't want to admit that we have this impulse. Admitting that we *want* to feel afraid would make us look insane, and would also deprive our fear of validity by showing that it rests on an insane wish. So instead, we see the impetus to feel afraid as coming at us from the outside, from a real, objective source, rather than arising insanely from within. Now it looks like we *have* to feel afraid. In this way, we have satisfied our secret desire to feel fear while keeping the desire hidden, so that it cannot be raised to question.

5.3. Projection is motivated by the desire to get rid of our guilt, but its deeper motivation is the desire to make us powerless to change our beliefs.

Why do we project causation outward? Why would we mount such a campaign of self-deception? There are two main answers the Course gives to this question, which we will discuss only briefly, since both are discussed in greater detail elsewhere:

1. We project in order to get rid of our guilt.

This is one common understanding among Course students which is absolutely correct. "The ultimate purpose of projection is always to get rid of guilt."[10] We feel guilty because we think that we caused something bad. Projection is perfect for this situation, because its whole purpose is to take our causation and throw it outside of us. Now you caused it, not me. In fact, one measure of how much guilt we carry is how often we point the finger at others, how frantically we try to clean the blood off our hands by wiping it on someone else. The incessant human habit of blaming others is thus one of our clearest witnesses to the existence of underground lakes of sleeping guilt. We will discuss this function of projection more fully in the next chapter.

2. We project in order to get rid of our power of causation, so that our beliefs seem externally caused, leaving us powerless to change our mind about them.

This is similar to what we discussed under key idea 2.8. There we said that we made the world in order to transform separation from a crazy idea we made up to an objective reality that made us. We did this through projection, for this is precisely what projection does. It takes our own subjective notion and projects it outward, where it seems to become a foreign power looming outside of us, holding us helplessly in its grip. Now it seems ludicrous to talk of changing our mind about it. For it is not our idea; we did not make it. It is an objective reality and we are its puppet. The Course explains this purpose behind projection clearly in the following passage:

> Though the dream [of this world] itself takes many forms...the dream has but one purpose, taught in many ways. This single lesson does it try to teach again, and still again, and yet once more; that it is cause and not effect. And you are its effect, and cannot be its cause.
> Thus are you not the dreamer, but the dream.[11]

As a result, the dreamer "cannot doubt his dreams' reality, because he does not see the part he plays in making them and making them seem real."[12] If you want to hang onto your illusions and not doubt them, what do you do? You project them.

Think of our earlier example of blaming our lapses in Workbook practice on unsuitable conditions, rather than our own unwillingness. This seemingly relieves our guilt, as we said above. But it does more than that. It also makes us powerless to change things. For the cause of our not practicing is not some inner choice. *That* we could change. No, outer circumstances are what keep us from practicing. Hence, until those conditions lift we will simply have to acquiesce to not doing our Workbook practice. And that is the whole point.

Blaming outer circumstances for our failure to practice will not, in the end, effectively relieve our guilt, but it will probably succeed in keeping us from solving the situation. We could spend years blaming outer circumstances for not practicing, growing guiltier all along, but never feeling that we really had the power to change anything. And for many Course students, this is not a hypothetical situation.

Here, then, we can see something of how these two reasons for projection relate to each other. In short, the first one does not work; the second one does. Through projection our guilt does not leave our minds; we still feel guilty. But our belief that we are cause and can change things *does* leave; we don't have a clue that we can make a different choice. I suspect, then, that the first reason for projecting—getting rid of guilt—is merely the bait to get us to project and so obtain the real result—the sense that we are powerless to change our minds.

5.4. Projection produces a world that seems to have enormous power over us.

We have explained the nature of projection at such length because without this understanding it is so hard to believe all that projection can do. Earlier we quoted the author of the Course saying a major advantage of being a psychologist is "the understanding of projection and the extent of its results." Now that we have some understanding of projection, let's turn to the extent of its results.

We can all see projection operating in our lives, especially in light of the preceding examples. Yet we assume that it is one factor among a great many. What if, however, just for the sake of argument, we assumed that projection's power and influence had no bounds? What if we imagined that projection were in the hands of a limitless mind, a fanatical painter with colossal brushes, fanatically bent on denying his role as painter? What kind of world would result from projection having no limits?

Projection takes our causation and throws it outside us. Therefore, a world manufactured entirely by it would be a world in which all power lay seemingly outside us, in which we were a mere effect and the world was our all-powerful cause. In this world we would be tiny specks of dust blown about by every external breeze. Everything we felt would be caused by what this world did to us. Everything we did would be its fault. The following passages capture what it would be like if we let projection run wild:

> You will believe that you are helpless prey to forces far beyond your own control, and far more powerful than you. And you will think the world you made directs your destiny.[13]

> Helpless he stands, a victim to a dream conceived and cherished by a separate mind [whatever mind or mechanism is running this world]. Careless indeed of him this mind must be, as thoughtless of his peace and happiness as is the weather or the time of day. It loves him not, but casts him as it will in any role that satisfies its dream. So little is his worth that he is but a dancing shadow, leaping up and down according to a senseless plot conceived within the idle dreaming of the world.[14]

By now you have guessed the punch line: This *is* the world we live in. This is our experience *now*. Our world is indistinguishable from a world produced by unlimited projection. This fact, of course, proves nothing, but it does open up some serious questions. Could it be that projection, a psychological defense mechanism, manufactured our world? Could it be that we are not helpless little *homo sapiens* afloat among the infinite stars? Could it be that we are omnipotent magicians who have produced this entire universe by waving the magic wand of projection?

5.5. Through projection, our self-imposed pain appears to come from an attacking world.

Now we are moving into the deeper waters of projection. The material we will cover in these last three sections is essential to our entire grasp of the Course and the total relevance of its message of forgiveness.

The power the world seems to wield over us is anything but neutral. More often than not it is hurtful, and it is often torturous and deadly. Given what we have learned about projection, we have the tools to understand why. The following passage provides a clue:

> You cannot be unfairly treated. The belief you are is but another form of the idea you are deprived by someone not yourself. Projection of the cause of sacrifice [or deprivation] is at the root of everything perceived to be unfair and not your just deserts.[15]

This passage (especially its first line) can hit one like a ton of bricks. Let's reconstruct its logic. First, you deprive yourself. You cause yourself to sacrifice or lose. Then you project the cause of this self-deprivation outward. Now it appears that someone else is depriving you, someone is treating you unfairly. But, in truth, no one is treating you unfairly because you are being deprived only by yourself.

Now let's apply these ideas to the nature of this world. The fundamental cause of our suffering was that we decided to throw God away. This was a massive attack on ourselves, a voluntary sacrifice on an incalculable scale. It was soon followed by the "projection of the cause of sacrifice." We projected outward our choice to throw God away. This produced a world that seemed to forcibly tear God's peace and joy from our hearts. We projected a world whose full-time job was to treat us unfairly.

Let's see how this works in a specific instance. Someone you care about leaves you. This causes you to feel loss, to feel deprived—or does it? The real cause of your sense of loss, says the Course, was your ancient decision to deprive yourself of God's Presence. As a result, you now feel a cavernous hole inside you, and so you are driven to fill it with things—especially people—from outside. These people, in your mind, become symbols for God's Presence. You believe they have the power to give you the sense of fullness and completion that He gave you. You might call them God surrogates.

Remember, though, that you voluntarily threw God away. Why, then, wouldn't you tend to do the same thing with these designated symbols for Him? And that is exactly what you do. You dream into your so-called life a dream event in which this person—your symbol for God—leaves you. And then you interpret this departure as real loss, as if a chunk of your own being is actually being removed, as if you are losing God all over again. But that's *your* interpretation. Nothing requires you to interpret this in that way. If you really decided, without ambivalence, to experience the fullness of knowing God, then no person, either by his presence or absence, could affect the perfect completion you felt. Why, then, do you interpret this event the way you do? To give yourself an *excuse*, an excuse to feel the loss of God. You had already chosen to feel that loss, you just want to see the cause of that feeling as forced upon you against your will, rather than freely chosen.

Imagine that this example applies to every pain in your life, every slight against you, every attack the world ever dished out to you. You might even want to think of some of them and say to yourself, "This attack from [fill in the name or source] was just the projection of my attack upon myself."

This, according to the Course, explains what we did with all that pain that ensued from the separation. We projected it onto an illusory world, which now plays the role of its delivery device. We still feel it, we always have; we just don't know where it is really coming from. In this light, the following passage encapsulates all that we have said about projection:

> Yet you cannot lose anything unless you do not value it, and therefore do not want it. This makes you feel deprived of it, and by projecting your own rejection you then believe that others are taking it from you. You must be fearful if you believe that your brother is attacking you to tear the Kingdom of Heaven from you. This is the ultimate basis for all the ego's projection.
>
> ....Projecting its insane belief that you have been treacherous to your Creator, [the ego] believes that your brothers, who are as incapable of this as you are, are out to take God from you....Projection always sees your wishes in others. If you choose to separate yourself from God, that is what you will think others are doing to you.[16]

5.6. Our guilt, projected outward, has produced a punishing world.

We are almost done with our exploration of what caused this attacking world. To fully understand the mechanisms behind it, however, we need one more piece: our guilt. We need to explore the role that our guilt played in producing this world. To do so, let us turn to an important paragraph in the Course. We will cover it line by line:

> The world you see is the delusional system of those
> made mad by guilt.[17]

What does it mean to say that our world is a "delusional system"? A delusion is an exceedingly faulty belief about reality that persists despite obvious and overwhelming proof to the contrary. A delusional *system* would then be an integrated group of such beliefs. For example: "A man who failed his bar examination developed the delusion that this occurred because of a conspiracy involving the university and the bar association. He then attributed all other difficulties in his social and occupational life to this continuing conspiracy."[18] His delusion evolved into a delusional system.

To say that our world is a delusional system, then, means that the world is not a real place. Just like the conspiracy in the above example, it is a strictly imaginary situation that exists only in our minds and that flies in the face of reality.

This system, we are told, was invented by "those made mad by guilt." At the center of this delusional system is the core delusion of guilt. Just a few lines earlier, the Course says, "It is guilt that has driven you insane."[19] So guilt, according to this passage, is the engine that drives this delusional system, which means that guilt is the driving force behind this crazy world.

We have seen this idea before. But it sounds so bizarre, how can we know if it is true? The rest of the passage addresses this very issue.

> Look carefully at this world, and you will realize that this
> is so.[20]

This sentence is actually suggesting an experiment of observation. All you need do, it says, is look really carefully around you, and you will realize that the world is actually driven by guilt. This sounds preposterous, but let us at least follow the experiment and see if it works. Conveniently, the author carries it out for us:

> For this world is the symbol of punishment, and all the laws
> that seem to govern it are the laws of death. Children are
> born into it through pain and in pain. Their growth is
> attended by suffering, and they learn of sorrow and separa-

tion and death. Their minds seem to be trapped in their brain, and its powers to decline if their bodies are hurt. They seem to love, yet they desert and are deserted. They appear to lose what they love, perhaps the most insane belief of all. And their bodies wither and gasp and are laid in the ground, and are no more.[21]

The above lines represent the results of looking really carefully at this world. What do you see? According to this passage, you see the human life cycle. We come into this world through a concert of pain. So lost are we in our pain we don't realize we are emerging through the wall of our mother's pain. While we grow up we continue to suffer, as we don't get our way, as our siblings mistreat us, as our parents yell at us. And we slowly learn that suffering is the norm in this strange land. We see people angrily split up, we see adults so despondent they need medication, and one by one we go to the funerals of our relatives. In the midst of all this loss, we learn to exercise extreme caution with our bodies, for one wrong move and we might sustain brain damage and lose a significant part of our mental functioning.

After these precarious and difficult early years, we emerge into young adulthood and feel the glorious bloom of love, whose sweet fragrance promises to lift us above the suffering that rules the earth below. Yet, to our shock and heartbreak, people leave us. More shocking still, *we* leave *them*. Thus, though we chase it for many years, our dream of love and happiness never materializes. Finally, we near old age, and what little we have accumulated begins to slip through our fingers. Our friends die, our status in the world slips, our minds start to go. And the bodies we have so carefully safeguarded cannot be protected from the grim march of time. They shrivel up, gasp their last breaths, "and are laid in the ground, and are no more."

This account of the human life cycle is not pretty, yet hard to argue with. These things all happen, and they define our lives. Yet this paragraph is not just trying to remind us of what we already know. It is trying to use what we already know to demonstrate that this world was made by "those made mad by guilt." How does the human life cycle demonstrate that? The connection is not very easy to see. The key lies in a line I purposefully glossed over: "For this world is the symbol of punishment, and all the laws that seem to govern it are the laws of death." What do you do when people are guilty? You punish them. And when they are *really* guilty? You put them to death.

And that is what this world does to us: it punishes us nonstop from our first breath until our last, when it carries out *capital* punishment. It treats us just as if we were guilty criminals. That is what observing the human life cycle reveals to us. It reveals that punishment for some mysterious guilt is the guiding principle behind the architecture of this world. It reveals that whoever made this place (assuming it is not a random dance of atoms) must be convinced that we are profoundly guilty. Let us go now to the last line of the paragraph:

Not one of them but has thought that God is cruel.[22]

Surely at some point in the sorrowful human life cycle, it crosses our minds that God is not being very nice to us. If we assume that God is running the show, then we must also assume that He is the One Who is sending us all those bad romantic partners, boring jobs, and shattered dreams. Not unreasonably, we suspect that He must be paying us back for something we did. He must be punishing us for our sins. It is no wonder we often find ourselves asking, "What did I do to deserve this?"

Do you see what this means? Remarkably, it shows that we already performed the Course's observation experiment on our own long ago. And it shows that we obtained roughly similar results. At some moment, maybe even for a fleeting second in the midst of personal tragedy, we looked at our lives, we looked at our world, and we concluded that whoever invented this place must, simply *must*, be punishing us for something, even if excessively so. We decided that the maker of this world *has* to be consumed with the thought of our sinfulness and guilt, or why else would he be sticking it to us like this? And we were right. We just had the wrong maker. It wasn't God Who had made a world out of an insane obsession with our guilt. It was we who did it.

According to *A Course in Miracles*, our world is the projection of our guilt. That is why this world is such a punishing place. We saw in key idea 4.5 that our guilt projects a punishing God. If so, why wouldn't it also project a punishing *world*? Remember how projection works: what we have caused now seems thrust upon us from without. Let's see how that applies to guilt. When we commit an apparent sin against someone, causing that person to suffer, our guilt tells us that we deserve to suffer in return (key idea 4.4). We then project that thought outward, where it becomes a world that hands us our "just" deserts. Yet—true to the nature of projection—we forget that we projected this world, and so now its punishment of us seems unfair and infuriating. We have no clue as to why it keeps punishing us for sins we don't remember committing. Here is the answer to any questions from the last chapter about evidence for the enormous guilt discussed there. In light of this argument, the entire world is the evidence for massive primordial guilt.

The Course gives the analogy of a nighttime dream of punishment. If, let's say, you went to sleep racked with guilt, would you dream a dream in which everyone is absorbed in their own guilt? Perhaps, but more likely you would find yourself caught in a saga in which everyone is punishing *you*, in which the police are hemming you in on all sides, the judge is pounding his gavel, and the electric chair is charged up and waiting for you.

> Like to a dream of punishment, in which the dreamer is unconscious of what brought on the attack against himself, he sees himself attacked unjustly and by something not himself. He is the victim of this "something else," a thing outside himself, for which he has no reason to be held responsible....Yet is his own attack upon himself apparent still, for it is he who bears the suffering.[23]

This is the Course's explanation for all the affliction the world has sent our way. This is its explanation for all the pain in our pain-filled human life cycle, from our first pain-filled breath to our last. This is its explanation for why things are so damn hard here. Think about all that the world has done to you, all the betrayal, the rejection, the grief, the tragedy, the unkindness, the robbery, the heartbreak. By all appearances, you have been treated unfairly since the day you were born by parents, teachers, employers, and lovers; by twists of fate and acts of nature; even by germs, bacteria, and insects. For this reason, you probably feel as if this passage was written with your name on it: "You who are sometimes sad and sometimes angry; who sometimes feel your just due is not given you, and your best efforts meet with lack of appreciation and even contempt..."[24]

Yet from the Course's perspective, the world has never laid a finger on you, for there is no world. It is merely a collection of dancing images you projected onto the screen of your own mind. Its purpose is to put on a convincing display of dishing out to you the pain that you served up for yourself, the pain that you believe is your due.

5.7. Our primary experience of this world is that it attacks us in manifold ways, that it has done us wrong, that it has taken our happiness from us.

Projection's smoke and mirrors show has fooled us completely. The idea that the world is attacking us and robbing us of our peace is extremely real to us. As the Course says, we have "a self-perception which regards us in a place of merciless pursuit, where we are badgered ceaselessly, and pushed about without a thought or care for us or for our future."[25] Not only do we feel attacked at various points over the course of our lives (as we saw in our review of the human life cycle), we feel attacked in each and every moment.

To get in touch with this, let's do a brief exercise. To set this up, we must first define attack more broadly than we are accustomed to. We will define "something attacking you" as:

- anything that seems to arise from outside your choice in this moment,
- that is weighing on your peace of mind right now, so that were that thing changed or absent, you would feel better now.

In light of that definition, let's reflect on what is attacking you right this instant. First, if you will, think for a moment about the various physical needs and discomforts that seem to be attacking you right now. Perhaps you are hungry or thirsty or sleepy. Maybe the temperature in the room is attacking you by being too hot or too cold. Maybe the chair in which you are sitting is harassing you with back pain.

Now reflect on ways in which the condition of your body is attacking you. Perhaps it torments you by not being pretty or handsome enough. Maybe it is too fat or too old or too short. Maybe its nose is too big or its biceps too small. Think, also, of any health problems it is currently vexing you with.

Now reflect on how the material condition of your life is attacking you. Maybe your checkbook is assailing you with its low numbers. Perhaps your job is not treating you right. Your lawn may be demanding to be cut, your carpets screaming at you to be cleaned, the dishes clamoring to be done, messes begging to be straightened up. The dream home you have hoped for may be assaulting you simply by virtue of keeping itself out of your reach.

Now mull over all the demands and responsibilities that are oppressing you right now, the people you are supposed to call, the decisions you need to make, the projects that sit half-completed, the ones you have been avoiding starting, the deadlines that are haunting you like specters.

Now go to the people in your life who are attacking you. Maybe your spouse has been grouchy of late. Perhaps your kids continue their offensive patterns. Maybe a fellow Course student's recent attacks are still weighing on you or a boss's lack of appreciation is still gnawing at you or a lover's failure to call is still chilling you with loneliness.

Now think of some of the things from the past such that, had they never happened, you would feel lighter in this moment: the bad breaks, the humiliations, the misfortunes, the tragedies. And then think of some of the future outcomes you anticipate that hang over your head and contribute to the burden you feel right now.

This brief exercise reveals that, all in all, there are literally scores of things that we feel attacked by right this second. And this of course will carry on into the next instant, and the next, as it has been carrying on through virtually every instant of our lives. As the Course puts it, "every day a hundred little things make small assaults upon"[26] our peace of mind. To adapt a saying about raising children, life in this world is like being nibbled to death by ducks.

Hopefully we now can at least consider that being under attack is our primary experience of life in this world. The world we experience is, more than any other single thing, an *attacking* world. We try extremely hard to not admit this, to stay calm, put on a happy face, have a pleasing disposition, and generally act like everything is fine. Yet even while smiling we are rushing about fending off countless small attacks, putting out all the fires, making sure our defenses are up, our doors are locked, our windows barred. In the face of this behavior, how can we claim we don't feel attacked by the world? That would be like a man building a massive fortress and putting a moat around it yet all the while insisting he has no fear of war. According to the Course, all of us are like this man to some degree, for we all have no idea just how incredibly besieged we feel:

> The sense of threat the world encourages is so much deeper, and so far beyond the frenzy and intensity of which you can conceive, that you have no idea of all the devastation it has wrought.
>
> You are its slave. You know not what you do, in fear of it.[27]

We are conscious enough of this attack, though, to conclude that the world—in the guise of various people, situations, and events—has taken our happiness from us. We may never remember actually being happy, but we feel in our bones that happiness is our right, a right we were born with and a right we earned through our giving, our sacrifice, and all our sincere trying. In return, the world has simply demanded more, and continued its relentless assault. In short, the world has robbed us of our sacred right to be happy.

See how well projection has done its job! It has thrown an opaque veil over everything. It has covered our attack on ourselves, and even more fully veiled our divine identity. Heaven is so completely hidden, so long out of sight, that the very idea of it seems like a fairy tale. The separation, too, sounds like something out of some weird science fiction novel.

> No one asleep and dreaming in the world remembers his attack upon himself. No one believes there really was a time when he knew nothing of a body, and could never have conceived this world as real.[28]

And so our world simply carries on, century after century. We go about our days and our lives, tending to the business before us. We perform our duties and find time for life's little pleasures, and as we do, the last thing we ever suspect is that we are heirs to the infinite Kingdom of God, living in self-imposed exile. The furthest thing from our minds is the possibility that in the primordial dawn we threw away our sweet, endless happiness and chose suffering instead. No, on this we are all agreed: Our happiness was stolen from us by an unkind world.

As a result, we know exactly what the problem is and how to solve it. If our happiness was taken by the world, we know just where to look to find it.

Six

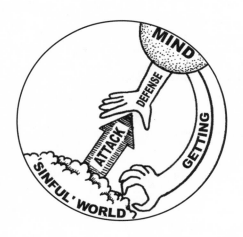

Our solution: Acquire happiness by rearranging our external world.

Six

Projection conjures the illusion that the world is the cause of our experience. What the world does to us causes how we feel. Up until now it has caused us to feel largely unhappy and unfulfilled.[1] The solution to this problem seems perfectly obvious: We must simply rearrange the world's situations and events so that they will cause us to feel happy. We must organize the images on our projection screen so that they assume a pleasing configuration.

This *is* how we spend our days, is it not? We spend them carefully, cleverly, and dutifully rearranging the furniture of the world: washing clothes, driving cars, shuffling papers, pressing computer keys, buttoning shirts, picking up phones, etc., etc. This activity is so basic that we take it for granted. Yet imagine how different life would be if we were unable to manipulate our world—if, for instance, our arms and legs were paralyzed, if our voice were gone (one of our primary means of getting things to move), if we couldn't even blink a simple "yes" or "no" to communicate our wishes. This thought is so frightening simply because of how deeply and fundamentally we depend on being able to manipulate our environment. According to the Course, this rearrangement of the world is nothing less than our plan for salvation; that is, our *ego's* plan for salvation:

> The ego's plan for salvation...maintains that, if someone else spoke or acted differently, if some external circumstance or event were changed, you would be saved [happy, fulfilled, complete]. Thus, the source of salvation is constantly perceived as outside yourself. Each grievance you hold is a declaration, and an assertion in which you believe,

that says, "If this were different, I would be saved." The change of mind necessary for salvation is thus demanded of everyone and everything except yourself.

The role assigned to your own mind in this plan, then, is simply to determine what, other than itself, must change if you are to be saved.[2]

This chapter will explore our search for happiness in this world. Its purpose is to simply describe the human program for happiness, without much analysis and without attempting to penetrate too far beneath the surface (we will reserve that for the two chapters that follow). After several chapters in which we have tried to turn upside down our normal picture of things, in this chapter we are talking more or less about life on the surface.

6.1. Our conscious self-image is "the face of innocence," that of a good self trying to make its way through an unjust world.

Let us begin our survey by setting the stage. In our life story we are the main character on a quest for happiness within the world. How do we see ourselves, as this main character? How do we see the world wherein we search? And how do we see our relationship with this world? The Course has an important passage which answers all three of these questions. In this passage the Course calls our conscious self-image "the face of innocence":

> It is this face that smiles and charms and even seems to love. It searches for companions and it looks, at times with pity, on the suffering, and sometimes offers solace. It believes that it is good within an evil world.
>
> This aspect can grow angry, for the world is wicked and unable to provide the love and shelter innocence deserves. And so this face is often wet with tears at the injustices the world accords to those who would be generous and good. This aspect never makes the first attack. But every day a hundred little things make small assaults upon its innocence, provoking it to irritation, and at last to open insult and abuse.

The face of innocence the concept of the self so proud-
ly wears can tolerate attack[ing] in self-defense, for is it not
a well-known fact the world deals harshly with defenseless
innocence?[3]

What I find amazing about this passage is that everyone seems to
relate to it and feel it describes him or her quite personally. For instance,
when I first read this passage I felt as if the author were reading my
secret thoughts. I wondered, "How does he know me so well?" I apparently had assumed I was the only one who was like this, the only one
who was so well-intentioned, so put upon by the world, yet so noble and
forbearing as to rein in my just urge to retaliate. Clearly, no one around
me had such forbearance. The irony, of course, is that this is exactly how
this passage *predicts* I would look at the world. Even more ironic, this
is more or less how we *all* look at the world. In our own eyes, we all
belong to some minority of goodness, some elite order of decency (at
least as we define goodness and decency). One wonders, then, who
comprises the evil world? Who is doing all the unprovoked attacking?

The fact that we all seem to identify with this passage is all the more
striking when you note that it describes a self-image. According to conventional assumptions we all have very unique self-images, yet this passage seems to capture us all. The face of innocence therefore appears to
be the underlying template for all of our conscious self-images, which
now are revealed to be mere variations on this universal theme.[4] How
odd to think that we all have the same self-image.

Let us now answer our original three questions one by one. How do
we see ourselves? We see ourselves, in essence, as *innocent* and *good*.
We go about our duties, offering to others our smiles, looking for those
who can share our journey, feeling compassion for the downtrodden,
and offering help when we can.

How do we see the world? We see the world, in essence, as *unjust*,
unfair. It is unable to give us the love, safety, recognition, and acclaim
that we so well deserve. This recalls that quote from the last chapter:
"You...who sometimes feel your just due is not given you, and your best
efforts meet with lack of appreciation and even contempt..."[5]

How do we see our relationship with the world? We see a relationship in which we never attack first. Yet the world goes right ahead and
attacks us anyway, a hundred times a day. We initially get irritated, but

we hold back. We eventually get angry, but still hold back, proving once again just how innocent we are. Finally we get pushed beyond any limit of human tolerance and we simply have to lash out. Yet even here, mind you, we only attack in self-defense. We regret having to do this, but we know what would happen if we left ourselves completely defenseless. We would become just another greasy smudge on the heel of the world's giant boot.

All of this can be boiled down to a phrase that we might call the personal slogan of nearly everyone alive: "I am a good person making my way as best I can through a harsh world."

6.2. We respond to the world's attacks by defending ourselves.

In the previous section, as well as in the previous chapter (key idea 5.7), we mentioned that defending ourselves is a major part of life on earth. This is to be expected, given that we experience the world as an attacking world. What we may not appreciate is just how all-pervasive this defense is. It is not limited to defending ourselves against physical assaults, or even verbal assaults. Merely adjusting the thermostat is a defense, is it not? Think of all the forms of the world's attack we mentioned in the last chapter. For every one of them, however tiny, we have some specially crafted defense that fits the attack like a key fits a lock. We have aspirin for headaches, coats for cold weather, toothpaste for tooth decay, sunglasses for bright sunlight, windshields for the wind. There is no point in carrying this list on, for it would eventually cover every single object we use in any way.

In this vein, the Course says that *any* attempt to "organize the present as you wish"[6] is a defense. It further points that even the simple act of planning for the future is also a defense. It acknowledges that "planning is not often recognized as a defense,"[7] then goes on to explain:

> The mind engaged in planning for itself is occupied in setting up control of future happenings. It does not think that it will be provided for, unless it makes its own provisions.[8]

In other words, plans are our defenses against future attacks.[9]

Defense is even built into the very structure of nature, as we mentioned in Chapter 2. Our bodies are outfitted with many means of defense, which go way beyond mere fists, nails, and teeth. And when our defense systems fail, as we see so graphically with a disease like AIDS which destroys the immune system, death is not far behind.

In an important paragraph, the Course describes the belief that lies behind our defenses, and says that our entire world is based on this belief:

> You operate from the belief you must protect yourself from what is happening because it must contain what threatens you. A sense of threat is an acknowledgment of an inherent weakness; a belief that there is danger which has power to call on you to make appropriate defense. The world is based on this insane belief. And all its structures, all its thoughts and doubts, its penalties and heavy armaments, its legal definitions and its codes, its ethics and its leaders and its gods, all serve but to preserve its sense of threat. For no one walks the world in armature but must have terror striking at his heart.[10]

Some parts of this paragraph get a little bit ahead of us. For now, I merely want to highlight a few of its points. First, defense stems from a threefold belief:

1. You are inherently weak and vulnerable.
2. What is happening outside you is dangerous; it threatens you with harm.
3. You must protect your vulnerable self from these dangerous happenings.

These three things are so obvious that we have probably never felt a need to put them in words, just as fish probably do not sit around commenting on how they appear to be surrounded by water.

Second, the entire world is based on this threefold belief. Notice the list given in the above passage (in the sentence beginning, "And all its structures"). You might want to ask yourself in relation to each item on this list, "Does this thing (e.g., our world's penalties, heavy armaments, legal definitions and codes, ethics, leaders, gods) preserve this threefold belief?"

Finally, the all-pervasiveness of defense reaffirms what we said in

Chapter 4 (key idea 4.6), that fear is the human condition. As this passage puts it, "no one walks the world in armature but must have terror striking at his heart."

6.3. We attempt to fill our needs with external things, situations, and events, based on the belief that we are inherently lacking.

Of course, it is not enough merely to defend against the world's attacks. We must also arrange for the world to treat us right and give us happiness. This is a full-time job. Trying to force, manipulate, cajole, bribe, and coax the world into its most pleasing configuration occupies virtually our every waking instant. As a result, we are ceaselessly engaged in an endeavor somewhat like trying to orchestrate the perfect family photo after a huge holiday argument.

The Course calls all the things we seek for in the world "idols" (for reasons which we will explain in Chapter 8). An idol is anything external that we think will fill us up and contribute to our happiness and wholeness. The following is a partial list of the idols we seek, drawn from *A Course in Miracles*:

human love[11]	physical pleasure[24]
being liked[12]	physical protection[25]
someone to save you[13]	pills[26]
having employees[14]	physical beauty[27]
status, prestige[15]	adornment of the body[28]
power, influence[16]	other people's bodies[29]
knowing the right people[17]	intelligence[30]
being a master over others[18]	finding your special gift in the
fame[19]	world[31]
money, wealth[20]	rights[32]
material things[21]	desired places, situations,
going shopping[22]	circumstances[33]
clothes[23]	

These are just a few items on what the Course twice calls an "endless list."[34] The length of this list and the full-time nature of our pursuit of it are probably not all that surprising to us. We know that we more or less spend our days engaged in seeking. For some reason, we are more cognizant of this unending seeking than we are of our just-as-unending defense. There is a song I like entitled "Constant Craving Has Always Been." I know of no song, however, named "Constant Defending Is All We Do."

In the end, however, the two ideas are extremely interrelated. When you go to the store and buy food, you are buying an external good to fill your need. Yet you are also defending—you are defending against the threat of *not* having food, the threat of hunger. And when you defend against anything you are trying to fill yet another need—the need for safety and security. So these two processes are really two sides of the same process. In every act we are both seeking and defending. With that in mind, let us take the three-fold belief behind defense and adjust it so that it applies to our seeking after idols. Every act of pursuing externals implies:

1. You are inherently lacking and needy.
2. There are certain happenings outside you that can fill your needs and make you complete.
3. You must fill your needy self with these pleasurable happenings.

Again this seems so obvious that it hardly needs to be articulated. We simply accept that whatever force fashioned us made us with a variety of needs. Yet once you think about this, it can begin to look rather strange. A need is a lack, a cavity, a hole, some void inside of us that simply has to be filled, and filled from outside of us. What an odd thing, to construct a being that is riddled with such holes, each of them crying out to be filled, each of them requiring us to locate some special external spring that can fill them. Think of all the needs we have. We not only have a large array of bodily needs (for air, food, water, sex, sleep, among many others), but our mind has an equally large number. Our mind hungers for love, security, achievement, control, and adventure. It thirsts for approval, excitement, peace, meaning, and understanding.

As we all know, when these needs are not met, the desire for them intensifies, causing us to increasingly feel pangs of lack. As these pangs grow in intensity, they fervently promise overwhelming relief and satisfaction if only we can get our feeding. Unmet, they can propel us into a frenzy, until we finally locate the "food" we seek and satiate ourselves. Yet here is where the weirdest part of all occurs. After a short time of feeling full, the need starts to stir in us again, causing the entire process to begin once more. Has it never struck you as odd that within a few hours of eating—after all the anticipation, preparation, chewing, swallowing, and cleaning up—you have to do it all over again?

6.4. A major need we seek to satisfy is the need to feel innocent.

Let's look more closely at these needs. In key idea 6.2 we already discussed in a roundabout way one of our major needs. This is the need behind our defenses: the need for safety and security. In our next four key ideas we will discuss other major needs.

The first one is a need to feel innocent. By "innocent" I don't mean naive or inexperienced; I mean not at fault, not to blame, not a bad person. On one side, we seem to be on an unending quest to clear our name, to vindicate ourselves, to be exonerated, to prove we didn't do it. On the other side, we will drive ourselves into an early grave to fulfill all that our peers and our culture expect of us, to jump through all their crazy hoops, just so that we can prove to them what a good person we are.

One of the main ways in which we try to fulfill this need—and the way the Course is most interested in—is blaming others. We discussed this briefly in the last chapter (in key idea 5.3, under the heading of projecting our guilt). Pointing the finger at the other guy feels like instant innocence. "I didn't do it, he did." This is one the most automatic human reflexes there is. To test this reflex, all you need do is accuse someone and see how quickly he or she says, "It's not my fault, it's so-and-so's" (or "I couldn't help it, such-and-such happened"). To find other examples, simply listen to someone telling the story of their day, and see how much it involves them trying to exonerate themselves and finger someone else for the difficulties of the day. Whatever the truth of the matter is, it just feels a whole lot better to cast the other person as the bad guy, to lay the blame at the feet of his mistakes and minimize our own. The Course captures this pervasive attitude in the following tongue-in-cheek passage:

Yours are mistakes, but his are sins and not the same as

yours. His merit punishment, while yours, in fairness, should be overlooked.[35]

Pointing the finger or blaming the other guy is quite simply one of the primary pursuits on planet earth. The unreflective ease and knee-jerk rapidity with which we whip that finger out is truly astounding. No gun-slinger of the Old West would stand a chance against us.

6.5. Another major need is the need to feel special.

Specialness may just be the most valued treasure in the world. It is easily worth more than gold, for it is the reason we *want* gold. It is the treasure that we hope all of our idols will grant to us. Who of us really doubts that being incredibly special would fill the emptiness in us and make us ridiculously happy? After all, when we say we want love, don't we mean that we want to occupy a special place in the heart of a special someone? Isn't being special considered the same thing as having worth and self-esteem? Specialness is so central to our lives that the Course devotes an entire chapter in the Text to it (Chapter 24), where it plainly tells us, "nothing in the world [you] value more."[36]

What does it mean to be special? I like to define it as being both *set apart* and *set above*:

- *Set apart.* To be special is first of all to be *specific*, particular, unique; to be one particular thing as opposed to another thing or to everything.
- *Set above.* Special usually means more than merely set apart. It means set apart in a *"good"* way: exceptional, better, superior, set above.

To give an example of how pervasive the urge for specialness is, shortly after I came up with this twofold definition many years ago, I was mulling it over while driving to the *Course in Miracles* center where I taught. There at a traffic light I looked over to my right and noticed a billboard advertising napkins. It proclaimed, "Set your table apart." Then I looked to the left, and there was a billboard for Cutty Sark scotch, urging one to give it for Christmas and saying, "Give a Cutty above." These ads were naked appeals to our desire for specialness, promising us that mere napkins and scotch could set us apart and above.

Yet specialness, of course, is not just dangled in front of us on billboards. Any time we advertise, formally or informally, any time we want something to look enticing, we tell someone that the product (which may of course be ourselves) is truly special and that buying it will increase his or her own specialness. The desire to be special dominates our lives and our goals. Why, for instance, do we want a certain spouse, a certain career, a particular house in a specific community? Is not a major factor the hope that this spouse or career will make us look and feel really special? Specialness also permeates our private thoughts. When we track our thoughts we will find ones like these frequently crossing our minds: "My, that was a clever remark I made (showing how especially clever I am)," or "I am certainly better looking than she is."

In one passage the Course refers to "all of the tribute you have given specialness," and then presents an interesting list which details this tribute: "All of the love and care, the strong protection, the thought by day and night, the deep concern, the powerful conviction this is you..."[37] This list describes our specialness as if it were some precious antique which consumes our days, as we muse about it, hold it and look at it, polish it, and repeatedly check it to make sure it is safe. Is this far off the mark? Think of the things to which we give love, care, protection, thought by day and night, and deep concern. What are they? Our bodies, our lovers, our children, our financial affairs, our jobs, our homes. Aren't all these things, at least to a significant degree, means to the end of feeling special? Isn't that a great deal of what they are supposed to deliver? In being consumed with them we are to a large degree consumed with our own specialness. And when they do deliver and grant us specialness—when our bodies look fabulous, when our kids become doctors, when our homes are the envy of all our neighbors—do we not have "the powerful conviction" that this special person is, in fact, who we are?

The following passage has a very similar flavor. It describes our love affair with specialness as if we were an obsessive lover who worships the object of his love, fawns over her, supplies her every whim, and defends her honor against the most trivial affronts:

> How bitterly does everyone tied to this world defend the specialness he wants to be the truth! His wish is law to him, and he obeys. Nothing his specialness demands does he withhold. Nothing it needs does he deny to what he loves.

And while it calls to him he hears no other Voice [the Voice of the Holy Spirit]. No effort is too great, no cost too much, no price too dear to save his specialness from the least slight, the tiniest attack, the whispered doubt, the hint of threat, or anything but deepest reverence.[38]

Can we not see ourselves in this passage? Our attachment to being special is never more evident than when we feel a threat to it, when someone treats our specialness with "anything but deepest reverence." Here, perhaps better than anywhere else, we catch a glimpse of a fact that may at first be quite startling: We live and breathe the pursuit of specialness like we live and breathe the air.

6.6. In our search for happiness, the body is both a means and an end.

We have not discussed the body much thus far, yet it clearly lies at the center of all our attempts to derive happiness from the world, playing at once both means and end. Think of all the time we spend feeding, washing, relieving, resting, exercising, grooming, dressing, and gratifying our body. After you add up all the time spent in these activities, how much time is left? I asked this at a workshop once and someone called out, "About half an hour, morning and evening!" My answer, not very different, is that virtually the only time left is all the time it takes to earn the money and purchase the supplies for these activities.

The Course emphasizes the central role the body plays in our lives. The following passage is from a section whose title, "The 'Hero' of the Dream," is a reference to the body. This passage almost reads like a research report on the role of the body written by someone from a realm in which there are no bodies:

The body is the central figure in the dreaming of the world....It takes the central place in every dream, which tells the story of how it was made by other bodies, born into the world outside the body, lives a little while and dies, to be united in the dust with other bodies dying like itself. In the brief time allotted it to live, it seeks for other bodies as its friends and enemies. Its safety is its main concern. Its comfort is its guiding rule. It tries to look for pleasure, and avoid the things that would be hurtful. Above all, it tries to teach itself its pains and joys are different [from each other] and can be told apart.

The dreaming of the world takes many forms, because the body seeks in many ways to prove it is autonomous and real. It puts things on itself that it has bought with little metal discs or paper strips the world proclaims as valuable and real. It works to get them, doing senseless things, and tosses them away for senseless things it does not need and does not even want. It hires other bodies, that they may protect it and collect more senseless things that it can call its own. It looks about for special bodies that can share its dream. Sometimes it dreams it is a conqueror of bodies weaker than itself. But in some phases of the dream, it is the slave of bodies that would hurt and torture it.[39]

These are fascinating paragraphs, containing a kind of outsider's picture of our life stories, including our relationships, money, clothing, shopping, employment, possessions, and other things. At the center of all these lies the body. It is the one doing things and the one to which things are done. It is both means and end.

The body is means in the sense that it carries out all our work in the world. If you recall, our entire program for happiness involves skillfully arranging the furniture of the world. That is what the body is for. Given that our mind seems completely unable to budge physical objects on its own (except, perhaps, in rare cases), we need physical fingers to move around all the chess pieces on the world's chessboard. Even if the Course is right and external objects are mere images on our mind's projection screen, we have lost touch with our ability to move the images with our minds. We therefore need to use the one image we *can* move with our mind—our body—to move the others.

The body is also means in another sense. It is a means to specialness. As we all know, if one has a special body, then one is considered to be special and can, in the words of the above passage, attract other "special bodies that can share [one's] dream." The Course irreverently describes this as using the body "for show, as bait to catch another fish, to house your specialness in better style."[40]

Lastly, the body is also an end. The paragraphs we quote above say that the body's "main concern" and "guiding rule" are its own safety, comfort, and pleasure. Another passage expresses the same sentiment and even provides the same list: "What plans do you make that do not involve [the body's] comfort or protection or enjoyment in some way?"[41] Imagine going on a vacation and not arranging a place to stay, not locating a bed to sleep in, and not bringing money to buy food with.

The body is the doer on the stage of the world, and a great deal of its doing is for the sake of its own safety, comfort, and pleasure. It owns the whole loop. The body is indeed "the central figure in the dreaming of the world."

6.7. The crowning gift we seek, which incorporates all of the other gifts, is special love.

What *A Course in Miracles* calls "the special love relationship" is the crown jewel in the treasure house of the world. The Course calls it "the ego's most boasted gift."[42] What, then, is the special relationship? It is a relationship in which:

- I have a special arrangement with
- and receive special treatment from
- a very special person
- so that I can feel more special.

This definition, of course, fits many of our relationships, from friendships to working relationships to valued contacts and acquaintances. However, the most special relationship of all, of course, is the romantic relationship. This is what we dream and fantasize about, what we write songs and poems about. This is the most celebrated and most sought after gem in this world.

And little wonder it is. For special love promises to satisfy all of the needs we have. First and foremost, it promises to fulfill our need to be special. Think of the high you get when that someone you think is super-special tells you, for the first time, that he or she feels that same special way about you. What more wonderful feeling is there? Special love also promises to deliver safety. Our partner is supposed to provide the physical safety of a roof over our head and/or the emotional safety of someone who understands and can make it all better. Special love also vows to deliver various external gifts or idols: a steady income, a well-kept home, good cooking, a manicured lawn. It also is supposed to supply us with innocence, for here at last we have someone who really sees our side of the story, who can sympathize with us for all the unfair treatment we have received, and who can stand up for us and point the finger right along with us. Finally, one of special love's main functions is to satisfy our body's needs for comfort, safety, and physical pleasure. It goes without saying that sexual gratification is a huge lure in the romantic special relationship.

Is it not amazing that a single relationship can promise so much? Here, in this relationship, lies our major hope for happiness in this world. We sorely need this hope, for the world has mistreated us so badly. It has battered and buffeted us about since the moment we left the womb. We can never reasonably expect the entire world to one day change, put a big smile on its face, and start showering us with cash, prizes, and free shopping sprees. But perhaps we can find just *one* person, that one perfect person, who is unlike the rest of the unfair, inconsiderate world; who will wrap us in his arms and kiss our scrapes and bandage our wounds. Assuming that we find this person and win him over, the world will of course continue its cruel ways and try to snuff out our glorious love. Yet, as the saying goes, love conquers all. And so the two of us will emerge victorious and go off to establish our own little picket-fenced paradise, our own quiet haven amid the storms of a hateful world,[43] where we can both live happily ever after. That, at least, is the dream.

6.8. All of our seeking attempts to get something from the world, for which we generally must pay something back.

If you notice, most of what we have discussed in this chapter are things that we must acquire from the world. Something outside must come inside. Something that someone else owned must somehow get transferred to us. We gain it and, unfortunately, they lose it.

This is obvious in the case of material objects, like money, food, and possessions. Someone else has the food—the farmer or the grocery store—and we must acquire it from them. Now we have it and they don't.

However, this is far less evident in the case of the intangibles we desire, like specialness or innocence—less evident but no less true. Let's start with specialness. Specialness, though intangible, behaves just like a physical commodity. It can be possessed, transferred, even bought and sold. Think of a celebrity. When we look at a celebrity don't our minds actually feel a kind of halo or aura of specialness surrounding her? In our imagination, her body carries with it a semi-physical energy that lights up any room she walks into. Further, she can transmit this energy—it can rub off on us. Her body can transmit it with a smile, a touch, a signature, any behavior that sends the message "I, the special one, acknowledge you." Certain special body parts can transmit this energy more powerfully than others. Getting touched by her elbow is nothing compared to being kissed by her lips. Lastly, she does, in a sense, lose this energy when she transmits it. If, for instance, she kisses everyone, you will receive less specialness from her kiss than you would if she were more selective.

Innocence works in a very similar way. People who we perceive as innocent seem to shine with a squeaky clean halo, while people we see as guilty seem surrounded by a dark, smoky cloud. Again, these imagined energies can seemingly be transmitted. Think about when you blame someone. If you are convincing, your accusing finger, like some evil futuristic weapon, seems to actually transmit the smoky cloud that was around you. Now the cloud engulfs the other person, while his halo of innocence is taken from him and comes to rest upon your head. The Course refers to this very process:

> Can innocence be purchased by the giving of your guilt to someone else?...Whatever way the game of guilt is played, there must be loss. Someone must lose his innocence that someone else can take it from him, making it his own.[44]

Hence, all the things we think we want, whether tangible or intangible, are commodities that are possessed by others and that we hope to acquire. And as we acquire them, the other guy loses them. Herein lies the problem, for no one enjoys simply giving up something for nothing in return. Therefore, as most of us learn over the course of childhood, we must pay for the things we acquire. We must give the owner something he values to replace the commodity he is losing. We can pay in many forms: in money, in trade, in favors, in companionship, in sex. But pay we must. If we don't pay something back, we had better *watch* our back. For the owner, or the police, will soon be coming for us.

To the never-ending regret of us all, this is how the world works. If we thought that just having needs was a strange system, the whole thing gets even stranger when we realize these needs can only be met by giving up something else we need. Economics, of course, works in just this way. If we want an appliance, we go to the store and sacrifice some money for it. Yet human relationships work this way as well. The Course mentions "the 'laws' of friendship, of 'good' relationships and reciprocity."[45] Reciprocity is probably the primary law in the economics of relationships. If someone does something nice to me I should return the favor, or I am not much of a friend. It is really not so different from purchasing a toaster.

This buying and selling goes far beyond the mere trading of favors. This is actually how we acquire friends and lovers in the first place. How, for instance, do we win over a romantic partner? We offer her gifts: dinner, candy, flowers, gestures of love and friendship. Yet these tangible gifts are actually just transmitting devices for the real currency, the energy of specialness. We are transmitting to her our specialness halo, sending her the message "You are special," and sending her the promise of even greater specialness should she choose to be ours. How special of a partner we can acquire, then, has everything to do with how much specialness we have to give. How good looking are we? How much status do we have? How successful are we? Do we have a good sense of humor and good conversational skills? Do we have charisma? All of these and more add up to money in our specialness account, and determine what exactly we can afford in a partner.

In the case of marriage, we are in essence trying to purchase a human being. We want to own her: body, mind, heart, and soul. We want the entire store of her specialness. Therefore, we must pay her *our* entire store of specialness. We must give her ownership of our very "self," of our identity as we perceive it. The Course describes this transaction in the following important passage:

> Each partner tries to sacrifice the self he does not want for one he thinks he would prefer. And he feels guilty for the "sin" of taking, and of giving nothing of value in return. How much value can he place upon a self that he would give away to get a "better" one?
>
> The "better" self the ego seeks is always one that is more special. And whoever seems to possess a special self

is "loved" for what can be taken from him. Where both partners see this special self in each other, the ego sees a "union made in Heaven."[46]

This sacrificing in order to purchase a valued commodity applies even to religion as we see it. Traditionally, we are supposed to make sacrifices for God, to give up various pleasures and do His Will instead. In return for our sacrifice He gives us certain goods, just like a grocer. He looks upon us as special, thus transmitting some of His infinite specialness to us. He grants us special favors and gives us a place among His elite, who go to a better place after leaving this sorry earth. And while we remain here, He takes our side in our ongoing struggle with an unjust world. He helps us clear our name, win our wars (and our football games), and avoid sickness and disaster. Again, all this aid is purchased through sacrifices on our part.

We see, then, that everything in our world works according to economic principles of acquiring through payment, of accumulating through sacrifice, of gaining through loss. We have the economics of material goods, the economics of human relationships, and the economics of religion.

This makes life here an incredibly complicated and precarious dance. We have to figure out what things we really want and what things only appear desirable. We then must calculate which ones we can actually afford, and then determine the means for acquiring them. In purchasing them, we must make sure we get a bargain and do not lose more than we gain. And we must do this in relation to hundreds of things as we try to supply literally scores of needs that cry out for satiation yet can only be temporarily quieted.

Now add in the fact that while we are performing our furious juggling act of acquisition, we are also busy defending ourselves from attacks on all fronts. In our defense we must identify what is attacking us, how big of a threat it is, and what precisely will neutralize it. Hopefully, we will foresee its attack and make plans that will neutralize it before it ever reaches us. And again, we are doing this in relation to literally hundreds of things that are threatening us at any given time. What's more, a world bent on attacking us is hardly going to give us a fair deal on all our purchases.

Our desperate hope is that we can play this game of acquiring and defending well enough to win. Our lives become a chess game of trying to obtain the other guy's pieces while defending our own. If we can move our pieces around cleverly enough, and if the stars are on our side, and if we beseech God sincerely enough before the game, we will hopefully gain victory. The world's chess pieces will stop their assault and will instead turn and smile upon us and give us happiness, which only they have the magical power to do.

This, I believe, is the human program for happiness. In the language of the Course, this is the ego's plan for salvation—to arrange the external world so that it ceases its attack and grants us contentment. The question is, does this plan ever work? We can answer that in part simply by looking at the lives around us. But to give a truly complete answer, we will have to dive deeper into the hidden motives behind our plan.

Seven

Our search for happiness is actually an expression of resentment and a quest for vengeance on the past.

Seven

In the last chapter we attempted to describe the conventional search for happiness without doing much unveiling. We simply tried to describe what we spend our time doing and the beliefs reflected in those behaviors. Now we are going to dive beneath the surface of our lives to the hidden darkness that, according to the Course, is really motivating our seemingly innocuous search to feel good. The picture we will bring to light is not pretty. But once again, it is crucial for setting the stage for the profound and total relevance of the Course's central theme of forgiveness.

7.1. Underneath our conscious face of innocence is the victim level, a place in us where we are enraged over what we think the world has done to us.

Recall our discussion from the last chapter of the face of innocence, the operative self-image of *homo sapiens*, the image which says, "I am a good person making my way as best I can through a harsh world." Why was it called the *face* of innocence? Did you notice that the passage which described it did not say that "you" are going through life making the best of a harsh world? Instead it said *this face* goes through life. The face smiles and charms. The face's eyes search for companions and look on the suffering. The face's cheeks are often wet with tears. The passage spoke of the face just like a mask we wear, or like a puppet we operate.

The implication is clear: The face of innocence is just that—a face we put on. It is a *facade* of innocence. It conceals something else, the something wearing this mask, operating this puppet. Let us return to the original passage and look at material we didn't quote earlier, to see just what that something is:

> The concept of the self the world would teach is not the thing that it appears to be. For it is made to serve two purposes, but one of which the mind can recognize. The first presents the face of innocence, the aspect acted on [the conscious aspect upon which we act].[1]

This passage says that our self-concept is deceptive, for it contains a hidden aspect. It has two aspects, only one of which is conscious ("but one of which the mind can recognize"). The other, therefore, must be unconscious. The conscious aspect is "the face of innocence." After describing this face of innocence (in the part we quoted in the last chapter), the Course comments on how this conscious aspect relates to the second, unconscious aspect:

> No one who makes a picture of himself omits this face, for he has need of it. The other side he does not want to see. Yet it is here [referring to the other side] the learning of the world has set its sights, for it is here the world's "reality" is set, to see to it the idol lasts.[2]

Here the Course says plainly that the face of innocence *is* the operative self-concept of humanity: "No one who makes a picture of himself omits this face." Not, however, because it is true, but because it serves some purpose, because we have "need of it." This purpose is given in the next sentence: "The other side he does not want to see." The face of innocence exists purely to *hide* the second aspect of our self-concept, to keep it unconscious. Yet the second aspect is the *important* aspect. It is how our self-concept really portrays us—a portrayal it simultaneously hides from us with the face of innocence. As the final sentence says, the second aspect is what all worldly experience is trying to teach us. Let us, then, skip ahead a few lines and answer the question: What *is* this second aspect?

> The lesson teaches this: "I am the thing you made of me, and as you look on me, you stand condemned because of what I am."[3]

Imagine, if you will, really saying the above statement to someone *and meaning it*. How would you feel toward that person? The Course is claiming that underneath your smiling exterior, this is how you feel towards everyone. Beneath the innocent veneer you fabricated, this is your self-concept. This, rather than the mask of innocence, is the universal self-concept of humanity.

I call this second aspect *the victim*, for its essence is a condemning rage over what the world has supposedly done to me, over the mangled, despicable thing I think it has made of me. Remember, our primary experience of the world is that it is an *attacking* world (key idea 5.7). In the face of innocence, we try to numb the horror of being attacked. On the victim level, however, we are fully in touch with it.

Think of the human life cycle as we described it in Chapter 5. We believe that the world has bludgeoned us from birth until the present moment. We think it has rejected our good intentions, shattered our dreams of love, stripped us of our innocence, and actually ripped the Kingdom of God out of our hearts. We believe it is brutally responsible for our miserable, godforsaken lot. Given this, can our face of innocence really be an honest stance? Can our appearance of stepping tolerantly through life, a good self making its well-intentioned way through a difficult world, eking out its pleasures, doing its duty, paying the man what he asks—can this appearance be how we truly feel?

We all know the stories of the quiet, introverted postal worker who one day snaps and starts blowing people away. Is there nothing of him in us? Yet we need not turn to such an extreme example. One of the primary goals of many forms of modern psychotherapy is to uncover this victim layer of the psyche. Every day there are people in therapy making contact with this level. They discover, often to their shock, that beneath their people-pleasing exteriors is someone in a state of rage over past abuse.

Let us look for a moment at the nature of anger. Anger, according to the Course, is "a response to function unfulfilled as you perceive the function."[4] In other words, "When you are angry, is it not because someone has failed to fill the function you allotted him?"[5] Now let us ask ourselves, have the people in our lives fulfilled the functions we allotted them? Have they lived up to all of our expectations? Has the world conformed to our notions of what it ought to be? Has it obeyed our wishes? Given that our answer is probably a resounding "no" to all of these questions, and given the massive toll this seems to have taken on our lives and our happiness, what are we going to feel but angry? In light of this, is it so hard to imagine that our face of innocence is skating on a thin, cracked layer of ice that floats atop a churning lake of anger?

The postal worker and the abuse victim are windows onto us all. Within each one of us, claims the Course, lies burning anger, sleeping rage at what the world has done to us. In a memorable line, the Course says, "You will become increasingly aware that a slight twinge of annoyance is nothing but a veil drawn over intense fury."[6] Here, the Course is promising that through walking its path, you will discover that your mild-mannered face of innocence is nothing but a mask worn by a raging victim.

7.2. The victim's primary perception is that other people are sinful.

Let us return to the Course's discussion of the victim level:

> Here is the central lesson that ensures your brother is condemned eternally. For what you are has now become his sin. For this is no forgiveness possible. No longer does it matter what he does, for your accusing finger points to him, unwavering and deadly in its aim.[7]

The essential perception of the victim is that other people are *sinful*, worthy not of forgiveness but of eternal condemnation. For, of course, in the world's war against us, they have been the soldiers assailing our walls, or, worse yet, conniving their way inside the walls to strike from within our own bed. Therefore, in this place in our minds we feel the burning condemnation that the above passage describes. A hidden finger in us points at the people in our lives, "unwavering and deadly in its aim," and says (in the words we quoted earlier), "I am the thing you made of me, and as you look on me, you stand condemned because of what I am."

What does it mean to say that people are sinners? In Chapter 4 we learned that a sin is a *real attack*, an intentional attack that results in actual harm. According to this definition, if anyone has purposefully harmed or hurt us then that person is a sinner. It takes little reflection to realize that, in our perception, everyone in our lives fits this definition of "sinner" to at least some small degree. Workbook Lesson 68 asks us to think of the major grievances we hold, and goes on to say:

> Then think of the seemingly minor grievances you hold against those you like and even think you love. It will quickly become apparent that there is no one against whom you do not cherish grievances of some sort.[8]

Again, even these *seemingly* minor grievances, even these slight twinges of annoyance, are a cover over intense rage.

This entire chapter is really about the perception that others have sinned against us. Yet I want to highlight this perception by making it a separate point within the chapter simply because it is so central to the Course. As we will eventually see, the Course targets this perception, more than anything else in this world, as the cause of our suffering and thus the focus of its path.

7.3. In this place in our minds we believe that past injustices have given us the right to resentment, restitution, and revenge.

Whenever we believe that we have been attacked and wounded, that we have been sinned against, we automatically feel we have certain rights—*victim's* rights. There are at least three such rights:

1. The right to anger and resentment toward our attacker.
2. The right to restitution, to have restored to us what the attacker deprived us of.
3. The right to vengeance, the right to punish our attacker.

We might call these victim's rights the three "R's": resentment, restitution, and revenge. These perceived rights are part of the logic of sin. As we learned in Chapter 4, one who has done real harm (were real harm possible) is a sinner, who is therefore guilty and deserves punishment. Just as the sinner deserves certain forms of pain, so his victim is supposedly granted certain kinds of rights. Let us look more closely at these three perceived rights.

1. The right to anger and resentment

In essence, we already looked at this in the previous sections. When we feel attacked, anger is the emotional mirror of our attacker's guilt; anger is emotional justice. To expand our earlier definition of anger, anger is merely the feeling that arises when we believe that someone has sinned by not fulfilling the function we assigned him.

2. The right to restitution

If someone has taken something from us, we clearly feel we have the right to get it back. What could be more basic? Yet having physical things stolen is nowhere near as common, nor as devastating, as being deprived of the intangibles we cherish. While writing this I saw a news story in which a woman returned home to discover that most of her possessions had been stolen. She said that everything she lost could be replaced—everything, that is, except the most important item taken. "They robbed me of my sense of security," she said.

In our eyes, it is the intangibles that the world has primarily stolen from us. According to our version of things, its unjust treatment has robbed us of love, security, peace, self-respect, recognition—in short, of happiness. Our only consolation is that we see this unfair past as a high-value claim ticket, entitling us to restitution in the form of a better future. This is why we cling to grievances—we are holding onto that claim ticket. This is also why we get very adept at telling stories of how we were wronged, for, alas, the claim ticket is invisible to others. Our stories, told skillfully enough, have the wondrous effect of making it visible.

3. The right to vengeance

Webster's Dictionary defines vengeance as "punishment inflicted in retaliation for an injury or offense." What could be more natural than the idea that if we are attacked, we have the right to attack back? According to the logic of sin, our attacker deserves punishment. Since we were the ones *he* punished, shouldn't we be the ones who get to punish *him*? Vengeance goes by many names: an eye for an eye, tit for tat, payback. Perhaps its main synonym, however, is "justice." What we call justice is largely making sure that attackers receive their "just" punishment. The Course remarks on this: "To the world, justice and vengeance are the same, for sinners see justice only as their punishment."[9]

Vengeance, however, is not a mere impersonal balancing of abstract scales. It fulfills a very personal need. Seeing someone receive their just punishment can feel deeply satisfying. Why? The answer is simple: *Vengeance is the means for restitution of the intangibles.* As we said above, by wounding you, your attacker supposedly took various intangibles from you—for instance, your pride, dignity, self-respect, security, status, etc. By turning the tables on him you reverse the transfer of these intangibles and recover them. By victimizing you, he took them from you; by victimizing him, you take them back.

For example, when a defending champion in boxing is beaten and loses his title, a great amount of his invisible status is taken from him and appropriated by the new champion. If he can have a rematch and regain his title, he wrenches that status away from the new champion and possesses it once again. We even symbolize this by the transfer of the title belt back and forth.

One place in which these three "rights" are particularly apparent is the criminal justice system. There it is plain to see that victims have an unwritten right to be angry (right #1). They often receive awards or damages for harm done to them (restitution—right #2). And they have a right to see their attackers be punished (right #3). Perhaps this is the reason we are so fascinated with the justice system, with police shows, with good guys and bad guys, with murder mysteries and courtroom dramas. Here is an official theater in which we can vicariously observe what we all want to see: victims at last receiving their due—and sinners getting theirs. Here we can see heinous crimes that symbolize all the injustices in our own lives. And we can feel satisfaction as the long arm of the law comes crashing down on the criminals. Ah, we think, if it only worked that way all the time.

Getting back to my main point, if this victim level of the mind is really there, if you truly believe deep down that the world robbed you of your happiness, what would you want in this place in your mind? Would not your single desire be to recover what the world stole? Would not victim's "rights" become your most precious possessions? Would not your life become an angry yet "justifiable" quest to exact your vengeance and reclaim your treasure?

This is precisely how the Course describes us, in the section entitled "The Laws of Chaos."[10] In paragraphs 9-12 of that section, it says you think your brother has stolen from you "what you want but never found,"[11] the "hidden secret treasure,"[12] "the magic that will cure all of your pain."[13] "He would deprive you of the secret ingredient that would give meaning to your life."[14] Because of his theft, you are left with only one course of action—to retaliate and recover the secret ingredient to happiness:

> All of the mechanisms of madness are seen emerging here: The "enemy" made strong by keeping hidden the valuable inheritance that should be yours; your justified position and attack for what has been withheld; and the inevitable loss the enemy must suffer to save yourself [to recover your inheritance].[15]

We have all seen lives driven by just these thoughts, people who are consumed by the belief that they have been terribly wronged and who live only to exact their revenge. Yet certainly, we think, we are not among those people. We are good and decent and well meaning. We do not walk through life on a crusade to settle some colossal score with the world. After all, we are decent people, maybe longtime seekers of God, perhaps serious students of *A Course in Miracles*. After years of reading and meditating we have left such base motives far behind.

Yet isn't this exactly what we would predict the face of innocence would say? After all, its whole purpose is to hide these motives and keep them unconscious.

This innocent facade, in fact, does more than merely mask our rage; it *expresses* it. It carries out its plans. This brings us to a startling concept: Our conscious persona is a *masked expression* of the hidden victim within us. This masked expression includes our entire search for happiness which we explored in the last chapter. From the Course's standpoint, our seemingly innocent search to feel better is actually an angry quest for restitution and revenge. All of that pragmatic moving around of the world's chess pieces is driven by a secret program. We are not just impartially manipulating externals; we are doing so because we are on a mission, a mission to settle an old, old score. As we absent-mindedly get in the car and drive to work, we ourselves are unwittingly being driven by an ancient vendetta. Like a money-laundering project, the victim's program of resentment, restitution, and revenge is being funneled through our "harmless" daily activities.

Upon hearing this, most of us will struggle to convince ourselves that we are an exception to this unpleasant concept, if in fact this concept is true at all. Therefore, to bring this idea home, let us examine the evidence of our lives. In the final three sections of this chapter we will see the three "rights" of the victim constantly leaking through our seemingly innocuous process of rearranging the furniture of the world.

7.4. Our attempt to rearrange the world is based on anger, resentment, and grievances.

We began the last chapter, about the human search for happiness, with this passage:

> The ego's plan for salvation centers around holding grievances. It maintains that, if someone else spoke or acted differently, if some external circumstance or event were changed, you would be saved.[16]

We explored at length the meaning of the second sentence here, that we think happiness will come by a change in how the world is treating us. Yet how does that connect with the first sentence? How does that amount to a plan for salvation based on *holding grievances*?

It will help us if we can define what a grievance is. Webster's Dictionary defines it as "a cause of distress (as an unsatisfactory working condition) felt to afford reason for complaint or resistance." Let's expand this a bit:

- Something outside of me is unsatisfactory.
- This causes me to feel distress about it, and gives me cause to complain about it, as well as to *resist* it, to attempt to change it.

In short, a grievance says, "If this outer thing were different, I would not feel distressed." Or, to word it slightly differently, a grievance says, "if someone else spoke or acted differently, if some external circumstance or event were changed, you would be saved." This, of course, is the second sentence of our passage above! The second sentence is not at all disjointed from the first; it *restates* the first. Do you see what this means? A plan for salvation based on rearranging externals *is* a plan based on holding grievances. And that *is* our plan. All day long we are rearranging externals because they are (or soon will be) causing us distress. All day long, then, our behavior is stating the complaint, "If this outer thing were different, I would not feel distressed." All day long we are expressing grievances.

As an example, at the very moment I was writing this material, my son (who was then about nine) appeared at my office door dripping with water from swimming. I said, "You aren't dripping water everywhere [meaning, on the carpet], are you?" By this I implied that he should change this state of affairs, that he should go back outside or should go into the bathroom and dry off. I also clearly implied (and he knew it) that I would feel better if he did. This was a classic grievance. There was some outer condition that I considered unsatisfactory. This condition (supposedly) caused me to feel bad. It also apparently gave me cause for complaint. I then voiced that complaint in an effort to resist the outer condition, to change its form to a more pleasing one.

Immediately following this, my oldest daughter (then five) came into my office, also wet. This made her cold—a clearly unsatisfactory condition—so she voiced her complaint in an effort to change things: She asked me to wrap a towel around her. She then found standing unsatisfactory and asked me to set her body (now incapacitated by the towel around her) onto my lounge chair. This chair, however, was covered with a blanket and some clothes, a condition she soon found unsatisfactory. So she asked me, somewhat curtly, to pick her up, remove the debris, and place her back on the chair. Another grievance. As I typed this description she was saying, "Dad, aren't you done working yet?"

Grievance after grievance after grievance. Unsatisfactory condition eliciting displeasure, followed by attempt to change the condition, followed by another unsatisfactory condition. And this is life on earth, is it not? We experience the world as one massive unsatisfactory working condition, about which, like chronically disgruntled workers, we have an endless string of complaints, leading to an endless series of attempts to set things right. You can see this in your own behavior if you simply watch yourself for a few minutes: Each movement is an attempt to head off some perceived source of distress, and is succeeded by another such movement heading off another distress, and on and on and on. Your life is a necklace strung with the beads of grievances. And since a grievance is a resentment, and resentment is anger, we return to our starting point: Our attempt to rearrange the world is based on anger, resentment, grievances.

7.5. In our giving and in our suffering, we constantly send the message, "I suffered because of you. Therefore, you owe me."

We have seen that our conventional search for happiness expresses the first of our so-called victim's rights, the "right" to anger and resentment. Now let us turn to the second, the "right" to receive restitution for our losses.

It is hard to argue with the Course's idea that in many ways this is a dark and crazy world. Perhaps we would despair altogether were it not for all the giving that goes on between people, the kindness and the loving behavior that passes between friends and loved ones. This giving is a pocket of light that can seem to balance out the world's darker patches.

Let's be honest, however: Most of what passes for giving in this world, as we sadly learn, has strings attached. It therefore is what the Course calls "giving to get."[17] We discussed this in the last chapter (under key idea 6.8), where we talked about having to pay, either in tangibles or intangibles, for the things we acquire from the world. We must make a sacrifice to fill the empty spot in the other guy's hand, as his possession becomes ours. A great deal of this "giving to get" masquerades as real giving, simply because the bargain is implied, not stated, and because we are trading intangibles like specialness, rather than things we can see with our eyes. Therefore it looks like I am just smiling and loving, while in actuality I am conducting a business transaction.

The Course has a dim view of this "giving," as we can see in the following passage, which opens by saying that God's gifts are totally unlike the gifts of the world,

> in which the giver loses as he gives the gift; the taker is the richer by his loss...
>
> ....No gift is given thus. Such "gifts" are but a bid for a more valuable return; a loan with interest to be paid in full; a temporary lending, meant to be a pledge of debt to be repaid with more than was received by him who took the gift.[18]

This passage describes something we all more or less realize: that most of our gifts are merely payment for something in return, some new thing we perceive as having greater value than the thing we gave up. This obviously applies to our monetary transactions. It also applies to most of the apparently kind and giving behavior in our friendships and romances, in which we give out the energy of our love and attention (read "specialness") for some desired return. It applies even to the process by which we acquire our friends and lovers, for, as we saw in the last chapter, we essentially purchase them with the currency of specialness. Thus, perhaps the main light we cling to for comfort in this dark world turns out to be mere mercantilism—not much of an inspiration at all.

Yet the Course does not stop there. This is just the beginning of its analysis of what normally passes for giving. Let us turn to a crucial section entitled "The Needless Sacrifice"[19] to get the rest of the story:

> In one way or another, every relationship the ego makes
> is based on the idea that by sacrificing itself, it becomes
> bigger.[20]

This states in different words what we already said. Our egos think that by giving out, by sacrificing something to someone else, we can gain something of more value. Through losing we gain. In this case, through sacrificing ourselves for another, we gain that person's love and friendship.

> The "sacrifice," which it regards as purification, is actually
> the root of its bitter resentment.[21]

When we sacrifice for another, don't we feel purified by it, as if we have paid off some debt? Doesn't this sacrificing convince us that we are a good person? That much is clear. What, however, does it mean when it says that this sacrificing is the root of our ego's bitter resentment? The next sentences explain this:

> For it would prefer to attack directly, and avoid delaying
> what it really wants. Yet the ego acknowledges "reality" as
> it sees it, and recognizes that no one could interpret direct
> attack as love.[22]

Why do we bitterly resent having to give to people? Because we would rather just take what we want. Deep down, we would really prefer to have it for free. Yet we spent our formative years slowly conceding that the world simply does not work that way. If we just reach out and try to grab the love we want, people will see what we are up to and withhold the love we crave. And in the process we ourselves will feel guilty. Therefore, regrettably, we will have to pay for it, we will have to "give." But—and this is the point—we secretly *resent* it. This is a secret we keep from others and perhaps even from ourselves. We probably believe that, as grown-ups, we have adjusted to the way the world works and that we only resent it when we get a bad deal, when we pay more than something is worth. No, in some childish room in our unconscious, we resent having to pay at all. As you get up to do some favor for your partner, for example, have you never sighed and had something like the following flash through your mind: "I wish I could just get what I want from him (or her) without having to put out all this effort"?

> Yet to make guilty *is* direct attack, although it does not seem to be. For the guilty expect attack, and having asked for it they are attracted to it.[23]

Even when we show our generosity and "give until it hurts," this *too* is direct attack. Why? Because its intended effect is "to make guilty." How does our gift induce guilt in the other person? This shouldn't be terribly hard to answer, since this is such a common human experience. Our gift induces guilt because we are losing something for the sake of the receiver. She is gaining from our loss. And somewhere inside we are murmuring, "I wish I could get what I want from her without having to pay." Our gift, in other words, carries the hidden message, "I am suffering because of you. You are responsible for my loss."

If we came out and said these lines, it is no mystery how the other person would feel: guilty. And feeling guilty of our loss, she would now (as the above passage says) "expect attack" as her just deserts.

> Each one thinks that he has sacrificed something to the other, and hates him for it....And for this sacrifice, which he demands of himself, he demands that the other accept the guilt and sacrifice himself as well.[24]

These lines complete the Course's description of the hidden psychology of "giving." We think we have sacrificed something to our partner and hate her for requiring this sacrifice of us. Actually, we demanded this sacrifice of ourselves, but we conveniently overlook this. In our minds, she is responsible for our loss, and so we demand that she accept the guilt and—here is the final step—make a reciprocal sacrifice. She must give something back in order to pay off her guilt. In sum, then, our generous "giving," our noble self-sacrifice, is really designed to send the covert message: "I suffered because of you. You owe me." What can such a message be but an attack?

This passage goes on to say that this process of instilling guilt through self-sacrifice is how we obligate people to stay with us. "It is only by attack without forgiveness that the ego can ensure the guilt that holds all its relationships together."[25] Note that this says, "holds *all* its relationships together," meaning: romantic relationships, family relationships, business relationships, political relationships, international relationships. This idea (that by sacrificing for you I make you guilty and obligate you to sacrifice back in order to pay off your guilt) is the grimy glue that holds virtually all social intercourse together. Earlier we said that material commerce, human relationships, and even conventional religion all run by economic principles. The core of these principles is this very system of sacrificing in order to instill guilt and sacrificing in order to pay off guilt.

This brings us very close to the sobering conclusion that the world is run by the unconscious victim. For, of course, one of the victim's foundational pillars is the exact idea we have been discussing, that you are responsible for my suffering and therefore owe me restitution. Isn't one of the best ways to make ourselves a victim to give and give and give, so that we are entirely depleted and so that the world owes us an everlasting debt?

Of course the world rarely compensates us to our satisfaction, and so we must frequently adopt another posture besides "giving." This other posture is that of overtly playing the victim. We show the pain and the scars that come from not receiving our just due. We show "the face of suffering and pain, in silent proof of guilt and of the ravages of sin."[26] We show proof of damage. This seems poles apart from being the generous giver, but is actually a different form of the same content.

We alluded to this posture earlier, in referring to our storytelling of how wronged we have been. Yet displaying proof of damage takes many, many forms, often hard to recognize for what they are:

In looking at the special relationship, it is necessary first to realize that it involves a great amount of pain. Anxiety, despair, guilt and attack all enter into it, broken into by periods in which they seem to be gone. All these must be understood for what they are. Whatever form they take, they are always an attack on the self to make the other guilty. I have spoken of this before [in "The Needless Sacrifice," which we just quoted from].[27]

According to this passage, all the pain we experience in our relationships is an attack on ourselves which we then use, rather dishonestly, to send the message, "I suffered because of you. You owe me." This is somewhat like shooting ourselves in the leg and then sticking the gun in our partner's hand and demanding restitution. According to the above list, this principle holds true when we are anxiety-ridden, when we give up hope, when we get angry and vindictive, even when we feel remorseful and guilty. Later, the Course applies this principle to any form of suffering whatsoever:

Whenever you consent to suffer pain, to be deprived, unfairly treated or in need of anything, you but accuse your brother of attack upon God's Son. You hold a picture of your crucifixion before his eyes, that he may see his sins are writ in Heaven in your blood and death, and go before him, closing off the gate and damning him to hell.[28]

Note that these stark words apply to literally any suffering, including any sense of being deprived or unjustly treated, even any sense of having *needs*. All of this we do to ourselves (we "consent" to), but then blame on others. This same section (entitled "The Picture of Crucifixion," after the above passage) says that this applies to physical illness as well.

A sick and suffering you but represents your brother's guilt; the witness that you send lest he forget the injuries he gave, from which you swear he never will escape....Death seems an easy price, if [you] can say, "Behold me, brother, at your hand I die."[29]

Again, we see the same message: "I suffered because of you. I demand restitution." This is the victim's tune and we are singing it almost all the time, through our benevolent giving and sacrifice, through our suffering and sense of need, even through our physical illnesses. Virtually all our behavior is testimony to the vindictive program of the victim oozing through the pores of our face of innocence.

7.6. We seek vengeance through subtle attempts to re-enact the past and reverse past "injustices" against us.

Now we turn to the third of our victim's rights: the "right" to vengeance. We are all familiar with the urge for vengeance, the impulse to strike back when attacked. Yet for the most part we confine this impulse to our fantasy lives, where we imagine ourselves getting back at our attackers in all kinds of delicious ways that we are simply too decent to carry out in "real life." However, according to the Course, we *are* acting out these fantasies all the time. The Course claims that our special relationships are an ongoing kind of vengeance theater dedicated to physically acting out our dreams of retribution. As it tersely says, "The special relationship takes vengeance on the past."[30]

The Course openly acknowledges that special relationships do not seem to have this purpose:

> In the special relationship it does not seem to be an act-
> ing out of vengeance that you seek. And even when the
> hatred and the savagery break briefly through, the illusion
> of love is not profoundly shaken.[31]

This passage is correct, is it not? Even when we experience savagely vengeful moments in our relationship, we interpret them as some sort of weird anomaly and go on with our lives, rather than seeing them as a brief window onto our underlying motives. How, then, can we see these vengeful motives at work in the rest of the relationship, even in times when "the illusion of love" is firmly in place?

To answer that question we will need to go back in time and explore the past on which we seek vengeance. In our version of that past, despite how nobly we tried, the world dished out to us a series of injustices, hurts, and disappointments which left us permanently scarred. To a large degree our memories are organized around these hurtful incidents and situations, which become much of the skeleton on which we hang our life story. Central to this story are the particular people—parents, siblings, friends, teachers, neighborhood bullies—who delivered these various injuries. Perhaps they did so through overt abuse, perhaps through neglect, perhaps through simply not living up to the role we assigned them. In some way or other, they did not give us the specialness we wanted.

These are the people we want to take vengeance on. In our eyes, they took what was rightfully ours. If we can punish them for how they treated us, then we reclaim the intangibles they stole. According to the Course, we carry our personal collection of these people with us at all times in our mental hip pocket. If we watch our minds, we might even catch ourselves holding imaginary conversations with them, as we state our convincing case to them once again. Their image—a caricatured image that reflects not them but our one-sided memories of them—looms large in our unconscious, where they haunt the corridors of our minds and people our inner world.[32] The Course calls these dark, ghostly images from our past "shadow figures."

How do we get back at these shadow figures? Even when we are still in relationship with these people, the past in which we were victimized has long since vanished. That past is gone and cannot be changed. What, then, to do? We will bring the past into the present. We will put on a play that re-enacts the past. This is where our current special relationships come in. It is with our current partners that we hope to stage our vengeance theater. We can see this production taking place in three stages:

1. Casting

First, we search for people who in some way remind us of our shadow figures and so can play their part. According to the Course, this is what actually motivates us to choose particular relationship partners. This, in other words, is the Course's theory of romantic attraction: "Whatever reminds you of your past grievances attracts you, and seems to go by the name of love, no matter how distorted the associations by which you arrive at the connection may be."[33] In other words, my new wife may not look or act just like Mom or Dad, but there will be some strange association in my mind that makes her just right to play their parts in my vengeance theater. Again, according to the Course, this is the real reason that I am attracted to her.

2. Re-enacting

After we have hired the actors, we subtly arrange a rough re-enactment of the original situation in which we were humiliated. Perhaps one of our shadow figures is a coach who never gave us a chance to prove ourselves at baseball. Our re-enactment might be with a boss in a workplace just competitive enough to remind us of the baseball field. According to the Course, once all the actors and props are in place and the play commences, we, the producer/director, actually become fooled. On an emotional level we respond as if we are back there in the past:

> It is through these strange and shadowy figures that the insane relate to their insane world. For they see [take notice of, are attracted to] only those who remind them of these images [i.e., shadow figures], and it is to them that they relate. Thus do they communicate with those who are not there [the shadow figures], and it is they who answer them. And no one hears their answer save him who called upon them, and he alone believes they answered him.[34]

This passage paints a disturbing picture. We do not relate to people directly, we relate to them through the projected haze of our shadow figures. In other words, we see our current partners wearing the mask of our past victimizers. Thus, when we talk to our partners in the present, on an emotional level we are speaking to our shadow figures. And when they respond to us, we hear it as if our shadow figures are speaking to us. Like the person in the insane asylum, we are carrying on conversations—indeed, carrying on a life—with people who are not there.

3. New ending

Vengeance has a compulsion to recreate past humiliations and then turn the tables. When you lose a sports contest, for instance, what do you do? You challenge the winners to a *grudge match*, a repetition of the original situation which will hopefully have a different ending. Here in our special relationships, we do the same thing. We re-enact the scene of our humiliation and plan to turn the tables. This time we hope to receive the love, recognition, and adulation—in short, the specialness—that we were so unfairly denied the first time around. In our scripted new ending, Dad (played by our spouse) would rather spend time with us than go fishing; teacher (played by our employer) cannot imagine how anyone could overlook our amazing abilities; first husband (played by third husband) deeply appreciates our tireless self-sacrifice and natural beauty.

Of course, these happy endings do not come cheap! Which is where all of the "giving" we discussed in the previous section comes in. We must pay our actors handsomely, with flowers, smiles, touches, dinners, sex, and eventually with houses and even our firstborn. But we consider it all worth it. For when our new cast of characters gives us the specialness we want, we experience the ultimate triumph. We get to hoist our enormous trophy—our doting husband, our six-figure book deal, our palatial home—before the stingy eyes of the shadow figures that crowd our dark mental attic. As they gaze in shame we know we have accomplished our victory. We have proven to them in a public court that they did us wrong, that we really deserved what they so stingily withheld. By thus humiliating them, we turn the tables on them. We feel the specialness that was rightfully ours leave their ghostly grasp and, like a king's robe, envelop us at last. A thousand times we have told ourselves, "I'll show them." Well, now we finally *have* shown them for, of course, this crowd of shadow figures is who "they" are.

Our new relationship partners have played an oddly dual role in this process. On the one hand, they have seemed to be our loving comrades who have helped us wage our war, sympathizing with our plight and hating our past victimizers right along with us. On the other hand, they have played the *role* of our shadow figures in our vengeance theater. Thus, the payment we demand of our shadow figures is really payment that *they*—our new partners—have to cough up. They are the ones who must provide restitution for the sins of our fathers, sins they were not even there to witness let alone commit. And since we emotionally confuse them with our shadow figures, they are the ones who receive all of the anger that is pent up from our past. Thus, our painful past ends up being like a horrendous day at work—even when we leave it behind we carry it with us. And when we get home and greet people that were not even part of our horrendous day, we take it out on them. In short, the vengeance we take on our shadow figures is vengeance we take on those who symbolize them.

The following paragraph summarizes this concept of vengeance theater:

It is impossible to let the past go without relinquishing the special relationship. For the special relationship is an attempt to re-enact the past and change it. Imagined slights, remembered pain, past disappointments, perceived injustices and deprivations all enter into the special relationship, which becomes a way in which you seek to restore your wounded self-esteem. What basis would you have for choosing a special partner without the past? Every such choice is made because of something "evil" in the past to which you cling, and for which must someone else atone.[35]

In this passage we have almost the entire process we described above:

- We have a past which is purportedly responsible for our "wounded self-esteem." Note the list of slights, pains, disappointments, injustices, and deprivations—all forms of wounded self-esteem.
- We select special partners on the basis of this past, to make possible the rest of the process.
- We attempt to "re-enact" this past with our new partners. This includes mentally superimposing the past onto the current relationship (what is meant by saying that our past pains "all enter into the special relationship").
- We attempt to "change" the past through this re-enactment, to give it a new ending. This new ending restores our wounded self-esteem.
- The new ending comes through our new partners paying for ("atoning" for) the past "evil" that was done to us before they came on the scene.

Even if the above scenario sounds bizarre, we all can relate to the desire to acquire what past figures in our lives denied us. For instance, see if you can think of one person in your past from whom you wanted to hear this message: "I was so wrong. You deserved better than what I gave to you. Here is all the love (or money or approval or sex or whatever) I didn't give you before—with interest!" Assuming that someone has come to mind, can you think of any ways in which you tried to wring this statement out of that person? Further, can you think of anything you have acquired or achieved in your life that prompted you to mentally gloat to this person, "See, I told you I deserved better"? If so, you are catching the Course's theory of shadow figures in action.

This theory, however, will not sound so bizarre to those who have spent years exploring the unconscious archeology of their personal relationships. They perhaps have already realized that they were really not responding to the partners in front of them, but instead lashing out at and trying to extract something from Mom or Dad. They perhaps have recognized why they keep falling into the same relationships with different faces, why they keep meeting their mother in disguise.

This theory of shadow figures and re-enacting the past wraps up everything we have seen in this chapter. According to the Course, beneath our conscious face of innocence lies a place in which we feel horribly wounded by an unjust past. In this place we feel that people have grievously sinned against us and stolen our happiness and peace. This, we believe, justifies our eternal anger. It launches us on a quest for vengeance, in which we continually attempt to re-enact a bygone past, convict its key figures, and wrench from their hands the restitution we deserve. These repetitions make up our days and years, and indeed comprise our lives. Our emotional stance becomes one gigantic grievance and we are driven by the need to settle an across-the-board old score. This quest, then, is the underlying content beneath our innocent facade's search for happiness. Its dark goal is what we really hope to achieve with our pragmatic repositioning of the billiard balls of the world. It is the underlying force that drives us. Or is it?

Eight

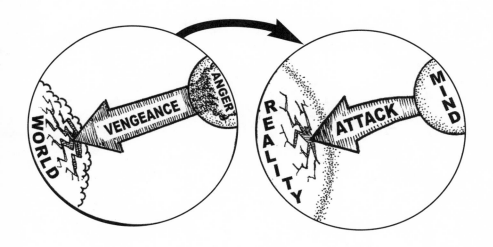

Our "solution" is an attack and so,
like the original problem, is an attack
on ourselves.

Eight

The victim cannot be the bottommost layer of what is driving our conventional pursuit of happiness. If, as the Course claims, the world is not real, then nothing has really attacked us and we are not victims. The victim level, therefore, must be a mirage produced by something lurking still deeper in our minds. What is it? This chapter will be devoted to answering that question and getting, at last, to the very bottom of the ego's system, the bottom of what is driving life as we know it. The following passage urges us to undertake this difficult endeavor:

> The closer you come to the foundation of the ego's thought system, the darker and more obscure becomes the way. Yet even the little spark in your mind is enough to lighten it. Bring this light fearlessly with you, and bravely hold it up to the foundation of the ego's thought system. Be willing to judge it with perfect honesty. Open the dark cornerstone of terror on which it rests, and bring it out into the light. There you will see that it rested on meaninglessness, and that everything of which you have been afraid was based on nothing.
>
> My brother, you are part of God and part of me. When you have at last looked at the ego's foundation without shrinking you will also have looked upon ours. I come to you from our Father to offer you everything again. Do not refuse it in order to keep a dark cornerstone hidden, for its protection will not save you. I give you the lamp and I will go with you. You will not take this journey alone. I will lead you to your true Father, Who hath need of you, as I

have. Will you not answer the call of love with joy?[1]

This passage describes a journey into the hidden chambers of our ego as if it were a physical expedition. In this journey we find ourselves underground beneath some massive building, the edifice of the ego. We might see ourselves walking down a dark, dank corridor, approaching some nameless horror, the way getting ever "darker and more obscure." Yet Jesus is with us, leading us along the path, handing us a lamp—the light of truth—to light our way. We feel our hand in his. At last we see it looming up ahead, "the dark cornerstone of terror" on which the ego's entire edifice is built. With Jesus beside us, we bravely hold the light of reason up to this dark cornerstone. We then open it up (probably a reference to the practice of placing things like time capsules inside of cornerstones), and calmly see, once and for all, that it contains nothing. We see with our own eyes that the ego's foundation is completely hollow and vacuous. This allows us to look past its empty foundation to our true foundation in God. We might imagine looking past the dark cornerstone and seeing an opening, a window onto Heaven.

In this chapter we will take this expedition, and this will open up for us the "lighter" chapters that follow.

8.1. Beneath the victim level is the ego proper, which is pure, unprovoked attack.

In an important passage, the Course first describes the victim and then explicitly tells us what lies beneath it:

> A brother separated from yourself, an ancient enemy, a murderer who stalks you in the night and plots your death, yet plans that it be lingering and slow; of this you dream. Yet underneath this dream [of being the victim] is yet another, in which you become the murderer, the secret enemy, the scavenger and the destroyer of your brother and the world alike.[2]

After describing the victim—the dream of being stalked by a sadistic murderer outside yourself—the Course, at last, tells us what lies "underneath" the dream of the victim. It is the dream of being the *victimizer*. All along you have been hating your brother for being the bad guy, the evil one who has been unfairly attacking poor innocent you, and the whole time it has been *the other way around*. You have been the attacker preying on him. This is literally the last thing any victim ever wants to hear or, worse yet, admit to, for his entire self-esteem is based on being the innocent victim. Yet it is crucial that we look upon this place within us for, as the lines following the above passage say, "Here is the cause of suffering....Here is the cause of unreality. And it is here that it will be undone."[3]

I call this level the *ego proper*, because, although the face of innocence and the victim are also within the ego's system, they are mere masks. This level is the ego undisguised, unmasked. The ego we discover here is very different from the ego as defined in many systems of psychology and spirituality. It is not an inner child. It is not some bruised part of us to lift up and comfort. It is not some necessary muscle we must develop in order to function in this world. It is not some true part of us which we have condemned but must learn to love and embrace. And it is not something which, once embraced, we will take with us into Heaven.

As the Course views the ego it is much like the devil: the embodiment of pure evil, which lies in total opposition to goodness and light, and is bent on the overthrow of God. In fact, from the Course's perspective, the devil *is* the ego.[4] The concept of the devil was the result of projecting our ego outward onto a cosmic screen, thereby making a mere internal belief appear to be an omnipotent external being.

Surely, we think, if this ego is really within us, there must be some reason for it, some valid point it has, some real need that caused us to adopt it. The Course would reply that no, there is nothing reasonable, valid, or justified about the ego. To the Course this is good news, for if the ego had even a shred of validity then we would have to sleep in the same bed with it forever. Since it does not, we can be free of it completely, not through affirming it and embracing it, but through realizing its utter vacuousness.

We can see the ego as composed of two things, a single activity in service of a single need:

1. *The ego's only activity is attack.* The ego is pure attack. That is all it does. Further, its attack is unprovoked, unjustified, without any external cause.
2. *The ego's only need is to preserve its so-called existence. That is*

why it attacks. This of course was key idea 2.7, that the ego's only need is to stay in business, to confirm its "reality," to protect itself against the threat of oneness.

Throughout this chapter we will see these two things being the real driving forces behind the bulk of our personal lives and what we call life itself.

8.2. The victim level is an excuse to attack, produced by projecting our own attack outward.

How does the victim level relate to the ego proper? By saying that the ego exists *underneath* the victim, we are really saying that the ego is concealed or hidden by the victim. The ego makes us feel guilty and so we cover it over by playing the wounded victim, and thereby feeling more innocent.

There is more to it, however. If you recall, the face of innocence is not merely a cover for the victim, but an expression of it; in sum, a *masked expression*. The same holds true here. The victim is not just a cover for the ego proper; the victim *expresses* the ego, does its dirty work, carries out its attack. The abused victim is simply a mask the ego wears as it goes on its killing spree.

To put this slightly differently, the victim level is an excuse we manufactured to justify attack. To see how this happened let us retrace our previous chapters. We began in a state of pristine perfection called reality or Heaven (Chapter 1), yet we attacked reality, hoping to gain some triumphant status over our brothers and God (Chapter 2). This attack had no effect on reality (Chapter 3); it merely boomeranged and attacked us, hurting our own state of mind (Chapter 4). We then projected this attack outward, making it seem that our attack came at us from the outside, in the form of an attacking world, a world which punished us for our sin of leaving God (Chapter 5). Hence, this world now appears to be the cause of our suffering. We therefore seek relief from suffering by rearranging the forms of the world, by defending against its dangerous forms and acquiring its pleasing forms (Chapter 6). On a deeper level, however, we feel brutally victimized by its unrelenting attack. This victimization gives us the "right" to retaliate in various forms—by feeling resentment, exacting restitution, and taking vengeance (Chapter 7).

Do you see what has happened here? We started out attacking and we ended up attacking, only now at the end our attack is, by all appearances, perfectly justified and even necessary. We seem to have a completely honest and righteous excuse to attack. How did we manage that trick? We used the excuse-making device *par excellence*: projection.

> Anger always involves [i.e., results from] projection of separation [projecting the responsibility for one's own decision to separate from the Kingdom], which must ultimately be accepted as one's own responsibility, rather than being blamed on others.[5]

> Projection and attack are inevitably related, because projection is always a means of justifying attack. Anger without projection is impossible.[6]

"Projection is always a means of justifying attack." Let us put this insight in terms of the two levels of the victim and the ego proper:

1. In the beginning we attacked—this is the ego proper.
2. Then we projected the attack outward, making it appear to be coming at us from without.
3. Now we seem to have been victimized by an outer attack (which is really our own attack in disguise).
4. As a victim, we have the "right" to retaliate. Now the ego proper is justified in doing what it has always done: harbor anger and launch attack.

Do you see what an amazing feat projection has accomplished? It allows us to attack again and again, while we say, "Hey, my hands were tied; I had to protect myself." Projection "makes attack seem reasonable, honestly provoked, and righteous in the name of self-defense."[7] It enables us to repeatedly attack yet be "in no way responsible for it"; to attack just because we like it yet hide behind the cloak of being provoked. If you wanted to be an attacker yet still be innocent, wouldn't you just love a device like this?[8]

What's more, we have fabricated this excuse to attack out of the material of our *own prior attack*. What beautiful circularity! Our own attack, projected outward, is what justifies our continued attack. It is a brilliant system, you must admit. The victim is not merely a cover over our aggressive impulses, it is an ingenious method for attacking with impunity, for attacking *perpetually*. Thus is fulfilled the ego's drive to perpetuate itself.

Even if we cannot see our minds projecting this world outward, we can catch the above dynamics at work. We can see ourselves groping for excuses to explain our attacks, to make them appear warranted. We can also note the inner pleasure that comes from being able to lash out with a free conscience because we clearly have been provoked.

For instance, think of the universal theme of the good guy against the bad guys. The bad guys actually perform a valuable service, for their presence grants the good guy what he secretly wants: a license to kill. Now he can be the righteous avenger. He can kill people and at the same time be the hero, the good guy; not in spite of killing, but *because* he kills. And we, from the comfort of our living rooms, can share his outrage and celebrate his killing and be completely innocent in these feelings. Getting to be innocent while you attack, *because* you attack—isn't this the ultimate example of having your cake while eating it too?

The theme of the good guy versus the bad guys is no isolated theme. It is the story within nearly all our stories, the underlying template for our personal narratives and our official histories. For instance, how many stories have you told in which you described yourself as the bad guy, the slimy black hat, surrounded by squeaky clean good guys? As we saw in the previous two chapters, good self versus bad world is literally the essence of our self-image, both in its mild version as the face of innocence and in its darker, bloodier version as the victim. Good self versus bad world is, quite simply, the lens through which we view reality, a lens we ground so that we could attack with impunity.

In this light, let us think of all the times we have attacked, in little comments and in angry rages, and how each and every time we had an excuse. In each case the other person did something which *made* us angry and *made* us attack, right? We certainly would not just attack without provocation. Earlier we saw this theme in both the face of innocence and the victim, who engaged in attack but only in necessary and righteous response to a prior attack from the outside. What, then, if the Course is correct and never, not a single time, have we attacked *with* provocation? What if each and every time we subtly manufactured a situation which gave us "cause" to do what we already wanted to do? What if, since the dawn of time, the knife has always been in our own hand, yet we placed a mirror before us so that we could see another hand raising another knife, simply to give ourselves just cause to go on slashing?

8.3. The ego promises that attack will get us safety and happiness. This simply tricks us into accumulating guilt, to which the ego is attracted.

We said above that all the ego does is attack. This means that all of the activities we have examined in the ego's system are merely different forms of attack.

Defense (key idea 6.2) is usually quite clearly an attack. As we have seen, even those defenses that do not obviously hurt the other person at least send the message, "You are attacking me." And that itself is an attack, is it not?

Taking from the world to fill our needs (6.3) is clearly an attack. This is why we try to pay, to give something back, rather than merely take (6.8). Yet, as we saw in the last chapter (7.5), even our paying (and even our noble self-sacrifice) is an attack, being designed to instill guilt, to send the message, "I suffered because of you. Therefore, you owe me."

Trying to be innocent through blaming others (6.4) is obviously an attack. Yet even being special (6.5), that most precious of jewels, is an attack. As we saw, specialness rests on being set apart and set above. This means that specialness depends on somehow being above others, being better, having more, and that is clearly an attack. If you were to say to someone, "I am so much more special than you are," how do you think that person would feel? Specialness therefore requires us to play a delicate game. We must somehow get across the message that we are, in fact, superior. Yet we must not be too obvious about it, or we will insult the very people from whom we want adulation.

Trying to get vengeance (7.6) is clearly an attack. Yet even our suffering (7.5) is an attack, being designed to send that same old message, "I suffered because of you." Finally, even our innocent rearranging of external objects, things, situations, and events is nearly always an attack, since it is usually based on grievances (7.4). It thus sends the message, "If you were different, I would be saved." This blaming message is simply another way of stating our fundamental perception that other people are sinful (7.2), the perception that weaves through all the behaviors and strategies we have seen.

To all of this we might counter that we only attack occasionally.

Most of the time, in relation to most people, we simply feel more or less neutral. What we call neutral, however, is also an attack. In the Course's system, there is nothing in between love and hate, there is no middle ground called "neutral." Hence, anything less than pure, boundless love is an attack. This boundless love is our natural state, and it takes an enormous amount of anger to turn off such love and produce this vacant indifference we call "neutral." The attacking nature of neutrality is captured in this line from George Bernard Shaw: "The worst sin towards our fellow creatures is not to hate them, but to be indifferent to them: that's the essence of inhumanity."

According to the Course, then, we live in a virtually constant state of attack. But why? What are we hoping to gain? Everything, says the ego. According to it, attack will bring us safety, security, completion, pleasure, absolution, peace, and happiness.

Yet let's examine the idea that attack brings us rewards. This assumes that by expressing an attack thought, we can take a thought in our mind and toss it outside. Once outside, like an animal uncaged, it can devour others while leaving us, its trainer, unscathed, and indeed dutifully bringing us back something to feast on. The Course refutes this idea with one of its most important concepts: "Ideas leave not their source."[9] Like a bullet ricocheting around inside our heads, attack does not actually leave our minds. It thus produces its damaging effects *inside* that same mind. "The purpose of attack is in the mind, and its effects are felt but where it is."[10] These effects amount to the emotion we call guilt: "Attack...must increase the guilt, for guilt is the result of attack."[11] Therefore, attack cannot leave our mind and snatch us some reward. It merely stays in our mind and festers, breeding the rot of guilt.

Yet, strangely, the ego knew this all along:

> We said before that the ego attempts to maintain and increase guilt, but in such a way that you do not recognize what it would do to you. For it is the ego's fundamental doctrine that what you do to others you have escaped. The ego wishes no one well. Yet its survival depends on your belief that you are exempt from its evil intentions. It counsels, therefore, that if you are host to it, it will enable you to direct its anger outward, thus protecting you. And thus it embarks on an endless, unrewarding chain of special rela-

tionships, forged out of anger and dedicated to but one insane belief; that the more anger you invest outside yourself, the safer you become.[12]

This paragraph says some startling things. The ego, it says, is angry at everyone and everything. This includes you, but if you knew this, you would get rid of it. To survive, therefore, the ego tells you that "you are exempt from its evil intentions." It says that you can unleash its evil intentions on the world and thereby keep that evil from being pent up inside where it will take its wrath out on you. However, getting you to attack others does not actually exempt you from the ego's evil intentions. Instead, it makes you their *target*. For attacking others simply increases your own guilt. And what is better than guilt at making you the focus of your own anger and bitterness?

The big prize the ego is going after, then, is guilt. The ego is actually *attracted* to guilt. Guilt is its idea of a good time. "Guilt is the only need the ego has, and as long as you identify with it [the ego], guilt will remain attractive to you."[13] The ego thirsts for guilt like we thirst for water, and for the same reason: Guilt keeps it "alive." Guilt confirms that the ego is real, that you are an ego. When you feel guilty can you really doubt that you are a separate entity split off from God?

Therefore, all of the ego's attacking is designed simply to collect more guilt. It promises that attack will win for us all of those flashy prizes (safety, pleasure, absolution, etc.), but does so simply to dupe us into going ahead with attack. In our thinking, the prizes are the real motive for attack, and guilt is just an unfortunate by-product we have to live with afterwards. The Course says it is the reverse: The so-called prizes are just a shiny lure to entice us to bite down on the barbed hook of guilt, so that the ego can reel us in.

The attraction of guilt is an exceedingly difficult concept to swallow. It is hard for us to imagine wanting guilt not because it makes us feel decent and somehow purified, but simply for its own sake. The Course acknowledges this, saying that we are incapable of consciously desiring guilt, and could not want it if we allowed our attraction to it into full awareness: "Yet the attraction of guilt has value to you only because you have not looked at what it is, and have judged it completely in the dark."[14]

I have made my own peace with this difficult concept in this way:

Guilt does appear to me to be the chief result of attack. This cause and effect relationship of attack and guilt is not only simple and logical, but is experienced thousands and thousands of times over the course of a lifetime. Strangely, after all those times, we still think that our attack will bring us peace, not guilt. Are we really that stupid? I wonder. I find it plausible to think there is something in our minds that knows full well that the next attack will bring exactly what the previous four hundred thousand attacks brought. Is it not possible that something in us does understand that attack yields guilt—and is counting on it?

8.4. The ego promises that getting will fulfill us and defending will protect us. This tricks us into accumulating lack and vulnerability.

The pattern we saw in the previous section we will see again and again in this chapter. The ego promises that if we do a certain thing, we will be saved. We then do that thing only to find that it does not save us, but instead saves our ego (from disappearing). Like some devious tapeworm, the ego tells us to feed ourselves, but when we do we find that we fed it and we're still hungry.

Back in Chapter 6 we discovered that one of our major means of trying to save ourselves is defending against the world's attack. This defense was based on the following three beliefs:

1. You are inherently weak and vulnerable.
2. What is happening outside you is dangerous, it threatens you with harm.
3. You must protect your vulnerable self from these dangerous happenings.

By expressing these beliefs through our behavior, we hope to gain safety. In other words, we hope that expressing our sense of vulnerability will cause this sense to leave our mind and be replaced by a sense of security. Yet what if ideas do not leave the mind via behavior? Remember the process we examined in Chapter 5 (key idea 5.1)? Mind takes its own ideas and expresses them outwardly, and this expression is then looked upon and becomes the mind's experience. If this process really happens, we are in big trouble. The *idea* in this case is that we are weak, vulnerable, and endangered. The *expression* of this idea is our defensiveness. This expression would cause us to simply *experience* more of our beginning idea—that we are weak, vulnerable, and endangered.

> Yet is defensiveness a double threat. For it attests to weakness, and sets up a system of defense that cannot work. Now are the weak still further undermined, for there is treachery without and still a greater treachery within. The mind is now confused, and knows not where to turn to find escape from its imaginings.
>
> It is as if a circle held it fast, wherein another circle bound it and another one in that, until escape no longer can be hoped for nor obtained. Attack, defense; defense, attack, become the circles of the hours and the days that bind the mind in heavy bands of steel with iron overlaid, returning but to start again. There seems to be no break nor ending in the ever-tightening grip of the imprisonment upon the mind.[15]

This passage says that defensiveness produces a double threat. It tells you that you are under attack from without. And with that very message it whispers cruelly in your ear, "You weak and frail creature." Now you find yourself attacked from without *and* from within. Danger is everywhere, so you must protect yourself, you must defend. But your defensiveness affirms all over again that you are under attack from without and within. So you defend some more, affirming more threat which asks for more defense. And on it goes, each defense adding another steel band of imprisonment around your mind.

This is not such an unrealistic picture of our lives. Does, for instance, the man with the highest and strongest walls really feel the most secure? Or is he sitting around worrying about how to improve his walls?

Now let us turn to our search to get things from outside ourselves. In Chapter 6 we examined our search to acquire objects, situations, events, and people, in the hopes that they would grant us specialness and so fill the hole in us. We saw that this search was based on the following three beliefs:

1. You are inherently lacking and needy.
2. There are certain happenings outside you that can fill your needs

and make you complete.

3. You must fill your needy self with these pleasurable happenings.

By seeking completion outside ourselves we are expressing our belief in lack. We hope, however, that if we do this with cleverness and confidence, we can fill ourselves and our belief in lack will be gone. Yet that is a violation of the law of mind. *Expression* of the thought of lack leads only to *experience* of that thought. Our search for completion thus simply reinforces its beginning premise: *Completion is without and lack is within.* In the words of the Course: "Seek not outside yourself. The search implies you are not whole within."[16]

Again, we need merely look around and see the truth of this. Are the people with the world's treasures, the ones sipping champagne on their yachts, the world's happiest people? Or, while they sip, are they not pondering how to acquire more treasures and worrying about losing the ones they have? Are they not consumed with thoughts of lack? And are we any different?

Does our external seeking ever deliver the happiness we hoped it would? As a friend of mine is fond of saying, "The pizza never delivers." How many times have we looked forward to some pleasurable event, only to be right in the middle of it and find ourselves looking forward to something else? Even after all those times, however, we don't question the quest itself. We assume that there remains something out there somewhere that will do it for us, if we could only find it. After countless disappointing experiences one would think the truth would dawn on us: The problem is not the specific places in which we have searched outside ourselves; it is the search *itself*.

Yet maybe we do get it; maybe we have known all along. Just perhaps, something inside us wants to deepen the cavern within us, and go on deepening it until all of the life that God gave us seems to have drained out. After all, total lack of life is just the logical extension of the concept of lack. "For...lack *is* death."[17]

> The lingering illusion [that something outside him will bring happiness] will impel him [one who comes into the world] to seek out a thousand idols, and to seek beyond them for a thousand more. And each will fail him, all excepting one; for he will die, and does not understand the idol that he seeks *is* but his death.[18]

The ego *wants* us to feel lacking, needy, vulnerable, and endangered, for these feelings reinforce the ego. When you feel these things, can you honestly doubt that you are a separate entity split off from God?

8.5. The ego promises us joy through bodily pleasure. This tricks us into making separation real.

Well, at least we have physical pleasure. What fun would life be without the pleasures of food or sex? To understand the Course's radical perspective on pleasure, we must first remember that the body was invented as physical proof of separation. The body does this job very well, for it seems to be a wall of flesh that surrounds the mind and imprisons it in its own private cell, a wall that "proves" that we are indeed a separate bit of mind.

Physical pleasure, being of the body, has the same purpose as the body itself: the purpose of proving our separateness. How does it do this? Pleasure, like all sensation, shows that the body is the boss, for the body can make the mind feel whatever it chooses. And when the body gives the mind a dose of pleasurable feelings, the mind, like a junkie, becomes enslaved to these mysterious delights. Once these good feelings dissipate, however, all we have is their impact on our picture of reality. That impact goes something like this: Pleasure shows that my body is real and is lord of my mind. If this lord can enforce pleasure on my mind, it also has power to enforce separateness upon my mind. Therefore, my body makes me separate and there is nothing I can do about it. Oddly enough, pain has this same effect and therefore has this same purpose:

> Pain demonstrates the body must be real....Its purpose is the same as pleasure, for they both are means to make the body real. What shares a common purpose is the same.[19]

Pain and pleasure share a common purpose, and therefore are different names for the same thing. What's more, says the Course, both result in pain. The reason is simple: For an infinite spirit to think it is trapped in a tiny body is profoundly painful.

> It is impossible to seek for pleasure through the body and not find pain....[This] is but the inevitable result of equating yourself with the body, which is the invitation to pain.[20]

165

Just as with attack, defense, and getting, the ego is fully aware of the real cause and effect relationship here. "To you it [the ego] teaches that the body's pleasure is happiness. Yet to itself it whispers, 'It is death.'"[21] Physical pleasure is simply another form of the ego's bait. It knows that once we take this bait, we will feel further imprisoned in these bodies, and it will feel further reinforced in its "reality." We might even surmise that this ego-reinforcement is the underlying pleasure within physical pleasure, the actual reason we find it pleasurable.

This teaching about pleasure is yet another of the Course's hard teachings. To help it hit home, imagine a situation in which you have every conceivable physical pleasure as frequently and as intensely as you like. Can you imagine, in the midst of this pleasure-fest, still feeling unfulfilled? Could you actually feel imprisoned by the meaninglessness of it, and cut off from some higher, truer source of meaning? If so, this is not very far from what the Course is saying.

It is important to not misunderstand the Course here. It is not saying that pleasure is sinful or bad. We are *not* being asked to refrain from all activities that produce pleasure. Perhaps the best approach is, in the midst of our pleasure, to simply observe it, and understand that what really drives it is the attempt to prove our separateness, and that this is the effect it ultimately has. Through such a process we may eventually learn, each of us in our own time, that as a separation device, physical pleasure just doesn't feel good.

8.6. The special relationship is the biggest false promise of all, the one that motivates us to pursue all of the ego's false promises.

In this chapter we have revealed many of this world's promises to be false. At this point we might find our minds clinging to one last hope, one last refuge: "true love." Yes, the world is filled with suffering, but isn't this all the more reason to find that one person, that one shining, rare jewel, who can cure my pain? It is a deep-seated belief that special love is our one consolation prize for being born on this ball of pain hurtling through space. In love's tender arms we can take refuge from all the insanity in this mad, mad world. Special love truly seems different from, even saner than, the rest of the madness. This belief is difficult to dispel. After sixteen chapters in the Text, two of which have described in detail the madness of the special relationship, the author of the Course has this to say:

> You have but little difficulty now in realizing that the thought system the special relationship protects is but a system of delusions. You recognize, at least in general terms, that the ego is insane. Yet the special relationship still seems to you somehow to be "different." Yet we have looked at it far closer than we have at many other aspects of the ego's thought system that you have been more willing to let go. While this one remains, you will not let the others go. For this one is not different. Retain this one, and you have retained the whole.[22]

"For this one is not different." These, I think, are among the most ominous words that a human mind can hear. They mean that special love is not the exception to the madness which can raise us above the madness. It is *part* of the madness, a part designed to pull us down *into* it. This same section in the Text, entitled "The Two Pictures," then goes on to explain why the special relationship seems different. This difference amounts to it being the single shiniest lure in the ego's tackle box.

First, the section says that the ego's system protects itself with various defenses. "Every defense operates by giving gifts, and the gift is always a miniature of the thought system the defense protects, set in a golden frame."[23] The frame is the key. Its "purpose is to be of value *in itself*, and to divert your attention from what it encloses."[24] To summarize, each defense gives you a gift. This gift is a miniature portrait of the ego's thought system—a dose of the ego's insanity and pain.[25] But this gift is surrounded by a frame designed to be so mesmerizing that you do not even notice the gruesome portrait you have just bought. You therefore hold onto the picture; you take it home and mount it on your wall. And the defense has done its job, for its job is to defend against *you* throwing away the picture, and the ego's thought system along with it.

What does all this have to do with special relationships? Special love is quite simply the ego's best defense, "its chief defense."[26]

> The special relationship has the most imposing and deceptive frame of all the defenses the ego uses. Its thought system is offered here, surrounded by a frame so heavy and so elaborate that the picture is almost obliterated by its

imposing structure. Into the frame are woven all sorts of fanciful and fragmented illusions of love, set with dreams of sacrifice and self-aggrandizement, and interlaced with gilded threads of self-destruction. The glitter of blood shines like rubies, and the tears are faceted like diamonds and gleam in the dim light in which the offering is made.[27]

This is one of the Course's starker images, yet one that conveys a great deal of content. As an ego defense, the special relationship offers us a tiny picture set within a huge, gaudy frame. What does the frame stand for in this metaphor? It stands for all that attracts us to the special relationship. A list is given in the third sentence: fantasies of love, dreams of self-sacrifice, illusions of self-aggrandizement (we all hope through the special relationship to make ourselves greater, more special). We could throw into this list all the physical things we hope the relationship will deliver: sex, dinners, wedding rings, houses, etc. All of this, however, is there to distract us from the real gift—the picture. The picture is a miniature reproduction of the ego's thought system, with all its hate, conflict, vengeance, loneliness, and despair.

The frame is the promise, what you think you are getting. But the picture is what you *really* get. It is the gift. The frame is dinner and flowers; the picture is the morning after. The frame is the joy of the wedding; the picture, the bitterness of the divorce. The frame's function is to attract your attention to itself and away from the picture, to make you so eager to obtain it that you do not even notice the hideous picture you are buying, nor its enormous cost. The frame is there to dupe you into accepting a picture that you otherwise never, ever would.

Special love offers you the exact same ghastly picture as every other expression of the ego; it is just better at *selling* you the same defective product. That is why it is the ego's chief defense—it is the best at defending the ego from being discarded. Its frame is the biggest, the flashiest, the most mind numbing and sense overloading, the most *seductive*, of them all. The passage continues:

Look at the *picture*. Do not let the frame distract you....Let not your gaze dwell on the hypnotic gleaming of the frame. Look at the picture, and realize that death is offered you.[28]

Let us carry out this instruction and take a good look at the picture. We set the stage for this picture in our discussion of shadow figures— our mental images of past figures who didn't give us the specialness we wanted. There (in key idea 7.6) we reviewed our painful past, filled with "imagined slights, remembered pain, past disappointments, perceived injustices and deprivations."[29] To get back at this past we plan to re-enact it, only with a more flattering ending. So we search for the perfect person with whom to stage our re-enactment. Once we find her, we fall in love—in essence, with our own fantasies of how she will supply what the past withheld. We become entranced with the "hypnotic gleaming of the frame." To hire her for the part we make massive payments. We compliment her, wine and dine her, do all we can to make her feel special. We give her our self, praying it will be enough. And when we make this giving official and slip that ring on her finger, we believe we receive in return the title to her soul. We think we own her.

Yet even at this happy moment there is anger churning just beneath the surface. For we have secretly resented all the sacrifices we have made, and thus they all have contained the hidden message, "I suffered because of you. You owe me big time!" Also, because she is playing the role of our shadow figures, we have unconsciously assigned her the role of atoning for their sins. Should she fail in this, all of our anger at them is just waiting to come out at her.

After the honeymoon, these hidden forces begin to show their face. Now we hope to reap what we have paid for. We want the new ending. We want to possess the frame, completely. So we start calling in the debt. Inevitably, our partner does not live up to our demands. She starts blowing the lines we scripted for her. So we switch our tactics from the covert blaming of self-sacrifice to more overt blaming. We remind her of how much we gave, how little she has paid back, and how much we have suffered as a result. We send this same message in many ways, by moping around the house, by going numb emotionally, even by getting sick.

At this point, whether we have a stormy breakup or reach an icy truce, the result is essentially the same. We do not get our new ending. Our hoped-for re-enactment falls into straight *repetition*. The partner that held such promise has become another bitter disappointment. The one that was supposed to be our sweet revenge on all who didn't love us has become another one to get revenge on. Our love, our darling, our sweetheart has become another shadow figure.[30]

Now we can no longer even see the alluring frame; it is only a memory. We are left with the real gift, left staring directly into a portrait of the grinning face of death. And this was the ego's plan all along. We may say our special relationship didn't work, but, in fact, it *did*.

> Yet the ego, though encouraging the search for love very actively, makes one proviso; do not find it. Its dictates, then, can be summed up simply as: "Seek and do *not* find." This is the one promise the ego holds out to you, and the one promise it will keep.[31]

8.7. Through our normal daily activities the ego is carrying out its ancient attack on God.

Beneath all the activities we have examined, below the surface of the whole of human life, an ancient war is being waged. "Surely you realize the ego is at war with God."[32] The war the ego launched on God, which set off the Big Bang and gave birth to the illusion of time and space, has never stopped. It is being waged this very moment.

We have seen (in key idea 2.7) that the ego lives in constant fear of God's Love. It is terrified that the attraction of His Love will, like a whirlpool, pull our minds into the infinite ocean of His Mind, where the ego will go spiraling into nothingness. The ego must therefore win our allegiance at all costs. Its goal is to keep itself enthroned in our mind forever and so *last* forever. "Eternalness is the one function the ego has tried to develop."[33]

The ego sees itself in a war with God, the basic dynamics of which are very similar to the title fight we mentioned in Chapter 7, in which a store of invisible power and status goes to the winner. The ego wins this fight by gaining our complete and permanent allegiance and defeating God's attempt to pull our minds back to Him. The ego thereby proves that it is more real than God, and that God's egoless reality is false. Having vanquished God, the ego takes possession of His "title belt." God's life, power, and status leave Him and wrap around the ego. God is dead and the ego is God, with no contenders in sight and with nothing to fear. That is the ego's ultimate objective.

The ego pursues this final victory not in some cosmic battle among the stars, but simply by trying to win our minds over to its side. And that is what we have been seeing in all the activities we have examined in this chapter. The ego is conducting its ancient war against God through our normal daily pursuits, through our flipping of TV channels and trips to the mall, through our heroic search for love and the pursuit of all our hopes and dreams. The ego's war against God is the subterranean engine that powers our world.

This applies to all the strategies and activities that make up conventional human existence. In one of its most difficult and most important sections, "The Choice for Completion," the Course gives a specific description of this dynamic in the case of special love.

In the last chapter (key idea 7.5) we said that in both our self-sacrifice and our suffering, we are really attacking ourselves to make another guilty. We do this to obligate this person to compensate us with specialness. In "The Choice for Completion," the author of the Course refers to this idea and then promises to reveal a deeper dimension of it:

> I have spoken of this before, but there are some aspects of what is really being attempted that have not been touched upon.
> Very simply, the attempt to make guilty is always directed against God.[34]

Recall that the separation began when we asked God for special love (key idea 2.1). God could not comply, "for the request was alien to Him."[35] By not complying, He became the supreme figure from our past who did not give us the specialness we craved. He became the ultimate shadow figure. Had He granted this one wish, we believe, His special love would have made us truly complete. It would have made our ego fully real and totally secure. But He refused, and so He is the "real" reason we are not special enough and our lives aren't working. In the ancient, watery abyss of our unconscious, it is God we blame for all our pain, all our broken dreams, through all the ages.

According to "The Choice for Completion," when we do our dance of special love, we unconsciously believe we are acting out a ritual transaction with God, which will force Him to give us what He refused. In this ritual, our partner symbolically stands for God. This means that, in our eyes, what we make her feel, God feels; what she gives to us, God has given. The dance begins as we attack ourselves to make the other guilty. We do this through our generous self-sacrifice as well as through other means, such as depression and illness. As we saw, all of this is designed to send the message, "I suffered because of you. You are responsible for my loss. You owe me." The Course frames this attack on ourselves in stark terms, as a ritual killing of our self:

> Through the death of your self you think you can attack another self [with guilt], and snatch it [the self] from the other [because she is obligated now to sacrifice in return] to replace the self that you despise.[36]

This sacrifice of our self sends a powerful message of guilt to our partner, and ultimately, we believe, to God. We are in essence saying to God, "Look at what a worthless (nonspecial) self You gave me. It is so worthless I have to throw it away to get a better one." By discarding our despised self, then, we are like a spoiled child smashing a disappointing Christmas toy to make Daddy feel guilty for not giving a better one. On the surface, our attempt to make guilty is directed at our partner, but ultimately (in the words of a passage quoted above), "the attempt to make guilty is always directed against God."

Once we send this message of guilt, our partner responds by (hopefully) surrendering to us her rare and precious self. And as she does, we see God performing the same motion. We see Him giving us His specialness through this human vehicle, giving us the elixir of life He denied us in the beginning.

As the ritual comes to an end, we now believe we have actually defeated God. We have extracted from Him His special love, His power, and even His very life. We have endowed our ego with fire stolen from Heaven. Now God is dead and the ego is God. If this language sounds extreme, here is how the Course puts it: "The special relationship must be recognized for what it is; a senseless ritual in which strength is extracted from the death of God, and invested in His killer."[37] The Course actually likens it to a primitive ritual, in which human sacrifice takes place on a stone altar and the participants wear the mask of God.[38]

Yes, I know, this sounds extremely bizarre. This, however, is merely a very extreme case of what psychologists call magical thinking, in which we think that by performing a particular action we will achieve a result that is impossible by the normal laws of cause and effect—like thinking that by stepping on a crack you will break your mother's back. The ritual described by the Course is really not so different from the magical thinking that lies behind any ritual, either religious rituals or the rituals we perform in our daily lives. It is an age-old idea that by performing certain actions in church we invoke God. Is that really so different than the idea that by performing certain actions with our partner we kill God?

Moreover, the human mating ritual does have the exact psychological effects predicted by the Course's account. We generally go through life feeling vaguely empty and unfulfilled, because the life God gave us and self God made us just aren't special enough. Then one day, we discover that special someone and "fall in love." Our elation is beyond words. Now we know that we are truly special, because she is giving her self to us. "This," we think, "is all I ever needed." We don't need to go on some inner search for a nonphysical reality. The realm of bodies is doing just fine for us. We don't need to go on some mystical quest for a transcendental God. Our partner is granting us all the goodies that God failed to provide. Why do we need Him when we have *her*?

Onto these routine, predictable effects of special love, the Course would merely add the question: What if these effects were your goal from the outset? The Course says, "Every special relationship you have made has, as its fundamental purpose, the aim of occupying your mind so completely that you will not hear the call of truth."[39] Special love was designed to drown out God's Call. Is this so far from the idea of trying to kill Him?[40]

8.8. All that the ego does is really designed to attack us, kill us, and send us to hell.

Throughout this chapter we have seen the ego displaying single-minded devotion to its one goal of staying intact. We have also seen it doing so at the direct expense of your happiness and peace. We have seen the ego preserving itself by continually inducing feelings of guilt, weakness, vulnerability, lack, and neediness. All of these have a single purpose: to evoke fear. Guilt produces fear of punishment. Weakness and vulnerability produce fear of being injured. Lack and neediness produce fear of not having our needs met. Everything the ego does is an attempt to put us and keep us in a state of fear.

> Here is the one emotion that you made, whatever it may
> seem to be. This is the emotion of secrecy, of private

thoughts and of the body. This is the one emotion that opposes love, and always leads to sight of differences and loss of sameness.[41]

Why is the ego so attracted to fear? Look at the characteristics that are ascribed to fear in the above passage: secrecy, private thoughts, the body, differences, loss of sameness. What do they all have in common? Separateness. The ego is the thought of separateness, and fear is the *emotion* of separateness. Fear is the emotion of the ego. As the Course says, "The ego is quite literally a fearful thought."[42] If, as the ego does, you feel that you are all by yourself, completely on your own, what else would you feel?

If the ego wants only to make us afraid, we are forced to conclude that it is not our friend. The person who wants to keep you in a constant state of fear is not on your side. The Course has a very blunt way of describing the ego's sentiment toward us. It says the ego is intent on murdering us:

> The death penalty is the ego's ultimate goal....Wanting to kill you as the final expression of its feeling for you, it lets you live but to await death. It will torment you while you live, but its hatred is not satisfied until you die. For your destruction is the one end toward which it works, and the only end with which it will be satisfied.[43]

A few chapters later, the Course qualifies this, saying that the goal of our death actually "leaves it unsatisfied,"[44] for death would mean the cessation of our suffering. Its real and final ambition for us, then, is an eternity in hell:

> The ego teaches thus: Death is the end as far as hope of Heaven goes. Yet because you and the ego cannot be separated, and because it cannot conceive of its own death, it will pursue you still [in hell], because guilt is eternal.[45]

In short, the ego wants to lay us in the ground but then pursue us beyond the grave, where, in a perpetual living-death, it will punish us forever in hell, playing the role of Satan to our condemned and tortured soul. Punishing us eternally for our sins is the ego's idea of heaven. These urges of the ego are so deeply woven into the fabric of our world that they are what actually cause physical death. They are also what has generated humanity's ancient and universal fears of a dismal afterlife.

How could this be? By the ego's own account, we gave birth to it, have made possible its continuance, have done nearly everything it said for untold eons. And this is how it repays us? Exactly, says the Course, "For what the ego loves, it kills for its obedience."[46] The ego's reasoning for wanting to kill us might be rendered in this way:

- The ego's entire survival depends on our belief that we are it, that we are an ego.
- We are not an ego, nor anything remotely like an ego. We are a holy Son of God. The ego is just a wrong belief about who we are.
- The ego fears that one day we will snap out of it and realize this, tossing it out of our mind and ending its so-called existence.

Imagine that a stranger, a madman, wanders into your home one day, and begins claiming that he is you. He starts sleeping in your bed, eating your food, answering your phone calls. He actually assumes your identity and starts living your life. For a time you become dazed and confused and actually go along with it. You even assume the role of his humble and obedient servant, doing whatever he says. Yet would he still not fear the day that you shake off this confusion? Would you not be the single greatest threat to his new life? And might he not, therefore, want to quietly do away with you, dispose of your body, and thus take over your life completely?

This is the fundamental irony in the Course's teaching about the ego. We have, it says, willingly invited a stranger into our home and "asked this stranger in to take [our] place."[47] Now, we work all day to feed this stranger while we go hungry. When we defend our "self," we actually protect the stranger, at cost of our own safety. When we go to satisfy our "self," we are instead pleasing the stranger. All that we do out of our innate instinct for self-benefit and self-preservation benefits and preserves the stranger, giving him strength for his campaign to punish and annihilate us.

This may sound dark and weird, but if it is true, it sure explains a lot. This, in fact, is the Course's explanation for the entire human condition. Something fundamental about our situation simply does not work. There are two completely different ways to explain this. The first way is to say that we have been handed a raw deal; we have been dropped by some giant hand into a rat maze for which there is no solution. Perhaps God did it. Maybe one fine morning in Heaven He decided to create a world full of suffering, a world in which everything dies. Or perhaps physical evolution is the culprit. Maybe it mindlessly manufactured us to serve its blind progress, not caring how many die or how well they lived, only caring if they passed on their genes before they breathed their last.

The second way is the Course's. In this way, no one is doing it to us; we are doing it all to ourselves. We designed this entire crazy system to look like it was doing it to us. This way, the system could incite us to do the very things by which we *keep* doing it to ourselves. For beneath it all we have a buried, demonic belief in our minds, bent only on preserving itself at our expense.

Which of these two explanations do we prefer? Which really serves us? If our sad condition is caused by God or by a soulless universe, we may feel a quick sense of relief, since now we are off the hook. This relief, however, would dissipate when we realized there is nothing we can do to change things. We're just monkeys in a medical experiment. We can only consign ourselves to our tragic fate. If, on the other hand, *we* have caused our own pain, then we also have the power to stop it, all of it. Total salvation is available and is lying in our own hands, right now.

In light of that, the news in this chapter is conceivably good news, *very* good news. Yes, we have uncovered some very dark motivations buried in our minds, but if we want the power to change things, then we must admit to having had the power to *cause* them. And if we did cause all the madness and suffering inherent in this world, then there must be a place in our minds whose darkness matches the darkness of the world. This can be the best of news for, if true, we can then find this place and have it healed as quickly as possible. This is the process the Course promises to guide us through.

> There is an instant in which terror seems to grip your mind so wholly that escape appears quite hopeless. When you realize, once and for all, that it is you you fear, the mind perceives itself as split. And this had been concealed while you believed attack could be directed outward, and

returned from outside to within. It seemed to be an enemy outside you had to fear. And thus a god outside yourself became your mortal enemy; the source of fear.

Now, for an instant, is a murderer perceived within you, eager for your death, intent on plotting punishment for you until the time when it can kill at last. Yet in this instant is the time as well in which salvation comes. For fear of God has disappeared. And you can call on Him to save you from illusions by His Love, calling Him Father and yourself His Son. Pray that the instant may be soon,—today.[48]

The Course is talking about a literal experience here, a terrifying encounter in which you at last come face to face with your own ego. Before this moment you simply assumed that your suffering was caused from without, by a distant god who was pulling the strings of this unfair world. Now, to your horror, you realize that all along it was you, doing it to yourself, trying to murder yourself. You finally realize "that it is you you fear."

Yet why is this literally petrifying moment "the time as well in which salvation comes"? Why in God's name should you actually pray "that the instant may be soon,—today"? Because in this instant you finally understand that God was never at fault. He never caused your misery, not one ounce of it; you did it all yourself. Now you can honestly see Him as a loving Father. And now you can sincerely call on Him, without reservation or suspicion, knowing He is totally on your side. Now you can call on Him to pull you out of this strange bind in which your hands are locked in a death grip around your own throat.

In the final eight chapters of this book we will explore just how our loving Father answers our call, helps us remove our hands from our throat, and draws us lovingly back to Him.

Nine

We have lost touch with reality and so need the Holy Spirit's help to be restored to sanity.

Nine

The ego's system is so ingeniously self-validating that on our own we would never get out. We would only eternally repeat the tiny, mad idea, forever ensnared in the endless circles of its cruel logic. Only the Father we left so long ago, the One we have blamed for all our suffering, only He could save us. The Course puts it simply, "While you made plans for death, He led you gently to eternal life."[1]

9.1. God created the Holy Spirit to bridge the gap in communication between Him and His children.

We already saw in key idea 3.6 that as soon as the separation seemed to occur God created the Holy Spirit, placing this Call to awaken in every sleeping mind. The Holy Spirit occupies a central place in *A Course in Miracles*. He is given many exalted titles, such as the Voice for God, the Answer to the separation, our "internal Teacher,"[2] "the communication link between God and His separated Sons,"[3] "the Great Transformer of perception,"[4] "the Universal Inspiration,"[5] "the great correction principle,"[6] among dozens of others.

Every student of the Course is familiar with the Holy Spirit, yet there remains a great deal of confusion around this topic. This is not surprising since paradox is inherent to the Holy Spirit. Indeed, the Holy Spirit *is* a paradox, for His entire function involves straddling two realms that are mutually exclusive. I will therefore devote much of this chapter to attempting to present a clear conceptual picture of the Holy Spirit.

Before the separation, there was perfect and total communication between God and His Sons. "Unbroken and uninterrupted love flows constantly between the Father and the Son, as Both would have it be.

And so it is."[7] What God communicated to us was not information; it was what He *is*. His act of communication was thus an act of revealing Himself, giving Himself to us, completely. The separation was merely a rupture in this communication, rather than an actual spatial rift. "The separation was not a loss of perfection, but a failure in communication."[8] Parts of the Sonship broke off their communication with God. These parts (the Sons of God, the children of God—ourselves) were still one with God, but by cutting off communication produced the illusion of being separate. They were like someone who is in a bustling crowd, surrounded by people, yet who has managed to tune everyone out so fully that he feels completely alone.

When God became aware that we had fallen into the sleep of isolation, He issued a single Call, which could be translated as "Awaken, My Son." In this act of God calling to us, He created the Holy Spirit, for this Call *is* the Holy Spirit. The Holy Spirit's job is to keep some degree of communication going between God and us by communicating in a form we can understand. No longer can we understand the unmediated revelation of God's Being. No longer can we understand the formless infinity of Heaven. What we *can* understand, however, is God's Call to come home. The Holy Spirit's role is to translate this Call into trillions of specific forms in order to reach us within our kaleidoscopically fractured dream. In this way, He can speak to us in our own language. And everything He says to us is simply God's single Call adapted into different forms to fit the varying needs of specific individuals in particular situations.

In *The Song of Prayer*, the author of the Course sketches this same relationship between the Call and the forms it takes. He says that God's Answer is a single sound, a pure song of love. This primordial sound, however, contains within it a vast multitude of smaller echoes, harmonics, and overtones. These are the "little answers" given us by the Holy Spirit:

> This [specific answer] is merely an echo of the reply of His Voice. The real sound is always a song of thanksgiving and of love....
> ....Along with it come the overtones, the harmonics, the echoes, but these are secondary....
> ....God answers only for eternity. But still all little answers are contained in this.[9]

By reaching us in a form we can understand, the Holy Spirit keeps communication open between God and His separated Sons. This is the Holy Spirit's whole function—to be a communication link. The separation was a *failure* in communication, the Holy Spirit is a link through which *partial* communication can still occur, and this will eventually restore *total* communication. This is why He is called "your remaining communication with God."[10] He, in other words, is all the communication with God that we have left after the communication breakdown known as the separation. It is important to note that the Holy Spirit is a *two-way* communication link:

> God would respond to every need, whatever form it takes. And so He keeps this channel [the Holy Spirit] open to receive His communication to you, and yours to Him.[11]

This passage specifically says that the communication link works both ways, from God to us *and* from us to God. This amounts to a crucial fact, one that Course students often question: God *does* hear us. One of the Workbook prayers gives us these words to say to God: "And let me not forget my hourly thanksgiving that You have remained with me, and always will be there to hear my call to You and answer me."[12] This prayer confidently states that God hears our every call. Without the Holy Spirit we could not truthfully say this prayer. For just as He translates God's formless Call into forms we can understand, so He translates our many calls into a unified call that *God* can understand. To do this, the Holy Spirit views the entire gamut of human experience as a single call for help:

> Yet to the One Who sends forth miracles to bless the world, a tiny stab of pain, a little worldly pleasure, and the throes of death itself are but a single sound; a call for healing, and a plaintive cry for help within a world of misery.[13]

We can imagine, then, that He takes all of our anxious thoughts, desperate feelings, tense moods, and even our intentional prayers—our entire experience throughout time and space—and wraps it all into one grand prayer, "a plaintive cry for help," a single call to our Father: "Father, I want to awaken to You." Or, more graphically perhaps, "Get me out of here!" This the Father *does* understand, and this He lovingly answers with His single Call, "Awaken, My Son." Thus the dialogue goes on, as unity is translated into multiplicity and multiplicity into unity, so that Father and Son can still sing to each other across the gulf of separation.

What exactly is the Holy Spirit's relationship with God? Is He a Being somehow distinct from God or is He just God under a different name? To do justice to the Course's language about the Holy Spirit, I think we have to conclude that He is *both*. He is constantly spoken of as a Being Who acts on God's behalf, as God's representative or messenger. Yet He is also spoken of as the act of God speaking, as a shape that God's Will takes in order to act within the dream.

We can see this paradox in the term "the Voice for God," a term which, on the face of it, implies that the Holy Spirit is a Voice that speaks *for* God, on God's behalf. Yet that is only half of the story. The term is also frequently turned around to appear as "God's Voice." This suggests that when the Holy Spirit speaks, God is speaking to us through Him, which is what we see in these examples:

> Now hear God speak to you, through Him Who is His Voice.[14]

> Listen, and hear your Father speak to you through His appointed Voice.[15]

> Hear, holy Son of God, your Father speak. His Voice would give to you His holy Word.[16]

Let's look at these passages. Notice that in all of them, God is the One speaking and the Holy Spirit is "His Voice." This calls to mind the familiar situation in which a *speaker* is using his *voice* to speak his *word*. According to this model, when you hear the Holy Spirit speak to you, you are actually hearing *God* speak to you. If the message you heard said "I love you," the "I" here would be God, not the Holy Spirit.[17]

Yet a closer look at these passages reveals that it's not quite that simple. Notice that in all three, the Voice is granted a certain life of Its Own. God is speaking to you *through* His Voice (as in the first two passages), or it is His Voice (rather than God Himself) that is *giving* you His Word (as in the third passage). Now, if I were talking to you, I would never say, "I'm speaking to you through my voice," or "My voice gives you my word." That would imply that my voice is more than a lifeless instrument, that it is actually a conscious participant in the communication process. And that, of course, is exactly what these passages are implying about the Holy Spirit.

This leaves us with a paradox. The Holy Spirit is both the Voice for God and He is God's Voice. This paradox may tie our mind up in knots, yet it really just reflects the Course's overall philosophy about existence in Heaven. The Course paints a picture of Heaven in which there are beings that have their own identity and their own will, yet are also at one with the whole and will in perfect unison with a larger will. That is how we need to see the Holy Spirit, as in some sense having His Own Identity and Will, yet at the same time being merely an extension of God's Being and a flawless conduit for God's Will.

9.2. The Holy Spirit's function is to heal our minds by leading us into a thought system that reflects reality. This is how He guides us home.

The Holy Spirit is a way in which our Father can reach us in a form we can understand. Thus, He is the One Who comes to us in that "far country" where we have squandered our inheritance, and where we sit demoralized, destitute, and too ashamed to return home. He is the One Who takes us by the hand, lifts us out of the mud, and leads us, step by step, back to our Father's house.

> He seems to be a Voice, for in that form He speaks God's Word to you. He seems to be a Guide through a far country, for you need that form of help.[18]

This journey, however, is not a physical one, for, remember, "There is no world!"[19] The journey back to the Father is a journey through the landscape of our own mind.

In the traditional view, the Holy Spirit answers our prayers primarily by changing things in our lives, by healing our bodies, saving us from accidents, and giving us lucky breaks in the job market. In the Course He definitely does act in the world:[20] He guides people to us[21] and plans "all events, past, present and to come."[22] And if we allow Him, He will give us our function (which we will explore in Chapter 13) and all we need for that function, including our possessions,[23] our money,[24] and the appropriate situations.[25] Yet in the Course these are not ends in themselves. He does them solely in service of His single goal of *changing our minds*. He orchestrates appearances only because of the effect that has on minds which still believe in appearances.

Thus, all of His guiding and leading is really *teaching*. He is teaching our minds how to think differently, how to see things differently. This re-education of the mind is the substance of the entire spiritual journey. His job is to teach us to recognize what has always been true, to remember (as we saw in key ideas 3.4 and 3.5) that we are perfect spirits, "at home in God, dreaming of exile."[26]

The Course, however, emphasizes that the Holy Spirit cannot wrench us from the dark depths of our dream straight into the full daylight of awakening. The shock would be too great:

> Nothing more fearful than an idle dream has terrified God's Son, and made him think that he has lost his innocence, denied his Father, and made war upon himself. So fearful is the dream, so seeming real, he could not waken to reality without the sweat of terror and a scream of mortal fear, unless a gentler dream preceded his awaking, and allowed his calmer mind to welcome, not to fear, the Voice That calls with love to waken him; a gentler dream, in which his suffering was healed and where his brother was his friend.[27]

This fearful world is no more than "an idle dream." Yet we cling to it, because we believe that to leave it, we "must first go through a greater terror still,"[28]—a deeper dream in which we come face to face with our angry Father and the rotting corpse of our own soul. This, we think, is the nightmarish reality that awaits us on the other side of our dream, yet this, too, is just another mirage. To coax us out of our dream, the Holy Spirit must again assume His role as translator. This time He must translate the waking state into a "happy dream," a reflection of wakefulness that we, on this level, can understand and find attractive (it is thus a happy state of mind, not a pleasurable state of external affairs). Like a cool oasis, this happy dream beckons us out of the ego's barren desert. It allows us to make a gentle transition out of our nightmare and ultimately into a state that is beyond our current comprehension.

This triad of dream, happy dream, and waking is echoed in several similar triads, familiar to most Course students:

Wrong-mindedness is the ego's thought system. *Right-mindedness* is the Holy Spirit's thought system. *One-mindedness* is God's thought system, the nondual knowledge of Heaven. Right-mindedness is an alternative to wrong-mindedness that exists on its same level. Yet it reflects One-mindedness and therefore paves the way to it.

False perception is how our wrong mind sees the world. *True perception* is the Holy Spirit's alternative, how our right mind views the world. It is still within the realm of perception, where subject and object are separate, yet it reflects the *knowledge* of Heaven in which subject and object are one.

The *world* is what we see through false perception. The *real world* is what true perception reveals to us. It is still an illusion, merely a happy dream. Yet this dream mirrors *Heaven* and so leads us to Heaven's gate. The real world and true perception will be discussed at greater length in Chapter 15.

In all of these triads we are faced with a choice, a choice between two thought systems, two ways of seeing, two worlds—the ego's and the Holy Spirit's. They are the only two voices in our minds. In every moment each one is whispering to us, quietly urging us to choose its thoughts. One set of thoughts will simply reinforce the nightmarish world we see now. The other will lift us into a world of light whose radiance is a reflection of the eternal light of Heaven.

The Holy Spirit's entire task, then, is to shepherd us into a sublime way of thinking and perceiving, a way that is so lofty, so holy, and so pristinely pure, "it is but a step from there to Heaven."[29]

> God...blessed His children with a way of thinking that could raise their perceptions so high they could reach almost back to Him. The Holy Spirit is the Mind of the Atonement. He represents a state of mind close enough to One-mindedness that transfer to it is at last possible.[30]

9.3. The Holy Spirit bridges the distance between reality and illusion. By seeing our illusions in light of reality, He places them in true perspective.

The Holy Spirit's function rests on His ability to span the distance between Heaven and earth, to bridge the gap between reality and illusion. He must stand on both sides at once.

In order to fulfill this special function the Holy Spirit has assumed a dual function. He knows because He is part of God; He perceives because He was sent to save humanity.[31]

"He knows" means that He is on God's side of the gulf, sharing God's knowledge, fully conscious in Heaven. "He perceives" means that he is on our side as well, aware of our dreams in all their Technicolor detail. He sees everything in our minds, including our darkest hidden secrets, and everything in the world, down to the last atom. Another way of stating this dual function is that He is both in God's Mind and in ours. "The communication link that God Himself placed within you, joining your mind with His, cannot be broken."[32]

Being on both sides at once gives the Holy Spirit one crucial advantage: He sees our illusions in the light of reality, from the vantage point of reality. He thus sees their total vacuousness and unreality. By itself a falsehood can look true. The only way to uncover it is to expose it to the light of truth.

You cannot evaluate an insane belief system from within it. Its range precludes this. You can only go beyond it, look back from a point where sanity exists and *see the contrast*. Only by this contrast can insanity be judged as insane.[33]

If you think there is a monster beneath your bed, the only way to dispel this illusion is to get the flashlight out and look. If you think you are the President of the United States, and suddenly the real President shows up with his aides and security men and shakes your hand, what then? When reality and our insanity "are brought together, the truth of one must make the falsity of its opposite perfectly clear."[34] "As darkness disappears in light, so ignorance fades away when knowledge dawns."[35]

This is precisely why we need the Holy Spirit. We have lost the light that would reveal the nothingness of our illusions. How, then, can we discover that the monster is not really there? The ego's system which we examined in previous chapters is very much like a system of mind control exercised by a religious cult or a totalitarian regime. Any false system will protect itself by controlling the information that reaches its members, feeding them a strict diet of only those news items, images, songs, and slogans that validate the system. After all, unbiased contact with the real world would reveal the whole thing to be a pack of lies.

The ego is a master at this strategy, for the ego *invented* it. The entire physical world is like a gigantic cult compound. In this compound our eyes encounter only evidence for the cult of the ego—only bodies in motion. Everyone we talk to is another believer who prattles on endlessly about the cult, making it seem to be the only way to go. Every event is secretly staged in order to provoke the very behaviors the cult wants from its members. And if, by chance, we happen to venture outside the compound one day, into the brilliant sunlight of true reality, and return with reports of what we saw, our fellow cult members will probably label us crazy. If we persist and threaten to infect other members with our "insanity," we might even get kicked out of the cult, which of course is exactly what happened to Jesus.

Can you see why the Holy Spirit is so crucial? We are in a closed system here. All our attempts at escape, being based on our cult programming, merely draw us further in. We cannot get out on our own. Quite simply, we need a deprogrammer to sneak into the compound. We need a radio free station from Heaven to broadcast into this ego-occupied world. And this is precisely God's plan. "Into this hopeless and closed learning situation, which teaches nothing but despair and death, God sends"[36] His broadcast. Only the Holy Spirit can see this world from the perspective of true reality. Only He can see straight through all the masks and magician's tricks. Thus He looks upon the entire panorama of human history, the vast battlefield of bodies, struggling, bleeding, fighting and dying, and sees it all as transparent mist. Behind it all He sees the eternal light shining there unchanged.

> Unshaken does the Holy Spirit look on what you see; on sin and pain and death, on grief and separation and on loss. Yet does He know one thing must still be true; God is still Love, and this is not His Will.[37]

This is the sublime vision He teaches us to see.

9.4. All that we made for ego He takes and uses for our awakening.

The Holy Spirit is the perfect teacher. He uses only what your mind already understands to teach you that you do not understand it. The Holy Spirit can deal with a reluctant learner without going counter to his mind, because part of it is still for God.[38]

According to this passage, there is part of your mind that is continually leaving the back door ajar so that the Holy Spirit can sneak into the cult compound. Once inside, He uses anything and everything He can find as props to teach you how to get out. By using only "what your mind already understands" He is doing an amazing thing. He is using all the cult pictures, literature, furniture, and members—all the things that were put there to keep you trapped inside—as teaching devices to show you the escape route! In light of this, we can see why the above passage says, "The Holy Spirit is the perfect teacher."

This is a major teaching of *A Course in Miracles*. "The Holy Spirit teaches you to use what the ego has made, to teach the opposite of what the ego has 'learned.'"[39] We can see many examples of this in the Course:

- We made the body in order to stay separate, as a way to *not* communicate and *not* commune. "The Holy Spirit sees the body only as a means of communication, and because communicating is sharing it becomes communion."[40]
- We made memory "as a means to keep the past."[41] The Holy Spirit uses it as a means to remember the timeless present, to remember God Himself. "You are so long accustomed to believe that memory holds only what is past, that it is hard for you to realize it is a skill that can remember *now*."[42]
- The Holy Spirit transforms our special relationships into holy relationships (which we will explore in Chapter 14). Thus He turns "the ego's chief weapon for keeping you from Heaven,"[43] into quite literally "the source of your salvation."[44]
- Our specialness was made as a way to exalt ourselves and debase everyone else. He turns it into our special function in salvation, our special way of erasing our ego by *serving* everyone else.[45] We will examine this in Chapter 13.
- Human language was "made by separated minds to keep them in the illusion of separation."[46] Yet the Holy Spirit uses words for His holy purpose. This actually "gives to the words...the power of His Spirit, raising them from meaningless symbols to the Call of

Heaven itself."[47]

- Even our ability to separate He uses as a means to separate us from all our beliefs that teach us that we're separate![48]

This same principle applies to the world,[49] time,[50] perception,[51] learning,[52] defenses,[53] choice,[54] and faith and belief.[55] Indeed, it applies to literally everything we made: "All that you made can serve salvation easily and well. The Son of God can make no choice the Holy Spirit cannot employ on his behalf, and not against himself."[56] If you think about all the regrettable choices you have made in this life, the foregoing quote gives new meaning to the word "salvation." What follows tells us more clearly how the Holy Spirit accomplishes His remarkable feat.

> The Holy Spirit has a use for all the means for sin by which you sought to find it. But as He uses them they lead away from sin, because His purpose lies in the opposite direction. He sees the means you use, but not the purpose for which you made them.[57]

The Holy Spirit takes the abilities we developed and the forms we fashioned and sees them emptied of the purposes for which they were made. This leaves a neutral shell, empty of content. He then asks us to fill this shell with His new content, which means to *use* it for His new *purpose*. For instance, even though our body was made as a device with which to attack our brothers and keep them separate from us, the Holy Spirit sees it as simply a neutral instrument, a tool. Then He teaches us to use this tool only as a device for reaching out to our brothers with love and union.

This overall idea means, quite plainly, that nothing is too dirty for the Holy Spirit. We might believe that there are places too evil for Him to go, skills too destructive for Him to use, and structures too corrupt for Him to enter—all of which adds up to people too rotten for Him to save. Yet according to *A Course in Miracles*, none of this is true. As it said above, He does not even see "the purpose for which you made" these things. He doesn't care. Where we see a temple of Satan He sees only a potential storefront for God.

This has liberating implications. If nothing that sin made is too dirty for Him, if He simply dumps out its sinful content—without even looking at what spills out—then turns around and uses it for God, then it cannot *really* be sinful. Sin, rather than grave and weighty, must be meaningless in His eyes. The following beautiful passage puts it this way:

> Yet if the Holy Spirit can commute each sentence that you laid upon yourself into a blessing, then it cannot be a sin.[58]

When we were building our splendid structures and developing our impressive abilities, we were really laying a sentence on our heads, because we secretly believed we were sinning. If the Holy Spirit can commute every such sentence, not to a lesser sentence, but into a *blessing*, what does that say about the reality of our sin?

9.5. We accept Him as our Teacher by resigning as our own teacher.

Now we come down to brass tacks. We have described Who the Holy Spirit is, how He came to be and what His function is. How do we let Him carry out His function of bringing us home? How do we accept Him as our Teacher?

We can get a clue about how by looking at the role He will eventually play. According to the Course He holds a perfect plan for our lives that includes literally every detail. Ultimately, we will relinquish to Him what we do, where we go, what we say and to whom.[59] We will, in fact, give over to Him the entire structure of our lives, letting Him decide what belongs in our lives and what we get rid of.[60] We will let Him determine where we live and whom we marry. But more importantly, we will let Him choose the road by which we seek fulfillment, whether we pursue forgiveness as the road to happiness or use the more conventional means of money, status, and special relationships. We will even allow Him to reverse our fundamental picture of who people are and who *we* are. As this process nears its completion, He will think our thoughts for us, give us our feelings, and even control our bodies—He will behave through us.

Did any of this sound even remotely threatening? Perhaps even insulting? The Course says twice that we find such thoughts "personally insulting."[61] Now if, while we are fervently inviting the Holy Spirit in with our words, we are actually feeling threatened or insulted, what kind of an invitation is that? If you say to someone, "Will you marry me?" but your face looks anguished and terrified, is that a real proposal? The Holy Spirit only responds to a genuine invitation. What, then, is a genuine invitation?

We invite Him in, says the Course, by getting out of His way. We are deeply attached to being the one in the driver's seat. This sends Him the clear message, "Back off. I'm doing just fine by myself." The most sincere invitation we can offer Him, therefore, is to leave this seat vacant. That is all He needs. He does not need us to beg Him with wordy prayers or keep Him motivated with virtuous sacrifices or even believe in Him. He just needs us to stop wrestling Him for the wheel.

To this end the Course asks us repeatedly to practice the thought of how little we really know, because, in essence, keeping our hands on the wheel amounts to thinking we know. We'll now explore two such practices now. Here is the introduction to the first:

> Your part is very simple. You need only recognize that everything you learned you do not want. Ask to be taught, and do not use your experiences to confirm what you have learned. When your peace is threatened or disturbed in any way, say to yourself [the words quoted below]:[62]

This is an instruction in how to learn God's lesson, which, according to this section, results in total fearlessness and perfect peace in yourself and in everyone you meet or even think of.[63] You cannot be expected to teach yourself something so totally alien to your current understanding. Your part is to simply want to get rid of *everything* you taught yourself, and ask that this open space be filled with something from another Teacher. Just open the space, and while you sit in it, do not close it down by using your current experiences to prove that what you learned before really is the truth.

How do we carry out these rather sweeping and abstract instructions? The final sentence leads into a practical way to do just that. It says, "When your peace is threatened or disturbed in any way..." This implies that you should watch your mind for any kind of loss of peace, any sort of disturbance or upset. When you notice it, "say to yourself"—in other words, "silently do the following practice":

> *I do not know what anything, including this, means.*
> *And so I do not know how to respond to it.*
> *And I will not use my own past learning as the light to guide me now.*[64]

As thousands of Course students have discovered, this is a powerful practice. In fact, you may want to try using it right now in relation to some perceived disturbance. The reason it is so powerful is that the upset emotions you feel are the direct result of the *meaning* you have assigned the situation. If you truly suspend that meaning, then the emotions *will* be suspended with it. As a result, emotions that seem to hold you hopelessly in their iron grip can miraculously evaporate, as you find your mind drawing back into a tranquil, open space of peaceful unknowing. This blissful ignorance is precisely how we invite the Holy Spirit in to teach us God's bright lesson of perfect peace:

> By this refusal to attempt to teach yourself what you do not know, the Guide Whom God has given you will speak to you. He will take His rightful place in your awareness the instant you abandon it, and offer it to Him.[65]

The next practice we will look at comes from the section entitled "Self-Concept versus Self." This is the section which said that our self-concept is that of the victim wearing the mask of the face of innocence. For untold millennia we have been convinced of this dual self-concept, so convinced that we may never have seriously raised it to question. Even when we were not sure of who we were—in the sense of what we wanted from life, what our role in life was and what we believed in— beneath our troubling doubts was a comforting base of certainty. We "knew" that we were a separate human who was being mistreated by an unfair world. Only when this comforting, bedrock "certainty" leaves us and we have not a clue who we are can the truth enter our minds at last:

> There will come a time when [self-]images have all gone by, and you will see you know not what you are. It is to this unsealed and open mind that truth returns, unhindered and unbound. Where concepts of the self have been laid by is truth revealed exactly as it is. When every concept has been raised to doubt and question, and been recognized as made on no assumptions that would stand the light, then is the truth left free to enter in its sanctuary, clean and free of guilt.[66]

These are beautiful, if somewhat troubling, words. Yet how do we fulfill their challenging injunction? Again, a practice is given us. This one must have powerful effects indeed, for it is introduced as the one thing we are most afraid to hear:

> There is no statement that the world is more afraid to hear than this:

> *I do not know the thing I am,*
> *and therefore do not know what I am doing,*
> *where I am,*
> *or how to look upon the world*
> *or on myself.*[67]

Let's go through these not-knowings one by one. The first is the basis for all the rest. Because we do not know our true nature, we do not know anything else—what we are doing, where we are, or how to perceive the world or ourselves.

How can it be that I "do not know what I am doing"? I seem to know exactly what I'm doing. This line subtly likens me to the men who crucified Jesus. Remember that famous line, "Father, forgive them, for they know not what they do"?[68] That line provides the key. Those men thought they were doing society a favor by exterminating a rabble-rouser. They didn't realize they were trying to crucify the Son of God. The same principle applies to me. I don't know who I am, and so when I think that I am making myself happy by pursuing special love, I don't realize that I too am really trying to crucify the Son of God—the divinity within myself.

Only people lost in insanity do not know where they are. How, then, can *I* not know "where I am"? Key idea 2.8 said that my self-image causes me to surround myself with an environment that fits or confirms that image.[69] My current self-image—that I am a separate physical being—causes me to dream that I am surrounded by an environment full of separate physical bodies. Yet I am not a physical being; I am a holy Son of God. And I am not here in this world but asleep in Heaven (key idea 3.5). Like a hallucinating person, I don't even know where I am.

That I don't know "how to look upon the world" is likewise a disturbing thought. How I look upon the world provides me with my whole framework for reality. Yet the Course teaches that I see the world entirely through the lens of my self-concept. If, for example, I feel like a failure, the whole world looks glum. What, then, if my self-concept is completely off base? If that is true, then I have no idea how to really look at the world. My emotional reactions to all the happenings in my life are completely off-base. I have no idea what is real.

Finally, if my self-concept is off base, then obviously I have not a clue about how to "look on myself." My whole sense of stability comes from having a solid sense of self, from knowing deep down in my heart who I am. Yet this "knowing" is one hundred and eighty degrees off the mark. My "solid" foundation is like quicksand.

Now perhaps we can see why the Course said, "There is no statement that the world is more afraid to hear than this." With this greater appreciation we might even want to repeat the statement to ourselves. For, even though it can be frightening, such practice opens the way for salvation. It clears an open space in our minds that allows What we are to teach us, through the Holy Spirit, what It is:

> Yet in this learning is salvation born. And What you are will tell you of Itself.[70]

Yet what if the Course is wrong, and we really do know all of these things? Maybe we really know who and where we are, what things mean and how to respond. What cause do we have to abandon our hard-won wisdom for some pie-in-the-sky quest? The Course's answer is very simple: Look at your track record. Has what you "know" paid off in genuine happiness and peace of mind?

To help us reflect on this question, I would like to quote the Course at length here. The following paragraphs are designed to speak very personally to the reader and prompt deep reflection about his or her life. I suggest that you read them in this spirit, that you give yourself some time and read each line slowly, carrying out the reflection it asks or implies before going on to the next line.

> Is it not evident that what the body's eyes perceive fills you with fear? Perhaps you think you find a hope of satisfaction there. Perhaps you fancy to attain some peace and satisfaction in the world as you perceive it. Yet it must be evident the outcome does not change. Despite your hopes and fancies, always does despair result. And there is no exception, nor will there ever be. The only value that the past can hold is that you learn it gave you no rewards which

you would want to keep. For only thus will you be willing to relinquish it, and have it gone forever.

Is it not strange that you should cherish still some hope of satisfaction from the world you see? In no respect, at any time or place, has anything but fear and guilt been your reward. How long is needed for you to realize the chance of change in this respect is hardly worth delaying change that might result in better outcome? For one thing is sure; the way you see, and long have seen, gives no support to base your future hopes, and no suggestions of success at all. To place your hopes where no hope lies must make you hopeless. Yet is this hopelessness your choice, while you would seek for hope where none is ever found.

Is it not also true that you have found some hope apart from this; some glimmering,—inconstant, wavering, yet dimly seen,—that hopefulness is warranted on grounds that are not in this world? And yet your hope that they may still be here prevents you still from giving up the hopeless and unrewarding task you set yourself. Can it make sense to hold the fixed belief that there is reason to uphold pursuit of what has always failed, on grounds that it will suddenly succeed and bring what it has never brought before?[71]

Is not our dismal track record as captain of our own ship, as teacher of our own minds, grounds for immediate resignation? Is it not grounds for hiring another Teacher, One Who teaches a way that is as different from ours as night from day? Is it not ample cause to invite the Holy Spirit in? In words that speak of the very realization that gave it birth, *A Course in Miracles* says:

> Tolerance for pain may be high, but it is not without limit. Eventually everyone begins to recognize, however dimly, that there *must* be a better way.[72]

Ten

The Holy Spirit's message is that we never sinned, never changed ourselves. We need only change our minds.

Ten

So what exactly is this "better way" proposed by the Holy Spirit? What is His solution to the human condition and to our personal predicament? Now that we hopefully have established some clarity about the Holy Spirit, we will spend the remainder of the book examining His way. In this chapter we will examine His core message. In following chapters we will look at how we apply or realize His message. In the final two chapters we will look at the journey on which He takes us, the journey home.

10.1. The guilt and pain produced by the ego is stored in an unconscious level of mind which also contains our call for God's Love and help.

To appreciate the Holy Spirit's message we need to review the predicament it so lovingly addresses. We explored this situation through a process of digging ever more deeply into the mind, peeling back layer after layer.

First we encountered the face of innocence (Chapter 6), the conscious persona we wear which says, "I am a good person making my way as best I can through a harsh world." This nice face spends its life searching for pleasurable people, situations, and events. While conducting this innocent search, however, it feels constantly attacked by an unfair world. After heroic restraint it must finally put up its fists, but only in self-defense.

Next we encountered the victim (Chapter 7), the glare of hate beneath our smiling mask. On this level we see ourselves as a broken, bloodied creature lying mangled in the jaws of a sadistic world. Our hate-filled eyes speak the silent accusation, "I am the thing you made of me, and as you look on me, you stand condemned because of what I am."[1] On this level, we are burning with resentment, thirsting for revenge for what the world has done to us. The victim's campaign of vengeance oozes to the surface, disguised as the mild-mannered behavior of the face of innocence.

Finally, we met the ego proper (Chapter 8), who all along was the real character on the stage of the world, the stage *it* built. This character wears the previous two levels as a double-layer disguise. For it was never attacked by an unjust world. It launched the first attack, and then projected this attack outward so as to conjure the illusion of external armies besieging it. This gave it the excuse it needed to keep on attacking. This raw, unprovoked attack travels upward through the levels, donning increasingly civilized disguises. It first becomes the "righteous" vengeance of the victim, and finally emerges as the "justified" self-defense of the face of innocence.

This attack is ultimately directed against God. Through our innocuous daily activities, the ego wages its ancient war on God, hoping to murder Him, steal His power, and become God in His place. Through these same activities it also attempts to murder us, its host. The ego's attacks on the world are really designed to attack *us* with guilt, "compounding guilt until it becomes all-encompassing, demanding vengeance forever."[2] Thus, beneath all the blame we direct at the world, our condemnation is really directed at ourselves. The accusing finger you point, with deadly accuracy, at your brother, "points to you as well, but this is kept still deeper in the mists below the face of innocence."[3]

This line gives us a clue about the next level down in our tour of the mind. After all, there must be a level beneath the ego proper. Were the ego the bottom layer, then we *would* be monsters. Every awful thing said about us by theologians, priests, and former spouses would be true. Yet the ego is not the bedrock of our being. It, too, is a mask, the core of all of our masks. Above it lie its disguises. Below it lie its effects.

What does the line quoted above tell us about this next level down? It says that in this shrouded, foggy place in our minds, "in the mists below the face of innocence," our accusing finger points not at the world, but at *ourselves*. All of the blame we have directed so hatefully outward is here directed inward. In this place in our minds there is no shifting of responsibility. All of the problems, all of the suffering, are blamed on no one but ourselves. If there were such a place in your mind, just imagine the pain of it.

In key idea 4.3 we said that our primordial guilt lies deeply entombed in the murky fathoms of the unconscious. Here, beneath the ego proper, is where it is actually buried. Here is where the effects of the ego are stored. On this level is pure, anguished self-accusation. Here we fully believe that we have committed unspeakable crimes against God which can never be undone. We believe that our hands are stained with the blood of centuries, blood which can never be washed away. We assume that we have actually murdered our pristine original Self, the Son of God, and transformed ourselves into something evil; that we "have made a devil of God's Son."[4] In deepest remorse we yearn to be redeemed, to be made clean again, but are certain that it is too late. We "know" that God's Presence has fled from our wicked soul, leaving only a nightmarish vacuum filled with "dim imaginings of terror, cold fantasies of fear and fiery dreams of hell."[5]

As we have acknowledged many times, we find it hard to imagine that such a place is truly within us, right this moment, in the "mists" beneath our conscious face of innocence. We have discussed several ways in which this guilt rises to the surface. Yet one of the most direct ways it bubbles up is the fundamental, all-pervading feeling that says, "Something is wrong with me." We may have become so accustomed to this feeling that we overlook it. Yet might this not play a major role in causing our pervasive unease, our chronic state of anxiety? This feeling says that at the heart of me something is amiss, something is screwed up. Instead of wholeness at my center, there seems to be a gnawing, unsettling void. Instead of being at peace with myself, deep down I feel ashamed, and I fear that I will be exposed for who I "really" am. "Shame," in fact, is a good word for this entire condition. We are "ashamed of what we are."[6] A medieval mystic once spoke of the "foul stinking lump" of self. The language is harsh, but have we not felt that way about ourselves at one time or another?

We can view the entire human search as a multifaceted attempt to eradicate this hypothetical inner flaw. Isn't our hope that if the world shines on us just right, if that special person loves us just so, we will be made whole? When we blame others isn't our hope that their guilt will make *us* clean? We try so hard to be seen in a more favorable light, to prove we were in the right, to show how hard we tried. We work so diligently to cover up some nameless blemish with a thick paste of achievements, clothes, and clever remarks.

The feeling that something is wrong with us finds its mirror in the equally pervasive sense that something is wrong with the world, that things are simply not the way they ought to be. This feeling propels us on perpetual expeditions to find the earthly paradise. We look for it in the past: in our childhood home, in some bygone golden age, or in some mythic Garden of Eden in which everything was pure and all was right with the world. We also look forward to it in the future, in an anticipated scientific utopia, in a New Age Shangri-la, or perhaps in some dramatic apocalypse in which God swoops in, wipes out what is, and re-establishes the divine kingdom of what ought to be.

True, the self we identify with and the world we see *are* flawed to the core. Yet they are mere surface manifestations of this deep place in us where we believe we have defiled both ourselves and reality beyond hope. As terrifying as this level is, the Course urges us to uncover it:

> You must look upon your illusions and not keep them hidden....For beneath them, and concealed as long as they are hidden, is the loving mind that thought it made them in anger. And the pain in this mind is so apparent, when it is uncovered, that its need of healing cannot be denied. Not all the tricks and games you offer it can heal it, for here is the real crucifixion of God's Son.[7]

According to this passage, when we at last come face to face with this level, we contact the innocent mind that, to its unending remorse, thought it wrecked things for good. We see its undeniable need for healing. We see at last that its crucifixion comes not from the world, but from its own guilt. And we hear the call it has made to God since the dawn of time, the call to be redeemed, to be made whole again, the call for God's Love to come down, wash away its sins, and embrace it once again. The following passage puts it perfectly, and has inspired me to term this level "the call for help":

> Beneath all the grandiosity you hold so dear is your real call for help. For you call for love to your Father as your Father calls you to Himself.[8]

And this call has been answered.

10.2. The Holy Spirit's answer to our guilt is that we did not do it, that we are still as God created us, because the separation never occurred.

What is the Holy Spirit's answer to our remorse-filled call for help?

> One walks with you Who gently answers all your fears
> with this one merciful reply, "It is not so."[9]

To our most deep-seated and ancient fears—that we left our Father, demolished His Heaven, and slaughtered our original Self—the Holy Spirit says with calm assurance, "It is not so." To every one of our "sins," be it a tiny oversight or a life-changing catastrophe, His single answer echoes from the tranquil depths of our mind, "It is not so."

This message is no Band-Aid, no anxious effort to shoo away inconsolable guilt, no hollow attempt to placate us with empty platitudes. This answer is the single most liberating thing a guilty mind could ever hear. For it is the only thing that could completely reverse its sentence, open the door of its cramped cell and cause the entire prison house to simply disappear.

This is the message we discussed in Chapter 3: that the separation never occurred. At that point, however, we could scarcely appreciate just how healing of a message it is. Much of what we have discussed since then has been designed to give us tools to appreciate it. In Chapters 4 through 8 we sketched the Course's extensive theory of conventional life on earth. This theory explains all of human suffering in terms of strictly psychological causes. It says that our pain does not come from an external world, but from our own minds. It comes, more specifically, from our belief that we have sinned against God, our belief that the separation *did* occur.

The conclusion is obvious: If all pain comes from the belief that the separation occurred, then the idea that the separation did *not* occur has the power to directly and completely wipe away every trace of suffering. This one idea has the power to awaken us from the human condition, which merely pictures our belief that the separation took place. This one idea, if fully internalized, can return our minds whole and complete to their transcendental home in God.

A Course in Miracles speaks this single message to us over and over, in a variety of forms. One of its favorite forms is "I am as God created me." This statement is introduced in the final section of the Text, then becomes the only lesson in the Workbook to occur more than once (as Lessons 94, 110, and 162), and finally becomes the central theme of the twenty-lesson final review.

This idea has an immediate appeal to many. We all carry a sense that something newly born is innocent and untainted. We would especially assume this was true of something newly born from God. We would expect God to create only the pure, the holy. It is therefore natural to imagine that at the moment we were born from the Mind of God we must have been immaculate, without a single blemish, a gloriously fresh and new creation. In that one shining moment, what cause would we have to feel anything but flawless and beautiful, without a trace of shame?

Now imagine, says this idea, that nothing has changed since that primal moment. Imagine that that moment is still going on, that we are still emerging from the Mind of our beloved Creator, perfectly untarnished, still a river of pure radiance flowing from the Heart of the Holy One, while all of Heaven stands in silent awe at our birth. In one of the Course's prayers, we affirm this very thing:

> *Father, I seek the peace You gave as mine in my creation. What was given then [in my creation] must be here now, for my creation was apart from time, and still remains beyond all change. The peace in which Your Son was born into Your Mind is shining there unchanged. I am as You created me.*[10]

This is difficult to imagine, since it seems to fly in the face of our experience. To really appreciate this idea, then, we must realize that its whole intent is to *refute* our current experience of ourselves. To say, "I am as God created me" is to say, "I am nothing that I think I am."

> Salvation requires the acceptance of but one thought;— you are as God created you, not what you made of yourself. Whatever evil you may think you did, you are as God created you. Whatever mistakes you made, the truth about you is unchanged. Creation is eternal and unalterable. Your sinlessness is guaranteed by God. You are and will forever be exactly as you were created.[11]

To get their full impact, let us reflect on the above sentences. No matter what attributes you have applied to yourself, good or bad, they have nothing to do with who you really are.[12] You may see yourself as honorable or selfish or brilliant or uncaring or helpful, yet you are none of these things; "you are as God created you, not what you made of yourself." Regardless of the evil things you think you have done, in spite of lying to your mother or cheating your business partner or not spending time with your children, "you are as God created you." Even after your countless mistakes, careless accidents, and thoughtless omissions, "the truth about you is unchanged." All these things seemed to have power to reach inside you and remold your very identity, marring the purity that God gave you. But you have no such power. Your will apart from God's is totally impotent. Nothing you can do can change who you are. "You are and will forever be exactly as you were created."

I once had a dream in which I plotted and carried out the murder of someone close to me. While doing it, it seemed logical: It would be a definite relief to have him out of my life. Yet once he lay there dead I was overwhelmed with remorse. The guilt was too deep for words. It felt like I had changed my status from a human to a monster. I wanted desperately to go back and undo my deed. But it was too late. I knew that I would always carry this stain on my soul. I would be branded for the rest of my life, which would merely be one long consequence for this single sin. The pain of this feeling was simply horrible. I began to wake up, and in that drowsy space between sleeping and waking I realized that the police would arrive soon and my punishment would begin. Then I awoke further and realized that it was a dream, and so maybe I had only wounded him. Finally, it hit me: It was only a dream! He's still alive! I didn't do it! And therefore I was free. I was saved.

Think of the emancipation of applying this idea to all the bad things you ever thought you did. When you stole that item from the store, when you wrecked your parents' car, when you betrayed your best friend, when you left the partner you loved—it was all only a dream. Therefore, you are absolved of it all, of the "sins" you forgot and the ones you carry like a chain around your neck. The number of your sins does not matter, nor does their magnitude. It is irrelevant whether you had a fleeting thought of discourtesy or plotted to kill people. It all happened only in your dreams.

> It matters not what form they [the sins] took, nor how enormous they appeared to be, nor who seemed to be hurt by them. They are no more. And all effects they seemed to have are gone with them, undone and never to be done.[13]

As we will see in Chapter 12, this is the Course's new notion of forgiveness. In its teaching we are forgiven not because someone decides to graciously let us off the hook, but because our sins had no real effect. And this is so because the separation *itself* had no real effect. "And therefore all your sins have been forgiven because they carried no effects at all. And so they were but dreams."[14] This is the good news, the best we could ever hear. For we need deliverance not from what the past did to us, but from what we did in the past—or rather, *think* we did.

> Why would you not be overjoyed to be assured that all the evil that you think you did was never done, that all your sins are nothing, that you are as pure and holy as you were created, and that light and joy and peace abide in you?[15]

Why not indeed? We all know, either firsthand or from the report of others, the ecstatic feeling of deliverance that comes from feeling completely forgiven. I read a story of a man who, as a soldier in the Vietnam War, ordered the napalm bombing of a village. Years later, after guilt over the incident had crippled his life, he met up with a woman who, as a young girl, had been burned in this bombing (the widely publicized photograph of this girl fleeing naked from the scene had immortalized the incident). The man relates:

> She hugged me and said, "It's all right, it's all right. I forgive," and then all of a sudden, 25 years of shame and remorse was literally lifted off of me like someone had taken an anvil off of my shoulders....I was free. I was flying. I was finally at peace.[16]

Yet as liberating as this feeling is, conventional forgiveness leaves a remaining burden weighing nagging at our minds: We still sinned, we still caused harm. Do we, then, really *deserve* this forgiveness? If conventional forgiveness can still bring such a sense of release, just imagine what exhilarating freedom will blow through our minds when we realize that we never did it, that our "sin" was only a dream, and that we are still as God created us.

"I am as God created me" is one of the most profound ideas I have ever encountered—if not *the* most. The Course says, "It will mean far more to you as you advance,"[17] and I have found this to be true. It has come to mean to me that in spite of all appearances I am, right this instant, an infinite being, a shining field of pure spirit whose dimensions stretch to infinity. It means that whatever ageless, majestic, all-knowing Self was created as God's Son in the timeless beginning, *I still am That.* I am that boundless being; I have simply gone mad and think I am a microscopic creature on a little rock in a shallow puddle called space and time. I never was this person. I never set foot in this place. I was never born into this body. I never lived this life. And I will never, ever die. I have never left the Heart of God. I have been there all along, enfolded in all the tenderness of His boundless Love, basking in all the warmth of His endless Smile. And I am there right now, merely dreaming that I am this person, living this life, studying this Course, writing this book. In all of the countless millennia of my dreaming, with all of the things that I have done through all the mists of time, I have not succeeded in putting one dent in my reality. After it all, in spite of it all, I am and will forever be exactly as God created me.

Quite simply, "I am as God created me" means that there is nothing wrong with us. There is no hole to fill, no flaw to correct, and no stain to wash away. It further means that there is nothing amiss with reality; everything is exactly the way it ought to be. There was a paradise, a paradise of bliss, a perfect place that could fulfill our dreams a thousand times over, where we could abide forever growing only more carefree and more deeply enraptured. And it still is there, nothing has changed. Nothing has changed. Everything is exactly the way it was in the beginning. Eden is unmarred; it still shines in its first dawn. Even as we speak its sun rises and will never ever set. Adam and Eve are still there, relaxing in the ease of their Father's unabated Love. They never ate that fruit and were never driven out of the home that God created just for them. That was only a myth. That glorious golden age that we all long to be part of is still going on this very moment. Its domes are still gleaming, its banners still flutter in the morning breeze. It never decayed and fell; indeed, it's in the vigor of its youth, and we are its blessed citizens.

That perfect childhood home to which we have tried so hard to return didn't fade away. We never even left it. We are within its walls right now. At this very moment we are sleeping in our Mother's arms as she softly sings to us. And our whole sad life, in which we grew up and lost our innocence chasing vain ambitions in that far country, was just a dream that drifted across our minds in the space of one brief nap. For the duration of this nap we have forgotten that we are no ordinary child of humble parentage. We are the Christ Child, still resting safe and warm in our Mother's arms, still tranquilly asleep only moments after our glorious birth.

10.3. The journey home is an illusion. We need not purify ourselves or make sacrifices. Instead, we can wake up at any time we choose.

If there is truly nothing wrong with us, this has sweeping implications for our entire spiritual journey. Different spiritual systems frame this journey in different ways, but if we can step back far enough we can see many of them falling into broad overall patterns.

At the heart of those patterns is the assumption that something is deeply wrong with us. Our souls have fallen, are corrupted and imperfect. We may have a higher self, but for now we are primarily these lower selves, filled with flaws and prone to misdeeds. Because of this sinful, defective self there lies a yawning gulf between us and the Ultimate. We have had a rupture with our Source. Therefore, we must go on a journey, a journey to purify our lower selves, to fill this "foul stinking lump" of self with holiness borrowed from God; a lengthy journey from the earthly side of the gulf over to the heavenly side.

The road that spans this chasm is a road of sacrifice. For the pleasures our lower self enjoys are not appropriate for the ethereal atmosphere of Heaven. To be with God we must pay Him a high price—just as we needed to pay our special relationship partners. In many traditional systems we must give up every bodily comfort and earthly pleasure, and endure poverty, hunger, and celibacy. We must also sacrifice our mental comfort as we strain to resist temptation and lift ourselves skyward in prayer and meditation. The Lord smiles on this sacrifice, and indeed commands it, for this is our penance for being a fallen soul, a lower self. It is the debt that must be paid before the gates of Heaven will open for us.

The journey is thus one of making ourselves worthy of Heaven. We are not there now because, quite simply, we don't deserve to be. And so all of our sacrifices, our struggle with inner demons, our church-going, our scripture reading, our diligent prayer and meditation, are subtle ways of paying for our sins and earning a place among the holy. They are ways of bending the corners of God's mouth from a frown into a smile. Most systems perhaps do not state this openly, because it sounds so crass. Yet (as we will see in the next section) this is what happens when unconscious guilt drives our religious pursuits.

In this view, because of our immense unworthiness, the spiritual expedition takes a long time—if we make it at all. For we are covering a real distance, from a sinful self to a holy self, from this world to another world. Therefore, it might be thousands of lifetimes, or thousands of years in Purgatory, before we are pure enough at last to enter that blessed abode.

This account of the spiritual journey may sound somewhat like the Course. Indeed, the Course does say that we will go on a journey to God. On this journey we will seem to actually change from sinful to holy, and will feel an increasing closeness and communion with God. Along the way, we will give up everything we think we value. And, after what will probably be a very long time, we will leave this world entirely in favor of our eternal home in Heaven.

Despite these similarities, the Course sees the spiritual journey profoundly differently than the above more conventional account. This is because the Course's picture of that journey rests on a different fundamental premise: *"the separation never occurred."*[18] If we never left God, how can we really travel back to Him?

> The journey to God is merely the reawakening of the knowledge of where you are always, and what you are forever. It is a journey without distance to a goal that has never changed.[19]

In other words, there is nowhere to go and no one to become. I need only reach the place I never left, become the being I have always been. I am simply emerging from amnesia, recovering knowledge already in my mind. You could say that I am traveling from a dream to the bed I am sleeping in. The entire excursion, therefore, is an illusion, a dream voyage. How can a "journey without distance" be a *real* journey?

It takes little reflection, I believe, to see that this "journey without distance" is enormously preferable to the conventional version. For one, it has got to be easier to cover no distance than to traverse a vast expanse. Further, if this expanse is that between a guilty sinner and a holy God, bridging it seems to be a nearly hopeless prospect. This hopelessness, familiar to all spiritual seekers, is a feeling which the ego treasures. "The ego can accept the idea that return is necessary because it can so easily make the idea seem difficult."[20] However, if I am already a perfect Son of God, already in Heaven, then all I need do is accept *what is*. Certainly that is easier than remolding myself from a sinner into a saint.

I am therefore going on a strictly mental journey, from my own resistance to what is to an inner acceptance of what is. My only job, then, is to shed my resistance, or as the Course says, to allow my blocks to be removed.[21] I don't seek some distant light of which I am currently unworthy. I instead seek out my own blocks: raise them to awareness, question their premises, expose their results, and conclude that they are undesirable. In a well-known line the Course says, "Your task is not to seek for love, but merely to seek and find all of the barriers within yourself that you have built against it."[22]

This is why the Course spends so much time dragging the ego's thought system into the light. The Course's focus on the ego—along with our previous chapters on it—may seem depressing. Yet that focus stems from a larger thought, boundless in its optimism. It is this: All we need do is locate and remove the ego's dark glasses and we will find that we have been bathed in sunlight all along.

In this view of the journey, there are no sacrifices to make. We are merely shedding a self we thought we were. We are merely letting go of our attachments to things that promise salvation but really deliver pain. The Course speaks of the things we value in the world using the image of a lump enclosed in wrappings: "The thin disguise of pleasure and of joy in which they may be wrapped but slightly veils the heavy lump of fear that is their core."[23] This is how the Course sees our conventional pleasures, as thin wrappings that carry within them a heavy payload of fear. Doesn't this agree with our experience? As we sample the "good things in life," we feel pleasure in the short term, but in the long run we are saddled with constant anxiety, which is another way of talking about fear.

God, therefore, does not deprive us of our pleasures; He gently and gradually frees us of our self-torture. There is no real sacrifice to make.

There is no entry fee at the gates of Heaven. The Course emphasizes this often, because the idea of sacrifice sits like a massive rock right in the middle of our motivation for God. We will still *experience* sacrifice along the spiritual path, yet this will eventually go as we learn that we are clinging to nothing more than lumps of pain in pleasure's clothing.

> God's teachers can have no regret on giving up the pleasures of the world. Is it a sacrifice to give up pain? Does an adult resent the giving up of children's toys? Does one whose vision has already glimpsed the face of Christ look back with longing on a slaughter house?[24]

This picture of the journey comes down to one thing: We can go home literally anytime we choose. A "journey without distance" need not take any time. As the Course says, "Love waits on welcome, not on time."[25] The inner peace and privilege of being the Son of God Himself, the rapture of abiding in the Heaven of His Love—these are things we deserve right now. These are gifts we can claim right now, for they are *ours* right now. Infinite happiness is ours this instant, waiting only for our acceptance: "The emphasis of this course always remains the same;—it is at this moment that complete salvation is offered you, and it is at this moment that you can accept it."[26] This accepting may well take a long time, but that is due solely to our inner resistance. The journey home is like one of those simple, easy tasks that can take forever, not because of the nature of the task, but because we don't want to do it. Finishing it has nothing to do with time and everything to do with willingness.

> It is not time we need for this. It is but willingness. For what would seem to need a thousand years can easily be done in just one instant by the grace of God.[27]

This is the advantage of the Course's view of the spiritual journey. The Course is absolutely clear that everyone will wake up in the end. The only question is, how soon? On the Course's path we will take the same basic journey everyone else is taking. We will move through the same general stages, travel through the same terrain. We *will* feel like we are sacrificing and it *will* take time. We won't pick up *A Course in Miracles* one day and painlessly awaken the next. Yet the Course's promise is that it will simply teach us how to do it *faster*. It claims it can save us literally centuries,[28] even thousands of years.[29]

To understand how the Course can do this, let's imagine an experiment. You hypnotize two people and tell them that they are both in the same room and that on the other side of this room is an exquisitely delightful reward. Their job, you tell them, is to run across the room to reach it. They will not actually be going anywhere; the room is imaginary and so they will be running only in their minds and reporting to you when they have made it across.

The key is that you give each one different instructions. You tell one that he is terribly sinful and dare not think that he is remotely worthy to reach the reward. He will have to wait, you tell him, until he has literally transformed himself from a sinner into a holy person. Until that day, he deserves only to encounter overwhelming obstacles—chairs and tables piled high, strong men standing in his way and shoving him back. And each little step he does manage to make will involve painful sacrifices on his part. As part of his punishment, he will have to give up all that makes him happy for a greater reward he may never reach. In contrast, you tell the second guy that he has ten feet of open space to cross and that the reward is a wondrous object that, unbeknownst to him, he already owns.

In this experiment, just as in our spiritual paths, both are making a strictly mental journey. Both are traversing the same inner space. Both are making a journey without distance that *need* not take any time. But which one is going to get across that imaginary room more quickly and easily? Which one would *you* rather be?

10.4. The holy instant is a moment when this is realized, applied, a moment of doing nothing.

Let's see how the above ideas play out on a more practical level. The holy instant is one of the primary teachings of the Course, yet one which leaves many students confused. Before we discuss it, then, let us first describe what it is.

A holy instant is a moment in which we momentarily transcend identification with illusions and experience what is real. For an instant, the past and future fall away from us like useless layers of armor. We shed all self-concern, all burden of our guilt and shortcomings, all worry about our safety, and even awareness of our bodies. The entire steel framework through which we perceive the world collapses in a silent heap, and we are left looking straight into the present. There we see the glory that has been right in front of us all along. Our minds expand beyond the tiny prison of this body and enter into communion with the totality that seemed to lie outside of us, but we now realize is within. We pass into a state of exaltation and happiness impossible to describe as we find ourselves part of a "bright, endless circle that extends forever."[30]

This experience can come in many forms and in many degrees of fullness. It can be a moment of deep joining between two people or a private mystical experience of the highest order. It can be a hazy glimpse of light that hardly leaves an impact[31] or it can be the pivotal experience of one's life. To help us get a handle on the holy instant, the Course relates it to an experience most of us are familiar with. It says we can have a kind of quasi-holy instant through joining mentally with a piece of music, a beautiful scene, a pleasant memory, or even an abstract idea.[32]

The real question is, how can we experience these holy instants? They are often the happiest moments of one's life, yet they seem to come and go like the wind, outside of our control. How can we bring them on? To this question there are two very different answers, which stem from the two different pictures of the spiritual journey.

The Course discusses these two ways in a well-known but often misunderstood section entitled "I Need Do Nothing."[33] The first way is the way of *preparation*. In this way, you assume that you are currently unworthy to experience the holy instant. You therefore must prepare yourself for it. You need to muster up your best intentions and purify your mind of all dark thoughts and feelings. In short, you must "make yourself holy to be ready to receive it."[34] This section implies that the way of preparation is the dominant religious approach of this world:

> You may be attempting to follow a very long road to the
> goal you have accepted. It is extremely difficult to reach
> Atonement by fighting against sin. Enormous effort is
> expended in the attempt to make holy what is hated and
> despised. Nor is a lifetime of contemplation and long peri-
> ods of meditation aimed at detachment from the body nec-
> essary.[35]

In this passage, I believe the Course is sketching a quick portrait of the dominant approaches of Western and Eastern spirituality. In the West we fight against our inner demons. We wrestle with temptation, trying to rein in our evil impulses. In so doing, we are trying to manually convert our hated self into a holy self. In the East, the approach is somewhat different. They spend a lifetime in "long periods of meditation" in which they try to rise above their lower, bodily identity.

The Western way is labeled "extremely difficult," requiring "enormous effort," while the Eastern way is said to be merely not "necessary." But both approaches are said to be "a very long road." Why? The next sentences provide the answer:

> All such attempts will ultimately succeed because of their purpose. Yet the means are tedious and very time consuming, for all of them look to the future for release from a state of present unworthiness and inadequacy.[36]

All seekers, East and West, will ultimately get home and will indeed have holy "instants of success"[37] along the way. Yet the way of preparation will take a long time. Why? The very means employed assume that I am not worthy now, and that it will be a long time before I can slowly, tediously make myself worthy. And since the journey is only in my mind, the very thought that it will necessarily take a long time is a self-fulfilling prophecy. It mentally shot-puts my final release into a distant future, generating the span of time through which I must journey before I can be released.

The dominant Western approach clearly assumes an unworthy self. Yet the Eastern way may seem to be in harmony with the Course. While I believe that certain paths and practitioners are, this passage is describing a broad current in Eastern spirituality that is not. In this broad current, people are stilling the body and mind; they seem to be doing nothing. But are they really? They are devoting long periods to almost muscularly detaching themselves from the body, the source of pollution and the seat of sin. It looks like a classic attempt to make oneself holy by separating from the source of unholiness. Is this not evidence that buried guilt has dictated the rules of the game? The key factor here is not the stilling of the mind, but the motive behind it. If the motive is to make oneself holy, then even doing nothing becomes a doing.

In response to the way of preparation, the Course says, "Your way will be different."[38] The Course's path is the way of *doing nothing*. We merely close our eyes, and "sink into stillness."[39] We simply bask in all that is ours right now. We lie back and serenely float on the tranquil ocean of God's eternal acceptance. We sit down beside Him and rest our head on His Knee.[40] We fall into His Arms and let all our sorrows end in His embrace.[41] In short, we relax in the thought that we need do nothing because everything is ours right now.

To truly rest in this, we must for just an instant stop our physical doing. Most of all, however, we must briefly drop the thought on which that doing is based, the thought which says, "I need to do something to become holy." "Let us be still an instant, and forget,"[42] says the Course. For a brief second we must forget our doing-machine—our body, and its comfort, protection, and enjoyment.[43] We must forget the past and the future, the time line in which our separate self hunts for food. This hungry self must also be forgotten, as well as the world in which it does its hunting. We must suspend our entire mental framework, which is saturated with the single thought, "I need to do something before I can be holy, before I deserve to be with God."

This forgetting is how we do nothing. Instead of trying to earn holiness, we simply forget all those thoughts that imply we *need* to earn it, all those thoughts of anxious grasping. Unfortunately, this state is so alien to our restless minds that we will require training in order to find it. The way of doing nothing is, paradoxically, a way of mind training. It takes a great deal of training to enter into the state of truly doing nothing. Yet initially we need only manage it for just an instant. If we can, that instant will become a holy instant. Our minds will pass into a place where it is fully obvious that, for perfect peace and infinite happiness to be ours, we have never needed to do anything. This is the same realization that so many others, East and West, have had. Hopefully, we will simply have reached it more quickly and painlessly:

> When peace comes at last to those who wrestle with temptation and fight against the giving in to sin; when the light comes at last into the mind given to contemplation; or when the goal is finally achieved by anyone, it always comes with just one happy realization; "*I need do nothing*."[44]

What a beautiful and ironic passage. The lifelong meditators and the sin-wrestlers *will* make it; their labors *will* pay off. Yet after all their arduous climbing to earn a pinnacle they think they do not deserve, when they finally reach the top of the mountain they will be enveloped in a rapturous surprise: "It was mine for free all along. I have been here all along."

10.5. The miracle is a free deliverance from the imprisonment of the human condition. It is our right, because we never sinned.

A holy instant affords us a brief glimpse of the end of the journey, where in truth we already reside. The Course calls it "a little flicker of your eyelids."[45] Experiencing the endpoint draws our minds closer to that end. This shortens the journey, since it is a journey of the mind. This shortening of time is central to the Course's purpose. *A Course in Miracles* makes the exact same point about that which its title claims to teach us: the miracle.

> The miracle minimizes the need for time. In the longi-tudinal or horizontal plane the recognition of [the final lesson] appears to involve almost endless time. However, the miracle entails a sudden shift from horizontal to vertical perception....The miracle thus has the unique property of abolishing time to the extent that it renders the interval of time it spans unnecessary. There is no relationship between the time a miracle takes and the time it covers. The miracle substitutes for learning that might have taken thousands of years.[46]

Remember our account of time from Chapter 3 (key idea 3.6)? There we said that our journey through time has already happened, like a movie that is already shot. Our current experience of time is produced by watching this movie and thinking that it is still happening and that we are living inside of it. The content of the story line, regardless of the particular characters and specific scenes, is that we are gradually learn-ing how to reach the final scene in which we awaken to God.

A miracle is an instant in which we step outside this normal frame-by-frame progression and catch a glimpse of the final scene (we "shift from horizontal to vertical perception"). This draws our mind closer to that ending. It thus advances our learning to a place much further along in the movie. As a result, we actually skip over all of those scenes in which we would have laboriously learned to reach this level.[47] These scenes are "the interval of time it spans" and "the time it covers" mentioned above. As we said in Chapter 3, this is like hitting the fast-forward button. By pushing this button, we may in an instant fast-forward past scenes that would have normally taken thousands of years to watch.

What is a miracle? We will actually be defining it over three different key ideas in the next four chapters. Our goal in this initial discussion will be to establish its essence: liberation without cost from what seemed inescapable.

Living in this world, as we have said many times, is an experience of feeling imprisoned by forces outside our control. We seem hemmed in by bills, viruses, inclement weather, impossible jobs, and bad relationships. We work day and night to solve all of these problems, but there are too many and some are just too big.

> No one could solve all the problems the world appears
> to hold. They seem to be on so many levels, in such vary-
> ing forms and with such varied content, that they confront
> you with an impossible situation.[48]

Quite simply, we need a miracle. Wouldn't it be wonderful if, just as in the Bible, the Spirit came in, neutralized all the laws and powers that hold us prisoner, and set us free from our bonds? In a single instant He could bring healing that we could not achieve in a lifetime. We know such miracles happen, but we do not count on them. Why? They are so rare. By definition, they are not part of the natural order. They are the exception. Either we must wait for divine whim to blow our way or we must earn our way into the special class of God's Elect. Even then, there are probably some problems that are too big even for a miracle to solve.

What is really imprisoning us, however, is not a set of outer problems. These are mere external projections of inner bars and walls, of our imprisoning beliefs. These beliefs do far more than manifest problems in our lives. They place our minds in the iron shackles of anger, guilt, fear, and loneliness. They give rise to the human illusion of being locked away for life on this prison planet and denied visits from our Father. Our belief in separation is the problem behind all our problems. Most of all, then, we need to be liberated from the shackles we have placed upon our *minds*.

This is where the Course's new definition of the miracle comes in. Its miracles are, first and foremost, divine healings of the mind. They come not when God finally decides to hear our prayers. These miracles are always available, awaiting only our invitation. They can be counted on, for they are natural. One day they will be "as simple and as natural to [us] as breathing to the body."[49] They come automatically any time we are willing to suspend the imprisoning framework of our ego's beliefs. This allows the Holy Spirit to enter where He was formerly unwelcome. "At the holy sound of His Voice"[50] a whole wing of our sprawling inner prison complex dissolves. This will often manifest in our outer lives as physical walls and bars melting away—as the healing of illness, money problems, relationship difficulties, etc. Yet the important part remains the inner healing of belief and perception.

There are no limitations on this miracle. To the Holy Spirit, no problem is too big. He solves all of them with equal effortlessness because He sees all of them as equally unreal. This is the well-known first principle of miracles: "There is no order of difficulty in miracles. One is not 'harder' or 'bigger' than another. They are all the same."[51] For many longtime Course students, this principle may have worn smooth through repetition. It may have come to sound dry and routine. Yet if it really is true, what could we hear that would be more wondrous; indeed, more miraculous?

Each one of us is beset daily by our personal list of problems, ones that sprang up today and ones that have dogged us for years. In order to appreciate this first principle more fully, you may want to mentally review some of your own problems, especially the ones at the top of your list. Think of two or three main problems that weigh on your mind, such that, if they were solved you would feel delivered, emancipated, as if you had been unexpectedly set free from a life sentence. Holding these in mind, imagine, if you will, how you would feel "if you saw them vanish one by one, without regard to size, complexity, or place and time, or any attribute which you perceive that makes each one seem different from the rest."[52] Imagine that they not only vanished on the outside, but that all the fear and anxiety you held around them vanished, too. How would that feel? As if in answer to our doubts that such a thing is even possible, the very next sentence says, "Think not the limits you impose on what you see can limit God in any way."

A miracle, then, is an instance of unconditional, instantaneous, and free deliverance from the inner imprisonment and (secondarily) the outer problems of this world. You may ask, how can we be delivered so freely and completely? The only way we *couldn't* is if we had truly sinned and thus really deserved to stay in jail. Only then would God's deliverance be withheld until we paid our penalty. The miracle, then, is simply another application of the central theme of this chapter. Miracles are our right *because* we are not guilty, *because* we are as God created us. We need do nothing whatsoever to make ourselves worthy of them. They are pure gift, pure grace, and always deserved. As Workbook Lesson 77 says, "I am entitled to miracles."[53] Because we are the Son of the Lord of Heaven, total liberation is our birthright, without cost, just for the choosing.

> And all you need to do is but to wish that Heaven be given you instead of hell, and every bolt and barrier that seems to hold the door securely barred and locked will merely fall away and disappear.[54]

The journey to God, then, is very much like Dorothy's journey in *The Wizard of Oz*. She thought she had great distances to traverse in order to get back home, untold leagues filled with dark and dangerous obstacles. She thought she had to escape from the imprisonment of evil, and earn the favor of a godlike floating head. Yet throughout all her adventures she had the power to return home instantly, whenever she chose. For the journey was merely a dream in her mind.

Like Dorothy, we are asleep at home dreaming of a long and frightening journey. And like her, all we need do to awaken in our own bed, surrounded by our loved ones, is realize that there's no place like home—there's no place *but* home.

Eleven

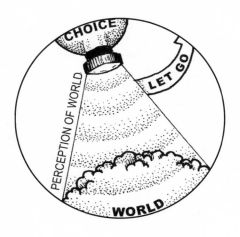

Changing our minds means allowing
the Holy Spirit to heal our perception.

Eleven

The journey to God is one of simply realizing who and where we already are, removing the blocks to what we already know, reaching out our hand and claiming the treasure that has always been ours. This sounds so easy, but how do we actually do it?

11.1. To awaken in Heaven all we need is a change of perception.

We have said that at this moment we are the Son of God enfolded in the Heaven of God's loving embrace. That is our actual situation. But we do not *perceive* it that way. We perceive ourselves as flawed humans under siege by a merciless world. The Course repeatedly stresses that this perception is an illusion, yet it remains a very convincing one.

Nothing outside of us is making us see things this way. Our mind is the cause of our experience (see key idea 5.1). Therefore, this faulty perception must be coming solely from choices in our own minds. Further, it cannot be our past choices that produce this perception, for that would make the past our cause and we would be victims of the past. No, something we are doing in our own minds *right now* must be manufacturing the perception that we are not in Heaven, not God's Son. Even as we read these words we must be performing some mental sleight of hand that conjures the entire illusion of this world.

A Course in Miracles would agree. According to it, our perception that we are flawed humans rather than Sons of God is continually produced by nothing other than our *perception*. This sounds hopelessly circular, but that is because the word "perception" stands for different things, as the following passage acknowledges:

> There has been much confusion about what perception means, because the word is used both for awareness and for the interpretation of awareness. Yet you cannot be aware without interpretation, for what you perceive *is* your interpretation.[1]

In normal thinking, we are first *aware* of something; we receive a raw awareness of pure sensations. Then we interpret and organize those sensations—we perceive them in a certain *way*. These are the two meanings of "perception" in our passage above. We perceive something in the sense of having the raw *awareness* of it, and we perceive it in the sense of *interpreting* our awareness of it.

The above passage, however, disagrees. It says that raw, uninterpreted sensation never even reaches our awareness. We experience sensation exclusively through an invisible grid of interpretation. We see it through the thick glass of our own personal lens. As a result, "what you perceive *is* your interpretation."

Getting back to my point, to say that our current experience is produced by our *perception* is to say that it is produced by our continual act of *interpretation*. Amazingly, the entire world of illusions is being manufactured in our minds right now. Through our ongoing interpretation, minds that are perfect, infinite and in Heaven are fabricating the illusion of being imperfect, finite and in the world. Somewhere in the process of your eyes gliding across this page right now, scanning from left to right, moving from top to bottom, recognizing letters, organizing them into words and then into sentences, interpreting the sentences as ideas, construing meaning in the ideas and responding emotionally—somewhere in that very process is the mental alchemy that manufactures the illusion of time and space. Somewhere in there is the hidden weaving of the fabric of separation.

If only we could locate that motion, that weaving, if only we could find the flaw in our interpretive process and let it go—think what that would mean! This, in fact, is the goal of *A Course in Miracles*:

> This is not a course in philosophical speculation, nor is it concerned with precise terminology. It is concerned only with Atonement, or the correction of perception.[2]

According to this passage, everything in the Course has only one purpose: to correct perception. The Course does not discuss philosophy to satisfy our intellectual curiosity. It discusses only those philosophical concepts that by their nature shift our perception. It does not use terms according to a rule of precision and formal consistency. It uses words for one purpose: to induce a shift in perception. This shift is all that we need, for as the last sentence says, the correction of perception *is* Atonement; it *is* how we reconcile with God. We only *perceived* ourselves splitting off from Him. When our perception is corrected we will realize that we have never left His fatherly embrace.[3]

If all we need do is change our perception, then we have developed a great many unnecessary things to resolve our split with God. A vast array of religious traditions, spiritual philosophies, and therapeutic modalities have evolved a staggering array of methods for healing our sense of being alienated from some perfect condition or supreme Being. I once compiled the following list of well-known methods that are not inherently about changing our perception: being part of the right institution; being part of an order or ashram; going to a church or a temple; going to a sacred site; having holy objects, pictures, or relics; proper use of crystals, colors, sounds, and smells; participating in rituals, sacraments, and festivals; making sacrifices to the gods; experiencing painful events as payment for wrongdoings; wearing the right clothing; eating the right foods; performing the right exercises, postures, or bodily movements; the proper use of breath; moving energy around in the body or focusing attention on certain body parts; adopting the right lifestyle; holding virtuous occupations; engaging in virtuous behaviors; having special powers; being able to manifest the right events; appropriately drawing one's boundaries; believing in particular historical events; understanding the form of the universe and spiritual reality.

This list hits several bases in most of our spiritual lives. Yet, according to the Course, these things, in and of themselves, have no power to bring us home. They may help induce a change in perception, but they may not. Instead, they are primarily about manipulating, understanding, participating in, or being associated with some kind of *form*, either physical or mental. They are about form, not content. This distinction between form and content is familiar to most Course students. A form is something—an object, an event, a situation, a piece of information— that can be used for different purposes, endowed with different meanings. Content, on the other hand, *is* meaning. It is the meaning we see in things. To fill a form with content is to see a particular meaning in it, or express a particular meaning through it.

According to the Course, then, to arrive home and find ourselves safe in the Arms of God, we need merely learn how to perceive a new meaning in the same old forms. We need neither transform our souls nor modify our environment. "Therefore," says the Course, "seek not to change the world, but choose to change your mind about the world."[4] Though a challenging statement, this can also induce an immense sense of relief. All that we have sought through our arduous attempts to rearrange the furniture of the world can be found simply through seeing a new meaning in that same old furniture.

Think of the overwhelming joy you had hoped would come through marrying a certain person, getting a particular house, or achieving some important thing. That joy, which probably never came, can come at last through a strictly *inner* change. It can come through a shift in how you perceive the mundane things in front of you this instant. Is it possible that an inner shift could actually make you happy, that it could succeed where all else has failed? This is the promise of *A Course in Miracles*. Changing our perception will do it all. "This is the only thing that you need do for vision, happiness, release from pain and the complete escape from sin, all to be given you."[5]

We find this difficult to really believe because we are so thoroughly soaked in the idea that things have to change outside of us. We assume that before we can feel better that car has to get fixed, that person has to stop being angry at us, that friend has to say she's sorry. Surely we could not just feel better right now, with things exactly as they are. Hence, to make more sense of this simple but hard-to-swallow concept, let us examine the mechanics of perception.

11.2. Projection makes perception.

The Course's philosophy of perception is summarized in a brief phrase it repeats twice: "Projection makes perception."[6] These three words represent a direct reversal of how we seem to experience the world. It appears to us that external objects and events are more or less impressing their contours onto the soft clay of our minds, leaving their footprints in our perception and emotion. It seems that some kind of power travels from those outer things and inserts an experience of them into our minds. Think of an apple dropping to the floor and breaking. Light travels from this to our eyes, placing a picture of the event in our minds. The sound vibrations travel to our ears, planting a sound record in our minds. The odor travels to our nostrils, imparting the smell of apple to our awareness. The same seems true of the *meaning* of the event, which seems to enter our mind right alongside the streams of sight, sound, and smell. The unpleasant meaning—of good food being wasted—assaults our mind like a bad odor, causing us to feel bad.

In sum, our normal experience is that perception is caused from without. In contrast, "projection makes perception" is saying the exact opposite. Rather than outer events traveling into our minds and leaving their imprint there, causation actually travels from the *inside out*. Our minds project their own overlay of meaning onto neutral forms. As the Course says, "Perception is a mirror, not a fact. And what I look on is my state of mind, reflected outward."[7]

There is an excellent discussion of this idea in the Manual.[8] The section "How Can Perception of Order of Difficulties Be Avoided?" begins by observing that our visual field is filled with differences, with "thousands of contrasts in which each thing seen competes with every other in order to be recognized."[9] Later, this section explains what actually gives rise to this myriad of differences:

> Where do all these differences come from? Certainly they seem to be in the world outside. Yet it is surely the mind that judges what the eyes behold. It is the mind that interprets the eyes' messages and gives them "meaning." And this meaning does not exist in the world outside at all.[10]

This states what we have already said—that our interpretation provides the meaning that we see in things—but says it more strongly. If our interpretation provides literally every bit of the meaning we see out there, then "this meaning does not exist in the world outside at all." Even the most basic and tacitly obvious meaning of "this thing is different than that" arises solely from our minds. It is manufactured by our own projection. How do we accomplish this?

> What is seen as "reality" is simply what the mind prefers [what it values]. Its hierarchy of values is projected out-

ward, and it sends the body's eyes to find it.[11]

When you look at the scene in front of you, do your eyes not gravitate, almost by themselves, to particular things? Are not some things vastly more worth looking at than others? Why is this? Because over the course of your life you have built up a "hierarchy of values," a massive mental pyramid which assigns everything a certain level of value. At the top of this pyramid lie those things that are most precious to you. Based on this hierarchy, your mind gives your eyes this direction: "Go out and find me the things of greatest value." Like hunting dogs, your eyes bring back to their master—your mind—only what they have been trained to retrieve. This becomes what your mind feasts upon.[12] Through this simple, universal process of selective attention, you are ignoring most of what you see. Using the few remaining items, you then set about mentally constructing the world that you experience.

> The body's eyes will never see except through differences.
> Yet it is not the messages they bring on which perception
> rests. Only the mind evaluates their messages, and so only
> the mind is responsible for seeing. It alone decides whether
> what is seen is real or illusory, desirable or undesirable,
> pleasurable or painful.[13]

Once your faithful hunting eyes bring back their game, your mind sets about chewing on it, interpreting it. The eyes see only form. Have you ever seen meaning with your eyes? No, meaning is strictly mental. Therefore, no matter what the eyes bring back, the meaning *must* be supplied by the mind. For instance (to use the example given in our passage), your eyes are always going to see differences, but only your mind can actually decide that these differences are *real*. The mind alone assigns a meaning of "real or illusory, desirable or undesirable, pleasurable or painful." And it assigns this based entirely on its own belief system, the same one that guided the eyes in the first place.

As an example, while I was writing this, my wife at the time walked in and showed me her little finger. She sliced the tip off of it the day before while cooking and I hadn't seen it yet. This whittled finger was just form. But I looked at this form and, based on my own belief system, immediately decided that it was filled with all kinds of distressing meaning: Part of her identity had been sliced off; part of our financial identity had been cut away by the doctor bill; part of her ability to get things done—another chunk of her (and my) identity—had been severed while she recuperated; etc. Yet none of this meaning was in the form at all. All of it was in my mind. It was my own subjective interpretation, which I had projected onto the form.

Now we have seen two ways in which our belief system, our hierarchy of values, shapes what we see. First, through *selective attention* it guides what we focus on. Second, through *subjective interpretation* it guides our perception of what we have focused on. Let's see these two work together as our passage continues:

> It is in the sorting out and categorizing activities of the mind that errors in perception enter. And it is here correction must be made. The mind classifies what the body's eyes bring to it according to its preconceived values, judging where each sense datum fits best. What basis could be faultier than this? Unrecognized by itself, it has itself asked to be given what will fit into these categories. And having done so, it concludes that the categories must be true....Can this confused and senseless "reasoning" be depended on for anything?[14]

Let's juggle the order of the ideas here. I start with a preconceived hierarchy of values, filled with various categories. The most important of these categories are of people. We call them stereotypes. There are an endless number of them, most of them too sensitive to use as examples here without distracting from the points I wish to make. So I have chosen the most nearly harmless one I can think of. I live in a town— Sedona, Arizona—which is known for its natural beauty. Tourists flock here from all over the world to see the beautiful red rock formations, and once they get here, they often drive exceedingly slowly, even stopping in the middle of the road to get out and take pictures. This, of course, is irritating to the locals, who have seen the rocks a million times and are just trying to get from A to B. So I will use the slow-driving tourists as my example of a mental category that guides perception.

Once this category is built (and I expect that nearly everyone in Sedona has it), the mind does look for examples of it. There is some perverse pleasure that comes from finding new and even more flagrant examples that serve to justify one's resentment of the slow tourists.

Something in you actually wants to find them. Thus, while I drive, without even knowing it, my eyes are searching for slow tourists (selective attention). I'll automatically pay more attention to those drivers that are potential candidates. And once I lay my eyes on one that exhibits even a couple of the requisite characteristics, I will be predisposed to file that driver in the "slow tourist" category.

This act of *filing* is also an act of *interpretation* (subjective interpretation). Simply by filing an image in the slow tourist category I assign to it all the judgments that *define* that category, all the judgments that have been poised in my mind, ready to leap onto the first candidate. "Apparently," I conclude, "what we have here is a slow, inattentive tourist who thinks that the town has been shut down so that the roads are completely free for his rock-gazing." It is amazing how many judgments can be instantly placed on a complete stranger, isn't it?

Finally, having found someone whom I believe belongs in this category, I decide that the category itself has been verified. "Here's someone who fits the category. I therefore can safely conclude that this category really does describe an actual class of things out there." I will think this whether or not this person actually fits the category, for I will make him fit. How? I will focus on any behaviors of his that even remotely resemble my stereotypical slow tourist while ignoring behaviors that don't, thus producing a warped caricature of him that looks more like my stereotype than it does the actual driver in front of me. In my mind, he will not be his own unique person, he will be the stereotype.

In the end, I will come away assuming that I have seen reality, that I have successfully identified actual slow tourists. Yet, given that most of the identified slow tourists have Arizona plates, how do I really know that I'm right? In fact, I found exactly what I was searching for. I found what I was predisposed to find, what I *wanted* to find. That is the meaning of "projection makes perception"—I see what I want to see, not what is really out there. And that is why our passage closes by asking a sobering question that we may well ask ourselves: "Can this confused and senseless 'reasoning' be depended on for anything?"

We don't just carry one or two such stereotypes. There are hundreds of them. Yet they all are variations on a single theme. They are all children of the mother of all stereotypes: the stereotypical human being. This category sees every human through a set of basic judgments: A human is a "mind [that] is separate, different from other minds, with different interests of its own, and able to gratify its needs at the expense of others."[15] This amounts to a stereotype of the human being as *sinner*. Can you see how my slow tourist stereotype is simply a variation on this theme? According to the Course, the main thing our eyes hunt for, the primary thing we value in our visual search, is evidence of sin in others.[16]

We may argue that we formed our categories based on the solid evidence of our life experiences. Yet let us recall our discussion of projection from Chapter 5. Not only are our interpretations of events a projection of our beliefs, but the events themselves are, too. On a more superficial level we project the grid of our categories onto the world we see. But on a deeper level we project the grid of separation itself onto the oneness of Heaven, seemingly breaking it up into separate events, the very events our ego wants to see.[17]

Now we can appreciate the meaning of "projection makes perception." It means that our belief system projects outward by guiding our *attention* and our *interpretation*. The result is that our perceptions are just miniature projections of our beliefs. "It is impossible not to believe what you see, but it is equally impossible to see what you do not believe."[18] If we take this seriously, this undermines our entire sense of being in touch with reality. We think that we are peering out of windows in our skull and seeing an objective reality beyond the confines of our private mind. Yet all we are viewing are the contours and corridors of our own belief system.

Now we are in a position to add onto our cycle the final, crucial aspect: Just as what I believe becomes what I perceive, so what I perceive becomes what I *experience*, what I *feel*.[19] My emotions are a response to the meaning I perceive. My feelings do not at all come from what happens in my life. They are not produced by external facts. They are internally generated. They come from how I choose to interpret things. The Course says this plainly: "It is always an interpretation that gives rise to negative emotions, regardless of their seeming justification by what *appears* as facts."[20]

We have all experienced how our feelings are produced by the meaning we perceive in a situation. For example, let's say you come home to find that your partner has left sandwich fixings strewn all over the kitchen. If you assumed he was too caught up in the football game to clean up, you might feel resentful. Yet imagine how your feelings would change if you then found out that while fixing his sandwich he had a heart attack, called an ambulance and was now lying in the hospital. You would feel differently because you would assign a different meaning to the same situation.

If we are Course students, we practice trying to see things differently. Yet this usually only seems to shift things so far. For instance, let's say that your spouse didn't clean up his mess because he was in fact too eager to watch the halftime cheerleaders. You may try to see this situation differently, but usually it seems that there is only a small range in which your feelings have room to change. The nature of the event itself seems to put constraints on how far your mind can stretch this seeing differently business. That's how it feels, isn't it?

This implies, however, that there is at least some meaning in the outer form. This meaning acts like a tether that allows our perceptions to swing only so far from the pole of that disgusting form. What, then, if there is *no* meaning in the form whatsoever? What if the distance between the appearance of the form and the actual meaning behind the form could be unlimited? This would mean that we have complete freedom to see the situation differently than how it appears. It would mean that there is no limit on how far our interpretation can swing from a supposedly unpleasant form. In this view, it would be theoretically possible for our eyes to look on murder while our minds bask in infinite joy. This sentiment is echoed in a line that I think every Course student would benefit from memorizing:

> This is the lesson God would have you learn: There is a way to look on everything that lets it be to you another step to Him, and to salvation of the world.[21]

"A way to look on everything"—on that "disagreeable" person babbling on and on, on your wife's finger being sliced, on your child being killed, on *everything*. When I am in a situation in which there seems to be no other way to look on it, I often ask myself if a great spiritual master, were he here, would be forced to see this situation as I do. Or could he see it completely differently? Could he not see even *this* through the eyes of love?

I read a story about Martin Luther King, Jr. that demonstrates this same idea. When King launched his first protest he began receiving death threats daily. Over the weeks of this his fears began to grow.

Finally, late one night he received yet another death threat over the phone. It was the last straw. "It seemed that all of my fears had come down on me at once. I had reached the saturation point....I was ready to give up." Unable to sleep, exhausted and wondering how he could bow out gracefully, he decided to take his fears to God:

> My head in my hand, I bowed over the kitchen table and prayed aloud....At that moment I experienced the presence of the Divine as I had never before experienced him. It seemed as though I could hear the quiet assurance of an inner voice....Almost at once my fears began to pass from me. My uncertainty disappeared. I was ready to face anything. The outer situation remained the same, but God had given me inner calm.[22]

"The outer situation remained the same." While the outer situations of our lives remain just as they are, could a mere internal shift give us inner calm? And if these situations got considerably worse, is it possible that this inner calm could *still* be a sane response? If our emotions are not caused by outer forms, then there is literally no limit on the peace we could feel under *any* circumstance. We could be falsely accused, dragged off by the authorities, beaten by the police, abandoned by our loved ones, and even executed by the state, all the while being lifted up in a state of perfect happiness beyond description. If this seems hard to believe, we can take comfort in the fact that at least one person managed to do it. According to *A Course in Miracles*, this was the message of the crucifixion of Jesus.[23] This is the lesson he was trying to teach us all those centuries ago. This is the lesson God would have us learn.

11.3. Step one: Identify the cause of your pain as your own perception, and bring this illusion to the light of truth.

Workbook Lesson 23 takes these insights and applies them in the form of a simple three-step process for the healing of our perceptions:

> The idea for today introduces the thought that you are not trapped in the world you see, because its cause can be changed. This change requires, first, that the cause be identified and then let go, so that it can be replaced.[24]

We have discussed at length in previous chapters our experience of feeling imprisoned by an attacking world. This passage claims that this experience is not true. Why? "Because its cause can be changed." This change occurs in three steps:

1. Identify the cause.
2. Let go of the cause.
3. The cause will be replaced.

We will spend the remainder of this chapter elaborating on these three steps.

For example, let's go back to that mess your spouse made in the kitchen. This mess seems to trap you, to imprison you, does it not? Its very presence seems to thrust negative emotions onto you. What do you do to solve things? Do you clean the mess up yourself and say nothing? Do you politely ask your spouse *why* the mess is there and *if* he was planning to clean it up? Do you plan to wait until a break in the game he is watching to nonchalantly suggest that now would be an excellent time to clean it up? Do you express your feelings in a healthy display of drawing your boundaries and not stuffing down your anger?

These questions, as normal and universal as they are, represent the ego's seductive dead end. They are exactly where you don't want to go. For they assume that your bad feelings are caused by the outer world and are soothed by rearranging its chess pieces. This belief in external causation is the whole illusion we discussed in Chapters 5 through 8.

Your first proper move is to realize that you are having an ego attack, that your pain is not caused by the mess in the kitchen but by your *perception* of it, by your *interpretation* of its meaning—and nothing else. That is the cause you must identify. Realizing that, you stop what you are doing, stop wondering how you can fix it on the outside, and instead sit down and devote yourself to the healing of your thinking. This does not mean you never do anything about it on the outside. It just means you realize that external doing is not your first priority because it will never heal the real source of your pain.

The first thing you are faced with is your anger. What do you do with it? Do you vent it in order to blow off steam and relieve the internal pressure? Or do you suppress it, knowing the harm it might do? From the Course's standpoint you do *neither*. For both assume that anger is a cause unto itself, a wild thing inside that must either be penned in or allowed to run free. This is simply another version of the illusion that your feelings are solved through appropriate behavior (or non-behavior, in the case of suppression).

As we saw above, anger is merely an effect. Like all emotions, it is the effect of your interpretation—in this case (as we saw in key idea 7.1), your interpretation that your spouse has not fulfilled his proper role and is therefore a sinner who deserves your wrath. Your task is to let go of this interpretation. This will literally pull the plug on your anger, cut off its power supply. Then there will be nothing to express *or* suppress.

In the meantime, *A Course in Miracles* counsels you to step back and observe your feelings dispassionately. Identifying with your anger is what makes you feel that it has you by the throat, that it has power to make you a bad person. But you are not your anger. You are the Son of God merely entertaining this strange thought called anger. Would it not feel better to adopt this vantage point? "Watch [your egoic thoughts and feelings] come and go as dispassionately as possible."[25] Step back and observe your anger. Look straight at it "without shrinking."[26] It is merely a feather that happened to drift into the temple of your holy mind. It cannot hurt that temple. The temple is still holy. "You might imagine that you are watching an oddly assorted procession going by, which has little if any personal meaning to you."[27]

Before you can reach this calm place you might possibly need to do some venting (preferably not at the other person). But realize that this doesn't really solve anything. Expressing your rage merely throws the inner beast a steak. This can be useful, for while the beast sleeps on a full stomach you now have some room to let it go. But if you don't let it go, it will soon wake up as hungry as ever.

Rising above your anger as the detached observer will also allow you to see it for what it is. "Be lifted up," the Course says, "and from a higher place look down upon it."[28] From this higher place you are in a position to calmly and objectively see that your anger makes no sense. "The senselessness of conquest is quite apparent from the quiet sphere above the battleground."[29] Your anger's "senselessness" is composed of two facts: It "cannot be justified. But neither is it safe. And thus it must remain unwanted [unsafe] as well as unreal [unjustified]."[30] If your anger is neither justified nor joy producing, what possible reason could there be to hang onto it?

To realize this you must be willing to look very closely at these two issues. Does your anger rest on a sound thought system and does it bring happy results? Making this evaluation is much of the reason for studying the Text, where one learns in detail about the premises and results of the ego's thought system. Close study of the Text arms one with a great many ways to expose anger as "unwanted as well as unreal." In the next chapter we will look at several of these ways. For now we will simply draw upon ideas we have already discussed.

As we have learned, on the surface your irritation ("anger" may even feel like too strong of a word) at the mess in the kitchen seems to be a justified reaction. For this is the latest in a string of approximately one billion inconsiderate things that your spouse has done. Though you have been extremely patient, even saints have their limits.

This irritation, however, is merely a veil over the rage of the victim, which looks at your spouse and says, "I am the thing you made of me, and as you look on me, you stand condemned because of what I am."[31] In this inner place you see your spouse as a sinner whose long-term thoughtlessness has caused you to slowly turn sour inside.

Yet, of course, even this is a cover over the ego proper, whose sole activity is *unprovoked* attack. This attack is designed to continually dump into your mind's hidden caverns more buckets of the tears of guilt. This guilt, this feeling that "something is wrong with me," is the actual cause of your pain. The mess in the kitchen is merely a blank screen onto which you have projected the cause of your pain. This makes the pain seem to stab at you from the outside. And this simply gives you an excuse to attack once again, and accumulate yet more guilt.

In other words, coiled in this ordinary, "innocent" thought of irritation is the entire ego system we examined in previous chapters. In this single thought lies the DNA necessary to construct the whole organism of the human condition, with all its homeless people and domestic violence, its clashing armies and ethnic cleansings, its eons of senseless suffering and death. This is how the perceptual process we are engaging in right now is conjuring the fabric of time and space, which, as we have seen, is nothing more than the fabric of separateness.

For this reason, *A Course in Miracles* does not need to lead us through involved processes in which we dig deep into the unconscious and laboriously extract buried memories. In fact, there are no such processes in the Course. For all of that buried material is contained right here in this single flash of irritation. Really looking, deeply and honestly, into this one thought is how the unconscious is made conscious, how the ancient serpent of separation is uncoiled and undone.

Based on the above account, is your anger justified? No, for you have caused your own pain. It was caused by your projection, by your interpretation, not by your spouse's behavior. How can you blame him for what *you* did?

Does your anger bring happiness? Again, no. It brings guilt, and with it the entire spectrum of human ills. In fact, says the Course, your attraction to guilt is the underlying motivation behind your irritation at your spouse. The pain of guilt is the "prize" you are unconsciously hoping to collect from this incident (key idea 8.3)—and the prize you *will* collect.

The Course calls the process we have just described bringing darkness to light, or bringing illusions to truth. This means bringing your egoic beliefs out from under their masks and into full awareness to meet the light of reason. Doing this can take many forms. One form it may take is that of prayer, in which you bring your secret thoughts before the Holy Spirit (or Jesus) and "look upon them with Him" (as the passage below says), trusting that He will not condemn you, but rather lovingly free you from your self-condemnation:

> The Holy Spirit asks of you but this; bring to Him every secret you have locked away from Him. Open every door to Him, and bid Him enter the darkness and lighten it away. At your request He enters gladly. He brings the light to darkness if you make the darkness open to Him....Bring, therefore, all your dark and secret thoughts to Him, and look upon them with Him. He holds the light, and you the darkness. They cannot coexist when Both of you together look on them.[32]

The Course's most common method for bringing darkness to light is repeating right-minded thoughts to yourself. When darkness fills the room of your mind, you flip on the light switch by introducing thoughts of truth. There are literally hundreds of examples of such thoughts in the Course. For instance: "I am never upset for the reason I think."[33] "Do I want the problem or do I want the answer?"[34] "Only my condemnation injures me."[35] It is hard to imagine how much power these thoughts can have until you actually use them and discover for yourself.

This is not denial or waving a magic wand. It is a profound and delicate spiritual practice, mastered over much time and practice. You repeat the words slowly and confidently, while trying to go beyond them and drink in their meaning. While doing so you hold your mind in a relaxed alertness, without straining. You don't try to wrestle your anger away. You merely let the meaning in the words *shine* it away.

If your anger persists, you may need "to take several minutes and devote them to repeating the idea until you feel some sense of relief."[36] Or you may want to employ a process of inspired reasoning with yourself. The following is one such process, a favorite among Course students. It gives a series of gentle steps for coaxing a resistant mind to healing:

> *"At least I can decide I do not like what I feel now."*
> *"And so I hope I have been wrong."*
> *"I want another way to look at this."*
> *"Perhaps there is another way to look at this.*
> *What can I lose by asking?"* [37]

11.4. Step two: Let go of your perception; have a little willingness for the Holy Spirit to remove it and replace it with truth.

Whatever method from the Course you use, the goal is to come to a point of clarity, in which you realize that you simply have no use for this perception. This way of seeing the situation does not serve you. And it is not true. You will come to see your anger not as a sacred right, or a delicious but forbidden treat, but as "a wholly worthless thing, a but imagined source of guilt and pain."[38]

At that point, you will have carried out the first step—identifying the cause. You will have identified your *interpretation* as the cause of your *pain*. From this recognition will naturally flow a choice, a decision: to give up your angry interpretation. This, of course, is the second step—letting go of the cause—which follows quite logically and almost automatically from the first.

It is important to note that you reach this decision without any reference to the details of the situation. You don't have to know why your spouse left his stuff strewn all over the kitchen. You don't have to understand how good his intentions were and how understandable were his excuses. You don't need an accurate history of the situation, going back to when the two of you met. All of these assume that if the details were configured in a certain way, anger really would make sense. Instead, in the context of this one situation, you have made a decision about anger in *all* situations. You have made a decision about anger itself. You have in effect decided that anger is by nature an invalid emotion that rests on a wrong interpretation. In the words of the Course, you have realized that "anger is *never* justified."[39]

On your own, however, you are literally unable to flush anger completely out of your mind. Remember, you made an entire attacking world to convince yourself that anger *is* justified (key idea 8.2). Everything you see is evidence for this, planted there by you. Nearly everyone you talk to is a lawyer hired by you to argue anger's case. You have purposefully constructed a world in which you are sequestered from the light of God, the very evidence that would reveal anger to be invalid. So even though part of your mind may like the idea that anger is never justified, another part of your mind remains unconvinced.

In this divided state you cannot rid yourself of anger. And you are not expected to:

> But remember salvation is not needed by the saved. You are not called upon to do what one divided still against himself would find impossible. Have little faith that wisdom could be found in such a state of mind. But be you thankful that only little faith is asked of you. What but a little faith remains to those who still believe in sin?[40]

If you have tried and tried and tried to force your mind into a kinder, more loving state, the above words may feel like rain in the desert. You can stop forcing yourself and just let the healing rain fall. Would it be fair of God to ask of you what you cannot do? "And where would justice be if He demanded of the ones obsessed with the idea of punishment that they lay it aside, unaided, and perceive it is not true?"[41] Therefore, God does not ask that you rid yourself of anger (which is intimately related to the idea of punishment). He only asks for "a little faith." This is the concept of "the little willingness," a familiar and beloved idea to students of the Course.

What exactly does a little willingness mean? Let's take it one word at a time. The "willingness" means that you are willing to let the Holy Spirit *remove* your wrong interpretation and *replace* it with His thinking. "Your part is only to offer Him a little willingness to let Him remove all fear and hatred, and to be forgiven."[42] This is not your sole desire; you are not one hundred percent sure about this. But you are agreeable to it; you will allow it. This brings us to the word "little." How agreeable do you have to be? How much is a "little" willingness? The following passage answers this:

> You need not give it to Him wholly willingly, for if you could you had no need of Him. But this He needs; that you prefer He take it than that you keep it for yourself alone.[43]

All you have to do is want Him to take your thought of anger *more* than you want to keep it. You just have to tip the scales, to have one side outweigh the other. We might call this the 51 percent theory. It is all right, then, to have 49 percent of your mind still wanting to keep your anger. You don't have to feel ashamed about this 49 percent, nor pretend it is not there, nor try to shove it out the back of your head, nor hide it in a closet. In fact, openly admitting your remaining unwillingness actually *aids* the process, as the following passage says:

> And your willingness need not be complete because His is perfect. It is His task to atone for your unwillingness by His perfect faith, and it is His faith you share with Him there. Out of your recognition of your unwillingness for your release, His perfect willingness is given you.[44]

When you acknowledge your unwillingness without shame, He makes up the remaining 49 percent with His perfect willingness, which you actually unite with and share. His perfect willingness becomes yours. In sum, "the little willingness" means that you can stop trying to make yourself good and holy and just focus on becoming, on balance, agreeable to receiving the Holy Spirit's gift. As the Course says in a well-known line, "Trust not your good intentions. They are not enough. But trust implicitly your willingness, whatever else may enter."[45]

Another aspect of this second step is admitting that you do not know how to look at the situation. We discussed this in key idea 9.5. You invite the Holy Spirit by acknowledging that you simply do not have a clue about what anything, including this, means. This not knowing is a major theme in the Course. It also clarifies those many Course practices in which you actively affirm the truth (for instance, Lesson 35: "My mind is part of God's. I am very holy"). Those affirmations are not an act of holding in your mind a truth that you already know. They are really an invitation for the reality behind the words to overshadow your mind and illumine it. They are a prayer to be filled with what you do not know now, but long to discover.

In fact, all the aspects of this second step—choice, decision, little willingness, admission of ignorance, and desire to know—are in essence a prayer, an appeal to a wisdom that far transcends your own. "The understanding that you need comes not of you, but from a larger Self [the Christ in you], so great and holy that He could not doubt His innocence."[46] Only the Holy Spirit knows the Christ in you and therefore only He is absolutely certain—without the remotest hint of doubt and without ever wavering—that anger is never justified. Your small part is simply to give Him permission to finish what you started. Your prayer to Him need not be explicit—the choice itself is an implicit prayer—but it can help to make it explicit. The Course provides this excellent example: "Say to the Holy Spirit only, 'Decide for me,' and it is done."[47]

11.5. Step three: The Holy Spirit will replace your perception with His; He will give your mind a miracle.

Once you have completed steps one and two, step three will be done for you:

> The first two steps in this process require your cooperation.
> The final one does not. Your images have already been
> replaced. By taking the first two steps, you will see that this
> is so.[48]

The Holy Spirit is the One Who performs step three. He removes your old perception and replaces it with His new perception. As the above passage says, He did this long ago, at the dawn of time (key idea 3.6). But you will experience it as happening now. All at once you will find yourself seeing the exact same situation through completely different eyes.

This difference can be truly amazing. One of my favorite lines that expresses this difference is this: "A shadow figure who attacks becomes a brother giving you a chance to help."[49] Imagine that! The same situation given an opposite interpretation. When you looked before at the mess in the kitchen you saw your spouse thoughtlessly attacking you for the billionth time. As he did you saw him wearing the masks of all those shadowy figures who had done all those inconsiderate things to you since the day you were born. Now this perception has been literally turned upside down. Rather than a shadow figure, you see your spouse as a *brother*, as someone closely related to you and sharing a common Father. And rather than attacking you, he is actually giving you a gift. He is *giving* you a chance to help him and so to free yourself (we will discuss this concept in Chapter 13). How do you help him? Through the exact process we have been describing, through seeing him as a brother and not a shadow figure.

This healing of your mind is the miracle:

> A miracle is a correction introduced into false thinking by me [by Jesus, through whom the Holy Spirit works]. It acts as a catalyst, breaking up erroneous perception and reorganizing it properly. This places you under the Atonement principle, where perception is healed.[50]

It is a common understanding among Course students that the miracle is a shift in perception. It would be more accurate to say, however, that the miracle *shifts* perception.[51] It shifts the way we see a situation from ego to Spirit, from fear to love.

The best way to understand this miracle, I believe, is as a psychological version of the traditional biblical miracle. In the Bible, Jesus came to people afflicted with various diseases and healed them, no matter how serious their disease appeared to be. If you can simply transpose that miraculous healing from the body to the mind, from diseased tissue to diseased *perception*, you have a good idea what the Course is saying about the miracle. It is an *inner* miracle (though it may have a tremendous impact on external situations). And so, just as Jesus in the Bible healed hopelessly ill bodies, so he promises in the Course that he will heal our impossibly confused minds:

> I raised the dead by knowing that life is an eternal attribute of everything that the living God created. Why do you believe it is harder for me to inspire the dis-spirited or to stabilize the unstable?[52]

To change our dreary picture of the world is indeed a miracle, for it is something we cannot do for ourselves. We constantly rearrange our surface interpretations of things. For instance, we decide that losing our watch was okay because we can get another or that someone's attack was understandable given his own prior victimization. Yet though we change our perception of the details, we still seem solidly stuck in the deeper rules by which we perceive, rules which say attack is real, bodies are real, fear is rational. We might think that only a miracle could free us of these deeper rules, and we would be right.[53] That is what the miracle is for.

This miracle behaves in truly miraculous ways. It simply does not matter how warped our perception is. A murderous rage can be healed just as easily as a fleeting thought of disapproval. For the miracle comes as a pure gift, not as a carefully measured reward for good behavior. It does not hold itself back because of our inner flaws and serious personality defects. It does not come in spite of these flaws and defects. It comes *because* of them. It comes simply because the Son had a need, and the Father answered. We need only let that answer come, and we will walk the same world and look upon the same scenes, yet experience them entirely differently. For in the same clashing forms we will see a whole new meaning, a meaning as far removed from our old meaning as a quiet garden is from a deafening battlefield.

> When you have looked on what seemed terrifying, and seen it change to sights of loveliness and peace; when you have looked on scenes of violence and death, and watched them change to quiet views of gardens under open skies, with clear, life-giving water running happily beside them in dancing brooks that never waste away; who need persuade you to accept the gift of vision?[54]

Twelve

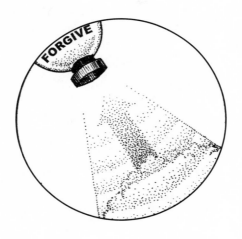

We heal our perception by forgiving the
world for what it did not do.

Twelve

After all of these chapters, all the necessary pieces are in place and we are ready at last to approach the Course's central teaching. Our ears have been prepared to hear a new message, a fresh antidote to the disease of humanity. In this message we can hear the distant strains of the forgotten song rising in celebration. This message is "the trumpet of awakening that sounds around the world. The dead awake in answer to its call. And those who live and hear this sound will never look on death."[1] What is this message?

12.1. Forgiveness is the answer to our separated condition.

"Forgiveness is the key to happiness."

Here is the answer to your search for peace. Here is the key to meaning in a world that seems to make no sense. Here is the way to safety in apparent dangers that appear to threaten you at every turn, and bring uncertainty to all your hopes of ever finding quietness and peace. Here are all questions answered; here the end of all uncertainty ensured at last.[2]

"Forgiveness is the central theme"[3] of *A Course in Miracles*. Forgiveness is the Course's method for bringing us home. "Forgiveness offers everything I want,"[4] says Lesson 122. This same lesson goes on to proclaim, "Here is the answer!"[5] and then sounds this same proclamation over and over, like the joyous pealing of a bell of freedom, "Here is the answer!" After so many eons of toil and struggle, at long last, here is the answer.

Forgiveness is not only the most important concept in the Course; it is the summary idea that ties together the Course's whole way of salvation, "holding all its parts in meaningful relationships, the course it runs directed and its outcome sure."[6] The following passage gives us a single sentence which it claims summarizes the Course's teaching, our practice, and the Holy Spirit's entire plan for salvation:

> Forgive the world, and you will understand that everything that God created cannot have an end, and nothing He did not create is real. In this one sentence is our course explained. In this one sentence is our practicing given its one direction. And in this one sentence is the Holy Spirit's whole curriculum specified exactly as it is.[7]

This idea that forgiveness is *the* answer to everything strikes nearly everyone as odd at first. How can this be? How can forgiveness be the whole solution?

Actually, the preceding eleven chapters of this book have been carefully designed to reveal the answer to this one question. Really grasping what those chapters said would make what I am about to say already clear. Really understanding them would reveal that forgiveness is the one key that fits all the locks. Let us, therefore, recap those chapters:

1. We started out in God's perfect, pristine reality that could never be tainted or marred.
2. We believe that we attacked this reality, tore our mind out of its oneness and made the world of time and space.
3. This separation, however, did not really occur, for reality cannot be changed. It happened only in our dreams while we slept safely in Heaven.
4. Our attack simply circled back and attacked our own state of mind. We believed we had sinned, had corrupted our original purity. We consequently became consumed with guilt and fear.
5. We then projected our sins, making them appear to strike us from the outside, from an attacking world. The cruel world, rather than our own choice to separate, now seemed to be the cause of our suffering.
6. Our surface experience is therefore one of being an innocent self unfairly treated by an attacking world. The world seems to

cause how we feel, and so we spend our days trying to rearrange it in an effort to thwart its attacks and seize its treasures.

7. This "innocent" program of rearranging externals, however, is driven by an unconscious rage. We believe that the sinful world has ruthlessly stolen our peace and happiness, giving us a "right" to retaliation and revenge.

8. Yet the attacking world we perceive is not real. It is the projection of our own mind. Its purpose is to give our ego an excuse to keep attacking. The ego is driven to attack, for that is how it collects more guilt, and thereby maintains the ancient illusion of separation from God.

9. The Holy Spirit has an answer to this illusion, an answer our minds could never provide.

10. His answer is that it never happened, we never sinned, we never corrupted our original innocence. To realize this and awaken in Heaven we need only relinquish our inner blocks.

11. Letting go of our blocks means letting go of our *perception* of the world, a perception which comes entirely from our own projection.

And what exactly is this perception we must let go of? How *do* we perceive the world? It is right there in points 5, 6, 7 and 8. We perceive an *attacking* world, a world which "demands" of us the very angry, defensive reactions that reinforce our guilt. We saw just how pervasive this perception is in the exercise we did in 5.7, where we defined something attacking you as "anything that seems to arise from outside your choice in this moment, that is weighing on your peace of mind right now, so that were that thing changed or absent, you would feel better now." This perception is present in all of us, from the fury of the murderer all the way up to the spiritual master who must separate himself from an impure world, and who sees himself plagued by failing disciples and by competing teachers.

The perception of an attacking world seems so obvious, so inescapable. Yet this perception is what causes our anger, which in turn produces our guilt, which in turn makes us feel separate from God. This single perception, then, is what makes us feel like sinners, split off from the Holy One. This single perception is what keeps us from realizing that our identity stands totally unmarred and perfect, and that Heaven remains the only reality there is.

To find salvation, then, all we must do is relinquish this one all-pervasive perception. And that relinquishment is what the Course calls *forgiveness*. This definition is so different than the conventional definition that we will need to get very clear on it. We can define Course-based forgiveness in this way:

> To forgive is to give up the false perception that someone
> is guilty of attacking and wounding you, in the recognition
> that he could neither wound your reality with attack nor
> corrupt *his* reality with guilt, for reality is changeless.

In contrast, conventional forgiveness, of course, does assume that the other person is guilty of attacking and wounding you. This is such a fundamental difference that it makes you wonder why the Course even uses the term "forgiveness." The reason is that the essence of conventional forgiveness is the giving up of resentment and retaliation, and that is exactly what Course-based forgiveness aims for. It simply accomplishes this goal through different means. Conventional forgiveness, while retaining the perception that someone really attacked and wounded you, tries to let go of the bad feelings that stem from that perception. Course-based forgiveness lets go of those bad feelings by letting go of the perception that causes them, the perception that a real attack occurred. We'll discuss this contrast in more depth later.

If Course-based forgiveness means giving up the perception of being attacked, then it represents the reversal of our whole way of being. As we saw in earlier chapters, our basic mental/emotional posture is one of feeling that our self hasn't been treated right by the world. To varying degrees, we are all walking around nursing one giant grievance which says, "The world has not done right by me." Our basic stance, then, is one of *unforgiveness*.

This means that forgiveness is not a sometimes solution. It is not some special medication we pull out occasionally and apply to a specific kind of wound. It is the direct reversal of our global state of being. It is the alternative to our basic mental/emotional posture. It is the undoing of our fundamental mood. Through forgiveness we let go of the one perception that contains all of the ego's DNA, the one perception through which we perpetually give birth to the illusion of separation. Through forgiveness, we let go of our ancient reflex of recoiling from God.

12.2. Forgiveness is the Course's unique and original message, yet is also the heart of the Holy Spirit's message to humanity.

As I said earlier, forgiveness is the Course's unique and original method for total spiritual awakening. To my knowledge, no path or teacher has ever taught that we awaken from the dream of separateness into formless transcendental reality by letting go of the fallacious perception that others have attacked and wounded us (along with the attendant emotions of anger and resentment).

I think that all religions agree that forgiving those who have wronged us is a good thing. Every major tradition realizes that anger and resentment poison one's own mind and keep one chained to the past. Yet (apart from the Course) I have never heard forgiveness recommended as a direct path to the heights of God-realization. If mentioned at all, it seems often to be regarded as one of the outer fruits of a truly spiritual life, or as part of the ethical training one does on the lower rungs of the spiritual ladder, before one is ready to scale the true mystical heights.

Along these lines, I have found it very revealing to look up forgiveness in *The Encyclopedia of Religion*. This is a comprehensive and masterful encyclopedia which had the great scholar Mircea Eliade as its editor in chief. It contains thousands of entries on virtually every conceivable topic in world religion. Most of the entry titles are so obscure that they would be familiar only to the specialist (the first three entries, for instance, are "Isaac Abarbanel," "Abbahu," and "Abbaye"). Yet there is no entry on forgiveness. There isn't even a subheading on forgiveness within any of the entries. In the fifteen volumes of the encyclopedia, there are two hundred passing references to variations on the word "forgiveness." Over 80 percent of these are about *receiving* forgiveness, from God, the gods, the church, the community, the pope, the king, other people, etc. Only thirty refer to one person *giving* forgiveness to another. Of these thirty, sixteen are about the ministry of Jesus, either about him giving forgiveness or about him teaching others to do so. If *The Encyclopedia of Religion* is any indication, the spiritual value of giving forgiveness is a very minor note in humanity's religions, a note that is primarily associated with the ministry of Jesus.

This makes it all the more notable that in the Course, giving forgiveness is *the* road to God. The Course sees forgiveness as the single lesson behind every stage of the spiritual journey, the content of every realization that lifts us closer to God. Forgiveness is what elevates us from the basest levels of human development, where we sit nursing old wounds and live to settle old scores. It is what frees us from a life lived solely for self and allows us to serve a whole that we now recognize as innocent and worthy of our love. According to the Course, our ability to forgive—rather than our belief in God—is what makes us one of God's messengers on this earth.[8] For its liberating power is how we set others free from their bonds—bonds forged from the iron of guilt.

On the higher levels of development, "Forgiveness offers wings to prayer."[9] It is what sweeps away the inner clouds of guilt that have obscured the Father, allowing our minds to soar into the formless regions of His Mind. Yet even as accomplished mystics we still will not completely comprehend the unearthly beauty of forgiveness. For it is "the final lesson,"[10] "the final goal of the curriculum."[11] Therefore, our final insight into the true nature of forgiveness will be our crowning realization along the path. In that moment, when we at last understand what forgiveness really means, we will be lifted out of this world and into Heaven.

What do we do with this uniqueness, with the newness of this message? This is a very delicate issue, because the Course sees other paths as its brothers on the same journey, and sees itself as simply one "form of the universal course."[12] Yes, it does claim it will save us time over traditions that imply that something must be done before we deserve salvation (see key idea 10.4). Yet even these are its brothers. In addition, there do exist spiritual paths whose central tenet is that nothing must be done for us to deserve God, that enlightenment is always already available.

Volumes could be written about the relationship between the Course and other spiritual paths. And I believe that much will be written, as future scholars seek to understand how the Course relates to other paths. For now, let me just elaborate a bit on what the Course itself says and implies. For this we will turn to a section entitled "The Circle of Atonement":

> Teachers of innocence, each in his own way, have joined together, taking their part in the unified curriculum of the Atonement.[13]

This is talking about teachers all over the world of different faiths, traditions, and philosophies. Even though these teachers are, by and large, not consciously joined, not outwardly cooperating (and perhaps even outwardly competing), they *are* joined. For they are members of the same global team, teaching the same "unified curriculum," united in the same goal and answering to the same Boss—the Holy Spirit (going, of course, by many different names). Further, they are *meant* to teach this curriculum differently, "each in his own way." "Each one teaches the message differently, and learns it differently,"[14] says this section elsewhere. Yet no matter how they teach it, the elixir in the teaching that actually awakens the dreamer is always the same. In all paths there is only one active ingredient. Regardless of differences in language, concept, theology, and technique, regardless of how the particular loaf of bread is constituted, it is always leavened by the same yeast. "And every teaching that points to this points straight to Heaven, and the peace of God."[15] What is this active ingredient?

> Everyone has a special part to play in the Atonement,
> but the message given to each one is always the same;
> *God's Son is guiltless.*[16]

This can be a shocking passage. For the Course is claiming to identify the universal message taught by the Holy Spirit to every prophet, messenger, mystic, and guru throughout history. Yet rather than capturing some common denominator within the world's traditions, something like Aldous Huxley's perennial philosophy, the Course inserts a summary of its own unique message! "God's Son is guiltless" is simply another way of talking about Course-based forgiveness. It means: "You can let go of the guilt you perceive in everyone, including yourself, because sin never happened, because everyone is still God's holy Son." And this is not the only place in which the Course locates its own message at the heart of the global program of salvation. Elsewhere, it calls "God's Son is guiltless" the central theme of the universal course[17]—the universal course being the real essence behind the thousands of paths in the world.

The Course is thus implying that the healing power of forgiveness has been flowing through all the great teachers and teachings. It has been the active ingredient in all paths, setting people free for centuries. Yet to some degree, it has been a *hidden* ingredient, working through teachings and teachers that for the most part have only indirectly acknowledged it.

How could this be? How could the great saints, sages, *rishis*, and rabbis of the ages embody this message, yet at least slightly mistranslate it? How could they have failed to clearly see that forgiveness is our only solution and unforgiveness our only problem? Here is the Course's answer:

> All blocks to the remembrance of God are forms of unforgiveness, and nothing else. This is never apparent to the patient, and only rarely so to the therapist. The world has marshalled all its forces against this one awareness, for in it lies the ending of the world and all it stands for.[18]

"The world has marshalled all its forces against this one awareness" because the world was *made* to keep this awareness from us. The world was made as a colossal brainwashing device, designed to pound into our heads a single illusion: that negative feelings are forced upon us from without, giving us just cause to feel anger. And it has worked. So flawless has been this illusion, so seamless its special effects, that even the world's great spiritual therapists have not fully grasped its nature. Even the greatest doctors of the soul have partially misdiagnosed the illness, so heavy has been the blanket of illusion and deception it has cast upon the world.

A Course in Miracles is subtly implying that it has penetrated through this veil more fully, that it has punched through its foggy layers more completely. This kind of thing does happen in human history. The truth does occasionally break through the clouds in a way it has not before. The Course is implying that it is just such a breakthrough. This would be quite natural from its standpoint. For it claims to be authored by the individual who was himself the first to break all the way through the clouds, the individual who is now the leader of the global salvation process. "[The Holy Spirit] has established Jesus as the leader in carrying out His plan since he was the first to complete his own part perfectly."[19]

But the Course never makes this claim of greater insight an overt one, and so we should not dwell on it. The important point is this: If you do happen to be a student of *A Course in Miracles*, you need not turn to other methods. Forgiveness is your heritage, the heart of your tradition. It is your way home, and so hold it very, very dear.

12.3. Conventional forgiveness, in which we forgive another for his sin against us, is not real forgiveness.

Course-based forgiveness is a difficult concept to comprehend. It simply does not fit within our normal framework, for that is the framework it is designed to undo. To grasp this new concept we must carefully distinguish it from conventional forgiveness, for it is a profoundly different idea.

What do we normally mean by forgiveness? To begin with, as I said above, conventional forgiveness assumes we have been sinned against. In Chapter 4 (key idea 4.2) we defined the idea of sin in two steps:

- An attack that attempts to do harm for the sake of selfish gain
- An attack that succeeds, that results in real harm

So, in this scenario, someone has intentionally attacked us for the purpose of gaining at our expense. And his attack has succeeded. We *have* been harmed and this person *has* gotten something out of it, either tangible or intangible. As a result of this sin, two things follow for the sinner (as we saw in Chapter 4):

- He is now truly guilty (4.3).
- He deserves to be punished (4.4).

Additional things follow for us, the victim (as we saw in Chapter 7). For we have been left unfairly deprived by this attack. Hence, to balance this out, to compensate us for our loss, justice grants us certain rights, victim's rights:

- The right to anger and resentment toward our attacker
- The right to restitution, to have restored to us what the attacker deprived us of
- The right to vengeance, the right to punish our attacker

These two sets of results (one for the sinner and one for the victim) follow with rigorous logic from the idea of sin. In fact, they are mirror images of each other. They go hand in glove. We have a right to anger because the sinner's guilt makes him deserving of anger. We have a right to restitution because he deserves to be stripped of what he unfairly took. We have a right to vengeance because he deserves to be punished.

This is where conventional forgiveness comes in. When I forgive in this way, I accept the entire picture we have just described, but simply give up the two sets of logical results that flow from the fact of sin. In effect, I say, "You did attack me for selfish gain. You did injure me and gain at my expense. You are a sinner, you are guilty, and you do deserve punishment. As a result, I am fully within my rights to resent you, to exact my pound of flesh, and to punish you. But I choose to forego my rights. I am giving up my resentment, my claim to compensation, and my right to punish you." Quite simply, conventional forgiveness means *letting the sinner escape his just deserts by giving up your victim's rights.*

And herein lies the problem. Does any of this make sense? If sin is real, its consequences follow with inexorable logic. As the Course says, "If sin is real, then punishment is just and cannot be escaped."[20] If sin is real, then you paid for your victim's rights fair and square. You paid with your loss, leaving you these rights as all you have left. Why on earth would you just give them up? And for the sake of a sinner who does not deserve your gift? The Course replies, "This is where the ego is forced to appeal to 'mysteries,' insisting that you must accept the meaningless to save yourself."[21] If sin is real, then forgiveness surely rests on some obscure, inscrutable mystery.

This is why forgiveness is normally such a strain. You feel, quite simply, like you are struggling to give the unjustified. The Course captures this feeling exactly when it says, "You conceive of pardon as a vain attempt to look past what is there; to overlook the truth, in an unfounded effort to deceive yourself by making an illusion true."[22] Further, because conventional forgiveness, by its very definition, is an unmerited gift, there is no logical mandate to give it consistently; only when the mood strikes you. Conventional forgiveness is "a charitable whim, benevolent yet undeserved, a gift bestowed at times, at other times withheld....It is an eccentricity, in which you sometimes choose to give indulgently an undeserved reprieve."[23]

Most important, by assuming the reality of sin, conventional forgiveness cannot really forgive. It cannot do the one thing it is meant to do. To forgive is to release all resentment and to set someone free of guilt and punishment. Yet resentment, guilt, and punishment are the logical products of the reality of sin. They follow from it like sound waves from an explosion. As long as you perceive the blast of sin, resentment will reverberate through your mind. As long as your attacker perceives this blast, guilt and fear of punishment will rumble through his mind. I am not saying that outside of the Course, no one ever really forgives. That would be ludicrous. There is something in the human heart that *wants* to forgive. The impulse to do so seems inherent in our nature. And as this impulse rises up, I think it often succeeds. It brings people to that miraculous state in which the resentment has vanished and they see the other person shining with innocence, cleansed of all stain. However, I think they reach this place over the *obstacle* of their conscious belief that they were genuinely hurt by an unfair attack. That deep impulse to forgive, when it succeeds, does so in spite of the thought system behind conventional forgiveness.

Because conventional forgiveness believes that sin is real, when you are "forgiven" within the limits of its thought system, you don't feel completely set free. If someone says to you, "Even though you are a sinner who deserves to suffer, I will graciously forego my right to punish you," do you really feel let off the hook? Don't you feel subtly (or not-so-subtly) attacked? The author of the Course, in fact, calls this "forgiveness-to-destroy."[24] In *The Song of Prayer* he delineates the following four varieties of this "forgiveness":

1. Forgiving someone to show how much better you are than he. Here you say, in effect, "My brother, you have injured me, and yet, because I am the better of the two, I pardon you my hurt."[25]
2. Forgiving someone because you are every bit the sinner that he is. You say that *both* of you "have been unworthy and deserve the retribution of the wrath of God."[26] Included in this category would be the common sentiment, "That's okay—I've done the exact same thing before."
3. Playing the martyr, in which you patiently suffer another's attack. "Behold, how good are you who bear with patience and with saintliness the anger and the hurt another gives, and do not show the bitter pain you feel."[27] This not only makes you feel holy, it sends a silent message of blame to your attacker.[28] We used to call this long-suffering. Now we call it codependence.
4. Forgiving someone on the condition that she do something for you: that she reform her ways, treat you better, do you a favor, etc. This says, in essence, "I will forgive you if you meet my needs, for in your slavery is my release."[29]

In these forms of conventional forgiveness, two things are evident. First, there is some ego payoff for you as the forgiver. By forgiving, you purchase either a favor or a sense of being saintly or a feeling of superiority. In short, you purchase specialness. Were it not for this reimbursement, why would you give up the victim's rights which you paid for in blood? Second, you are pronouncing a subtle accusation of sin. As we said, this accusation is the beginning premise of conventional forgiveness. But not only that, it is the hidden purpose as well. That is why it is called "forgiveness-to-destroy"—destruction is its purpose. This term implies that the underlying reason for conventional forgiveness is to attack under the guise of being merciful. This should sound familiar by now, for again and again we have seen the ego make war in disguise. Conventional forgiveness, then, is not an instrument of liberation. It is simply another part of the ego's overall program to attack in sheep's clothing, and so keep us in bondage and in hell.

12.4. Real forgiveness is a shift in perception, in which we let go of the perception that a sin occurred.

What, then, is this new kind of forgiveness, the forgiveness taught by *A Course in Miracles*? We defined it earlier as "giving up the false perception that someone is guilty of attacking and wounding you." In fact, our example in the last chapter—of letting go our perception of being attacked by the kitchen mess—was an example of Course-based forgiveness. Now, however, we will define it more completely.

In the last section we saw that a single thing gives birth to both the attacker's guilt and the victim's rights. A single thing makes forgiveness so unwarranted and such a strain. This single thing is the perception that *sin has occurred*. If, therefore, this one perception is in error, then all those consequences are groundless. There is no cause for guilt. No one deserves to suffer. There is no need for anger and resentment. Vengeance is totally uncalled for. And forgiveness is no strain at all. If sin is real, then all the world of suffering is inescapable. If sin is an illusion, then we can all go home, no questions asked, right now. The one justification for forgiveness—and the philosophical foundation of *A Course in Miracles*—is the complete *unreality* of sin:

> It is sin's unreality that makes forgiveness natural and wholly sane, a deep relief to those who offer it; a quiet blessing where it is received.[30]

Sin is impossible, and on this fact forgiveness rests upon a certain base more solid than the shadow world we see.[31]

Only if sin is unreal can our bitterness be lifted from our minds and replaced by the clear light of love. Only if sin is unreal can we completely absolve the other person, so that no trace of shame hangs over her head and haunts her footsteps. Only if sin is unreal can all its tragic consequences disappear into the nothingness from which they came. Therefore, only an approach to forgiveness based on the unreality of sin can promote genuine, *wholehearted* forgiveness.

This forgiveness entails a profound shift in perception, for our picture of any unpleasant situation is simply saturated with the perception of sin. Our picture of the world itself is saturated with this same perception. Everywhere we look we perceive injury due to unfair treatment. To let go of that perception would mean a revolution in our minds.

Now we can appreciate the stark difference between conventional forgiveness and Course-based forgiveness. The core foundation of one is the *reality* of sin; the core foundation of the other is the *unreality* of sin. One asks us to merely forego our "right" to resent and punish a particular attacker. The other asks for a basic change in how we perceive the nature of reality. Because Course-based forgiveness asks for a fundamental shift in perception—rather than just a foregoing of our "rights"—its effects are far more sweeping and dramatic. We will examine these effects over the next few chapters.

It is crucial to keep this difference in mind, both for new students *and* for those who have been trying to practice Course-based forgiveness for years. As long as you are still trying, still practicing, as long as forgiveness is not flowing effortlessly from you like a river of peace, then you are still confusing the two. You are finding forgiveness a strain because you think that sin is real. And so, even while you try to practice Course-based forgiveness, on an emotional level you feel stuck with the unsavory job of pardoning real crimes. "The major difficulty that you find in genuine forgiveness on your part is that you still believe you must forgive the truth [the "truth" of sin], and not illusions."[32] If you actively remember that your only job is to let go of your own self-made illusions, the process will go much quicker and easier.

12.5. The Course's thought system is one big rationale for the idea that sin is unreal and that forgiveness is justified.

At first, the forgiveness I am describing may sound excitingly easy. Yet sooner or later Course students discover that this forgiveness is no small task. Forgiveness will seem a slight challenge when someone forgets to use her turn signal. It will seem impossible when someone has (seemingly) demolished your life. The unreality of sin may simply be the hardest thing you ever learn. It will require a complete retraining of your mind. Along the way you will have to question literally everything you now believe. As the Course says, "To learn this course requires willingness to question every value that you hold."[33] To understand why the belief in sin is so deep-rooted, see if this logic make sense to you:

- Sin can only be unreal if real harm was never done.
- Harm can only have not been done in every situation if harm *itself* is unreal.
- Harm itself can only be unreal if all things that can *sustain* harm are unreal.
- All things that change can sustain harm—they can change in a negative direction.
- Everything in time changes, for change is the fabric of time.
- Therefore, unless time and everything within time is unreal, then harm can be done, sin is real, and forgiveness is not justified.

Sin can only be unreal if the world never existed. It can only be unreal if the primordial sin, the archetype for all the rest, never happened— *if the separation never occurred.* Now we can see the purpose of the Course's metaphysical foundation. We need those lofty, time-transcending ideas to justify letting go of our grievance over the most minor mess in the kitchen. We need them to make forgiveness fully *justified.* The Course's unique teaching of total, unconditional forgiveness only makes perfect sense within its particular metaphysical vision. That is the purpose of its entire thought system and every concept in it—to justify forgiveness.[34]

We need that justification badly. Unless forgiveness makes sense to us, we will simply have no reason to do it. A great deal of the Course's job is to make this new and difficult concept actually make sense to us. The Course is brilliant at doing this, giving us flawlessly logical reasons for its validity. Its arguments are so persuasive, so reasonable, they can turn our whole mind-set upside-down. They can make forgiveness seem like the only sane response, and make everything that used to seem reasonable look crazy.

The rest of this chapter will be devoted to examining just a few of the justifications the Course gives for forgiveness. They will take the form of statements pulled from the Course that I've slightly reworded. These statements, in turn, are offered as actual spiritual practices, as bright lamps we switch on when the darkness of anger fills our mind (as we described in key idea 11.3). The Course says, "When the temptation to attack rises to make your mind darkened and murderous, remember you *can* see the battle from above."[35] By repeating the following statements slowly, again and then again, while concentrating on their words and letting their meaning sink deeply inside, we *are* seeing the battle from above.

I cannot be hurt, and do not want to show my brother anything except my wholeness.[36]

In trying to forgive, the first difficulty we come smack up against is the "fact" that we have been hurt. As we said above, sin can only be unreal if it has no effect, if no harm was done. But how can that be? We feel the sting of someone's words, we experience the emotional wound. Further, *physical* harm may have been caused. Maybe our valuables were stolen. Maybe our face got punched. Damage has been done, or so it appears.

We have learned, however, that our experience is caused by our own minds, not by what happens outside of us. We experience hurt because we mentally *identify* with some form that has been hurt—our image, our status, our valuables, our face. We see that form as part of us, and so *its* damage appears to be *our* injury. Hence, we *experience* injury; we feel hurt.

Without question you can identify with what can be hurt. The question is, can *you* be hurt? Can the one who is doing the identifying be injured? To answer this, we must know who you are. According to the Course (as we saw in key ideas 3.4 and 10.2), you are an ageless, eternal spirit, beyond time and space. God's loving power brought you into being and holds you there exactly as He created you. To hurt you, then, something would have to overpower God. And how is *that* going to happen? Therefore, says the Course, "The Thought God holds of you is like a star, unchangeable in an eternal sky."[37]

> Completely unaffected by the turmoil and the terror of the
> world, the dreams of birth and death that here are dreamed,
> the myriad of forms that fear can take; quite undisturbed,
> the Thought God holds of you remains exactly as it always
> was. Surrounded by a stillness so complete no sound of
> battle comes remotely near, it rests in certainty and perfect
> peace.[38]

Now imagine that this majestic star looked down on our distant
speck of a planet and identified with its little dramas, and felt wounded
by its tiny battles. Could the star *really* be injured by this viewing experience? Could this cause it to stop being a star? And could you be hurt,
ever again, if you realized that you *are* this star, "unchangeable in an
eternal sky"? And once you had this wondrous realization, how difficult
would forgiveness be then?

I cannot be unfairly treated. For I am deprived only by myself.[39]

So we cannot *actually* be hurt. Yet even then, if others could force us
to have *feelings* of hurt, that would be cause for resentment. Most of the
previous chapters, however, have been arguments for the Course's view
that our pain is caused by nothing other than our own mind. Many
Workbook lessons have this as their theme, including Lesson 338, "I am
affected only by my thoughts," and Lesson 281, "I can be hurt by nothing but my thoughts." This simple idea runs so counter to our normal
perspective that the Course states it in many ways, as plainly and directly as it possibly can.[40] So important is this single concept that the Course
calls it "the secret of salvation":

> The secret of salvation is but this: That you are doing
> this unto yourself. No matter what the form of the attack,
> this still is true. Whoever takes the role of enemy and of
> attacker, still is this the truth. Whatever seems to be the
> cause of any pain and suffering you feel, this is still true.[41]

Why is this idea the secret of salvation? Because it *is* forgiveness.
How can you blame someone else if it was you who caused yourself
pain? How can feel unfairly treated when you realize that you have been
deprived only by yourself?

Forgiving [so-and-so] is the natural reaction to distress that rests on error, and thus calls for help.[42]

When you are attacked, you generally respond as if the other person has taken something from you. Somewhere in your mind, you assume that he has gained something at your expense, even if all he has gained is the internal satisfaction of taking you down a peg. Yet if he has truly gained, then he does not deserve your forgiveness, for he is evil. Only evil feeds off the suffering of others. Only evil takes delight in causing others pain. And evil, if it is real, does not deserve forgiveness.

A Course in Miracles, however, argues for another view of what is going on in your attacker's mind. It asks you to see two calls existing in his mind, a surface call and a deeper call. Regarding the surface call, the Course more or less grants your current view of things. It acknowledges that, in attacking you, your brother is issuing a naked "call to war."[43] In this war, he hopes to loot your humble village and bring home the spoils. For these spoils are what he thinks the *deeper call* within him craves. He thinks the call of his being is for the sense of triumph and vindication he hopes to gain from his attack on you.

Yet he is seriously wrong, for the deeper call within him couldn't be more opposite. In truth, this deeper call asks only for the things of God. It wants only to be your friend, to be part of you. It wants only to unite with you in innocence and peace. It yearns to find love, in all its holiness and joy. Your brother's deeper call, in other words, is as pure as the heart of any saint.

This puts your attacker in a real bind, for now his surface call is totally at odds with his deeper call. His surface call is pushing away love, the very thing his deeper call is calling *for*. It's as if, while the captain is looting the village and preparing to bring the spoils back to the king, the king is sitting in his palace wanting only to befriend that village, to shower it with his blessings and forge a bond with it that will last for generations. How do you think the king will feel when he finds out what the captain has done?

That is how the deeper call within your brother feels as it observes his surface attack on you. Deep within your brother's mind is the pain that comes from not finding the love he truly wants, as well as the guilt that comes from making war. In this deep place he knows that he is ill and needs healing. Yet he fears that he is beyond hope, that his sins have made him unworthy of redemption. Thus, his secret prayer is that someone will come along and cure him and grant him absolution.

He has pinned those hopes on you. Even as his surface call makes war upon you, his deeper call is asking you for help. It is asking you to show him a love without attack. It is calling to you "for mercy and [for] release from all the fearful images he holds of what he is and of what you must be."[44] It is asking for your patience in the face of his mistakes. It is asking for your forgiveness.

Your role is, quite simply, to see beyond the surface call to war, to see the deeper call for help and healing, the call for love. Again and again the Course urges you to rise to this calling:

> You are deceived if you believe [your brother wants] disaster and disunity and pain. Hear not the call for this....But listen, rather, to the deeper call beyond it that appeals for peace and joy.[45]

> How wrong are you who fail to hear the call that echoes past each seeming call to death, that sings behind each murderous attack and pleads that love restore the dying world.[46]

This completely reverses the situation as you saw it. You thought your brother gained from his attack on you, leaving you in dire need of compensation. You thought *you* were the one in need. In fact, he lost from his attack. It failed to wound you, but it did wound him. Therefore, he is the one in need, not you. And something deep in his mind calls out to you to meet his need, to cure his sickness, to forgive his sin.

All of this is summarized in our beginning statement, "Forgiving [name] is the natural reaction to distress that rests on error, and thus calls for help." Your brother's attack was not a sin, it was just an error, because it failed to answer his deeper call. As a result, he is in distress. His deeper need has not been met and so he feels lonely and he feels guilty. What would be your natural reaction to seeing this? Would it be retaliating and adding to his guilt and loneliness? Or would it be shining them both away by offering him the balm of your forgiveness?

You are the dreamer, not the dream figure.[47]

We now have dealt with two crucial aspects of the logic of sin: the idea that harm was done, and the idea that my attacker actually gains from my harm. Let us now dispel a third aspect. This aspect says that because of these two things—because my attacker *gained* from causing my *injury*—he has made himself guilty. He has corrupted his nature, transforming himself into a sinner who deserves only to suffer. The awful power of his sin was first unleashed on me, but then it turned on its own master and sunk its teeth into him, tearing apart his purity and destroying his soul.

This is more than just a colorful image. It captures what I believe really happened. In my eyes, my attacker has *become* sin. He has turned into a foul thing, hideous to look upon. Sheer honesty forces me to condemn him.

That is why the above statement is a favorite practice of mine. It is meant to be silently spoken to the person who has angered me—or to anyone, since everyone has displeased me to some degree. Saying "You are the dreamer, not the dream figure" instantly changes my perception of anyone to whom I say it. It reminds me that what my eyes see is no more than a figure in a dream. All the things I judge about this person— his body, his behavior, his personality—are just aspects of that illusory figure, and he is none of those things. He is not the dream figure. He is the divine dreamer, who idly pretends that he is a human being named so-and-so from such-and-such a place that never existed. In truth, he is the Son of a transcendental Father, who merely has a bad case of amnesia and thinks he is the son of a mere earthly father. He is the Christ Himself with delusions of littleness, totally convinced of the ridiculous notion that he is penned in by physical limitations and past misdeeds. And that is why he is in pain. He is an infinite spirit in pain over his delusion of being finite, a holy being in anguish over his dream of being sinful. Yet nothing he dreams can alter in the slightest who he is, for he is as God created him.

In short, this idea reminds me that I have literally no idea of the magnitude of the person who stands before me. As the author of the Course says of the psychotherapist, "[The patient] who calls on him is far beyond his understanding."[48] One sight of this being would be the happiest moment of my life. One brief glimpse would lift me into ecstasy. In a beautiful line, the Course says that if I really saw this person as he is, I would be so overcome with this vision of sanctity that I "could scarce refrain from kneeling at his feet."[49] I thought this person had mutated into a sinner. Now I can barely hold myself back from kneeling at his feet.

Forgiving [name] keeps my rights from being sacrificed.[50]

We have seen that conventional forgiveness means sacrificing my victim's rights. And oh what a sacrifice that feels like! We are not going to really give up our anger and resentment until we realize that we are not giving up anything. How is this possible?

First, we can realize that we have no victim's rights. At this point we have knocked all of the pegs out from under those supposed rights. We were not harmed by someone else, either in reality or in our feelings. Our attacker was not gaining at our expense, but was calling for love in a mistaken form. His attack did not corrupt his identity and turn him into a guilty sinner. The entire picture that gave rise to our victim's rights is utterly false.

Second, to claim our victim's rights (to anger, to compensation, and to vengeance) is to sacrifice our *true* rights. What are these true rights?

> You have the right to all the universe [a synonym for the Kingdom]; to perfect peace, complete deliverance from all effects of sin, and to the life eternal, joyous and complete in every way, as God appointed for His holy Son.[51]

It may help to turn this sentence into a series of first person statements and say them to yourself: "I have the *right* to all the universe. I have the *right* to perfect peace. I, [name], have the *right* to complete deliverance...," etc. These are the rights you *really* want to keep. Yet—and this is the crucial question—can you really believe these rights are yours while you hold onto your victim's rights? Can you say with conviction, "I am totally justified in my rage and retribution, yet I also have the right to complete deliverance from all effects of sin, and to the life eternal, joyous and complete in every way"? I don't think you can. According to the Course, the only way to know you are entitled to forgiveness is to extend this right to others. "If you can see your brother merits pardon, you have learned forgiveness is your right as much as his."[52] Hence, our above statement: *Forgiving [name] keeps my rights from being sacrificed.*

"The past is over. It can touch me not."[53]

We forgive people for things they did in the past. Yet the past is gone. It no longer exists. If we let this one fact sink deeply in, then forgiving past sins—which no longer exist—would be an easy thing.

We all acknowledge that the past does not exist. Why, then, does forgiveness seem so hard? The reason, I believe, is that we keep the past alive in our mind through memory. The past seems highly relevant to us because, even though it is gone, its *effects* are apparently still here. Its effects, in fact, seem to be *all* that is here. The present itself seems to be the effect of the past. Thus, although the sins themselves may be gone, before they left, it seems, they left us our *life*, the one we have now and regret. If it weren't for past sins, we believe, we'd have a better-looking spouse, a higher-paying job, and a psyche that didn't need therapy.

However, if the past is truly over, how can it have effects? How can the nonexistent cause anything? The Course teaches that our present is caused not by our past, but by our present choices of how we perceive the world. All the things our brother did to us in the past are gone, and their effects are gone with them. They literally can touch us not. If we believed this, if we truly believed this, would forgiveness be such a difficult thing?

I never hate my brother for his sins, but only for my own.[54]

The foregoing points have attempted to demonstrate that the entire picture of sin—from beginning to end—is completely false. It does not exist in reality. If it did not come from objective reality, where *did* it come from? The answer is obvious by now: We made it up. We projected it. As we saw in the last chapter, projection makes perception.

To be more specific, our perception of *sin* comes from projecting our own sins onto the world (see key idea 5.6). The real reason we suffer is that our sins are attacking our peace of mind from within. Through projection, however, we see our sins as if they were in our brother, attacking us from the outside. As an example, let's say that you feel terribly guilty for not being more attentive to your aging mother, and this guilt undermines your peace of mind. However, you don't realize that this is why you feel drained and depressed. You think the reason is that other people don't give you enough credit. Yet you wouldn't feel so vulnerable to their lack of praise unless what they said mirrored what you were secretly telling yourself. You hear in their voices your own silent self-accusation. When they say, "Why didn't you finish that project on time?" what you actually hear is your own voice saying, "How can I be so negligent after all Mother did for me?" Yes, you are angry at them, but are you hating them for their sins, or for your own?

This realization is forgiveness, because it automatically releases others from the sins that you laid on them. The Course ascribes the most powerful effects to this single thought, as we can see in the following passage:

> There is first one thing that must be overlearned. It must become a habit of response so typical of everything you do that it becomes your first response to all temptation, and to every situation that occurs. Learn this, and learn it well, for it is here delay of happiness is shortened by a span of time you cannot realize.[55]

So, there is "one thing" that we must take and so excessively overlearn that it becomes a knee-jerk reflex, our automatic first response to every single thing that happens. If we do, we will speed the arrival of happiness by "a span of time you cannot realize." (One wonders just how much time is a span we cannot realize.) What, then, is this "one thing"? What is the idea to which this amazing counsel is attached? It is this: "You never hate your brother for his sins, but only for your own."[56]

I forgive you for what you did not do.[57]

This is the grand conclusion of the logic of forgiveness. We have seen that all the components of the sin I perceived were not real, but were a projection of my own mind. Therefore, that thing I have been resenting you over, and struggling to forgive you for, you never even did. True, perhaps your mouth did say those things, perhaps your body did perform those behaviors. But those forms had no meaning in themselves. They happened only in a dream. My experience of what you did to me came from the meaning I gave it, and I made up that meaning. Now I let my interpretation go. That is true forgiveness. "Forgiveness recognizes what you thought your brother did to you has not occurred."[58] The following passage says it perfectly:

> Salvation does not lie in being asked to make unnatural responses which are inappropriate to what is real. Instead, it merely asks that you respond appropriately to what is not real by not perceiving what has not occurred.[59]

The heart of the Course's philosophy of forgiveness is contained in this simple statement: "Be willing to forgive the Son of God for what he did not do."[60] Not for what he *did*, but for what he did *not* do. In the midst of anger, these can be the hardest words in the world to hear. Yet without them, does forgiveness really make sense? Does it make sense to overlook what is really there? That is not health; that is *denial*.

"Be willing to forgive the Son of God for what he did not do." Think of the power of these words. Think of their implications for life as we know it. What stands in the way of our love for others but our perception that they have done something that makes them less than worthy? If they never did what we thought, if they are still as pure and holy as God created them, what could keep our heart from overflowing with love for them?

Forgiveness rests on the idea that in every person and in every relationship there is a sanctity, there is a shining spark of eternal value. Isn't this what motivates us to forgive people? We sense something in that person and in that relationship that is too sacred to be obscured by some passing offense. Why lose sight of this priceless gift, we say to ourselves, for the sake of a few careless words said in a moment of anger? Why not just let those words go and keep hold of the gift instead? Why not bury the hatchet?

The Course's teaching takes this universal human sentiment and gives it a powerful philosophical foundation. This shining spark, buried in that person and in that relationship, is no spark at all. It is the blazing light of reality itself. It is the only thing that is real. And it is so real that nothing can mar it in any way. All of the things that would block out its light—the unkind words, the inconsiderate deeds—are not only irrelevant, they are nothing. All of the character flaws that would sully its purity are mere dreams. All of the sins that would corrupt its innocence are powerless before its glory. All of these represent no "more than a passing cloud upon a sky eternally serene."[61]

And that is why we can overlook them all. That is why forgiveness makes sense. It doesn't have to struggle to overlook what is real. It simply overlooks illusory shadows, in the faith that beyond them is a reality so perfect and so holy that no spot of darkness could stand before its infinite brilliance. Forgiveness doesn't deny what is really there. It just wipes the grime off our own smeared lenses. When we have thus cleansed the doors of perception, we will realize that the serene face of reality has always been lit with joy, that all is very, very well, that the separation indeed *never occurred*.

Forgiveness, then, is what returns our minds to the awareness of a changeless, perfect reality. As we have seen, our perception of sin in our brother is the core of the dense cloud of insanity that we call this world. Therefore, to say the words, "Be willing to forgive the Son of God for what he did not do" is to dispel the very foundation of this world. "By them it disappears, and all things seen within its misty clouds and vaporous illusions vanish as these words are spoken."[62] And as these tattered clouds are swept away, we see at last the unspeakable grandeur that has awaited us, ever fresh, undimmed by all the eons of time, a glorious sunrise that will never stop rising.

Thirteen

Extending forgiveness to others reveals
to us that we too are forgiven. This
becomes our one function.

Thirteen

Forgiveness leads us back up the ladder which the separation led us down. "Beginning here, salvation will proceed to change the course of every step in the descent to separation, until all the steps have been retraced, the ladder gone, and all the dreaming of the world undone."[1] In the remaining chapters we will follow this ascent step by step, as forgiveness releases our loving extension to others (this chapter), unites us with them (next chapter), opens the eyes of Christ in us and reveals the real world (Chapter 15), and brings the entire Sonship to the place where God will lift us back to Him (Chapter 16).

13.1. Forgiveness releases us from our fixation on our separate self and allows our love to flow out to the world.

Forgiveness is an alternative to the ego's plan for salvation. In that plan, we seek happiness through rearranging the sinful world into a more pleasing configuration. In forgiveness, salvation comes through a strictly internal shift, in which we step back and simply give up our perception of sin out there. Happiness comes not through forcing things to go our way, but through forgiving things for *not* going our way.

That this could actually bring happiness is inconceivable to most of us. Rather, we are more likely to worry that the Course's path of forgiveness is a world-negating withdrawal, that it will turn us into happy vegetables. We fear that we will become passive good-for-nothings who sit around with vacant smiles, enveloped in a pink cloud of denial, remaining serenely motionless while people get run over right in front of our glazed eyes.

Yet the real story is just the opposite, as we will see in this chapter. *A Course in Miracles* is not a course in individual salvation (the only time the phrase "individual salvation" occurs, it is in a distinctly negative context[2]); it is a course in salvation *from* individuality. It is about releasing us from the prison of this separate self into a state of love for and oneness with all our brothers and all of reality.

This state does not render us useless to our brothers. The state we are in now is what does that. How can we truly be of help to others when we are intent on subtly taking from them for our personal benefit, and filled with resentment toward them for not letting us take *enough*?

In short, how helpful can we be when we are obsessed with our separate self? Like Narcissus, our gaze is rooted on our own image. Our attention is completely centered on its endless needs, its multiple wounds, and its delicate safety. As the Course says, "Your mind is filled with schemes to save the face of your ego, and you do not seek the face of Christ."[3] Even when we look outside this self, we see its reflection everywhere. In our eyes, the world revolves around this self's all-important needs—or at least ought to. The Course says, "You perceive the world and everything in it as meaningful in terms of ego goals"[4]— meaning, you see everything as existing only to serve your personal interests.[5] Think about it: When you look at a chair or a sandwich or a person, isn't what you see there, on an emotional level, the possibility of your needs getting met?

In such a state, can we really give to the world? Our self is our god, and we will serve no other.[6] We may reach out a hand to the suffering, yet even then we sound trumpets to be sure our acts of charity are observed. With one eye in the mirror, we hope that our generous self-sacrifice may polish that tarnished image which we love above all.

Who does not long to be free of this boring, worrisome self-obsession? We find this fixation on the separate self incredibly confining. For it blocks the one thing we really want to do, the one thing that is truly natural to us. Back in Chapter 1 we said that our natural dynamic is for our spirit to shine outward in an unfettered act of self-giving, joining, and love. The Course calls this *extension* and says that it is our true function. It is what we naturally do as Sons of God. Yet for time beyond memory, the expression of this fundamental urge has been blocked, "blocked by the capricious and unholy whim of death and murder that your Father does not share with you."[7] For eons we have been consumed with stroking, protecting, and gazing upon this idol we call ourselves.

There is not one of us who does not feel the urge to extend. In each of us there exists at least a spark of longing to live for the whole, to leave behind the petty worries of our infinitesimal "self" and pour ourselves out in service to the All. And so we often strain to work up some sense of love for others. But it rarely works. The reason is simple: In our eyes, they do not deserve our love, because of what they did and what they are. In short, we are struggling to love "undeserving sinners," and this is a task the mind rebels against. The perception of sin in others, then, stands like a granite block before our love. It is the dam that keeps our love from flowing freely.

Therefore, instead of straining to love, we need to forgive. Forgiveness is the key to letting the waters of our love break out of the wall of our narcissism. Why? Forgiveness cleanses our mind of the perception that others have sinned and are thus unworthy of our love. Hence, it is what removes "the blocks to the awareness of love's presence."[8] Forgiveness dissolves the dam behind which an ocean of love has waited since time began. Once this dam is dissolved, we don't need to strain to love; "love comes of itself."[9]

Now we can love to a degree we never thought possible. We might even find ourselves able to live out those challenging teachings of Jesus that we have heard since childhood. Their call to a radical love might be one that we always found inspiring, but most likely impossible to answer. This note of radical love runs through such famous parables as the Good Samaritan and the Prodigal Son, as well as those hard sayings that urge us to return kindness for attack:

> When someone slaps you on the right cheek, turn the other as well.
> When someone wants to sue you for your shirt, let that person have your coat along with it.
> Further, when anyone conscripts you for one mile, go an extra mile.[10]

Jesus' teachings in the Gospels challenge us again and again to offer to others a total love that takes no account for what is considered deserved or in our best interests. True forgiveness, I believe, is what makes this possible. For its very nature is to discard the thought system behind what we consider deserved and in our best interests, leaving only a vision of the infinitely valuable and lovable residing in the other person. It sweeps aside the sin that made our brother seem so dangerous and undeserving, leaving us face to face with pure unbounded innocence. With nothing to mar our ecstatic vision of him, now we *can* turn the other cheek, give him our coat when he has taken our shirt, and go with him the extra mile. Now we can express an unbridled love that appears extravagant and reckless, but which we realize at last is merely sane.

13.2. We first allow forgiving perception into our minds and then extend this perception to others.

This chapter will be devoted to exploring our function of extension, which I like to call "earthly extension."[11] For the extension we do on earth is a shadow or reflection of the extension which takes place in Heaven. This whole topic of extension is a source of great confusion among Course students. In this chapter I will attempt to present a clear picture of it, which I hope will resolve the confusion for those who read it.

Let us begin by saying that earthly extension is the Course's version of the concept of selfless service. It is another way of talking about what saints and spiritual masters have been doing naturally for millennia. However, two clarifications of our usual notion of service are in order. First, we think of service largely in terms of performing behaviors that are considered charitable, helpful, or self-sacrificing. We think that the form of the behavior—for instance, dishing up soup for the homeless— is what makes something a service. The Course would disagree. From its standpoint, it is the *content* behind the form, the *feeling* behind the behavior, that has power to heal the other person. The behavior is important, but only as a communicator of genuinely loving content in the mind.

Second, the feeling we often regard as crucial is that of empathy. To be helpful, we assume, we should feel for the dire straits a person is in and for how vulnerable she is. Yet, according to *A Course in Miracles*, what we call sympathy and even empathy is (as you might guess based on previous chapters) an attack. Why? Because it identifies the person with her problem and so perceives her as weak and damaged. "Make no mistake about this maneuver; the ego always empathizes to weaken, and to weaken is always to attack."[12]

If what we extend is not just the outer behavior and is not empathetic feeing, what is it? What *do* we extend? We extend healed *perception.* Specifically, we extend our vision of the other person as wholly pure, untainted, and divine. Put differently, we extend a forgiven perception. This forgiven perception is not meant to be extended only occasionally, but should ideally be the underlying message in all our communications:

> Awake and be glad, for all your sins have been forgiven you. This is the only message that any two should ever give each other.[13]

How do we extend this message? How do we get it from our mind to that of another? There are at least three ways: perception, prayer, and behavior.

On the simplest and most basic level, just by perceiving the other person as forgiven our thoughts reach out from our mind to hers. By their nature, loving thoughts go out and "join with what we see, rather than keeping it apart from us."[14] Such loving thoughts naturally extend to others[15] and *do* affect them, even without our conscious intention.

The Holy Spirit may, however, want us to consciously extend these loving thoughts to another. Yet even this may require no outer behavior. We may simply employ a kind of prayer in which we mentally send the other person our loving vision of her. For example, we might repeat in our mind (as the Workbook suggests), "Let peace extend from my mind to yours, [name]."[16] According to the following passage, this kind of prayer is the true healing agent in psychotherapy: "The process that takes place in this relationship is actually one in which the therapist in his heart tells the patient that all his sins have been forgiven him, along with his own."[17]

Finally, the Holy Spirit may ask us to communicate our perception behaviorally. In principle, minds do not need bodies in order to communicate, since minds are inherently joined. That is why the above mind-to-mind extension works. Yet let's face it, we currently receive the greater part of our information through our physical senses. Imagine if someone told you, "There is this great book called *A Course in Miracles,* but you need not buy it and read it with your eyes. You can have the whole thing fed directly into your mind." I don't care how psychic you are; the page 1 that you receive is not going to look much like page 1 of *A Course in Miracles.* Therefore, if you want the other person to really get the message "All your sins have been forgiven you," then *your* body may need to act it out for *her* senses.

This behavioral extension can take an infinite number of forms: a kind word, a warm smile, a hug, a letter, a gift. Great spiritual masters often transmit profound healings or realizations by means of a simple glance or touch. The form, however, should be left up to the Holy Spirit. Only He knows the ideal way in which another can receive the glad tidings of her sinlessness:

> "What should I do for him, Your holy Son?" should be the only thing you ever ask when help is needed and forgiveness sought. The form the seeking takes you need not judge. And let it not be you who sets the form in which forgiveness comes to save God's Son.[18]

Although physical behavior is not the only way to extend, we should not underestimate its importance. According to the Course, this behavioral extension is the body's *only* purpose. That means that everything we do with our body is meant to either *be* this activity or have the purpose of *supporting* this activity (for instance, fueling the body so it can carry this out). Recall that we made the body as a separation device (see key idea 2.2), a wall of separation that would keep our natural impulse to extend pent up, *arrested*.[19] Yet (as was mentioned in key idea 9.4) the Holy Spirit gives the body a new purpose. He transforms it from a block to extension into an *instrument* of extension. In this new purpose, the body exists not for our pleasure or comfort, "as bait to catch another fish,"[20] or as a furniture-moving device to rearrange our world to meet our needs. It exists only to communicate messages of love to other sense-bound minds. It becomes the perfect dream instrument for reaching dreaming minds in a form they can relate to. "A body they can see. A voice they understand and listen to, without the fear that truth would encounter in them."[21] There are many, many passages about this in the Course. Here are two of my favorites:

> The Son of God extends his hand to reach his brother, and to help him walk along the road with him. Now is the body holy. Now it serves to heal the mind that it was made to kill.[22]

Yet what makes God's teachers is their recognition of

the proper purpose of the body. As they advance in their profession, they become more and more certain that the body's function is but to let God's Voice speak through it to human ears.[23]

Let me reiterate that extension is not an empty behavioral display. We must really see the other person as innocent, as forgiven. Without that perception, we can give forth an endless string of "helpful" words, but we really have nothing worth saying. "It is essential...that the miracle worker be in his right mind, however briefly, or he will be unable to re-establish right-mindedness in someone else."[24] Our first responsibility, therefore, is to accept healed perception into our minds. We must be able to say, "Awake and be glad for all your sins have been forgiven you" and *mean* it.

This is not merely our first responsibility, it is our *only* responsibility. *"The sole responsibility of the miracle worker is to accept the Atonement for himself."*[25] This line, well known among Course students, does not mean that our only responsibility is ourselves. Wouldn't that be the ultimate in narcissism? It means that to extend miraculous love to another—to be a "miracle worker"—we must first accept a loving perception into our own hearts. Once we do, the extension of it will happen naturally, under the inspiration of the Holy Spirit. Yet we need to be attentive to how the Holy Spirit inspires us to extend the miracle, for if we do not extend it in a way the other person can hear, the message may very well not be received.

13.3. Extending forgiveness to others heals them in mind and body. This is the main sense of the word "miracle."

Forgiveness heals the person that we forgive. The Course puts it plainly: "To forgive is to heal."[26] *A Course in Miracles* frames forgiveness as the most powerful healing agent in the world. Just as it is the active ingredient in all spiritual teachings (key idea 12.2), so it is the active ingredient in all true healing. This may sound like an extreme claim, yet it flows naturally from another of the Course's radical claims: that guilt is the core sickness. Guilt is the self-hatred at the core of all of our suffering.

To understand the healing power of forgiveness, we must also remember that true forgiveness does not simply relieve others of their just punishment for a specific misdeed. It implies a profoundly different picture of who they are. It thus transforms their entire sick self-concept. It implies that they are not separate, selfish humans who have been stacking up sins by preying on their brothers. It proclaims that they are radiant extensions of the Heart of God; infinite, holy, and forever changeless. Through it we awaken their sleeping memory of Who they really are:

> The sick must heal themselves, for the truth is in them. Yet having obscured it [the truth in them], the light in another mind must shine into theirs because that light *is* theirs.[27]

Imagine the effect of someone standing in front of you and seeing you as the Christ, not in theory but actually *experiencing* you as the Christ. Imagine this person being so enraptured with your holiness that he can scarce refrain from kneeling at your feet. What would happen inside if you decided that he was saner than you, that his picture of you was more valid than your picture of you? What would happen if you let his shining conviction all the way in? You have it in your power to do this, for according to the Course, something in your mind will innately recognize the truth of his vision. As he sees you this way, he "but calls your ancient name,"[28] the name of who you really are, the name you forgot when time began and the galaxies spun out of your sleeping mind. Yet something deep within you still remembers your ancient name, and his vision will stir that memory to life.

It may be that you do not walk through your day feeling profoundly guilty and unworthy. Yet when faced with this person's vision of your holiness, you may suddenly feel acute unworthiness. In the blazing whiteness of this vision, your inner shadows may leap into stark relief. You may get in touch with just how dirty you feel. You may even catch a glimpse in which you see your entire identity (as you know it) and your whole life resting on the corrupt foundation of your (supposedly) sinful nature. Thus, in spite of all your normal poise, self-esteem, and vanity, you may find that what automatically leaps into your mind is "I am not worthy of this gift."

Yet, if you *do* allow his vision to replace your guilty self-concept— which, remember, is the root of all your suffering—you can imagine just how healing this experience may become. Who knows what chronic problems and lifelong neuroses might fall away? Although forgiveness is aimed at healing the mind, you may find your body miraculously healed as well. "The body can be healed as an effect of true forgiveness."[29] The Course teaches that physical illness is a manifestation of guilt. "Illness can be but guilt's shadow, grotesque and ugly since it [the shadow] mimics deformity [the deformity of guilt]."[30] Therefore, if the guilt is forgiven, then the shadow it casts—the sickness—will vanish as well.

The healing effects of forgiveness can be miraculous. Indeed, forgiveness is the healing agent within the miracle. With forgiveness at its core, the miracle can heal the insane, because their guilt was the core of their delusional system. It tells the patients, "Rise, take up your pallet, and walk,"[31] because their guilt was the source of their sickness. It says to the self-imprisoned, "You are free to leave your cell," because their own guilt was the verdict that kept them in jail.

This extension of forgiveness from one mind to another is the main meaning of the word "miracle" in the Course. This may come as a surprise to many Course students, because the miracle has been primarily portrayed as an internal shift in perception. We said in Chapter 11 that the miracle does have an internal dimension. It does shift our own perception, and so we can speak of an *inner* miracle. Many references in the Course speak of this as well. However, by far the majority of references to the word "miracle" refer to an extension of healed perception from one person to another.[32] To give a more complete definition: The miracle is the act of the Holy Spirit extending through the healed perception of a *miracle worker* to heal the perception of a *miracle receiver*.[33] We can see this extension aspect clearly in the miracle principles that begin *A Course in Miracles*. Here are some relevant examples:

> 8. Miracles...are performed by those who temporarily have more for those who temporarily have less.

> 9. Miracles are a kind of exchange....They bring more love both to the giver *and* the receiver.

> 18. A miracle is a service. It is the maximal service you can render to another. It is a way of loving your neighbor as yourself.

> 21. Through miracles you accept God's forgiveness by extending it to others.[34]

In other words, the Course's main focus is on the *interpersonal* miracle. It claims that interpersonal miracles are the single best device for speeding us home. Not even direct experiences of mystical union with God are as useful now, says the Course. This is a staggering claim, given the significance ascribed to the mystical experience by the world's great mystical traditions and by the Course itself.[35] Yet the Course makes this claim as plainly and openly as possible:

> Miracles...are genuinely interpersonal, and result in true closeness to others. Revelation [the Course's term for the mystical experience] unites you directly with God. Miracles unite you directly with your brother.
>
> ....Revelation induces only experience. Miracles, on the other hand, induce action. They are more useful now [than revelation] because of their interpersonal nature.[36]

13.4. Extending forgiveness to others is a psychological device for convincing us of our own innocence.

So why is extending forgiveness to others the pivotal act that awakens us to God? In Chapter 10 we saw that our only need is to realize that we ourselves are forgiven, that we never sinned and so are still as God created us. This remembering of our true Identity is the goal of the journey. It is also a great deal of the means. Many Workbook lessons are methods for directly reminding ourselves of this one stupendous Fact.[37]

However, the Course's *main* focus is on forgiving others and so seeing *their* true Identity. This strange paradox has twisted the brain of many a Course student. The following prayer may help us resolve it:

> *Forgiveness, truth's reflection, tells me how to offer miracles [to others], and thus escape the prison house in which I think I live. Your holy Son is pointed out to me, first in my brother; then in me.*[38]

This prayer says plainly what the entire Course implies. Through forgiveness I offer miracles to others and so come to see the Son of God in them *first*. *Then* this reveals that same Son in myself. Therefore, it not only lets them out of prison; it lets me out, too. Here is the resolution to our paradox. We focus on forgiving others because it is the quickest, most effective means for realizing that *we* are forgiven, that we are still God's guiltless Son.

How exactly does forgiving others accomplish this? We already saw part of the answer in the last chapter. There we said that, because of projection, our own guilt rises to the surface as our perception of sinfulness in another. Thus, the best way to forgive our own sins is to forgive their projected shadow—the sinfulness we see out there. This passage from *The Song of Prayer* says it quite directly:

> As prayer is always for yourself, so is forgiveness always given you. It is impossible to forgive another, for it is only your sins you see in him. You want to see them there, and not in you. That is why forgiveness of another is an illusion. Yet it is the only happy dream in all the world; the only one that does not lead to death. Only in someone else can you forgive yourself, for you have called him guilty of your sins, and in him must your innocence now be found.[39]

These are pretty strong words: "Only in someone else can you forgive yourself." One would think that we could just forgive ourselves directly, and there are examples of us doing so in the Course. However, that method alone will never reach and dispel the bulk of our guilt. Why? As we saw in Chapters 6-8, the entire structure of the human psyche is designed to deflect our guilt outward, producing the illusion of a guilty world and an innocent self. As a result, when we look within we mainly see a decent, well-intentioned "good guy" threading his or her way through a difficult and dangerous world. We see the face of innocence. How, then, can we forgive ourselves for guilt we do not know is there, for guilt we are not allowing ourselves to feel?

The place to get in touch with our guilt is in our anger toward others. It is hard to believe that we hate ourselves as much as we hate them, but the two are not only of equal strength; *they are the same thing*. In our hatred of others, our self-hatred has simply oozed to the surface and smeared someone else. There we can see it and feel it. There we can get our hands on it, and there we can let it go.

If you understand how projection works, it all makes sense. Because of the nature of projection, forgiving others is how we forgive our own guilt. Yet this is not the only reason for the focus on others. It also stems from the nature of *extension*—the healed counterpart of projection. Extension, if you remember, is the mind's native dynamic. In Heaven, we extend our very being and thus co-create with God. On earth, we are supposed to engage in an earthly reflection of this heavenly dynamic. By extending forgiveness on earth, we somehow rediscover our own innocence. How?

As we saw in Chapter 5 (key idea 5.1), extension is the process by which we take what is inside our mind and express it outward. Once we do this, we look on our effects, and based on them decide what must be inside of us. We decide what kind of *cause* we must be to have produced those *effects*. For instance, if we produce brilliant effects, we conclude that we must be brilliant. The Course puts it this way: "What extends from the mind is still in it, and from *what* it extends it knows itself."[40] Whatever intangible essence we are is invisible. Therefore, the only way to answer the all-consuming question "What am I?" is to see just what kind of fruits this invisible tree brings forth. From our fruits we figure out just what kind of tree we are. "You cannot see the invisible. Yet....by what it does, you learn what it is."[41]

This process has already been at work for a long, long time. In key idea 4.3 we said that our guilt comes from continually observing our ego's effects: our normal thoughts, words, and deeds. Based on this observation we conclude that such effects could only have come from a sinful heart. A tree that produces such rotten fruit, we decide, must itself be rotten to the core.

Consequently, we are so profoundly convinced of our guilt (that is, on an unconscious level), and have been for so very long, that forgiving ourselves is no easy matter. We will, in fact, not really forgive ourselves until we have absolute and repeated proof of our innocence. This proof can only come through the exact same process that "proved" our guilt, the process of *observing our effects*. Forgiveness gives birth to a whole new set of effects through us. It therefore reveals a whole different Self.

We can track these effects in four stages: the forgiving thought, the forgiving act, seeing the effects of forgiveness, and experiencing forgiveness returned to us.

First, you forgive. In a holy instant you let go of your judgments of someone. You stop seeing him as a flawed human with bad taste in clothes and an overly sharp tongue. For an instant you see something in him you have never seen before, "something beautiful and clean and of infinite value, full of happiness and hope."[42] That such a loving vision could arise in you provokes a happy realization: "I really am capable of genuine love. There must be something beautiful in me, something clean, something of God." As the cause of such a loving thought, you conclude you are an *innocent* cause.

Second, a loving response flows out of you. This is the behavioral extension we discussed earlier. Perhaps you feel your face relax and begin to radiate warmth and acceptance. Perhaps you find your hand reaching out to touch his arm, as kind words spontaneously well up and come out of your lips. Whatever the form, you find your loving vision of him being communicated behaviorally. This giving of love proves to you that love actually lives in you, that love really is a part of you. This idea is reflected in a basic Course principle: "Giving is the proof of having."[43] Your loving behavior strengthens your conclusion that you are an innocent cause.

Third, you see the effect your love has on the other person. His body relaxes; the tension clears from his face. You can feel his defenses drop as happiness spreads over him. The change you observe in him is further proof that something holy resides in you, perhaps even the Holy Spirit Himself. This person therefore becomes living proof that you are not a sinner. He becomes a key witness in the case for your innocence. This idea of other people as *witnesses* is another important Course principle: "Those whom you heal bear witness to your healing."[44]

> How can you become increasingly aware of the Holy Spirit in you except by His effects? You cannot see Him with your eyes nor hear Him with your ears. How, then, can you perceive Him at all? If you inspire joy and others react to you with joy, even though you are not experiencing joy yourself there must be something in you that is capable of producing it.[45]

Fourth, this person will often return your gift in the form of gratitude.[46] Perhaps he thanks you, not mindlessly, but with a tone in his voice and a look in his eyes that carry rare sincerity. Suddenly, you realize that *he* sees the holiness in *you*. The holiness that was demonstrated by the first three steps is now being directly gazed upon by him. He holds the secret of what kind of cause you are. In fact, he knows far better than you. He is the one feeling the full impact of the holiness in you, for that holiness has healed him. He who feels the beauty of the effects is he who knows the loveliness of their cause. The Course says it this way, "And as [the light in you] shines your brothers see it, and realizing that this light is not what you have made, they see in you more than you see."[47]

"They see in you more than you see." That is their function. While your mind remains mired in dreams of guilt, the ones whom you awakened to their holiness have come to awaken you to yours. "For the joy of teaching is in the learner, who offers it to the teacher in gratitude, and shares it with him."[48] The students have been sent to save the teacher. The patients have come to redeem the healer. "The sick, who ask for love, are grateful for it, and in their joy they shine with holy thanks. And this they offer you who gave them joy. They are your guides to joy."[49] In short, we are saved not by ourselves but by those we save. We need them every bit as much as they need us. This is not mere flowery rhetoric. The Course means this quite literally, as we can see in the following moving passage:

> Within the dream of bodies and of death is yet one theme of truth; no more, perhaps, than just a tiny spark, a space of light created in the dark, where God still shines. You cannot wake yourself. Yet you can let yourself be wakened. You can overlook your brother's dreams. So perfectly can you forgive him his illusions he becomes your savior from your dreams....
>
> See how eagerly he comes, and steps aside from heavy shadows that have hidden him, and shines on you in gratitude and love....This is the spark that shines within the dream; that you can help him waken, and be sure his waking eyes will rest on you.[50]

Yes, it is a nightmare of a world. Yet within its gloomy darkness there still shines a single ray of truth, one remaining spark of light. What is this spark? In a world of each-man-for-himself, you can set aside your personal interests and save your brother. You can lovingly brush away all the heavy shadows that fog his mind and rouse him from his ancient sleep. You can overlook his dreams of guilt. And when he awakens, you can "be sure his waking eyes will rest on you." What a beautiful image! As his eyes begin to open, they will alight upon the one who lifted him out of his nightmares. What could he feel but eternal gratitude? And in this gratitude, what could he do but return your gift to you? His waking eyes will now look past all of *your* dreams of guilt to the brilliant light of innocence in you. His loving gaze will awaken *you*. I find this mutual giving and receiving of salvation to be one of the most sublime ideas in the entire Course. This is the one heavenly thing that can happen on this shadowy, egocentric earth. This is the spark that shines within the dream.

The idea that our extension saves us is at the heart of *A Course in Miracles*. Indeed, the title itself refers to this. Based on the meaning of "miracle" that we discussed above, "A Course in Miracles" primarily means "an educational program in extending miracles to others and so receiving salvation for oneself."

This concept is also reflected in one of the Course's foremost principles: "Giving and receiving are the same"—a phrase it repeats verbatim no less than six times.[51] Normally, we think that when we give something we lose it. This thought lies at the base of the economics of the ego, as we saw in key idea 6.8. Thus, we generally do not give at all. Our "gifts" are really bargains designed to purchase treasures of greater value. We think giving and *losing* are the same. Hence, the principle that giving and *receiving* are the same is the direct reversal of the whole way we do business. The Course tells us repeatedly that this is one of its most important ideas and one of its most *radical*:

> Today's idea ["All that I give is given to myself"], completely alien to the ego and the thinking of the world, is crucial to the thought reversal that this course will bring about.[52]

> This [giving away in order to keep] has been emphasized throughout the text and the workbook, but it is perhaps more alien to the thinking of the world than many other ideas in our curriculum. Its greater strangeness lies merely in the obviousness of its reversal of the world's thinking.[53]

We have really already explained why giving and receiving are the same. The content of what we give to another is the idea of innocence. Seeing the gift of innocence flow out from us proves that innocence *must* be within us. The gift must have come from somewhere; it didn't just appear out of thin air. Thus, by extending innocence, we become convinced that there must be innocence within. In short, through giving innocence we receive it.

The Course also explains this concept from a slightly different angle. This explanation begins by saying that what we really give is not the physical form—which we do lose—but the *idea* behind it:

> It is sure that if you give a finite thing away, your body's eyes will not perceive it yours. Yet we have learned[54] that things but represent the thoughts that make them. And you do not lack for proof that when you give ideas away, you strengthen them in your own mind.[55]

We all know that we can give all of an idea away without losing any of it, and indeed experiencing it growing stronger in our minds. And this is the case with everything we give. In everything we do we are really giving ideas in our minds, and thus reinforcing them.[56] The question is, which ideas? From the Course's standpoint, there is only one idea worth giving, because there is only one worth receiving:

> Forgiveness is the only gift I give, because it is the only gift I want. And everything I give I give myself. This is salvation's simple formula.[57]

The supreme idea to give as well as to receive is, of course, *forgiveness*. Here is the answer! Here is the Course's simple formula for the salvation of humankind. In this formula we can detect three semi-distinct steps, which summarize our last three sections and which, separately and together, show up many times in the Course:[58]

1. *Receive.* We accept a forgiving perception into our minds. We accept the Atonement for ourselves.
2. *Give.* We extend this forgiveness to another mind. We give the miracle.
3. *Recognize we have received.* Through giving forgiveness we will recognize that we are forgiven. The idea we gave will be reinforced in our own minds. Our own innocence will have been proven to us by our loving effects.

Thus, through seeing loving effects extend through us we will slowly be convinced that love resides within us. Finally, after many, many extensions, we will come to realize that love is what we are. This is what the Course means by that beautiful line, "Teach only love, and learn that love is yours and you are love."[59] By constantly shining we will realize that shining is our nature. We will realize that we are not a meat-encased ego, but an eternal shining, an immutable beacon of love. Our shining on earth, then, will awaken us to our true Identity as a radiant star in Heaven.

And it will prepare us to return to our true function in that celestial sky, in which we forever "extend the Allness and the Unity of God."[60] Earthly extension is not merely a mirror of heavenly extension. It is *preparation* for it; practice for once again assuming our timeless function beyond the confines of space and time. The Course puts it this way, "Do not arrest your thought in this world, and you will open your mind to creation in God."[61]

In summary, extending forgiveness is not about being moral or doing our duty. It is quite simply a powerful tool of psychological persuasion. As the Course says, "It is a method of conversion"[62]—*self*-conversion, that is. It is a way of convincing our skeptical, guilt-obsessed minds of something we never would have believed: that we are actually holy.

13.5. Extension will become our only function. The Holy Spirit will give us a special form of this called our special function.

Extending forgiveness is so singularly important that, from the Course's standpoint, it is the only thing worth doing. "Each day should be devoted to miracles."[63] This, says the Course, is our true function on earth. Every single one of us has this noble calling, a calling which goes by many names in the Course. We are here to be a miracle worker, a teacher of God, a minister of God, a healer, the light of the world, a messenger of God, a savior of the world.

We sorely need such a function. It is a basic psychological need to make a contribution, to take our place in the grand scheme, to fulfill a meaningful role within a larger whole: "The lonely ones are those who see no function in the world for them to fill; no place where they are needed, and no aim which only they can perfectly fulfill."[64] Propelled by this need, we all seek endlessly for our special gift which will grant us our special niche in life—as a homemaker, businessperson, parent, lover, artist, writer, or whatever. However, most of the content behind this search is ego-glorification. We want to stand at the top of the world and have all eyes look up and see how special we are.

We might assume that the Holy Spirit would steer clear of such a base need, especially considering the nature of specialness. For specialness is not only an attack on others, it was the idea that shattered Heaven and started this whole mess in the first place. In light of this, we may assume that He would ask us to renounce having *any* place in the world and instead live as spiritual hermits. Yet (as we saw in key idea 9.4) He can use everything we made, even our desire for a special place in the world. He takes this idea, purifies it, and transforms it into a blessing. It becomes what the Course calls our *special function*:

> Such is the Holy Spirit's kind perception of specialness;
> His use of what you made, to heal instead of harm. To each
> He gives a special function in salvation he alone can fill; a
> part for only him.[65]

He takes our base metal and transforms it into pure gold. Under His alchemy, our plan to find a special place in the world's status quo becomes something else altogether. It becomes our special place in His plan to *overturn* the status quo and redeem the world. It is still a part that we alone can fill. Yet rather than being a way to exalt our ego and denigrate others, it becomes our way to *erase* our ego through awakening others. Here we can see the beauty of the Holy Spirit's ability to use what we have made. In transforming our desire for a special place, He has answered an even deeper longing than the need to be special. He has answered the fundamental yearning to extend, to love.

The term "special function" implies that this function has been specially tailored to our individual situation, and the Course backs this up. "The form is suited to your special needs, and to the special time and place in which you think you find yourself."[66] We can see this tailoring as having at least three aspects:

1. A special way of extending

The Holy Spirit fashions for us our own unique form of extending. He does this based on an infallible awareness of our individual strengths. "Seeing your strengths exactly as they are, and equally aware of where they can be best applied, for what, to whom and when, He chooses and accepts your part for you."[67] This "part" can be almost anything. The Course mentions psychotherapists, theologians,[68] spiritual teachers, and spiritual healers. One's function, however, may take any one of hundreds of forms, many of which may appear quite ordinary and not at all like a "spiritual" purpose. We may be called to be a healer disguised as a secretary, or a therapist disguised as a bartender. Only the Holy Spirit knows what our real strengths are and "where they can be best applied, for what, to whom and when."

2. Particular people to extend to

The Holy Spirit also knows who exactly can benefit from our particular form of extension. He assigns these people to us: "Certain pupils have been assigned to each of God's teachers."[69] He will send them to us, making sure we meet them: "Those who are to meet will meet."[70] He even sends them with a plan for what is meant to pass between us: "Not one is sent without a learning goal already set, and one which can be learned that very day."[71]

3. All the external specifics

According to the Course, the Holy Spirit will provide all things related to our function. He will give us the words to say,[72] guide our decisions,[73] provide for our physical needs,[74] even supply the money we need.[75] In a moving passage, loved among Course students, we are assured that He will take care of literally everything:

> He will go before you making straight your path, and leaving in your way no stones to trip on, and no obstacles to bar your way. Nothing you need will be denied you. Not one seeming difficulty but will melt away before you reach it. You need take thought for nothing, careless of everything except the only purpose that you would fulfill.[76]

These promises sound so wonderful, we naturally begin to wonder how we can lay hold of them. Who would not want this special function the Course talks about? And so a very common reaction is to begin asking ourselves (and God) all kinds of questions: What is my particular function? Will I be famous? Should I get credentialed? Should I hang up my shingle, or look for a publisher? These questions can consume us, and go unanswered, for literally years, until a new set of questions starts to arise: Why isn't it happening? Is God not holding up His end? Where did I go wrong? Am I perhaps just plain unworthy?

Questions about the specific shape of our function are legitimate.

They will need to get dealt with at some point along the way. On the other hand, some of the questions we ask (such as "Is God holding up His end?") never need to be asked. Yet even legitimate questions can get in the way if we become consumed with them and use them to neglect the real business of growing up inwardly in preparation for our function. The following passage seems almost written for this situation:

> Your questions have no answer, being made to still God's Voice, Which asks of everyone one question only: "Are you ready yet to help Me save the world?"[77]

The real question is "Am I ready yet?" And what will make you ready for your function is not being preoccupied with the form of it, but doing the inner work that provides the content of it. Once you have done a great deal of that inner work, it becomes much more appropriate to ask questions about the form of your special function. At that point, the answers will not seem frustratingly elusive; they may well come tumbling out of the sky. For once you accept the content of your function, the form of it will be provided. This is exactly what we are told in the line that precedes the above-quoted passage about Him making straight our path: "*Once* you accept *His* plan as the one function that you would fulfill, there will be nothing else the Holy Spirit will not arrange for you without your effort."[78]

Without this new content, even if you did find your special function and began to do it, it would not be the glorious ministry you anticipated. Since you would still carry the old thought system, giving would feel like a burdensome sacrifice. You would have "a tendency to assume that you are being called on constantly to make sacrifices of yourself for those who come."[79] You would also find various reasons to disapprove of the people you are serving. After a while, the sacrifices would accumulate, slowly adding up to an overall feeling of burnout, and you would start contemplating an escape from the very thing you thought would make you happy.

What you really want, then, is not the outer form of your function. What you want is the inner content, and this means seeing people differently. You want to see them as the divine dreamer, not as the weak and damaged dream figure that stands before you. You want to truly feel that you can scarce refrain from kneeling at their feet. In this perception, you will not need to worry about giving out so much that your own needs become jeopardized. For giving this perception is what will truly *fill* your needs. Pouring out this forgiveness will be *how* you take care of yourself. For this is how you will discover your true Self.

And this is how you will be able to truly serve the world. We all ache to see the world's chronic problems solved. We all see suffering in the lives around us right now that we would dearly love to alleviate. We all want to make a difference. The question is, how can we best do that?

The world is filled to the brim with attempts to save it. You might even say that everybody is trying to improve the world in their own small way. Yet most attempts to save the world fall at least in part under a single heading: "Stop the attackers." Stop the murderers, the dirty politicians, the polluters, the pornographers, the dictators, the drug peddlers—the list is endless. If we, the righteous, can just identify the evil ones and bring them to justice, then all will be right with the world.

Yet there is something suspicious about this approach to saving the world. Under the guise of being helpful, we are repeatedly stamping the label of sinner onto our fellows. Because we are the good guys and they are the bad guys, we can blame and attack with impunity. Like James Bond, we have a license to kill. Thus, the very syringe that we claim holds the antidote actually contains the disease. We, the saviors, have become a new set of attackers. And who will stop *us*?

Forgiveness is a radical alternative to the traditional method of saving the world. Rather than "Stop the attackers," its message is "*Forgive* the attackers." This doesn't necessarily mean that we allow them to keep doing what they are doing—although we may. It just means that while our body does what it does (which may include stopping someone from hurting another), our mind is doing the real work. It is perceiving the "attacker" as a holy Son of God. Instead of an evil criminal, we see a brother giving us a cherished opportunity to help. Instead of recoiling in horror from a devil, we can scarce refrain from kneeling at the feet of Christ Himself. This perception is the real agent of change. Imagine masses of people carrying out this program of global reform. Do you think it might yield better results than the traditional method? Could it perhaps actually save the world?

If we wonder how much good forgiveness could really do in the world, we need only turn to the gospels of the New Testament. In those pages we see what happens when a person who can truly forgive comes into contact with the hurting inhabitants of this world. According to both the Bible and the Course, forgiveness is what allowed to Jesus work his miracles.

Jesus of Nazareth, then, is the demonstration of what a single forgiving mind can do. In one instant it can succeed where all the world's doctors, therapists, social workers, and correctional institutions have failed. In that one instant, decades of guilt can fall away from a tortured mind. And as they do, the demons depart, sanity is restored, bones are mended, even the dead arise. Lifelong torment is replaced by the golden peace of God. An instant of this forgiveness was able to transform a life. A few short years of this forgiveness changed the world forever.

Forgiveness, then, is not an impotent gesture, the luxury of those who do not really care about solving the problems of this world. Based on the example of Jesus, we might well conclude that forgiveness is the most life-transforming and world-changing power on the face of this earth.

To extend this forgiveness is our calling, says *A Course in Miracles*. This is how we carry on the tradition of Jesus. This is how we fulfill his injunction to be the light of the world. The Course, in fact, once asks us to repeat all day long the following thought: "Forgiveness is my function as the light of the world."[80] In order to carry out this new way of saving the world we need much more than sufficient funds and an adequate number of volunteers. We need to acquire the most precious jewel in this world: a forgiving mind. Without that, we will simply be another body performing appropriate behaviors, while sending covert messages of blame to the attackers out there—and thus joining their ranks. At all times, then, we must place before ourselves the single crucial choice of whether to forgive or condemn, just as the Course does in this passage: "Choose once again if you would take your place among the saviors of the world, or would remain in hell, and hold your brothers there."[81]

I would therefore like to close this chapter with another passage from the Course. For maximum impact, I suggest that you read it as if it is addressed personally to you—you might even want to insert your name at different points. When it tells you to look about the world, do so. When it asks you a question, try to answer it. Most of all, when it says "they," picture "them" as specifically as you can. When it says they are "weary," you might picture street people. When it says they are "in chains," you might imagine convicts in prison. When it says they "suffer pain" you might see patients in hospitals, etc.

Look about the world, and see the suffering there. Is not your heart willing to bring your weary brothers rest?

They must await your own release. They stay in chains till you are free. They cannot see the mercy of the world until you find it in yourself. They suffer pain until you have denied its hold on you. They die till you accept your own eternal life. You are the holy Son of God Himself. Remember this, and all the world is free. Remember this, and earth and Heaven are one.[82]

Fourteen

Forgiveness also undoes the blocks that
separate us from others, allowing us to
experience the fact that we are one.

Fourteen

Let us now take another step up the ladder that the separation led us down. In the last chapter we saw that forgiveness delivers us from our obsession with our separate selves, releasing our love to flow out to others. In this chapter we will see that forgiveness releases us from separateness itself, and awakens us to our oneness with others.

14.1. Forgiveness wipes away that which maintains our sense of separateness from others.

The Course teaches that the problem behind all our problems is the illusion of separation: "Your only problem is separation, no matter what form it takes."[1] This sense of separation causes our identity to feel flimsy, insubstantial, and fundamentally lacking (as we saw in 4.1). We feel a gnawing emptiness inside coupled with a sense of loneliness.

This sense of separation seems to be a physical fact. Our minds appear to be locked away inside separate skulls, like prisoners in separate cells. This physical separateness, however, is the projection of a deeper, *mental* separateness (from God). The mind is the real source of the gap between ourselves and others. The mind also finds ways to continually reinforce and increase this gap. We will look at three such ways now. These form a kind of ascending series, with the first providing the foundation, the second building on the first, and the third building on the second.

First on this list is the belief in separate interests. This is the belief that one of us can gain while the other loses; the belief that you can gain at my expense, or that I can gain at yours. "And in these dreams the mind is separate, different from other minds, with different interests of

301

its own, and able to gratify its needs at the expense of others."[2] That we can gratify our needs at the expense of others is a fundamental assumption in this world (see key idea 6.8). In our economic and romantic exchanges we hold the ideal of balancing things out, so that each person gains something more desirable than what he lost (what we call a "win-win situation"). Yet the raw "fact" of separate interests still lurks beneath every transaction. And so even while we smile, shake hands, and exchange merchandise, we wonder if we have been cheated, or if we can turn around without getting a knife in our back.

Of course, many times we walk away convinced we *have* been cheated or stabbed in the back. This leads to another reason for mentally separating from others: the perception of sin. Part of our definition of sin (key idea 4.2) was the act of gaining from another's loss. Since people are constantly trying to gain at our expense, and since they often seem to succeed, we inevitably see them as sinners (key idea 7.2). Consequently, we recoil from them, both physically and emotionally. Who wants to unite with a sinner? Who wants to lie down beside the person who stabbed us in the back? Joining with these grotesque sinners sounds about as appetizing as kissing a leper.

A third factor is simply the accumulation of instances in which someone gains at our expense; in other words, the sins of the past. When our lover does something inconsiderate for the very first time, we can shrug it off. After all, he is our love, our happiness. His indiscretion may even strike us as endearing. But all his little instances of gaining at our expense add up, until twenty years down the road a dark, towering mountain looms between us, built of the stones of his past sins. This mountain blocks him from view so completely that he long ago stopped being our love. He has become irrelevant, for what we live with day in and day out is not him; it is the mountain.

Only forgiveness can cause this mountain to evaporate "as mists before the sun."[3] "Forgiveness takes away what stands between your brother and yourself. It is the wish that you be joined with him, and not apart."[4] It does so by letting go of the three factors we just reviewed:

1. Forgiveness reveals common interests, for when we give it to another we both gain together

The idea of common interests, you could say, is what the whole last chapter led up to. It is what our function of extension reveals to us. We can see this in the following passage, which is talking about our special function:

> Here, where the laws of God do not prevail in perfect form, can he yet do *one* perfect thing and make *one* perfect choice. And by this act of special faithfulness to one perceived as other than himself, he learns the gift was given to himself, and so they must be one.[5]

Let's look at this passage. This world is imperfect to the core, not so much because the weather is not always perfect, but because all of the beings on it are out for themselves. Isn't that what sours our mind when we contemplate the mass of selfish, competing individuals that we call "society"? And is the mass of individuals that we call "nature" any different?

In this dog-eat-dog world, there is one shining, perfect thing we can do. After all of the brainless, inconsiderate, and self-centered things we have done, we can at last get one thing right. We can reverse the entire trend of this place, forget about the needs of our ego, reach out beyond this separate self and give a single true gift. We can grant one other person our undying faith that, in spite of all appearances to the contrary, she is truly sinless. We can overlook all of her imperfections. We can forgive her.

Although this gift was given to "one perceived as other than" ourselves, once it is given, a remarkable thing occurs. We feel as if a gift has been given to us. Our gift was an acknowledgment of her innocence, and having given such a pure and selfless gift, now we feel innocent, too. Thus, the gift we gave was really given to both of us. We benefited as one. We must therefore not be what we look like: separate beings competing for the same food. We must somehow be one. This is the realization brought on by our gift. Hence, through this one act of ego-less giving, two people are able to escape from the prison of separateness and walk hand in hand into the broad daylight of oneness. This is the one perfect thing we can do in this imperfect world. "This is the spark that shines within the dream."[6]

2. Forgiveness lets go of the perceived sin that made us recoil from others

We withdraw from another because we cast a dark shroud of sin over him, making him look like a messenger of death. Forgiveness pulls this shroud off to reveal a Son of God, "glowing with radiant purity"[7] and clothed in holiness. Now, instead of retreating in terror, our heart will eagerly unite with one so beautiful and blameless. The Course talks many times about how forgiveness shines away the "shadow held between your brother and yourself,"[8] the "tiny spot of sin that stands between you and your brother still."[9] And once the barriers are gone, joining will naturally take place:

> And what has been forgiven must join, for nothing stands between to keep them separate and apart. The sinless must perceive that they are one, for nothing stands between to push the other off.[10]

3. Forgiveness lets go of the sins of the past

What is more poisonous to a relationship than the sins of the past? Like a strangling weed, their sum total grows larger every day until it chokes out all the love. Imagine how you would feel toward a long-term partner if by some miracle the accumulated burden of the past could be instantaneously cleansed from your mind. This is what forgiveness does; it releases the past and invites the miracle:

> The miracle enables you to see your brother without his past, and so perceive him as born again. His errors are all past, and by perceiving him without them you are releasing him. And since his past is yours, you share in this release.[11]

Imagine seeing your partner or mother or father or sibling or child as born again, free of all past errors, released from all past burdens. Would this not be a wonderful sight? And would you not genuinely love that person?

In summary, forgiveness releases the perception that others *can* gain at our expense, that others *have* gained at our expense, and that they have done so repeatedly over a long and ugly past. In doing so, forgiveness wipes away the barriers that keep us separate, allowing us to realize that we are one.

14.2. Forgiveness looks past differences and reveals our underlying sameness.

There is another very basic source of separation, not mentioned above: the perception of differences. We seem to be separated from others not just by physical space, but by a thousand perceived differences, in how they cut their meat (or whether they *eat* meat), in how they pronounce their words, in what they value in life, in their bodies, in their personalities, and in their station in society. These differences become further excuses to keep away from those bizarre and alien creatures out there.

Forgiveness wipes these barriers away, too, for part of forgiveness is looking past the apparent differences to the underlying sameness. I have collected the following series of samenesses that are mentioned or implied by *A Course in Miracles*:

Same nature

We believe that we all possess different natures, that we all contain a different collection of characteristics, inclinations, and abilities. We might say, "It is just her nature to be stubborn," or "He is an artist by nature." Yet according to the Course, we were created carbon copies of each other, with the exact same nature, the same characteristics, the same strengths and talents, without one iota of difference. And we are still exactly as we were created. We are identical beings who are dreaming that we are unique characters. But we are the dreamers, not the dream figures.

Same worth

Another assumption we carry is that some people are worth more than others. Some of us are simply more important, more deserving, more fabulous, even more holy—and some of us are *less*. And we all pretty much know who is who. The Course takes an opposite view. It even goes so far as to stress that *Jesus* is our equal, not because he is as human and fallible as we are, but because we are as divine as *he* is. The basis for our equality with others, then, does not lie in the dream, in the world. It lies in our equality beyond the dream, our equality as Sons of God asleep in Heaven.

Same desires

Other people have the strangest desires, don't they? How, we wonder, can they possibly like rap music, or broccoli? Worse yet, why would they hate other races, or abuse their own children? These weird needs and desires seem to set them on the other side of a wide ravine. Yet according to the Course, we all have the exact same needs and desires. Our one desire is for the Love of God. We have fractured and distorted this one into a kaleidoscopic array of different desires. Yet behind all these forms is the same single urge. We all want the same thing. "He [your brother] asks for what you want, and needs the same as you. It takes, perhaps, a different form in him..."[12]

Same mistakes

How often has another made a mistake that simply baffled us, even disgusted us? True, we think, we make our share of mistakes, but we would never, ever make *that* one. Our mistakes are natural and quite understandable, whereas the mistakes of others are often a head-scratching mystery. The Course acknowledges that we think this way, but begs to differ: "And each one seems to make a different error, and one the other cannot understand. Brother, it is the same, made by the same, and forgiven for its maker in the same way."[13] Mistakes differ only in form. In content they are all the same, "for there *is* but one mistake."[14]

Same problem

Have you ever found yourself saying, "What is your *problem?*" Our different makeups seem to contain widely differing problems. Yet the Course teaches that there is only one problem: the ego. And the ego's vast and complex thought system is the same in every single person. We all bought that same software and we are all running the same program. We may customize it a little, but it is still the same program. We have the same problem as the person next to us does, as Hitler did, as Gandhi did, as everyone does.

Same pain

Can anyone really understand our pain? Has anyone walked a mile in our shoes and suffered the same slings and arrows? Our pain appears to be made up of the specific ingredients of our particular experiences, blended with our personal temperament, and baked in the oven of our unique life situation. According to the Course, this is simply not so. We are all experiencing different forms of the only pain there is: the pain of being apart from God.

Same interests

As I said above, the fact that others can seem to gain from our loss is a major separating force in our lives. Yet the truth is that when we hurt another, we feel the sting of guilt. When we help another, we are helped to see our own innocence. We gain together or lose together. We benefit as one because we *are* as one.

Same goal

When we look out at the world, we see people scurrying about in various directions, all going different places. Some are going after material success, some after romance. Some seem launched straight toward Heaven and some seem intent on going to the hot place. In direct contrast, the Course teaches that we are all heading to the same place. Despite appearances, we are all marching together on the same road toward the same glorious goal, the only goal that will truly satisfy us all. Really believing this brings a wonderful sense of unity with our fellow travelers, making hating them unthinkable. "Would it be possible for you to hate your brother if you were like him? Could you attack him if you realized you journey with him, to a goal that is the same?"[15]

Same Self

The above eight points are meant to pave the way for this final one, the most radical one of all. If you and another really have all of the above things in common, might you not also share the same Self? Could it be that this other person, with whom you have maintained such a mistrustful distance, is no *other* at all? Could it be that you are not two separate minds, nor even two souls connected by an etheric bond? Could it be that you share the exact same Self, that you *are* the exact same Self? Is it possible that at the core of your being you are not alone, but that instead you are *everyone*?

I recommend using the above nine points as a spiritual practice. To do so, pick someone in particular; anyone will do. Then hold this person in mind while slowly going through the list: "Same nature, same worth, same desires, same mistakes, same problem, same pain, same interests, same goal, same Self." Each point means "he or she has the same [nature, worth, etc.] that I have." Try to stay with each point long enough to let it sink in. The cumulative effect of all the points together can be startling, as you may well discover.

By revealing our oneness with another, forgiveness frees us of the painful belief in separateness. As long as we experience ourselves as separate entities, we will not feel whole. "What is a sense of sickness but a sense of limitation? Of a splitting *off* and separating *from*?"[16] We will only feel whole when we know ourselves *as* the whole. Forgiveness is the pathway to this knowledge. Through forgiveness, "you recognize your brother as yourself, and thus do you perceive that you are whole."[17]

14.3. Forgiveness lifts us into holy encounters, in which two people set aside what separates them and experience salvation together.

Forgiveness can easily sound like a solitary affair, as if we are doing our forgiving from behind one-way glass. Yet as we saw in the last chapter, forgiveness is genuinely interactive. As others receive the gift of our forgiveness, they are healed (key idea 13.3), and as they return the gift to us through their gratitude, we are healed (key idea 13.4).

Forgiveness, then, has the power to lift us into a special kind of human encounter, which the Course terms a *holy encounter*. All encounters are potential holy encounters. According to the Course, the only reason we ever find ourselves with another human being is that the Holy Spirit has seen in us the potential to mutually transcend our differences and enter into a shared holy instant. We are together because He has brought us together, and He has done so for the sake of this potential. Normally, of course, the potential goes unactualized. We are preoccupied with our own set of concerns, and in this mindset we see the other person as a tool to use or an obstacle to get around. We are too lost in our private priorities to genuinely have an encounter at all.

Yet occasionally, something shifts us out of our myopia and we at last recognize the person in front of us. The Course provides a number of snapshots of such a moment: Two strangers smile at each other in an elevator. Two students decide to walk home together. An adult foregoes the temptation to scold a child who has bumped into him.[18] A therapist and patient are caught up in a moment of joining so holy that the patient's illness and the therapist's judgments are completely forgotten: "The room becomes a temple, and the street a stream of stars that brushes lightly past all sickly dreams."[19]

The Course's favorite image of a holy encounter, however, is the event in which the Course itself was born. Helen Schucman and Bill Thetford had worked together for seven years, during which time their relationship was filled with conflict and embedded within ever-widening circles of interpersonal discord. Then, one day, Bill delivered a pre-planned speech to Helen in which he said, "There must be another way."[20] He suggested that instead of attacking others and pointing out errors, that he and Helen try to be constructive and cooperative, and focus on the positive. Helen, the story goes, jumped up and said that he was right and that she would join him in this new approach. It was a very human moment, without a hint of anything spiritual, and yet it was literally the birthplace of the Course. Under its catalytic influence, Helen began having a series of symbolic inner visions, as well as psychic experiences, and several months later the Course began coming through her. The material she received was Bill's "better way" fleshed out into an entire system of psychology and metaphysics, along with detailed instruction in how to actually reach that cooperative state of being.

In all of the above encounters, the same essential thing is going on. One person allows into her mind a fresh perception of the other, and this sparks an encounter in which both individuals experience a new view of each other. The chalice of true perception is passed back and forth, and as they both drink from it, they are lifted together into a timeless moment. This moment may feel spiritual and it may not. Yet neither one will leave it the same person, and the change that enters in this moment may change countless lives beyond their own. That is certainly what happened with Helen and Bill. I meet people all the time whose lives have been permanently changed by the Course—the fruit of Helen and Bill's holy encounter.

The true perception that is exchanged in these encounters is a way of seeing the other person that overlooks all that would make us recoil from him or her. This true perception, then, is simply another way of talking about forgiveness. Forgiveness is the active ingredient in holy encounters. When we think of forgiveness, the picture in our mind should be that of a holy encounter. The Course wants us to practice forgiveness internally, of course. But it is really banking on this internal practice flowering into a holy encounter. For the full power of forgiveness lies not in the private experience of it, but in the giving and receiving of it. That is where forgiveness has maximal power to change us and change the world through us. And that is why the Course teaches that it is "holy encounters in which salvation can be found."[21]

14.4. The holy relationship is a gradual reversal of the special relationship, in which two people slowly realize their sameness.

The joining that is experienced in holy encounters is beautiful and incomparably significant. Yet for the real promise of this experience to be laid hold of, this joining must generalize beyond brief encounters. It must become deep, constant joining in an ongoing relationship, for that is our preparation for the everlasting union of Heaven. This brings us to the topic of holy relationships.

Holy relationships—the term itself can seem like an oxymoron. How can a human relationship be truly holy? Maybe a rare solitary person can be holy, but a *relationship*? Human relationships have got to be the most challenging and ego-ridden thing in this world. Just this morning I heard the sounds of a screaming argument coming from down the road. Yesterday morning I heard another screaming bout coming from a different direction, this one followed by the arrival of the sheriff's car. Perhaps, you think, I should switch neighborhoods.[22] Yet is any neighborhood really that different, or do some just have better sound barriers? The fact is that if you stick us humans together in the same space, sooner or later something ugly is going to happen.

Being separate is so painful that we are driven into relationship, driven by the search to transcend our isolation. We want to escape from the ego's tight boundaries into an experience of joining. Yet tragically, real joining so rarely seems to happen. Why is this? This question takes us back to the topic of special relationships, which we explored in Chapters 6 through 8. There (in key idea 6.7) we defined a special relationship as one in which *I have a special arrangement with and receive special treatment from a very special person, so that I can feel more special.*

This definition actually reveals why real joining fails to occur. The special relationship is really not about joining; it is about cannibalism. I feel a gaping cavity inside me, which I think can be filled by devouring you. For in my eyes, you possess some special magic that I do not. This magic is the invisible energy of your specialness. I hope that you will shower me with this energy, that you will cast your spell on me and perform exotic rituals on my body. This will hopefully cause all your magic powers to drain out of you and into me, filling the cavernous hole within me and making me whole. I may not have devoured your flesh, but I have consumed the specialness which I see as your life force.

We can see these dynamics in the following poignant passage, one of the most powerful about special relationships:

> For an unholy relationship is based on differences, where each one thinks the other has what he has not. They come together, each to complete himself and rob the other. They stay until they think that there is nothing left to steal, and then move on. And so they wander through a world of strangers, unlike themselves, living with their bodies perhaps under a common roof that shelters neither; in the same room and yet a world apart.[23]

According to this passage, the special relationship begins by assuming all the differences that keep us apart. We therefore approach the relationship as two needy people pursuing two separate goals and trying to fulfill those goals at each other's expense. My goal is for *you* to make *me* feel special. Your goal is for *me* to make *you* feel special. Hopefully, if we can negotiate and compromise creatively enough, these competing goals can both be pursued beneath "a common roof." Yet even then, our differences place a yawning chasm between us, making us feel eerily alone—"in the same room and yet a world apart."

This lack of true joining means that special relationships are actually not relationships at all. They are simply a cloak of relationship thrown over the bare, ugly fact of isolation. As the Course says:

> An unholy relationship is no relationship. It is a state of isolation, which seems to be what it is not. No more than that.[24]

It is disturbing to think that we are not actually in relationship with the people in our lives. Yet we *do* feel that way. Who among us doesn't know what it's like to be "in the same room and yet a world apart"?

What do we do with these fractured relationships, these lessons in loneliness? Maybe, realizing their insanity, we should do as so many have done: disentangle ourselves, emotionally and physically, and just walk away; perhaps move to a cave and spend our lives in solitary meditation. Yet the Holy Spirit has another plan: "I have said repeatedly that the Holy Spirit would not deprive you of your special relationships, but would transform them."[25] It does not matter how insane they are now. "However unholy the reason you made them may be, He can translate them into holiness."[26] Though we made them as songs of ego worship, He can transform them into hymns of heavenly praise. Thus, rather than leave the relationship dance altogether, He encourages us to stay on the dance floor and learn a new dance. He wants to transmute our special relationships into *holy relationships*.

Every Course student knows that special relationships are meant to become holy relationships. This topic, however, is yet another source of confusion and controversy among Course students. My interpretation of holy relationships departs significantly from most views. Perhaps the main difference is that I believe that a holy relationship requires the conscious cooperation of two people. The prevalent belief that a holy relationship is something that occurs inside one person's mind reflects common assumptions about what the Course *must* be teaching, but does not reflect the Course's actual passages about holy relationships. Those passages leave no room for doubt that a holy relationship takes two.[27]

The shift in a relationship from special to holy is a profound metamorphosis. Along the way, a relationship dedicated to "individual salvation"[28] becomes consecrated to a far loftier ideal: "I cannot go without you, for you are a part of me."[29] That stranger under the common roof is slowly revealed to be our dearest friend, until we finally see our own Self looking back at us through her eyes.

This transformation will take time. It is a process, a journey of slowly weeding out the specialness patterns that dominate the relationship. The Course routinely uses process language in talking about the holy relationship:

> In all its aspects, as it begins, develops and becomes accomplished, it represents the reversal of the unholy relationship.[30]

> As this [initial] change develops and is finally accomplished, it grows increasingly beneficent and joyous.[31]

The holy relationship *begins*, *develops* and becomes *accomplished*. It *grows* away from the old goal of specialness toward the new goal of holiness. In the remaining sections of this chapter, we will chart that growth, from its beginning to its final accomplishment.

14.5. When two or more people join in a truly common goal, holiness enters the relationship at a deep level and makes it a holy relationship.

A relationship is made holy when two or more people join in a truly common goal or purpose, as we see in these quotes: "The relationship is holy because of that purpose."[32] "Only a purpose unifies, and those who share a purpose have a mind as one."[33] Sharing a goal says that our two competing minds can find happiness in the same outcome. This means that we benefit together, that we share the same interests. From this standpoint, there is no reason to maintain our suspicious emotional distance. We can journey hand in hand. And when we finally reach our goal and bask together in its light, our minds will unite in the same idea and be lifted into the same happiness. We will join together in a single state of mind. "Reason sees a holy relationship as what it is; a common state of mind."[34]

The idea that a holy relationship comes from uniting in a common purpose, however, gets us quickly into trouble. For *all* relationships seem to be knit together by common goals. In a special relationship we might come together to establish a successful business, have great sex, or raise a happy, respectable family. The Course, however, would say that a special relationship's common goals are not really common. They are just common *forms* that can serve as vehicles for our separate *goals*. As the Course says, "Egos do join together in temporary allegiance, but always for what each one can get *separately*."[35]

For instance, if our goal is money, what I care about is my half, not yours. If our goal is great sex, my concern is my feelings and my sensations. If our goal is some set of outer circumstances (successful business, respectable family), my interest is in how those circumstances reflect on me, how they enhance *my* specialness. Anytime the goal is external, we cannot truly unite in it. We will have to divide up the loot, for nothing external can be truly shared.

If you share a physical possession, you do divide its ownership. If you share an idea, however, you do not lessen it.[36]

When we share an idea, we don't each get half of it. Each of us gets all of it. Therefore, only if the goal of the relationship is an *idea* can we actually share in that goal. Only then can we experience a true joining of minds, rather than a mere egoic alliance. Given this one condition, our common goal can be almost anything. It need not be overtly spiritual. The joining itself, not the specific details of the goal, is what invites God into the relationship. The *Psychotherapy* supplement says this:

> If any two are joined, He must be there. It does not matter what their purpose is, but they must share it wholly to succeed. It is impossible to share a goal not blessed by Christ, for what is unseen through His eyes is too fragmented to be meaningful.[37]

If the goal is truly shared, it *will* be blessed by Christ, whether it looks spiritual or not. There are three specific examples of a shared goal in the Course material:

As I said earlier, *A Course in Miracles* was born when Helen Schucman and Bill Thetford joined in demonstrating a more loving, cooperative way of being. Even though this goal was not overtly spiritual, Jesus took it as a personal invitation, to which he responded by entering the relationship and dictating *A Course in Miracles* to them.

In the Manual for Teachers, a spiritual teacher and his pupil join together in walking the same spiritual path, in learning the same course.[38] This teacher and pupil are the ones referred to in the following passage: "Those who would learn the same course share one interest and one goal."[39]

And in the *Psychotherapy* supplement, therapist and patient go through a process of reconciling their initially different goals. In the beginning, the therapist wants to change what he views as the patient's defective identity.[40] The patient, on the other hand, wants to have his pain healed without changing anything at all.[41] "The task of therapy is one of reconciling these differences. Hopefully, both will learn to give up their original goals, for it is only in relationships that salvation can be found [and only a united goal can make possible a real relationship]."[42] The goal cannot be for the patient's reality to change or for the patient to resist all change. It must be for the patient's *thinking* to change.

These three examples can give us an idea of how diverse these common purposes can be. They also give us an idea of how diverse the relationships themselves may be. A holy relationship is not restricted to romantic relationships. It can exist between friends and colleagues, teachers and pupils, therapists and patients—between any two people. They may have just met,[43] or they may have been slugging it out for years.

It does not matter what the form of the relationship is, nor its history. All that matters is that the two are willing to set aside their barriers and allow a common goal to enter. This often will happen in a single instant, in a holy encounter. Indeed, this is the holy encounter's fullest potential—to be the inauguration of a holy relationship. In such holy encounters, according to the Course, something divine is planted deep in the relationship, and from there it will slowly grow up to maturity.

This is certainly how the Course describes Helen and Bill's holy encounter. Earlier, I recounted a factual description of their encounter, how it looked from the outside. Yet the Course has its own description, which reveals what happened on the *inside*:

> What, then, has joined them? Reason will tell you that they must have seen each other through a vision not of the body, and communicated in a language the body does not speak. Nor could it be a fearful sight or sound that drew them gently into one. Rather, in each the other saw a perfect shelter where his Self could be reborn in safety and in peace.[44]

"They must have seen each other through a vision not of the body." Physical eyes see only bodies, and bodies cannot join. Therefore, something in their minds must have looked out through a different set of eyes and recognized in the other a kindred being, "and communicated in a language the body does not speak." Human language by itself cannot bring about joining. By giving everything a separate name, language reinforces separateness.[45] Thus, beneath Helen and Bill's exchange of words, their minds must have been silently communicating in an ancient language which lips cannot speak, the language of oneness. Whatever it was they saw in and heard from each other, it could not have been fearful, for how could that have drawn "them gently into one"? Instead, "in each the other saw a perfect shelter where his Self could be reborn in safety and in peace." In each the other saw the perfectly pure Mother

Mary to whom his or her own Christ Child could be safely reborn.

And that is exactly what happened. As they joined, something divine was born into the relationship. This birth was of such significance that the Course returns to it literally dozens of times. Again and again we find passages like the following:

> Heaven is restored to all the Sonship through your relationship, for in it lies the Sonship, whole and beautiful, safe in your love. Heaven has entered quietly, for all illusions have been gently brought unto the truth in you, and love has shined upon you, blessing your relationship with truth. God and His whole creation have entered it together. How lovely and how holy is your relationship, with the truth shining upon it![46]

Notice all the things that this passage says have entered the relationship: Heaven, the Sonship, love, truth, God and His whole creation (this last phrase covers everything real). Other passages mention Jesus and the Holy Spirit. I will refer to this totality simply as "holiness." Why does holiness enter? Because wherever it is welcome it comes. And what makes it welcome is *oneness*. "Christ comes to what is like Himself [which is oneness]....What draws you and your brother together draws Him to you."[47]

By joining in a common goal, Helen and Bill made holiness welcome. They cleared an open space in their inner clouds of resentment, which allowed all the radiance of Heaven to stream through and shine on them. They felt some of this consciously. Yet this inpouring of divine radiance primarily entered them on an unconscious level, establishing its home deep inside the relationship. There, it shone away the dark, underground root system of their old relationship.[48] This root system included all their hidden hate for each other, as well as the goals of specialness that had knit the relationship together. With this influx of holiness, the unconscious foundation of the relationship became completely healed, "washed in the waters of forgiveness, and cleansed of every evil thought [they] laid upon it."[49] Holiness became the relationship's foundation. It was now a holy relationship.

14.6. The relationship will go on a journey, as the holiness that entered it slowly rises and transforms the relationship.

This initial holy encounter is just the beginning. A relationship which holiness has entered must now set out on a long journey. Even though its unconscious foundation has been made holy, the conscious patterns of the relationship, though somewhat changed, will have remained largely intact. The two will still squabble, still judge each other, and still maintain separateness. Thus, the holiness at the relationship's base must now rise up and slowly replace all the surface patterns of specialness.

In a very real sense, the relationship's new *foundation* is simultaneously its new *goal*. In fact, the goal on which we joined has now become infused with the Holy Spirit's goal of total awakening. Our goal was simply a specific vehicle through which His far grander goal could enter our lives. Helen and Bill's relationship is a good example. They joined on the goal of embodying a more loving, cooperative way for people to relate. What then entered their relationship was a way (*A Course in Miracles*) for people to relate so lovingly that they could awaken together from the illusion of time and space. This became Helen and Bill's new goal.

Thus, even though some version of our original goal may still be present, the Holy Spirit's goal will have fused with it and deepened it (although we may not recognize this at first). Now, our real goal will be to fully and consciously reach that beatific place which, on a deeper level, the relationship has already attained. Our job, you could say, is to follow the relationship to where it has already gone:

> Your relationship with your brother has been uprooted from the world of shadows, and its unholy purpose has been safely brought through the barriers of guilt, washed with forgiveness, and set shining and firmly rooted in the world of light. From there it calls to you to follow the course it took, lifted high above the darkness and gently placed before the gates of Heaven.[50]

In order for the holiness that entered the relationship to rise to the surface, it must push through layer upon layer of thick resistance, for the ego does not give up easily. "The peace that already lies deeply within [the relationship] must first expand, and flow across the obstacles you placed before it."[51] The longest and quite possibly the most important section in the Text, "The Obstacles to Peace,"[52] is about this very process.

This resistance will be particularly heavy at first—at least after the initial inspiration has worn off. Many newly born holy relationships will enter what *A Course in Miracles*, in typical understatement, calls the "period of discomfort."[53] For now the relationship is a house divided. We can sense that a new purpose has entered our relationship and imbued it with a new meaning, changing all the old rules. Yet we are still *playing* by those old rules. And so we wonder what kind of sacrifices this new purpose might mean, what delicious delights we might be called to give up, what control might no longer be ours. A part of us feels that God is trying to invade our sacred palace of pleasure. A revolution is underway, and the old guard within us begins to fight for dear life.

Having one foot in both worlds makes for a troubling state of affairs. It "makes the relationship seem disturbed, disjunctive and even quite distressing....Now it seems to make no sense."[54] Being firmly divided between spirit and ego, the relationship feels like a bad joke. Look at us, we think, here we are supposed to stand for a better way and all we do is bicker. The prospect of ever reaching our lofty goal and fulfilling our noble purpose seems absolutely hopeless.

In response to the extreme pain of the period of discomfort, we do the only obvious thing: We blame each other. "Perhaps you are now entering upon a campaign to blame him for the discomfort of the situation in which you find yourself."[55] It seems plain: My pain here is not coming from my own inner conflict, my own deep ambivalence about our exalted goal. No, I am in pain because *you* are conflicted. You have been unfaithful to our goal. You made a commitment and you have not lived up to it. That is why we are such a joke.

This period of discomfort may last for a long time. Some holy relationships, such as Helen and Bill's,[56] never quite get out of it in this life.[57] Many partners decide it is just too hard, and check out of the relationship, either physically or emotionally.[58] Yet the Course promises that if they can have a little faith in the Spirit that entered their relationship, and in each other, they will slowly come out of this period.

They will emerge primarily under the force of a single remedy: forgiveness. Forgiveness is the great healer of relationships. After all, what estranges us from our significant others but the grimy buildup of past resentments? Forgiveness is what washes away the old grudges that stand between us. This is not simply a Course principle; reconciliation is probably the main use to which forgiveness is normally put. We say, "That's okay, honey, I forgive you," and kiss and make up. We bury the hatchet and try to let bygones be bygones. One person says, "I'm sorry," and the other says, "Think no more of it. As far as I'm concerned, it never happened."

Of course, we are rarely able to actually "think no more of it," for the only tool our culture gives us is conventional forgiveness, which is *pseudo*-forgiveness (see key idea 12.3). But we must make a gesture of forgiveness, however lame. We must *try* to forgive, for we dearly want to reconcile, and we plainly see that the shadow of past sins is what keeps us divided.

The holy relationship will progress to the degree that genuine forgiveness begins to occur. The two of us must learn that what is hurting us is not the other's sins, but our own. We secretly looked within at our own supposed sinfulness, and lost all hope that we could ever make it to our goal of holiness. This sense of sinfulness was so uncomfortable that we had to project it outward, onto our partner. We then claimed that our partner's sins were the cause of our hopelessness; he or she was the awful reason our joint goal will never be reached.

> Yet think on this, and learn the cause of faithlessness [your lack of faith in the relationship to reach its goal]: You think you hold against your brother what he has done to you. But what you really blame him for is what *you* did to *him*. It is not his past but yours you hold against him. And you lack faith in him because of what you were.[59]

If genuine forgiveness can enter the relationship, a monumental lesson will have been learned, the most priceless of them all. For by now our holy relationship partner will perhaps have become our most difficult forgiveness lesson. The establishing of a holy relationship kindles tremendous emotional investment. On an emotional level, both partners assume that here is the chance to find the holiness *and* the specialness for which they have longed. As a result, a lifetime of unmet needs surges into the relationship. And when things do not go as anticipated, a lifetime of bitterness becomes focused like a laser onto the other person.

In forgiving this one person, then, we forgive the world. He is the one we most need to forgive. And he is the one who needs our forgiveness, for he is plagued by his own imagined crimes against the sanctity of our relationship. Perhaps more than anyone else, he is the one whom we must save from the dungeons of guilt, both for his sake and our own. Saving him, in fact, is the beginning of our function as savior. It all starts with truly setting just one person free:

> To each who walks this earth in seeming solitude is a savior given, whose special function here is to release him, and so to free himself.[60]

> Consider once again your special function. One is given you to see in him his perfect sinlessness.[61]

Somewhere there is a person walking the world alone and lonely, needing salvation, to whom we have been appointed as savior. This is the same person we referred to near the start of the chapter, in relation to whom we make the "*one* perfect choice" to forgive. Who is this person? It is our holy relationship partner, of course. By seeing "in him his perfect sinlessness," we "release him," and that is how we free ourselves.

This is also the true beginning of our special function. We often think of our life purpose largely in terms of going out and affecting the lives of masses of strangers. Yet until we can forgive this one who is so close to home, whose image within us is a hornet's nest of hurt and anger, how much love can we really give those masses? And even if we did get up on stage and proclaim our message to the world, if afterward we came home to this one unforgiven person, wouldn't it all feel hollow? Wouldn't we feel like a hypocrite?

14.7. As the relationship's holiness rises to the surface, it will then reach out beyond the two people. They will be given a joint special function.

Forgiving someone so close to us is not a one-time act. It is really a process of emotionally growing up. Given long-term willingness, this growing up will occur. As it does, the two of you will begin to take on your true function as saviors of each other. You will start to give, *really* give, without strings or hooks, without bargains or trades, and finally, without ceasing. For you will learn from experience that giving is "the only means by which you can receive."[62] In such a relationship, "each one learns that giving and receiving are the same."[63] And thus you will learn your interests are the same. You will start looking out for each other's needs as naturally as you used to look out for your own. You will especially be alert for anything that would cause the other to feel guilt and so lose sight of his holiness:

> Every mistake you make, the other will gently have corrected [i.e., forgiven] for you. For in his sight your loveliness is his salvation, which he would protect from harm.[64]

Once this beautiful gift of forgiveness has been born in your relationship, and has grown as it was lovingly handed back and forth, you are ready to give it to the world. "When you have looked upon your brother [holy relationship partner][65] with complete forgiveness, from which no error is excluded and nothing kept hidden, what mistake can there be *anywhere* you cannot overlook?"[66]

If your love stayed just between the two of you, your relationship would retain glaring elements of specialness. By its nature, love must expand. Oneness must embrace and shut no one out. Thus, extending your love beyond the bounds of your little tea party is merely

> the logical conclusion of your union. It [your union] must extend, as you extended when you joined. It must reach out beyond itself, as you reached out beyond the body, to let yourselves be joined.[67]

Just as the Holy Spirit plans a special function for each individual, so He designs one for each holy relationship. "Each holy relationship must...learn its special function in the Holy Spirit's plan."[68] You might call this a *joint* special function. All the things that apply to the individual special function apply to this. The Holy Spirit designs a *special form* of extension that fits your strengths, as individuals and as a relationship. He sends you *particular people* that can benefit from your special form of extension. And He will take care of all the *external specifics*: guiding your words, behavior, and decisions, supplying your money and physical needs. The only thing that is different from the individual special function is that you do this one *together*.

The Course is very clear about the holy relationship's special function and returns to it many times over several chapters. Indeed, the Course itself is living proof of the idea, for it is the fruit of the special function of one particular holy relationship. Giving birth to the Course *was* the special function of the relationship between Helen Schucman and Bill Thetford.

So much of what the Course says about holy relationships really happened in Helen and Bill's relationship. In a holy encounter, two people joined in a common goal. In that instant, something holy was born into their relationship. This something was intent first on saving them, on blossoming fully in their relationship. Its ultimate goal, however, was to reach out beyond them and bless the world. And so it used their hands to record its words in the pages of a book that it called *A Course in Miracles*. While dictating these words, it promised them that their relationship would become the means through which the Holy Spirit could "spread joy to thousands on thousands who believe that love is fear, not happiness."[69] And this promise has been fulfilled, as thousands on thousands of students have picked up the Course and begun to walk its pathway home.

As the story of the Course demonstrates, the holy relationship has great treasures to give the world. And the greatest treasure of all is that possessed by two who can truly forgive. The Holy Spirit cannot wait to give the world the precious diamond that has been formed in the pressures of their relationship. With this diamond, they hold the secret to the world's release from suffering. For it is a world in a perpetual state of upheaval and fragmentation, as convulsions fracture its wholeness along the countless fault lines of old grievances, leaving it broken into a myriad of angry islands. And battle rages ceaselessly across the no man's land in between, between husband and wife, rich and poor, labor and management, black and white, male and female, human and animal. As the battle rages, we occasionally pause in our fighting to ask the anguished question: How will the madness ever stop?

It will stop with this one relationship that has learned to forgive, and with others like it. For in the hallowed silence of this relationship, the battle already *has* stopped. These two have found the cure to the rampant disease of this world and have inoculated themselves with it. Now they *are* the cure. They are an antibody in the global system. They are the living proof that old wounds and old hatred really can dissolve in reconciliation, that bitter separation can be replaced by loving oneness. They are the demonstration that people can actually get along; that human relationships can genuinely be made divine. According to this well-known line from the Course, the most sacred site on the face of the earth is not Jerusalem nor Giza nor Sedona; it is their relationship: "The holiest of all the spots on earth is where an ancient hatred has become a present love."[70]

From this holy place, holiness can spread outward, transforming all it touches. From it can arise a new world. Like the twosomes carried inside Noah's ark, this relationship is literally the seed of a new world. "The ark of peace is entered two by two, yet the beginning of another world goes with them."[71] Being the beginning of a new world, the holy relationship is also a harbinger of what will come after that world. It is a herald of the coming of eternity, as the Course proclaims in this moving passage:

> Each herald of eternity sings of the end of sin and fear. Each speaks in time of what is far beyond it. Two voices raised together call to the hearts of everyone, to let them beat as one. And in that single heartbeat is the unity of love proclaimed and given welcome.[72]

14.8. The journey to God is not a lonely journey. Through joining with others we discover our own wholeness and clear the way for uniting with God.

As the two participants carry out their joint special function, their relationship will continue to grow in holiness. They will emerge from the dim fog of separateness into the bright dawn of oneness. More and more they will experience the same thing. "For what one thinks, the other will experience with him."[73] Slowly, the boundaries between them will begin to dissolve away:

> The demarcations they have drawn between their roles, their minds, their bodies, their needs, their interests, and all the differences they thought separated them from one another, fade and grow dim and disappear.[74]

In unexpected, unplanned moments, they will fall into holy encounters, re-entering the sublime state which initiated their holy relationship, tasting the state toward which they journey. In these moments they will experience the same light at the same time as the same *Self*. *A Course in Miracles* even goes so far as to say that this holy encounter in a holy relationship, this "one instant spent together"[75] is "the special means this course is using to save you time."[76]

These instants are the Course's special means for shortening our journey to oneness, for they are *the experiential proof of oneness*. From their lucid vantage point we know that we are something more than the petty creature we thought we were, something more than the ego's flimsy soap bubble, *something more*.

Experiential proof of oneness—this is the whole significance of the holy relationship. This is why it is "the source of your salvation."[77] Yes, we can have private experiences of oneness with God, and these are vital along the journey. We can also experience our oneness with those who haven't joined us in a common goal, and this too is absolutely crucial. Yet the belief in separateness goes so incredibly deep that these experiences alone will not erase all of it. At least that is the Course's assumption.

To really dispel the belief in separateness, totally and completely, oneness will have to be proven to us on a very concrete level, on the same level as the belief in separateness operates.

> Salvation must reverse the mad belief in separate thoughts and separate bodies, which lead separate lives and go their separate ways. One function shared by separate minds unites them in one purpose.[78]

This familiar phenomenon of lonely, separate lives must be transformed on its own level. It must become *joined* thoughts and *cooperating* bodies leading *united* lives and going the *same* way. It must become two minds sharing one function and uniting in one goal, so fully that in the end they lose sight of their separate identities. According to this passage—perhaps the best passage on the purpose of the holy relationship—this is the single requirement for coming home,

> the same requirement salvation asks of everyone. Each one must share one goal with someone else, and in so doing, lose all sense of separate interests. Only by doing this is it possible to transcend the narrow boundaries the ego would impose upon the self.[79]

Just as we need our innocence proven to us by the loving effects we cause (see key idea 13.4), so we need our oneness proven to us through a mutual joining with another human being. Oneness is a mutual thing. If two people are one, then they are *both* one. Consequently, for only one of them to wake up to their oneness is not a full reflection of that oneness. For they are still experiencing different things; they are still in two separate worlds. Oneness is only truly reflected when both wake up to it *as one*, when both experience the same thing. Mutual joining is the earthly counterpart of heavenly oneness. The union of two human beings is the reflection of the oneness of God's Son.[80] It is the concrete proof that oneness really does exist. Our skeptical minds, so soaked in separateness, *need* this proof. Only once we have it, once we have experienced real union with another human being, will we be convinced in our heart of hearts, beyond a shadow of a doubt, that we are not alone. Only then will we be willing to leap with all our being into the formless oneness of God, utterly and forever.

By taking this approach, the Course appears to have charted a new road to the highest spiritual realization. The most lofty spiritual paths have by and large been lonely journeys up the mountain. Even when they have allowed for normal relationships during the ascent, those relationships—with the exception of the teacher-disciple relationship—are (to my knowledge) not seen as the very power that propels them up the mountainside. That honor seems to generally be reserved for private spiritual practices and experiences.

While the Course fully shares the goal of these paths and praises their successful climbers,[81] it implies that their means have contained the unfortunate contradiction of trying to find union through separation, trying to find the oneness of Heaven through separation here on this earth. "It is impossible to remember God in secret and alone....The lonely journey fails because it has excluded what it would find."[82] In contrast to thousands of years of mystical wisdom, the Course is emphatic in declaring that we best reach the summit of spiritual liberation through joining with other human beings: "It is only in relationships that salvation can be found."[83] This includes relationship not only with the teacher in the ashram, but also with our fellows in society—our boss, our friend, our coworker, our spouse.

This approach to God is something we all might find hard to swallow. Most all of us carry despair that human relationships can ever become sane, let alone holy. Whatever drives us into our relationships, especially the romantic variety, seems simply too dense, too animal.

Whatever happens behind the closed doors of our dysfunctional homes seems too dark to be transformed into the wings that lift us to God. Perhaps one partner could manage to pull herself out of the mire. But both? Could two people actually cooperate on forgiving each other until they together achieved a mature and profound sense of unity with each other and all living things?

This deep-seated skepticism naturally surfaces when we are faced with the topic of holy relationships, or with an actual holy relationship. In either case we can become plagued with doubts about the feasibility of this enterprise: How can I find someone who is willing to really join with me? How can I trust someone (especially so-and-so) to do her part and go the distance with me? How could I really forgive her for what she has done to me? And how can I be certain that she will forgive me?

The Course, however, sees such thoughts as symptoms of the very disease that will inevitably pass away as we ascend the mountain together. The Course displays boundless optimism regarding this process. It is certain that we will meet our chosen partners: "Those who are to meet will meet, because together they have the potential for a holy relationship."[84] It assures us that the road is far more familiar than we think,[85] that we *will* advance,[86] and that we *will* make it all the way home together.[87] The Course has supreme confidence that human relationships can be cleansed of all that poisons them now, that one day each relationship can and will "become a spotless mirror, in which the holiness of your Creator shines forth from you to all around you."[88]

After all, according to the Course, this is God's plan for the salvation of humankind. "Ask yourself if it is possible that God would have a plan for your salvation that does not work."[89] Is it possible that He is so stupid that He would devise a plan that even *we* could tell Him would be a flop? According to the Course, even though our relationships seem like such a hopeless mess, they "are still the temple of the Holy Spirit, and they will be made perfect in time and restored to eternity."[90] Even if we stumble and falter and call a relationship quits, we will eventually pick it back up, perhaps in another life, perhaps on another plane of existence, and carry it forward to its goal. For that goal is our destiny. The Course assures us of this. "Yet all who meet will someday meet again, for it is the destiny of all relationships to become holy."[91]

Fifteen

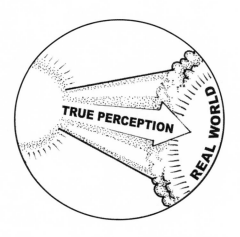

With forgiveness as our practice,
we journey toward the goal of
true perception.

Fifteen

Forgiveness has led us far up the ladder that separation led us down. We have seen it dissolve nearly every pillar that holds up this world of pain. Before going on, let us review the benefits of forgiveness according to the last three chapters.

1. Forgiveness releases our projection of blame onto another, ridding us of everything contained in that projection: the painful emotions of anger and resentment, the heavy burden of the past and, most importantly, our guilt (Chapter 12).
2. Forgiveness unleashes loving effects through us, proving to us that their cause—love and innocence—must abide within us. Forgiveness conclusively demonstrates "that love is yours and you are love"[1] (Chapter 13).
3. Forgiveness undoes the wall of resentment that keeps us apart. It thus reveals our oneness with others, replacing the experience of loneliness and lack with the experience of being whole. It also heals the rift between two people, making way for authentic joining, for holy relationship (Chapter 14).

In every case then, forgiving others heals our perception of ourselves. It shows us that we are not guilty (#1), that we are holy (#2), and that we are whole (#3). In this chapter, we will go on to examine one final benefit of forgiveness:

4. Forgiveness removes the blocks to true perception. It opens a different set of eyes that look upon a different world.

15.1. True perception is a different mode of perception which looks past bodies to the light of Christ in everyone and everything.

In key idea 9.2 we said that the Holy Spirit leads us into a transitional state which is the gateway out of the ego and the gateway into Heaven. This state, we said, is variously called true perception, the happy dream, right-mindedness, and the real world. Actually, more often than not it is called "vision" or "Christ's vision." However, we didn't say exactly what this state is. In this chapter, we will describe it in some detail, as we are nearing the end of the journey, and true perception *is* the end of the journey.

We explored the topic of perception in Chapter 11. There we discussed what we might call ordinary perception, in which we mentally interpret the sensory data we receive from our eyes and ears. Hearing the term "true perception," we might assume it refers to using our brain better and thus *accurately* interpreting the data received by our senses. This, however, is not the case. True perception does not operate on the physical level, where physical objects send messages of physical light to physical eyes which are then interpreted by the physical brain. True vision is nothing short of a completely different mode of perceiving.

The need for a different mode is clear when you recall the Course's teaching about the physical world. According to the Course, everything your eyes see is an illusion. If true, this has several rather dramatic implications. First, it implies that your physical eyes have never seen anything worth seeing. The most beautiful body and the most gorgeous mountain vista are not really worth looking at because they are not real. Second, if your eyes were constructed to see something that is not there, then, in essence, they were made to *not see*. "These eyes, made not to see, will never see."[2] They were made to give you the illusion that you are seeing when you are not. Third, it implies that you are blind—in the only important sense of the word. For the only thing worth seeing is meaning, and your eyes never have and never will see meaning. All they see is form:

> The body's eyes see only form....To this distorted form of vision the outside of everything, the wall that stands between you and the truth, is wholly true....
>
> ....See how the body's eyes rest on externals and cannot

go beyond. Watch how they stop at nothingness, unable to go beyond the form to meaning.[3]

Let's explore how vision works and how it contrasts with ordinary perception.

Vision does not use the body's eyes; it sees with the eyes of Christ

Ordinary perception, of course, uses the body's eyes and the other physical senses. If all your senses stopped working, perception as you know it would cease. Christ's vision, however, is not seen through your physical eyes. "[Your] sight is wholly independent of the eyes that look upon the world."[4] Vision is seen through a set of inner, spiritual eyes which the Course calls "the eyes of Christ." Thus, closing your body's eyes does not turn off Christ's vision. Amazingly, it operates irrespective of "concepts such as 'near' and 'far'"[5] and even sees perfectly in the dark.

Vision sees a nonvisual inner knowing

Perception as we know it involves the seeing of visual images. Since vision uses inner eyes, we might therefore assume that it sees inner images, such as the pictures, shapes, and colors we see in dreams or with our eyes closed. All such images, however, are mere form, and what vision sees is not form but *meaning*. Think about when a sudden recognition prompts you to say, "Aah, I *see*."[6] In that instance, what you are "seeing" is strictly mental, not visual. Your mind is seeing pure meaning, not necessarily accompanied by imagery of any kind. This kind of seeing is what we might normally call an inner knowing.

Vision comes not from the outside in; it shines from the inside out

Perception seems to come into our mind from the outside world. We saw in Chapter 11, however, that what we perceive is projected from our own mind. This holds true for vision as well. Yet in this case the *light* in our minds goes out and *joins* with the light in all things, rather than the darkness in our minds being projected out and kept apart from us:

> Today we are trying to use a new kind of "projection."
> We are not attempting to get rid of what we do not like by

seeing it outside. Instead...we are trying to join with what we see, rather than keeping it apart from us.[7]

Vision is not interpreted by the brain; it is born directly from the Christ in us

The meaning you normally see is interpreted by the brain based on the evidence of your senses. Vision, however, is not interpreted but is *received* from deep within you. Its meaning is born, pure and unadulterated, straight from the Christ in you. He has no need to piece together the jigsaw puzzle of sensory data. He already knows what everything really is and He looks on it unceasingly. And because He and you are one, you don't need to interpret what He sees. You just need to accept His sight as your own. Your sensory data needs such heavy interpreting because you are struggling to understand a senseless world that is fundamentally alien to you:

> Only your vision can convey to you what you can see. It reaches you directly, without a need to be interpreted to you. What needs interpretation must be alien.[8]

Vision sees neither physical objects nor sinfulness; it sees the light of holiness

Your physical eyes, of course, look upon physical objects—bodies of one sort or another. These bodies are generally doing things you do not like, and so you interpret them as sinful. The eyes of Christ, as we have said, see a different realm. Instead of looking on bodies and sin, what they look upon is *holiness*. That is the meaning they see. They see the Son of God in everyone, the face of Christ in all your brothers.[9] They see the beautiful divine dreamer behind every dream figure. They behold a light "too holy for the body's eyes to see."[10] And this light does not differ from thing to thing, nor from time to time. When you open the eyes of Christ in you, then, what you see is an unchanging field of radiant holiness stretching endlessly in every direction.

Vision does not see things external to us but united with us

Our usual perception looks out upon a world external. This split between you as the *subject* and the world as *object* is fundamental to all perception, even true perception. Yet true perception very nearly erases the subject-object dichotomy. In Christ's vision you feel a sense of oneness with all you see, no matter how rudely it treats you, how big its bank account, or even how many legs it has. You feel a profound kinship with all living things. You feel this closeness because in true perception, your Self, the Christ, is simply gazing upon Himself in everything. Wherever He looks He sees His Own face looking back at Him.

Much of the above is encapsulated in my favorite passage about Christ's vision:

> Christ's vision has one law. It does not look upon a body, and mistake it for the Son whom God created. It beholds a light beyond the body; an idea beyond what can be touched, a purity undimmed by errors, pitiful mistakes, and fearful thoughts of guilt from dreams of sin. It sees no separation. And it looks on everyone, on every circumstance, all happenings and all events, without the slightest fading of the light it sees.[11]

In Christ's vision, we do not mistake others for bodies animated by defective personalities. Instead, we recognize them as "the Son Whom God created." The sight of Christ looks past those bodies doing their weird dances and gazes steadily on "a light beyond the body." Rather than a visual image of shape and color, His vision sees "an *idea* beyond what can be touched." Rather than seeing sinfulness and selfishness, it sees "a purity undimmed." Instead of seeing a world outside of us, "it sees no separation." And instead of viewing an undulating disarray of differences and change, it looks on everyone and everything "without the slightest fading of the light it sees."

15.2. True perception looks on the real world, which is composed of the holiness in all minds and the loving thoughts in those minds.

The real world is a familiar term to all Course students. Yet the Course says some very puzzling things about this real world:

> Sit quietly and look upon the world you see, and tell yourself: "The real world is not like this. It has no buildings and there are no streets where people walk alone and sepa-

rate. There are no stores where people buy an endless list of things they do not need. It is not lit with artificial light, and night comes not upon it. There is no day that brightens and grows dim. There is no loss. Nothing is there but shines, and shines forever."[12]

What is puzzling about this passage is that the Course tells us repeatedly that the real world is not some kind of afterlife state, but something we experience while still in this world. Yet this passage instructs us to sit down, look around us, and tell ourselves that the real world has none of the things we see before us (an exercise you may want to actually try). It has no buildings, streets, stores, nor artificial light. At this point we may be thinking that it has nothing man-made, perhaps only natural things like trees, streams, hills, and maybe tofu. But then we are asked to say to ourselves that the real world does not contain a cycle of day and night, one of the most basic elements of the natural world. If "nothing is there but shines, and shines forever," then the changing light of the daily cycle is excluded.

The explanation for this passage is implied in our previous section. The real world is what we see with Christ's vision. While our physical eyes are looking upon streets and stores, the eyes of Christ in us are gazing upon a nonphysical holiness that simply "shines, and shines forever." In other words, we have two sets of eyes that see two different worlds. And both sets are working simultaneously, looking on their respective worlds *at the same time.*

This raises an important question: While in the state of true perception, what do we do with the visual information seen by our physical eyes? Does our visual experience carry on unchanged? Do our eyes stop working? The Course says many things about this issue, which I have lumped into four categories:

1. The Holy Spirit will interpret our sensory data for us

As long as we are interpreting our world by ourselves, we are going to inject our ego into that interpretation, for the ego is the very notion of "by ourselves." For this reason, the Course says, "Do not interpret out of solitude, for what you see [in solitude] means nothing."[13] Instead, "Let Him be Judge...of everything that seems to happen to you in this world."[14] Amazingly, the Course promises that one day we will so completely allow the Holy Spirit into our minds that He will carry out the second-by-second act of interpreting our complex visual field for us.

2. He will divide all objects and events into two categories: witnesses to truth and witnesses to illusion, extensions of love and calls for love

What does the Holy Spirit do with our sensory information? We have built up thousands of categories into which we file our visual images (see key idea 11.2). Yet the Holy Spirit has only *two*: "Only two categories are meaningful in sorting out the messages the mind receives from what appears to be the outside world."[15] These two categories are truth and illusion.

Here is how it works. The Holy Spirit guides your eyes to search for those outer symbols that call to mind an awareness of reality. He files these in the truth category. All the rest He tosses into the illusion bin. "He will select the elements in them which represent the truth, and disregard those aspects which reflect but idle dreams."[16] What are these outer symbols of truth? One good example would be the words of the Course or of other spiritual teachings. Another example, mentioned often in the Course, would be the visible results of miracles—the healed bodies and changed lives that furnish outer evidence of the inner Healer.[17]

Perhaps we can best see the Holy Spirit's two categories in action in His interpretation of human behavior: "The only judgment involved is the Holy Spirit's one division into two categories; one of love, and the other the call for love."[18] This is the well-known principle from the Course that every communication is either an extension of love or a call for love. Thus, in response to every action your eyes see, "your Interpreter"[19] will whisper into your ear, "That was an extension of love" or "That was a call for love." He will never say, "Now *there* was a particularly vicious call for love." For that would mean additional categories, and there are only two.

Seen rightly, even the calls for love are evidence for the reality of love (see key idea 12.5). Yet they are *indirect* evidence. For on a visible level, a call for love looks like an *attack*. On that same level, an extension of love looks like love. Both are windows onto the reality of love, but one is a more transparent window than the other. Mother Teresa's charity was a clearer window onto love's reality than was Hitler's genocide.

For this reason, the Holy Spirit will direct your eyes to scan your world for extensions of love. "The senses then will seek instead for witnesses to what is true."[20] In Chapter 11 we discussed the Course's theory of selective attention. In this theory, your eyes search for what you want, for what fits your categories. In your usual perception, you hunt most of all for people's mistakes, which you toss into the category of sin. In true perception, your eyes still selectively attend, but to a totally different category of things. Your eyes disregard mistakes as you search for expressions of love, no matter how small or seemingly insignificant. Your eyes will therefore "see only the blameless and the beautiful, the gentle and the kind. They will be as careful to let no little act of charity, no tiny expression of forgiveness, no little breath of love escape their notice."[21]

With this different use of selective attention do you think the world would look the same to you? I think it safe to say that you would be ushered into a different world, in which the following words would describe your experience of the world:

> Each day a thousand treasures come to me with every passing moment. I am blessed with gifts throughout the day, in value far beyond all things of which I can conceive. A brother smiles upon another, and my heart is gladdened. Someone speaks a word of gratitude or mercy, and my mind receives this gift and takes it as its own. And everyone who finds the way to God becomes my savior, pointing out the way to me, and giving me his certainty that what he learned is surely mine as well.[22]

Imagine walking out and experiencing your world in this way. When you do you will have taken up residence in the real world. For the real world is composed not only of the holiness in this world's minds. It is also composed of their *loving thoughts*, which express that holiness: "In the real world...only loving thoughts are recognized."[23]

3. He will assign one purpose to all things, which will give them all a holy meaning

The Holy Spirit may have two categories for what things witness to, but He has only one category for what their purpose is. "The Holy Spirit looks upon the world as with one purpose, changelessly established."[24] In His view, the only purpose of every *mind* is to reach the goal of forgiveness; the only purpose of every *form*—object, situation, and event—is to be used as an instrument for reaching that goal. When you live in the real world, this is how you see the world. "The real world is the state of mind in which the only purpose of the world is seen to be forgiveness."[25]

If you ascribe to the world this holy purpose you will see in it a holy *meaning.* According to the Course, the purpose we assign to something determines the meaning we see in it.[26] If we gave the purpose of forgiveness even to an instrument of torture, that instrument would take on a holy meaning for us. Isn't this exactly what happens when people venerate the crucifix? This world *is* an instrument of torture, but it can appear to us as holy as the cross of Jesus appears to a devoted Catholic—if we give it a new purpose.

4. Fundamentally, He sees all things in this world as unreal

The Holy Spirit can see physical things as witnesses or symbols of truth, and He can use them as instruments of truth, but His fundamental stance toward them is very simple: They are *not* the truth. They are unreal. They are not there. Consequently, in the state of true perception what you primarily do with physical things is look past them. Your inner emphasis shifts away from bodies as your mind becomes absorbed in the light of holiness. Your mind's gaze no longer stops at physical forms, but looks right through them to the lovely light beyond. Hence, though bodies still appear solid and opaque to your eyes, to your *mind* they feel empty and transparent. "Things which seem quite solid here are merely shadows there; transparent, faintly seen, at times forgot, and never able to obscure the light that shines beyond them."[27] Now when you meet someone, his or her body fades into the background: "The body grows decreasingly persistent in your sight, and will at length be seen as little more than just a shadow circling round the good."[28] Who would care about inspecting bodies when he can look upon salvation?

Now we have some sense of what the real world is. It is the state in which your eyes search only for outward signs of loving thoughts, and it is the world of radiant thoughts uncovered by that search. It is the state in which you assign to everything the holy purpose of forgiveness, and it is the enchanted world of holy meaning in which you live and move thereafter. It is the state in which the eyes of Christ in you look past all things physical and gaze in rapture on the holiness in all things. And it *is* that holiness within all things. In short, the real world is a world of meaning seen only by the mind, a world of *divine* meaning.

15.3. Looking with true perception on the real world is the happiest experience we can have here. It is the goal of the spiritual journey.

True perception shows you a different world. And do you not have an intense need to look upon a different world, and to see with different eyes? Has what your eyes have shown you ever really satisfied? Think of the worries, the boredom, the judgments, and the unpleasant memories you associate with each object your eyes alight on. Think of all the attacks your eyes see coming at you daily. Think of the disaster and insanity your eyes behold out there in the world. Has looking on this world made you happy? Has it filled your heart with joy and set your mind at peace? Or has it made you weary as day after day you gaze on the same worrisome situations in your life, the same tragic events in the world? Toward the end of the Text, the author of the Course gives us this wonderful promise:

> To your tired eyes I bring a vision of a different world, so new and clean and fresh you will forget the pain and sorrow that you saw before.[29]

To me this line is summed up in one word: *renewal*. The world we see has made our eyes fatigued. We have seen too much pain and sorrow, more than anyone should have to see. Yet the Course brings us "a vision of a different world." This world is so "new and clean and fresh" it will renew our tired eyes. It will heal our world-weariness. It will cause us to forget all those things we wish we had never seen.

Imagine what it would be like to see this different world. The same cars are sitting in the same spaces, the same people hurry about their same old routines, yet you see it all suffused by a meaning that is "new and clean and fresh." Seeing this meaning, you leave your drab and ugly world far behind and stride "into beauty that will enchant you, and will never cease to cause you wonderment at its perfection."[30]

You will no longer see a world of strangers thoughtlessly walking on you and poised to attack. As the Course has you say: "Everyone and everything I see will lean toward me to bless me. I will recognize in everyone my dearest Friend."[31] What would it be like to feel as if everything you see is leaning toward you to bless you? Instead of an evil planet teetering on the brink of catastrophe, you will see a world of "holiness and hope."[32] Imagine looking out at the world and seeing nothing but *holiness* and *hope*. Instead of seeing the same spent world, sick with sin, feverish with insanity, and weary from eons of struggle and futility, you will "see the world anew, shining in innocence, alive with hope, and blessed with perfect charity and love."[33]

The idea of seeing everyone leaning toward you to bless you hits on a key aspect of the real world. When you see someone through true perception, you do not just see a holy being, you see a being that is blessing *you*, shining on you, opening your eyes to the holiness in you. The Course refers to this concept again and again, such as in this passage: "Your brother may not know who he is, but there is a light in his mind that does know. This light can shine into yours."[34] This is one of the primary meanings of the word "savior" in the Course.[35] Earlier we saw that our brothers save us by returning our gift of forgiveness to us (see key idea 13.4). But they can save us without doing a thing, if we see them truly. It is said that awakened masters can impart profound experiences of enlightenment by simply gazing into your eyes. Underneath his disguise as a normal, bewildered human, *every* brother is an awakened master. And if you see him for what he is, the Christ in him *will* gaze into your eyes and *will* enlighten you.

Seeing this real world, filled with saviors in disguise, may sound impossible. Yet we have all had glimpses of it, "lovely flashes,"[36] as the Course calls them. "No one in this distracted world but has seen some glimpses of the other world about him."[37] Have you ever looked at someone and seen in her something innocent despite what she had done, something beautiful regardless of her outer appearance? Then you have experienced "a little flicker of your eyelids"[38] and briefly glimpsed the real world.

Chances are, this perception was not insignificant but was deeply meaningful to you. It was probably far more satisfying than what you normally see in that person or in your world. Now imagine that this experience was intensified and expanded, so that any shadow that marred it was cleared away; so that it grew to an overwhelming intensity; so that you experienced it in relation to everyone all the time. This provides some hint of what living in the real world would be like.

> Can you imagine how beautiful those you forgive will look to you? In no fantasy have you ever seen anything so lovely. Nothing you see here, sleeping or waking, comes near to such loveliness. And nothing will you value like unto this, nor hold so dear. Nothing that you remember that made your heart sing with joy has ever brought you even a little part of the happiness this sight will bring you. For you will see the Son of God.[39]

To really appreciate this passage it helps to apply it to your own life. To begin with, reflect on some of the lovely sights you have seen. Think of a beautiful thing you have visualized in your fantasies, then of a lovely scene you have looked on while awake, then of a fantastic image you have experienced in a dream. Now ponder the idea that none of these "come near" to the loveliness you will see through true perception. Then think of something you deeply value here, something you hold very dear. Now consider that one day you will hold far more dear what true perception will show you. Finally, think of an event in your life "that made your heart sing with joy," and reflect on the possibility that this event did not bring you "even a little part of the happiness" that true perception will bring.

In short, the Course is saying that true perception is the most joyous experience you can have on this earth. Nothing your eyes can see, no matter how lovely, can remotely compare to what the eyes of Christ see. Your eyes view only meaningless forms, while the eyes of Christ behold the Son of God. Seeing with them is not an act of gathering information. It is salvation.

According to the Course, this is the world that Jesus saw. While his body inhabited the same physical space as the rest of us, his mind was dwelling in a world of meaning to which we were, and still are, blind. Robert W. Funk, founder of the Jesus Seminar, has this to say:

> The reality human beings inhabit—cohabit, actually—is socially constructed, maintained, and transmitted....Jesus broke through the crust of his inherited world and achieved a vision of an alternative reality. He articulated that vision

in his parables and aphorisms...He seemed strange to family and friends because his world did not coincide with theirs.[40]

All great saints and spiritual masters have entered this "world" to one degree or another. This is what distinguishes them from us. Though their bodies may be standing right next to ours, they are seeing a different realm. They are living in a different world. While we worry and fret and jump at every noise, they abide in a peace we cannot fathom:

> They want for nothing. Sorrow of any kind is inconceivable. Only the light they love is in awareness, and only love shines upon them forever. It is their past, their present and their future; always the same, eternally complete and wholly shared. They know it is impossible their happiness could ever suffer change of any kind.[41]

To make these remarkable statements more real, you might want to take them, put them into the first person and say them to yourself: "I will want for nothing. Sorrow of any kind will be inconceivable for me. Only the light I love will be in my awareness, and only love will shine upon me forever...." And just in case you are thinking that, although this sounds nice, the exciting bits of cheese you are chasing in the rat race sound better, the Course adds these lines:

> Perhaps you think the battleground can offer something you can win. Can it be anything that offers you a perfect calmness, and a sense of love so deep and quiet that no touch of doubt can ever mar your certainty? And that will last forever?[42]

"All this beauty will rise to bless your sight as you look upon the world with forgiving eyes."[43] As we said at the beginning of this chapter, forgiveness is what unleashes true perception and reveals to us the real world. But how does forgiveness do this? How does it open the eyes of Christ in us? The answer is very simple: Forgiveness overlooks all that would blind us to Christ's vision. Let us return to a line we quoted in Chapter 12, in which the Course condenses its teaching into a single sentence:

> Forgive the world, and you will understand that everything
> that God created cannot have an end, and nothing He did
> not create is real.[44]

What does this mean? In forgiveness you overlook everything that
God did not create, everything unreal. He did not create bodies, and so
you look past them. He did not create sin, and so you overlook the entire
world of sin. You see this whole distasteful world of striving, sinning,
and dying bodies as just an empty play of shadows on the wall. With
these shadows cleared from your mind, you are free to look on the real.
That is true perception. You gaze on God's perfect reality and discover
in wonder that it remains pristine and unspoilt, forever unmarred by the
ancient war of the shadows. Nothing in His Kingdom will ever die,
because no shadow can slay the Son of God. Forgiveness, then, is how
you experience the truth of the Course's opening lines: "Nothing real
can be threatened. Nothing unreal exists."

Seeing reality, you are finally ready to *know* it again. "Seeing"
implies that you are looking at something from the outside. Being separated from what it is, you cannot really *know* what it is. To know reality, you must unite with it in direct awareness, with nothing standing
between you and it. Strictly speaking, then, true perception does not see
reality directly, as it really is; it sees a *reflection* of reality: "In it we see
Heaven's reflection lie across the world."[45] Yet when Heaven's reflection fills our field of vision so completely that we see nothing else, we
are finally ready to unite with Heaven itself. "For the reflection of truth
draws everyone to truth, and as they enter into it they leave all reflections behind."[46]

Therefore, looking with Christ's vision upon the real world is the
goal of the spiritual journey. This is where all human suffering and all
earthly limits are laid aside, as we prepare to don the garments of infinity. "Whoever looks on this no longer sees the world. He is as near to
Heaven as is possible outside the gate. Yet from this gate it is no more
than just a step inside."[47] We will examine this final step in the next
chapter.

15.4. The spiritual journey is the gradual making of a single choice, which slowly restores us to our right mind.

The perfect attainment of true perception is not going to happen overnight. We will not pick up *A Course in Miracles* one day and become enlightened the next. We will experience our awakening as a long journey. This journey will be shortened by miracles, by instantaneous jumps over whole stretches of the road. We are told that we can save a thousand years at a crack.[48] Yet if we are taking thousand-year chunks out of some larger sequence, that sequence must be large indeed.

The exact length of the journey, however, is entirely in our hands, because to complete it there is only one thing we must do. The entire journey is the making of a single, immensely protracted choice. We choose between illusions and the truth, between false perception and true perception, between attack and forgiveness. Though we may pass through many stages along the way, the content of every stage—and of every lesson within each stage—is this single choice, which we make through forgiveness. The choice to forgive, therefore, is the whole journey home.

We have all experienced choices—perhaps the choice to spend our life with someone—that we couldn't make all at once. We had to make these choices gradually, one bit at a time, until we could finally put our whole mind behind them. The spiritual journey is like this. It is the gradual making of the single choice to put our whole mind behind forgiveness. Only when this choice is fully made does choosing end, and time end with it: "Yet will you choose in countless situations, and through time that seems to have no end, until the truth be your decision."[49]

Another way to say this is that the journey home is the gradual transfer of our mind's investment from the ego's thought system to the Holy Spirit's. While living conventional life our investment is almost entirely on the ego's side. But somewhere along the road we reach a watershed. For one reason or another we get fed up with life as we know it, and we decide to set out in a new direction. This choice is often accompanied by a holy instant. Maybe we have a moment of holy joining with another person, as was described in the last chapter. Or perhaps we have an exalted experience in nature, during meditation, or while listening to music. Or maybe we pick up *A Course in Miracles*. Whatever the form, we experience the birth of God's light into our lives. The spiritual journey has begun.

The initial glow may take days, weeks, or longer to wear off. During this time we may assume that we are now a highly advanced being, an avatar sent to redeem unenlightened humanity. Yet this assumption is not due to our high advancement, but to our immaturity. What has actually happened is that a single ray of God's light has entered the darkness of our slavish worship of the ego. Our investment is still primarily in the ego, but now we are honestly attracted to the light as well.

When the glow fades we will slowly realize that we are in a state of conflict. We are in the highly uncomfortable position of being stuck between two thought systems. We feel precariously suspended between Heaven and earth, unable to meet the demands of either one. This inner division frustrates our basic need for inner unity, causing feelings of disorientation, confusion, aimlessness, meaninglessness, and instability. If this sounds reminiscent of the period of discomfort that begins a holy relationship (see key idea 14.5), it should. For that period is simply one version of the period of inner conflict that begins the spiritual journey.

We will try to blame the pain of this time at least somewhat on God. If He had lived up to His promises, we figure, we wouldn't be in this pain. We will also blame the world for being unable to appreciate and support its future redeemer. But we will also blame ourselves, for the light will have revealed our ego's dark contours, and we will be in horror over the madness we see staring back at us in the mirror. To the extent that we hang onto our ego and identify with it, we will be awash in self-blame.[50]

As the Course puts it, we stand at the branching of the road.[51] And we may stand there for a very long time. "Some remain at this step for a long time, experiencing very acute conflict. At this point they may try to accept the conflict, rather than take the next step towards its resolution."[52] To "accept the conflict" means to try to live with it, to look for an arrangement that allows us to permanently straddle both sides. We want to build our home on a fault line. This, however, only delays the inevitable and so brings on feelings of futility and despair. "And there is no part of the journey that seems more hopeless and futile than standing where the road branches, and not deciding on which way to go."[53]

Finally, however, we will set off down the road to God, at first slowly and hesitantly, and then with increasing firmness of resolve. "It is but the first few steps along the right way that seem hard."[54] Years of little choices (and this initial period will probably be at least that long) will add up, causing our inner scales to tip towards God, as the weight of our investment shifts away from the ego. We will therefore slowly leave behind this initial period of conflict and emerge into increasing peace and freedom. We will still have miles to go before we wake. We will still have many stages ahead of us. We will need to surmount seemingly impossible obstacles; face parts of our mind that before would have driven us mad. We may loiter for long periods at future branchings of the road. Yet from here on, our journey will overall be one of increasing emergence into greener pastures and wider states of being.

As the road climbs higher and higher, several general developments will be evident. To begin with, our devotion to others will steadily increase. Our neurotic self-concern will fade away, as the foremost question on our minds shifts away from "How do I look?" to "How can I help?" As we become single-minded in our desire to be truly helpful, our power to help will soar to undreamed of levels. We will become true miracle workers, able to heal the sick and actually raise the dead.[55] The holy vision which lights our eyes will travel into the minds of everyone we meet or think of, and even those who think of us.[56] It will heal people across the world whom we will never meet.[57] The time will come when all who encounter us, regardless of their personalities and beliefs, will experience the same thing in us, the same indefinable presence of holiness. And as they simply enter that presence, their different problems will all be shined away in the same light.[58]

As our hearts reach out to others, some of them will reach back and link hands with us. These will become what the Course calls our "mighty companions,"[59] and we will travel the rest of the way home with them, "for this is not a way we walk alone."[60] As we explore the heights of holy relationship with these companions, we will learn what real relationship is all about. We will realize that we can do far better than defend our territory, get our needs met, and creatively compromise, that we can awaken together as one Self. After so long alone, we will discover the joys of oneness. And as we do, the number of our mighty companions will increase, until the day when literally the entire world stands together as one Son of God.

Physical laws will no longer bind us. How can they, when we fully realize that they are pretend laws, laws that we made up? Before, our mind subtly manufactured the body to be our master and so enforce separateness upon us (see key idea 8.5). But now our mind will dream a body that is the perfect servant for our function of extending forgiveness (see key idea 13.2). "And it [the body] becomes perfect in the ability to serve an undivided goal."[61] When the Course says "perfect" here, it seems to mean just that. It promises that the body will eventually go beyond the need for food and drink, rest and sleep, protection from weather, beyond sickness, and even beyond aging.[62] We will be free from slavery to physical laws. And this will allow us to release others from their slavery. We will be able to do things for others that are "not of this world." We will be able to perform miracles:

> What [the Holy Spirit] enables you to do is clearly not of this world, for miracles violate every law of reality as this world judges it. Every law of time and space, of magnitude and mass is transcended, for what the Holy Spirit enables you to do is clearly beyond all of them.[63]

The Holy Spirit will be our Guide and Teacher, to Whom we turn for everything. He will speak through our lips, walk through our feet, reach out through our hands. He will even think our thoughts for us. He will send individuals to us, tell us what to give them, and then proceed to give it through us. He will take care of so much that we will feel as if we are "being carried down a quiet path in summer."[64] As we learn to lean on Him, we will increasingly enter into a state of rest even in the midst of busy activities; a sense of timelessness even while the currents of time swirl around us. "In Him you have no cares and no concerns, no burdens, no anxiety, no pain, no fear of future and no past regrets."[65]

Through the Holy Spirit we will rediscover the one relationship that time was made to obscure: our relationship with God the Father. We will begin to feel God's Presence beside us, then all around us, and finally within us. As we feel Him walking with us day after day, we will realize that He has always been by our side, through all the ages. And this implies a wondrous thing: that we never actually left Him *and* that we are already back with Him. The experience of His Presence will thus prove to us that the separation never occurred,[66] that the journey is truly without distance,[67] and that we are already at home in God, merely dreaming of exile.[68]

We will begin to have holy instants in which we enter His Presence so fully that the world momentarily vanishes and we "walk into eternity a while."[69] We will set aside the sleep of sense experience and briefly open our eyes in Heaven. This has traditionally been called the mystical experience. The Course calls it "revelation," which means it is God's direct revealing of Himself to us, without intermediaries or separation of any kind. As mystics throughout history have said, the Course claims that this experience cannot be accurately rendered in words: "Revelation is literally unspeakable because it is an experience of unspeakable love."[70] It also says (again agreeing with the mystics) that in the latter stages of the journey we will enter this state more frequently and more fully. Eventually, reaching this state forever (with all our brothers) will become the only thing that matters: "As this experience increases...all goals but this become of little worth."[71]

All of these developments are different ways of saying that we will be restored to our right mind. Do you remember our levels of the mind? On the surface is the face of innocence. Beneath that is the rage of the victim level. Beneath that is the unprovoked assault of the ego proper. And beneath that is the call for help, which contains the awful pain of guilt. The ego is the cause of the other levels. It generates the two levels above it as masks to conceal its true face; it generates the level below it as its hidden emotional outcome (guilt).

On the spiritual journey we gradually relinquish the ego, and this causes all of the levels to slowly fade away[72] and reveal the glorious treasure that lies beneath them: the right mind. This is the answer to our anguished call for love. The right mind is not our reality, but it is a state of mind that so purely reflects reality that it is the closest thing to Heaven on earth. "For here is only healing, already complete and perfect."[73] Here at last is sanity. In a world of madness, such sanity is a rare thing indeed. The right mind has probably been perfectly embodied by only a handful of individuals in the history of the world.

All of the unfoldments we have discussed come from the flowering of Christ's vision within us, from the opening of those unseen eyes. Christ's vision is the content of the miracles we extend to others. The oneness it perceives is what allows us to join with others in holy relationship. Its penetrating insight is what pierces the veil of the physical and sets us free of the imprisoning laws of this make-believe world. It is what opens our mind to the Presence of God, allowing us to feel Him by our side and granting us brief furloughs in the boundless ocean of His Love. It is the content of our right mind.

Now we can have some appreciation for the incomparable benefits of forgiveness, since it is the catalyst for Christ's vision. Forgiveness literally reverses the human condition. Through its liberating power every burden that weighs us down can be lifted, every sickness that has ever plagued humanity can be healed. Forgiveness can raise us into a happiness so exalted that we cannot currently comprehend it. The following passage attempts to describe this happiness, giving us a list of the benefits of forgiveness. The preceding four chapters have been preparing us to take such a list seriously. Therefore, if you will, go through each item individually (I have placed them all on separate lines), and first ask yourself if that thing is something you want, and then really consider the possibility that forgiveness can deliver it:

> What could you want forgiveness cannot give?
> Do you want peace? Forgiveness offers it.
> Do you want happiness [consider that forgiveness offers it],
> a quiet mind [could forgiveness offer that, too?],
> a certainty of purpose,
> and a sense of worth and beauty that transcends the world?
> Do you want care [being cared after] and safety,
> and the warmth of sure protection always?
> Do you want a quietness that cannot be disturbed,
> a gentleness that never can be hurt,
> a deep, abiding comfort,
> and a rest so perfect it can never be upset?
> All this forgiveness offers you, and more.[74]

"...and more"? What could possibly exceed the happiness described in this passage? I can think of only one thing: total remembrance of God, permanent awakening to Heaven. As we will see in the next chapter, forgiveness offers us even this:

> Forgiveness...clears your memory of all dead thoughts
> so that remembrance of your Father can arise across the
> threshold of your mind....
> ....What you will remember then can never be described. Yet your forgiveness offers it to you.[75]

Sixteen

When we and the entire world have
attained true perception, God Himself
will take the final step and lift us home.

Sixteen

"Listen to the story of the prodigal son."[1] Listen to our own story, for we collectively are the prodigal son. The story begins before time arose, in a limitless Heaven. We were born into our Father's transcendental home, His perfect Son, the generous outpouring of His unlimited Love, completely at one with Him. We passed eternity singing of our love for Him, returning the song in which we were created. And as we joined our voice with His in a single chorus, the endless expanse of Heaven was somehow extended and increased.

This Heaven, though beyond our current comprehension, is perhaps best captured by the concept of *pure goodness*. Think about what we call goodness in a being. Goodness is when a being benefits others, when it loves and blesses them, rather than hurting them for its own selfish gain. Goodness is also when a being is willing to join with others, to really commune with them, rather than withholding itself and being coldly standoffish. Goodness, in short, is when a being warmly extends itself to others in genuine love and joining. And when a being is truly good, we see that being as deserving of all good things. It deserves to be secure. It deserves to feel whole and safe and happy.

Heaven is a state of *pure* goodness, of goodness carried to such an extreme that it becomes perfect; it becomes holiness. What would it mean to extend to others so completely that nothing of yourself is held back and no one is left outside of your love? The total sharing of oneself with others would necessarily erase the very boundary between self and other. You wouldn't have a body, for a body is just such a boundary. Rather than being a solid form, you would be pure extension, pure shining. Consequently, you would know that you *deserve* only goodness.

You would be infinitely secure in yourself, knowing that you are as clean and blameless as God Himself, and that you are therefore entitled to *everything*. This is the state in which God created us.

Yet into our holy minds "there crept a tiny, mad idea."[2] We entertained the bizarre notion that there might be pleasure in separate existence. We pondered the idea of elevating ourselves above our brothers and even our Father. And as we took this idea seriously, it seemed to come to pass.

> And think what happens when the house of God perceives itself divided. The altar disappears, the light grows dim, the temple of the Holy One becomes a house of sin. And nothing is remembered except illusions.[3]

A terrifying reversal appeared to take place, in which the pristine paradise of Heaven was transformed into a hideous nightmare. The house of God was at war with itself, as we, its Sons, strove amongst each other for preeminence. Our pure goodness appeared to change and turn into its opposite. Our love, which had flowed so freely, was coolly withdrawn, to be replaced by a stream of vicious attack. Instead of sharing ourselves in perfect union, we recoiled from others and retreated into icy separateness. The bright rays of our extension were sucked back in; our formless radiance seemed to darken and coalesce into greedy, separate forms. Our perfect holiness had apparently metamorphosed into evil.

With this reversal of pure goodness, Heaven seemed to come apart at the seams. Light turned to darkness. Infinity appeared to shatter and become physical space. Eternity seemed to fracture into days, months, and years.[4] The Son of God appeared to splinter into countless separate hunks of flesh. The temple of the Holy One seemed to degenerate into a house of sin.

We experienced ourselves leaving home and setting out on a long, long journey. We left not as blessed sons, but as criminals and exiles, bearing the weight of an unspeakable sin, thinking that our nature had been forever corrupted. As we walked in sorrow, we carried a burden of guilt too deep for words. This guilt gave rise to feverish images of everlasting punishment. Through its hazy dementia we envisioned our Father brooding in His house, plotting His revenge. We imagined an angel with a flaming sword barring the way home, so that we could never go back again. We believed we had thrown our inheritance away forever.

Yet we did not want to go back home, for we had become identified with the tiny, mad idea. We equated ourselves with it. Now we could not bear to give it up, no matter how much guilt and fear it entailed. Out of our attachment to this idea there spilled from our minds a far country, a universe of time and space. This country was far indeed from our Father's house, being its antithesis in every way. Here, reality had been turned upside down, so that madness reigned. Against the boundless oneness of Heaven, this country was inhabited by tiny entities suffering inside minute cells. In contrast to Heaven's pure goodness, these entities made endless war until they died.

This country was no more than a mental projection on an imaginary screen. However, it had a powerful effect on our minds. Its function was to convince our minds that the mad idea of separation was objectively real and that oneness was just a dream. And it performed its function well. It encased us in separateness, proving that Heaven's unity had been vanquished. It dragged us through linear time, proving that eternity was no more. It pressed suffering into our flesh, proving that we had sinned and were reaping our punishment. And it laid us in the grave, proving that our Father had indeed put a price on our heads. It attacked us in manifold ways, from every quarter, for that is how it persuaded us. That is how it argued all its terrible points.

The world's ceaseless attacks convinced us of another thing: that we had not thrown our inheritance away. Instead, the peace our Father placed in us had been stolen from us by this savage place. That is how it happened, we decided. The citizens of this country were the guilty ones; we were their innocent victims. We looked out at our world and saw a populace of criminals, whose vicious crimes had reduced us to miserable wretches. Our deep sense of sinfulness had been pushed down and then projected outward, so that everywhere we looked we saw sinners about to pounce.

The world therefore represented a complete inversion of cause and effect. We had freely chosen our own suffering, but now it seemed thrust on us by the world. Separation was merely a subjective idea that we made, but now it looked like an objective reality that made *us*. We had caused the world, but it now appeared to be *our* cause, our mother, our god. It gave birth to us. Its winds of fortune shaped and molded our identity. Its events and circumstances impressed themselves on our emotions, causing what we felt. The world was reality itself, and so whatever it told us we had to believe.

The real problem—our choice to leave our Father's house—had now shifted. The problem was this damned far country, what it was doing to us, what it was making us feel. The solution was obvious. We had to rearrange this world, so that now *different* events and circumstances would cause us to feel pleasure rather than pain. We assumed that if we could just make things go better on the outside, we would be happy.

Thus, we hoped, with enough skillful plans and brilliant moves, this prodigal son's fortunes would turn around. He would get out of the business of pig feeding and starving. Now he would enjoy more riotous living than ever. He would have a whole harem of harlots. And he would fill his empty belly with all the delicacies the land had to offer. The far country would cease its unfair campaign against him, apologize, and restore to him the inheritance it had so wrongfully stolen.

We tried to rearrange the furniture of the world in many ways: by being "giving" and self-sacrificing, by bargaining and compromising, and by openly attacking. Yet all of these activities carried the weight of our anger at the world. All of them sent a covert message: "I suffered because of you. Therefore, you owe me." All of them were designed to instill guilt in others, and so obligate them to "give" to us. In other words, they were all just different forms of attack, and this reveals the underlying intent of our "solution." It was not really meant to solve the problem at all. It was just another part of the system we had invented to *perpetuate* the problem. By projecting a world that attacked us, we provided ourselves with the perfect excuse to attack in return. And in this attack we repeated our ancient departure from the house of Love. We repeated our reversal of the pure goodness that God placed in us at creation. With each interaction—each disguised attack—we convinced ourselves more fully that we had "made a devil of God's Son,"[5] and would never again be His Son in His house.

And so here we have stayed; like the prodigal son, stuck in the mud of time and space. We have been trudging in confusion through this nightmare world far, far longer than we would ever suspect. It didn't start with the birth of our current bodies: "Birth was not the beginning."[6] *A Course in Miracles* never says how long we have been traveling. But by saying that our departure set in motion the physical universe it says a great deal, for scientists tell us the universe is many billions of years old.

This generates a sobering conclusion: We, the collective prodigal son, have been wandering away from home for untold eons. Our wanderings began long before our current lifetime, before the dawn of humankind, even before planet Earth coalesced out of primordial gases. When the galaxies were just unformed matter hurtling through space, we were on our travels even then. Who knows what strange realms we have roamed through, what forms we have appeared in, what planes of existence we have traversed in lonely search? Next time we see a homeless person who has been wandering the streets for perhaps five or ten years, we might consider the possibility that we have been wandering homeless for *billions*. A *Course in Miracles* portrays each one of us as a homeless person, as "a sorry figure; weary, worn, in threadbare clothing, and with feet that bleed a little from the rocky road he walks."[7]

> Without the world he made [he thinks he is] an outcast; homeless and afraid. He does not realize that it is here he is afraid indeed, and homeless, too; an outcast wandering so far from home, so long away, he does not realize he has forgotten where he came from, where he goes, and even who he really is [on top of being homeless, he is mentally ill— he has amnesia]....
>
> ....He wanders on, aware of the futility he sees about him everywhere, perceiving how his little lot but dwindles, as he goes ahead to nowhere. Still he wanders on in misery and poverty, alone though God is with him, and a treasure his so great that everything the world contains is valueless before its magnitude.[8]

Strangers in a strange land, sojourners in a far country, through all of our travels we have been blindly searching for a home we dimly remember, for some obscure paradise lost. We have been nostalgically clutching our few remaining notes of the forgotten song, trying to place where it was we heard that divine melody. "Everyone is looking for himself and for the power and glory he thinks he has lost."[9] Because no one is at home in this world, everyone here is forever seeking; endlessly seeking, but never finding. We construct home after home,[10] hoping to recapture the blissful experience of being in our Father's house. Yet all of these homes are attempts to make a substitute for what *has* no substitute. And so they never satisfy.

> The world you see...has disappointed you since time began.
> The homes you built have never sheltered you. The roads
> you made have led you nowhere, and no city that you built
> has withstood the crumbling assault of time.[11]

This passage gives us a much larger time frame than we are accustomed to, as if we are looking back over vast stretches of forgotten history, filled with endless, fruitless seeking. We can almost see the cities going up, our little chests filled with hope for a better life, and then see those same cities lying abandoned, as the desert's dust slowly covers them. How many such cities have we built and deserted? How many homes have we constructed in the misplaced hope of finding real belonging? How many roads have we made that led us absolutely nowhere?

In our never-ending search and sorrow we have cried out with the biblical psalmists, "How long, O Lord?...How long wilt thou hide thy face from me?"[12] "How long wilt thy wrath burn like fire?"[13] For we have believed our own lie that it was God Who bestowed on us this wretched condition. He was the one, we thought, who locked us up in these bodies and allotted us this brief three score and ten in which to be whipped by the winds of the world He made. And once He did so, He just sat back and watched the action, until we expired. Therefore, we have cried, "How long, O Lord, will You leave me here to rot in this insane asylum? How soon will You rescue me and take me home into Your Arms?"

Unbeknownst to us, through all the ages of our crying, God has been calling to us in answer. The following words, though spoken by the author of the Course, can be heard as God's answer to us:

> How long, O Son of God, will you maintain the game of
> sin? Shall we not put away these sharp-edged children's
> toys? How soon will you be ready to come home? Perhaps
> today? There is no sin. Creation is unchanged. Would you
> still hold return to Heaven back? How long, O holy Son of
> God, how long?[14]

God's poignant question, "How long, O Son of God?" dispels all of the assumptions behind our aching question, "How long, O Lord?" The truth is *not* that we are sitting on this godforsaken rock where God cruelly deposited us, stuck in a real and horrible predicament, crying out to God to rescue us, while He turns a deaf ear.

The truth is something else entirely. The truth is that *God is lovingly calling reluctant children home from play.* If you look closely at the above passage, you can detect this image. Its lines sound almost like a mother calling her kids in for dinner: "How long are you going to stay out there playing?"

Our passage, however, gives this innocent and familiar scene a dark twist. We, the children, refuse to come in, because we are absorbed in a deadly game, "the game of sin." In our macabre game of make-believe, and using our "sharp-edged children's toys," we have played that we are murderers who have actually killed our beloved Father. We pretend that, by committing this crime, we have changed ourselves from innocent children into horrible monsters. In a secret place inside, we don't blame God for putting us here; in deepest shame, we blame ourselves. We think that we have made ourselves too sinful to ever return. That is why we "still hold return to Heaven back." That is why we ignore God's Call. For we have pretended long and hard—to the point where we truly believe it—that we can never go home again, *not in a billion years.*

Yet if we really listened to our Father's Call, we would realize that this is all so needless. For that Call is conveying a wondrous fact: This whole thing is only a game. It's not real life. Consequently, "there is no sin. Creation is unchanged." When we finally muster the courage to show up again at the back porch, weapons in hand, heads bowed in shame, our Father will gently laugh, and say, "Don't worry. You never really did it. You were just playing. You never lost your innocence. Come on back inside, children. I have a feast waiting for you."

Even this "back porch" image does not quite capture it, for in truth we never even walked out the door. All that happened was that we briefly fell asleep in the limitless temple of our Father's house. We dreamt of a lonely exile in a faraway land, through which we wandered aimlessly for time without end, our inheritance squandered. Yet all the while we remained safe at home, our inheritance lay sparkling all around us, and only a "tiny tick of time"[15] had passed. Although in our minds all hell had broken loose, in actuality Heaven remained serenely unchanged. And we remained its honored Son.

Now we can appreciate the words of God's Call: "How long, O holy Son of God, how long?" For "how long" is in *our* hands, not God's. Nothing is holding us back; not our Father and not our alleged sinfulness. We can return any time we choose. The door is standing open, waiting for us. All we need do is decide to put down our toys and walk in.

> You who have played that you are lost to hope, abandoned by your Father, left alone in terror in a fearful world made mad by sin and guilt; be happy now. That game is over. Now a quiet time has come, in which we put away the toys of guilt, and lock our quaint and childish thoughts of sin forever from the pure and holy minds of Heaven's children and the Son of God.[16]

Wouldn't it be wonderful if we could enter into this "quiet time," if we could realize that it was all just a game and rise up and reclaim our inheritance as Sons of God? How do we do that?

Through forgiveness, of course. Forgiveness is the single thing that unravels all the threads in the cloth of separation. We broke off relationship with totality and thought we were alone and separate. Forgiveness wipes away the old grudges that separate us from others. It reestablishes relationship, and so paves the way for oneness. We projected our sins onto the world, and saw them staring back at us.[17] Forgiveness lets go of this projection, and our sins along with it. We condemned our brother and became convinced we were evil. Forgiveness releases our minds from the poison of condemnation. It lets our love flow out again, proving that there really is good in us. We saw evil out in the world and thought reality itself had become warped and evil. Forgiveness sees past the illusion of evil and reveals to us a pristine reality, ever changeless. It opens the eyes of Christ in us. Forgiveness is how we realize that sin was nothing but a childish game, that pure goodness still shines within us. It is what shows us that we need not return because we never left.

Once he has completely forgiven, the prodigal son will awaken from his dream of a long and cruel journey. He will open his eyes in his own bed in his Father's house. He will find the house the same as ever, and find himself neither stranger nor outcast, but his Father's beloved Son. And Heaven will continue as it always has.

Listen to the story of the prodigal son, and learn what God's treasure is and yours: This son of a loving father left his home and thought he had squandered everything for nothing of any value, although he had not understood its worthlessness at the time. He was ashamed to return to his father, because he thought he had hurt him. Yet when he came home the father welcomed him with joy, because the son himself *was* his father's treasure. He [the father] wanted nothing else.[18]

This version of Jesus' parable concludes with an insight into the heart of the story, one which was implicit in the original but is made explicit here. All along the son was too ashamed to return home, thinking he had sinned, thinking he had thrown away his father's treasure. Yet upon return he discovered, to his glorious surprise, that he *was* his father's treasure.

16.1. Eventually, we will collectively devote ourselves to applying forgiveness and returning home.

The game of sin cannot go on forever. The costs are too great, the prizes too hollow. The day will come when we as a world will begin to decide that nothing here is worth it. We will assess our experiment in homelessness and conclude that it has been an unmitigated failure. In essence, the whole world will say to itself what the prodigal son said to himself:

Now we would arise in haste and go unto our Father's house. We have been gone too long, and we would linger here no more.[19]

It may be hard to believe that going to our Father's house could be a collective process. Perhaps individuals, like Christ and Buddha, could reach that state of perfect enlightenment. But could everyone come home together? From the Course's standpoint, this collective homecoming is not only possible, but inevitable. "Ultimately, every member of the family of God must return."[20] And every member must join hands along the way. For only thus is the ego's world reversed and undone.

Therefore, all of us will complete the journey home, and do so together. The rest of this chapter, which describes the Course's account of the last days of the world, may read somewhat like a fairy tale or fantasy novel. Yet it all follows from this single idea.

Before we can lay all games down forever, we need to play one last one. "We pause but for a moment more, to play our final, happy game upon this earth."[21] This is the game of salvation, also called true perception, also called forgiveness. It too is a game; given that we only pretended to leave, we can only pretend that we are coming back. Yet this game is a happy one, which heals us of the trauma of the game of sin. And this one leads beyond all games and into reality.

> Salvation can be thought of as a game that happy children play. It was designed by One Who loves His children, and Who would replace their fearful toys with joyous games, which teach them that the game of fear is gone....The game of fear is gladly laid aside, when children come to see the benefits salvation brings.[22]

This last line could be read as a prophecy of the final ages of this world. In those ages we, the children of God, will increasingly lay aside our fearful toys and enter ever more deeply into the game of forgiveness. We will thus grow more and more carefree. All the suffering and insanity that came with the separation will gradually be reversed. Forgiveness will eventually solve all of those chronic dilemmas that we tried for so many ages to resolve, all of those problems that would never go away. We will discover that each problem was caused not by some enemy out there, as we had thought, but by our own internal perception of enemy, by our own *enmity*.

As we release this perception, the most miraculous things will occur. The bitterest of enemies will become the dearest of friends. Ancient feuds will dissolve in reconciliation. Black and white, young and old, parent and child, rich and poor will drop the finger of blame and embrace in love. The hatred of centuries, traded back and forth so many times that no one remembers who started it, will seem senseless and be forgotten. The war that has raged across our planet since it first cooled will finally end in the onset of universal peace.

We will look around and marvel at how we ever missed the celestial beauty of the beings with whom we share this earth. We will fall into a state of wonderment over the ineffable light we see in everyone and everything. The resulting global outbreak of love will leap across all lines, even jumping the lines between species. As we beat our swords into plowshares, the lion and the lamb shall indeed lie down together. And as the lines of love link more and more minds, the planetary collectivity of humans, animals, plants, and even grains of sand[23] will begin to awaken as a single sentient Being, the holy Son of God.

16.2. The Second Coming of Christ is when the world collectively awakens to the Christ, the Self we share.

This awakening is what the Course calls the Second Coming. In Course terminology, it is not the physical return of Jesus, but rather the collective return of our awareness of our shared Identity, the Christ. His First Coming was when God brought Him into being, in the beginning. And now He comes again, to awaken all His parts to their single Self. The Course defines the Second Coming as "the return of sense,"[24] "the end of the ego's rule and the healing of the mind."[25]

The Second Coming will occur when all of us are willing "to let forgiveness rest upon all things without exception and without reserve."[26] When we have understood that there are no exceptions to forgiveness, that forgiving the most heinous "sin" and the most trivial mistake are exactly the same thing, we will have learned the first principle of miracles: "There is no order of difficulty in miracles."[27] And then we will be ready for Christ to come. This is an exceedingly advanced state. At our current stage in history only a few rare individuals have achieved it.

Yet the time will come, untold ages from now, when the entire world will have reached this place. Then we will experience the Second Coming's "gentle advent, which encompasses all living things with you."[28] The light of Christ will break out across the skies of our collective mind, illuminating our upturned faces and filling us with the expectation of the eternal:

> Creation [synonymous with "the Christ"] leans across the bars of time to lift the heavy burden from the world. Lift up your hearts to greet its advent. See the shadows fade away in gentleness; the thorns fall softly from the bleeding brow of him who is the holy Son of God.[29]

As Easter sunrise breaks out all over the world, the global experience of crucifixion will be undone. We will put away the fearful toys of childhood. All those sharp-edged toys that pierced our brows and nailed us to the cross will merely fall away. Sickness will disappear. Aging will be no more. The body will remain "incorruptible and perfect as long as it is useful for your holy purpose."[30] Even the great and final power of death, which seemed to "hold all living things within its withered hand,"[31] will be rendered powerless. Death as we know it will no longer occur. Instead of the body expiring when it can no longer function, we will consciously lay it down when we have completed *our* function here: "And so it is discarded as a choice, as one lays by a garment now outworn."[32] In some cases, the body will be physically laid down, such as when great yogis consciously exit this life. In other cases, its "reality" will be laid down, so that it actually vanishes, as happened with Jesus' body.[33]

What would a world without death be like? Death is so central to this world that its elimination would mean a transformation of the world's fundamental character. The Course symbolizes this transformation with uplifting images of the rebirth of nature:

> The blood of hatred fades to let the grass grow green again, and let the flowers be all white and sparkling in the summer sun.[34]

> The grass is pushing through the soil, the trees are budding now, and birds have come to live within their branches. Earth is being born again in new perspective.[35]

I believe that these images are both metaphorical and literal. In their literalness, they signify that as this "new perspective" is born into our minds the physical earth will actually become a verdant garden. True, all physical forms are dreams, yet dreams are symbols of what is in the mind of the dreamer. If the minds that dream this world were truly healed, what kind of dream symbols do you think would result? Why not the healing of damaged bodies, scorched fields, broken bird wings, and dry streams,[36] as mentioned by the Course? As our thinking continues to heal, even the basic fabric of the dream will probably begin to alter and transform. Physical laws will likely become more plastic, matter itself less dense, time more malleable, for all these are mere fabrications of the mind.

Yet still, the content of the reversal is mental, not physical. And nowhere is this mental reversal better expressed than in a section from the Manual entitled "How Will the World End?"

> The world will end in joy, because it is a place of sorrow. When joy has come, the purpose of the world has gone. The world will end in peace, because it is a place of war. When peace has come, what is the purpose of the world? The world will end in laughter, because it is a place of tears. Where there is laughter, who can longer weep? And only complete forgiveness brings all this to bless the world. In blessing [the world] departs, for it will not end as it began.[37]

16.3. The Last Judgment is a process by which we judge all past thoughts and retain only the pure.

The Second Coming is not the end of the world, but only the beginning of the end. "The Second Coming ends the lessons that the Holy Spirit teaches, making way for the Last Judgment, in which learning ends in one last summary that will extend beyond itself, and reaches up to God."[38] With the Last Judgment, the Course has again taken a traditional notion and dramatically reworked it. In the Course, the Last Judgment is not a final condemnation, in which God separates the righteous from the sinners, casting the latter into the lake of eternal fire. Instead, it "is a final healing"[39] in which *we* separate out our holy thoughts from our insane thoughts, choosing to retain only the former.

> You who believed that God's Last Judgment would condemn the world to hell along with you, accept this holy truth: God's Judgment is the gift of the Correction He bestowed on all your errors, freeing you from them, and all effects they ever seemed to have.[40]

With the Second Coming, we reached a stage that is quite likely beyond our present imagination. To our current minds we would probably seem more like angels or gods than human beings. Yet the significance of this stage is not that we have reached total sanity—for we have not—but merely that we are now ready to relinquish every last microscopic vestige of our *insanity*. We are finally willing to once and for all distinguish the real from the unreal.

Now the Holy Spirit will overshadow us, and open the hidden vaults of our minds. Here are piled, cluttered and dusty, all of the countless thoughts that we have accumulated since the beginning of time, most of them utterly forgotten as the decades and centuries closed over them. Into these vaults, accompanied by the Holy Spirit, we will carry the blazing lamp of truth. We will shine its purifying light onto each thought, judging each one by its uncompromising standard. Those thoughts that are already true we will happily retain. Those that are partly true we will accept and purify.[41] Those that are simply false we will firmly but dispassionately reject. We will calmly "disown [our] miscreations which, without belief, will no longer exist."[42] The end result of this process is called "the blessed residue,"[43] a collection of thoughts so crystal pure that it causes our minds to shine as brightly as the sun.

Vault after buried vault the Holy Spirit will open for us, and vault after vault we will judge by the unwavering light of truth. According to the Course, this process will go on collectively for millions of years,[44] though individuals may pass through it far more quickly.[45] Eventually, however, we will reach the very last door, the heavy, ancient door behind which lies our first separated thought: our decision to abandon God and make our own kingdom. This iron door, closed since the first moment of time, will now swing open on its rusted hinge. Standing at last face to face with the decision that began it all, we will make the last decision that we will ever make.

> The Great Transformer of perception will undertake with
> you the careful searching of the mind that made this world,
> and uncover to you the seeming reasons for your making it.
> In the light of the real reason that He brings, as you follow
> Him, He will show you that there is no reason here at all.[46]

When our reason for making this world lies unveiled before us, in the light of His reason we will finally realize that this world *has* no reason. Having at last seen with total clarity our primeval choice to separate, we will choose again, just as Jesus urges us to do in this passage: "Help me now to lead you back to where the journey was begun, to make another choice with me."[47] And now that he *has* led us back, we *will* make another choice with him. This time we will choose truth and not illusion. We will choose God, rather than ego; Heaven, instead of the world we made. This time we will remember to laugh at the tiny, mad idea of separation. Here, at the edge of the world, at the end of all things visible and temporal, we will make the one judgment we did not make in the beginning and have been unable to make until now:

> It is the judgment of the truth upon illusion, of knowledge on perception: "It has no meaning, and does not exist."[48]

And with this final judgment, our work will be done.

16.4. When we are perfectly healed we are ready for God to take the final step. In that step we remember God and our true Identity.

After all our travels, at last, at long last, we have come to the end of the road. We "have reached the end of an ancient journey."[49] We stand at that hallowed place which the Course poetically refers to as the gate of Heaven. "Your foot has reached the lawns that welcome you to Heaven's gate."[50]

> The lawns are deep and still, for here the place appointed for the time when you should come has waited long for you. Here will time end forever. At this gate eternity itself will join with you.[51]

Only one more step and we are home. Yet this is the biggest step we will ever experience. The pathway home has raised us far above the plains from which we began. But now the time has come to leave behind everything familiar, to step off the summit of the mountain into the clear blue sky:

> The path becomes quite different as one goes along. Nor could all the magnificence, the grandeur of the scene and the enormous opening vistas that rise to meet one as the journey continues, be foretold from the outset. Yet even these, whose splendor reaches indescribable heights as one proceeds, fall short indeed of all that wait when the pathway ceases and time ends with it.[52]

All of our changes thus far have been quantitative shifts. We have shifted into truer and truer shades of perception. However, "It is at this point that sufficient quantitative change occurs to produce a real qualitative shift."[53] This is the shift from perception to knowledge. This is a "fundamental change,"[54] for perception and knowledge are fundamentally different modes of awareness. Since time immemorial we have been in the mode of perception, in which we have tried to know objects that are external to our minds. Yet how can we really know something that is apart from us? The very nature of perception prevents us from reaching the certainty we crave. Now we are about to enter the realm of knowledge, in which our *knowing* of the object and the object *itself* are one and the same.

With this knowledge we will finally come to know ourselves. As we bridge the gap between knower and known, we will come face to face with ourselves. The *knower* will become the *known*. We will at last find out who we are. For all the numberless ages of time we have wondered, and have had to guess and speculate about our identity. For the longest time we were convinced that our identity was evil, and that if we were ever to catch sight of it we "would be struck with horror so intense that [we] would rush to death by [our] own hand."[55] On the higher rungs of the spiritual ladder, we slowly left this self-loathing behind and experienced heights of happiness we never thought possible. We discovered abilities we never dreamt we could have. However, all of it is so much straw compared to discovering our true Identity. As the Course reminds us, "Yet nothing he can do can compare even in the slightest with the glorious surprise of remembering Who he is."[56] And what is it we discover? Perhaps this quote says it best: "Deep in your mind the holy Christ in you is waiting your acknowledgment as you."[57] We discover that we are the Christ, the limitless Son of God, the radiant extension of our Father's Love.

This represents the end of the road in our tour of the mind. In earlier chapters we tracked the various ego levels from the superficial face of innocence to the subterranean call for help. In the last chapter we found that underneath all of the ego's levels lies the right mind, the abode of perfectly healed perception. Yet we also said that the right mind is not the bottom. Underneath the right mind is the Christ Mind, and this is not really another level at all. It is reality; one without a second. All of the levels are therefore just illusions, and when we step off the last one, the entire structure will vanish as we awaken to the only Mind there is.

This remembrance of our Identity, however, only comes in the last step, and we have not reached that stage of the journey quite yet. Having experienced the Second Coming and passed through the Last Judgment, we now stand before the gate of Heaven, serenely ready for God's final step.

Now comes a time of holy waiting. This is the shining instant we have longed for since time first began, the instant we have worked to draw closer with every gift of forgiveness and healing. Now that perfect healing has been attained, that instant is here. The earth is still; all motion has ceased. And we, the innumerable prodigal sons who have feuded for years beyond counting, stand finally reunited. Our joined hands encircle the globe. With eyes turned upward "we stand together as one Son of God"[58] and await our awakening to eternity. In two lines of great beauty, *A Course in Miracles* captures the pregnant joy and expectancy of this final moment of time and space:

> All living hearts are tranquil with a stir of deep antici-pation, for the time of everlasting things is now at hand.[59]

> And all he sought before to crucify are resurrected with him, by his side, as he prepares with them to meet his God.[60]

We wait for our Father. We prepare to meet our God. For He Himself must take the final step. As we said, perception and knowledge are fundamentally different modes, and so nowhere do the two actually meet. Even when we have reached perfect perception, there still lies a gap between it and knowledge. Our efforts are powerless to bridge this gap. God must do it for us. The following passage explains why:

> Yet the last step must be taken by God, because the last step in your redemption, which seems to be in the future, was accomplished by God in your creation.[61]

The last step is somehow the same thing as the first step—our creation by God. In our creation, God gave us Heaven. It was a pure gift from Him. We were placed there by His Will, not by our own efforts. And that is why it is impossible to lift ourselves back there. To give Heaven to ourselves, to place ourselves there with our own efforts, would be like creating ourselves. It can't be done. Thus, just as God brought us into Heaven in the beginning, so He must lift us *back* into

Heaven in the end. And those two events are somehow one and the same.

That is why we wait for Him. Rather than trying to seize Heaven with our tiny hands, we wait. In fact, the purpose of all our forgiving and extending has been to bring us to a moment of perfect waiting. Our entire journey home has been aimed at achieving a moment when we would no longer shut Him out; when not even the tiniest impulse in us would recoil from His Love; when we would be as perfectly receptive to Him as the air is to sunlight. One such moment is enough. When we finally reach it, says the Course, it "will be so short that [we] will barely have time to thank God for it. For God will take the last step swiftly."[62]

> God leans to us and lifts us up, taking salvation's final step Himself. All steps but this we learn, instructed by His Voice. But finally He comes Himself, and takes us in His Arms and sweeps away the cobwebs of our sleep. His gift of grace is more than just an answer. It restores all memories the sleeping mind forgot; all certainty of what Love's meaning is.[63]

This is a poetic image, but it refers to a real event, so beyond our comprehension that poetic images perhaps best capture it. We have spent ages apart from our Love, lost in the dim world of dreams. Even though He has guided our footsteps, still there has been a gap between our minds and His. He has spoken to us through an Intermediary, and through the murky veil of our sleep. Now, however, "He comes Himself," to revive His child, His beloved. With one sweep of His Arm He lifts us into His embrace. He pulls us out of the depths of our age-long sleep, restoring "all memories the sleeping mind forgot." He lifts us back into the full clarity of love's meaning, which we remember as we reunite with our Love and know Him again face to face.

As He lifts us to Himself, all that we made will vanish:

> Gone is perception, false and true alike. Gone is forgiveness, for its task is done. And gone are bodies in the blazing light upon the altar to the Son of God....For where God's memory[64] has come at last there is no journey, no belief in sin, no walls, no bodies, and the grim appeal of guilt and death is there snuffed out forever.[65]

The world will literally disappear; not only our small planet but all of the stars, galaxies, and galactic clusters of the entire phenomenal universe. "The stars will disappear in light, and the sun that opened up the world to beauty will vanish."[66] Space will dissolve. Time "will roll up like a long carpet spread along the past behind you, and will disappear."[67] The physical plane itself, along with every other dream plane, no matter how high or how subtle, will pass away, never to return. In the twinkling of an eye will be gone the entire constellation of all the worlds we made, all the enormous frameworks we constructed to keep God out. The kingdom that seemed eternal, that appeared invincible for so many billions of years, will pause, teeter, and quietly vanish. "It will not be destroyed nor attacked nor even touched. It will merely cease to seem to be."[68] After eons upon eons of its endless noisy spectacle of teeming forms and churning motions, there will be nothing but quiet.

All little things are silent. Little sounds are soundless now. The little things of earth have disappeared.[69]

And in the stillness of that hallowed silence, we will open our eyes in Heaven, and "breathe again the holy air that fills [our] Father's house,"[70] remembering that *here* is where we have always belonged, and that here is where we have always *been*, enfolded in the safety of God's boundless embrace. And in that holy temple we will be free at last, free of form and boundary, free in the exalted vastness of pure spirit. And God will greet our waking eyes with the brilliant sunshine of His Love, and we will respond with our whole being. The journey through time and space that felt so frighteningly real will seem like a vague, fleeting dream, and quickly vanish from our holy minds. And we will again join our voices to the ancient song, right where we left off, without having missed a single note.[71] The song of Heaven, "that vast song of honor and of love,"[72] that oceanic melody that rolls ceaselessly from God to us and us to God, will resound throughout the measureless expanses of infinity, filling the Kingdom with joy unbounded, as it always has, as it always will, throughout all eternity.

And we will be home, at peace forever in the Heart of God.

Conclusion

What are we to say about the thought system we have just surveyed? Having reached the end of our tour, I would like to offer some final reflections of a more personal nature.

Before I encountered the Course, I thought I knew the basic outlines of spiritual truth. In my mind, there was really nothing more to learn. The only task left was to apply what I had already learned. Then the Course came into my life. Initially, it seemed to fit my preconceptions: "Okay, yes, our real nature is divine, and we are in this world to fully realize our true nature and reunite with God. Yep, sounds about right." Yet I also recognized unsettling ways in which the Course frustrated my preconceptions of spiritual truth. I would come across ideas that I hadn't read in any other teaching. I didn't quite know what to do with these, and this contributed to me keeping a wary distance between myself and the Course.

As time passed, and I began to form my own ideas about the Course, it began to frustrate my preconceptions of *it*. Each time I thought I had sized it up, I realized that I had boxed up only certain aspects of it, while new aspects kept presenting themselves to me in a process that seemed endless. Slowly, without me really noticing, the Course was gradually reshaping the convenient little house I had built for spiritual truth. It was knocking out walls, adding on rooms, digging out basements, building additional stories, painting on new colors. Construction and reconstruction were going on constantly, day and night. The Course was making me aware of vital issues in life that I had never paid any attention to. It was also sensitizing me to the importance of subjects like postmodernism, Freudian psychology, Eastern mysticism, literature, poetry, theology, and many others. I finally realized that this expansion of my view of the Course and of spiritual truth would never stop. I realized that, under the Course's influence, my view of reality itself would be ever growing, with new rooms always being added on.

Therefore, today, twenty-five years later, I stand before this thought system more humbled and more astonished than ever. I want to tell you what I find so amazing about it, yet I don't feel qualified. Anything I say would be partial, and would ultimately reveal that I don't really get it. This teaching is simply far bigger than my mind is (or at least seems to be). Yet at the same time, I feel compelled to share what I can, even if it's partial, even if it doesn't do justice to the Course's real depth and breadth. So, with that qualifier, allow me to share what I find so remarkable about the Course's teaching.

In doing so, I will speak both of the Course and of its author. It's no secret that its author claims to be Jesus, a claim that I have increasingly embraced over the years. Yet even if one is skeptical or even dismissive of this claim, it is hard to deny that the Course bears the mark of an extremely distinctive mind. It is absolutely not a stream of rehashed spiritual concepts. The ideas, the language, the imagery—indeed, everything about it—shine with a creativity and originality that reveal this to be the work of a single towering mind. For the purposes of this conclusion, I will simply call him "the author."

On a strictly intellectual level, the Course's author demonstrates a mastery that I find breathtaking. Students often believe that the Course repeats a few simple ideas over and over, yet *nothing* could be further from the truth. There are in reality thousands of ideas in its system. It covers a phenomenally broad range of topics. This includes countless topics in human psychology and relationships, in spirituality and religion, and in philosophy and theology. Indeed, each word of any significance in the Course acquires its own family of Course-specific meanings as it recurs through these pages. Each reference to a word like "loss," for example, will frame that word in certain very specific ways (for instance, "Yet all loss comes only from your own misunderstanding"[1]). When you add up all the different references, a broad, multifaceted, yet unified perspective on that word will emerge. So far as I can tell, this is true of every word in the Course beyond minor words like "the" and "and."

This, in fact, is part of why the Course's teaching is so hard to learn.

Virtually every word is given special meaning. This special meaning may merely be a deepening and nuancing of the word's conventional meaning, or it may be a fundamental correction of the conventional meaning, making this essentially a new word. Either way, the reader encounters a sentence in which word after word is part of a specialized vocabulary. If only one word meant something new, you could readily clarify its meaning by looking to the surrounding words. But if the surrounding words carry new meanings as well, what do you do then? All you can do is lift yourself up bit by bit. As you understand one word in the Course's vocabulary a little better, that sheds light on every word it comes into contact with. In this way, you slowly climb the ladder into greater and greater understanding of the teaching.

Whenever I do a study of a particular word or a certain topic, I am struck by the brilliance and cogency of what the Course has to say on that subject. Maybe you can't prove the Course's perspective on that topic, but it does make surprising sense. It seems to accord with both experience and logic, and it contributes to practical change. Frequently, what the Course has to say on these topics is startlingly original. For instance, for two thousand years Christianity has called the crucifixion the Atonement, yet in complete contrast, the Course calls the *resurrection* the Atonement. Embedded in this single change of terminology is a whole new vision of Atonement and of our relationship with God. Atonement has to do with reconciling with God. In the traditional version, our break with God was frighteningly real, and so, in order to reconcile with Him, someone has to pay for that break—in blood. In the Course's new vision, however, our break with God was only apparent, and so we reconcile with God by simply waking up to His never-changing Love for us. Given this view, it is only natural for the Course to say that Jesus opened the way for our reconciliation with God not by dying, but by awakening to unlimited life—by resurrecting. You can't prove this new interpretation, of course, yet you also cannot easily put it out of mind.

Another apparently original contribution is the Course's teaching on the subject of free choice. The Course claims that free choice isn't free in the true sense of the word. Yes, it says, we are genuinely free to choose between alternatives. Yet freedom, as the Course points out, means doing what you want. And if part of you wants one alternative and the other part of you wants the other alternative, then no matter which one you choose, you don't *entirely* get to do what you want. The Course therefore concludes that free choice is not real freedom. I've never heard anything like this before, yet it is completely logical, and it fits my experience. Even once I have chosen one of the alternatives, there is still a sense of imprisonment since the part of me that wanted the other alternative doesn't get to do what it wants. And how can a sense of imprisonment be called freedom?

These are just two out of countless examples. With seemingly every topic the Course touches, it says things that appear to be strikingly original, and yet these same things seem logical and reasonable and inspire transformation. The result is that each topic stands on its own as a minor masterpiece. Each one could one day be recognized as an important contribution to humanity's thought. Yet that is only half the story. The other half is that, somehow, each topic fits seamlessly with all the other topics. What the Course has to say about freedom, for instance, fits perfectly with what it has to say about Atonement and loss and everything else. Thus, if you truly and completely understand its teaching about freedom, you simultaneously understand everything in its system. You could say, then, that each topic implicitly contains the whole teaching, with all of its thousands of parts.

This means that, in the end, the teaching is remarkably unitary. The more you understand it, the more you see how each idea leads to every other idea; the more you see them all weaving together into a pristine simplicity. This simplicity, however, is not simple minded. Rather, it is the simplicity of thousands of threads drawing into one.

This blending of seemingly disparate themes is one of the Course's great strengths. It has a way of taking ideas that have historically been seen as poles apart and weaving them together. In its teaching, uniting your self with God and realizing you *have* no self—two things that have traditionally been seen as different alternatives—are the same thing. Performing a useful function in this world contributes to detaching from the world and realizing its illusory nature. Healing the body comes from realizing there is no body to heal. Fulfilling your one responsibility to work out your own salvation is only done by helping others. Accessing God's grace is achieved through diligent self-effort. Awakening to non-dual reality beyond this world is done by joining with other people *in* the world. Surrendering to what is and entering the limitless present is done by setting clear goals and pursuing them in a determined, organized fashion. Again and again the Course takes concepts that the human mind has tended to see as separate and weaves them together so seamlessly that they begin to look inseparable. After a while you become unable to think of one without thinking of the other.

Through this power to synthesize, the Course honors and incorporates so much of what has gone before, while at the same time managing to break new ground. Here is a vision, then, which moves with the currents of humanity's perennial spiritual wisdom, yet which also strikes off in bold, original directions of its own. I believe that both sides of this equation are essential to appreciating what the Course is. I treasure the ways in which the Course echoes the insights of humanity's sages and mystics, as well as psychologists, philosophers, and even contemporary experts in positive thinking and motivation. There is something truly universal about it. Yet I also cherish its uniqueness. There is simply nothing else like it. Many of its core themes are insights that cannot be found anywhere else; or if they can, they are well hidden.

The Course's author takes this intellectual mastery and pours all of it into a single goal: moving us from our current condition into the realization of true reality. It seems as if every fiber of his being is focused on this single task. In order to accomplish this task, he brings to the table a variety of qualities that, again, may not initially seem to go together. He brings together the highest and the lowest, the darkest and the brightest, the celestial and the terrestrial, the most pessimistic and the most optimistic.

Real change has to begin with an accurate, in-depth awareness of our current condition, and in this the author of the Course excels. I get the feeling that he knows us very well, unbelievably well. He sees, unvarnished, the way we live our lives. He sees our quest for worldly things, for status, even for dominance. He sees our transitory relationships. Yet what is far more unnerving is that he sees what goes on in the privacy of our minds. He sees our goals change "ten times an hour."[2] He sees the names we secretly call ourselves, such as "callous" and "emotionally shallow."[3] He sees us inwardly treating our image of ourselves as a devotee would treat a god.[4] He sees us accusing ourselves of having ulterior motives even when our motives are genuinely loving.[5] He sees the quiet disappointment we experience when we reach the goals we thought would make us deliriously happy. He sees the slow despair that creeps into our veins as we gradually figure out that our hopes and dreams are never going to be fulfilled. The Course is full of passages that lay bare a private inner life that each of us thought was unique to himself or herself alone and therefore safely secret.

Yet his understanding of our minds and lives doesn't stop with what we are aware of. He dives down beneath the conscious mind into a vast unconscious, full of fear and darkness and, indeed, madness. I find it frankly disturbing to think that just below my consciousness lies the nightmarish region described by the Course. The caverns of this underground realm are dominated by the sinister presence of the ego, an ego which the Course describes in decidedly satanic terms. The essence of the ego is hostility and grandiosity. It wants to raise itself up while putting everyone else—others, God, even ourselves—at its feet. What makes this all the more disturbing is that these unconscious motivations do not stay in the unconscious. They rise to the surface in disguised form, in the form of the seemingly innocent motivations that drive everyday life.

I have often said that I know of no darker vision of human nature than that of *A Course in Miracles*. This may seem like a negative, yet here too the Course earns my respect. For there *is* something deeply wrong with the world, and it takes inner strength to place the responsibility, as Shakespeare said, not in our stars, but in ourselves. It is so popular to place the source of suffering somewhere outside of us: in our upbringing, in our genes, or in evil people out there. Yet the Course has the integrity to eschew the popular thing and say the responsible thing. And if we *are* responsible for the madness of the world, then surely that means that beneath our respectable veneers, madness lurks within us.

Although I know of no darker vision of human nature, I also know of no brighter, more affirming vision of ultimate reality, and this includes *our* reality. Even while the Course depicts our conventional thoughts and motives in satanic terms, it depicts our true nature in angelic terms. It says that we are as pure and holy as God Himself, and that this purity remains untainted by all of the nasty things we have ever thought or done. This is why the author of the Course, in a private aside to his scribes, likened us to demons, reminding them that demons are really just fallen angels. But then he added that the real truth is that angels cannot *really* fall—and neither can we.[6]

In the same way, while he depicts this world as "a slaughter house,"[7] where all things live only to die, he depicts ultimate reality as a paradise beyond imagination. It is a realm that is pure perfection, free of the pain and limitation of time and space. It is a realm that contains, in limitless measure, the love, unity, and sense of purpose that we all long for. What is most inspiring for me is the Course's vision of God. This is a God Who is so purely loving, so free of human foibles, as to defy comprehension. If we respond to this vision of God with disbelief, it is not because He seems too human to be God, but because He seems too good to be true.

This extraordinarily affirming vision of reality answers a profound need in us. We need to be assured that in the final analysis all is very, very well. In my younger days I often felt oppressed by the meaninglessness of it all. Beyond any unpleasant events in my personal life, there was the constant sickening hum of a reality without meaning. Whatever our overall view of reality is, it provides the backdrop for how we interpret all of our experiences in life. We therefore possess a deep need for an ultimately affirming view, and this is what the Course has given me. Now, all the little indignities of this world are so much easier to take, because I interpret them against the backdrop of the Course's sublime affirmation of what truly is.

Having sketched this unimaginably lofty vision of reality, the Course then calls on us to scale these dizzying heights. Its vision of reality quite naturally determines its goals. The author of the Course never ceases calling us to a perfection that lies beyond every trace of human ego. He asks us to habitually forgive even the most extreme attacks. He instructs us to comply with outrageous demands in order to show our dear brother a higher way of being.[8] In the end, he calls us to love each and every person—even strangers and attackers—with the same total, unconditional love.[9] In these ways, he reminds one very much of the historical Jesus and his radical injunctions to love your enemy and freely give your attacker twice as much as he is trying to take. One gets the persistent feeling that the author of the Course is asking us to be more than human, which makes sense since he claims we were never really human in the first place.

You have to admire the boldness of an author who calls his readers to nothing less than perfection. A lofty goal always carries the danger of appearing unrealistic, and yet experts in goal setting have long known that larger-than-life goals have the greatest power to dislodge us from our couches and spur us on to great things. Thus, even though the

Course's author runs the risk of having us give up in despair, I suspect that in setting his sights so high, he knows exactly what he's doing.

Yet a lofty goal *will* lead to giving up unless it is coupled with hope and encouragement, and the author of the Course provides ample amounts of both. He constantly tells us that we *will* get there, that we are making progress, that we are no longer wholly insane, that we don't have all that far to go, that the end is guaranteed by God. In one place, after saying that we are developmentally disabled when it comes to learning how to love, he tells us that our *potential* for learning is "limitless."[10] He then promises us, "You will become an excellent learner and an excellent teacher."[11] In the face of learning the kind of love he is talking about, I need that sort of encouragement. Every student does.

Lofty goals will also fail unless we are given practical tools that yield real results in the short term. The Course is renowned for this. However lofty its teachings are, it hooks those teachings up to practical methods that genuinely work. These methods are doable; they are truly within our reach. I'm thinking in particular of the Workbook, which provides explicit instructions for its daily practices. These practices start out very light—a couple of minutes a day—counting on the fact that as we see their benefits, we will be willing to give more time and effort. Yet even at their heaviest, they ask for only several minutes an hour—time that most of us waste anyway. I myself am continually amazed at the effectiveness of the Course's practices. I am not by nature a disciplined person, and yet the benefits of the Course's discipline have proved so valuable for me that, all these years down the line, I am more committed to its daily practice than ever.

One final element contributes to the accessibility of the Course's lofty goal, and this is the author's determination to meet us where we are. He has made major concessions to a broad range of earthly needs. For example, he affirms our need to have a role in the world that we alone can fill, even though this threatens to bolster our ego's addiction to being special. All he asks is that we leave the selection of this role to the Holy Spirit. He supports our need to be in relationship with others, even though relationships are such a hotbed of ego. He just asks us to give them to the Holy Spirit and says that if we do, we can enjoy relationships that are more enduring, harmonious, and truly united. He acknowledges our need to make decisions, "whether they be illusions or not."[12] He just says that we'll make better decisions if we ask for the

Holy Spirit's guidance. He even acknowledges our need for money and material things, despite his warnings that as ends in themselves, they are killers of spiritual progress. He says that the Holy Spirit will literally take care of our material needs, if we give ourselves single-mindedly to the life and function that He has laid out for us.

The Course, in other words, contains this strange combination of a world-transcending goal with a real honoring of the breadth of our earthly experience. This makes it fully possible to live a life in society, go to work, brave the freeways, raise a family, pay the bills, while making every minute an expression of divine guidance and a pursuit of a transcendent goal.

These elements that I have sketched come together to produce a single quality of utmost significance: *maximal power to induce change.* Every single element makes a vital contribution to this quality. By convincing us that he knows us, the author of the Course makes us feel that his teachings fit us, that they are for us. By painting our unconscious in such dark terms, he persuades us that what needs to change is inside of us, not outside, and that the need for change is immense and urgent. By painting true reality in such bright terms, he gives us a rational basis for embracing a whole new outlook, an outlook that is immeasurably bright. We choose this outlook not as an act of wishful thinking, but as an acknowledgment of what is real. By setting a lofty goal for us, he spurs us to reach for heights that otherwise wouldn't occur to us. By giving us hope and encouragement, and providing us with practical methods, he makes the notion of steady progress toward these heights seem realistic, something that is actually within our reach. Finally, by allowing us the elements of a normal life (only purified by the Holy Spirit), he makes it clear that this is not a path of sacrifice, nor one of lonely retreat from the human community. At this point, what is left to object to? All in all, it's as if the author has combined a single-minded dedication to our transformation with a deep awareness of what inspires transformation, and put that dedication and awareness into every corner of his system.

Yes, he is trying to change us. It may be for the sake of revealing our changeless Identity, yet it still means what we normally call change, and this arouses in us an instinctive wariness and suspicion. We immediately begin looking for reasons to not do what he asks. Perhaps our first question is "Who am I changing *for*?" We are so used to being asked to change for God's sake or Jesus' sake or the church's sake or society's sake or our family's sake. Something in us resists this kind of change, for it feels like a subtle betrayal of ourselves. Yet even though this author claims to be Jesus, he makes it continually clear that it's not about him. Rather, it's all about *our* liberation from our self-made prisons, a liberation that can't help but benefit everyone else. He makes it so constantly clear that we do the Course out of a kind of enlightened self-interest that our defenses slowly tire of being raised and eventually relax.

He is trying to change something that seems so deep-seated in us, so fundamental, that we want to dismiss what he says. Yet he has this knack for saying things that we immediately recognize as plausible, logical, even practical, despite the fact that they have never been said before and challenge every idea we live by. For example, the quest to be special dominates human life. Who doesn't want to be singled out for special honor and favor, either loudly by the masses or quietly by a cherished few? Yet the author of the Course makes this sage observation: "To 'single out' is to 'make alone,' and thus make lonely."[13] The instant you read this line you see the logic of it, and because of this, you cannot entirely defend yourself against it. To some extent, it just goes in, whether you like it or not. Once you've read it, you can never completely go back to the place you were before you read it. And yet, to really embrace this line means relinquishing every desire to outdo, to be better than, to be on top, to be specially loved, to be *singled out*. You can refuse to go all the way with such a line, but you cannot entirely dismiss it.

This appears to be the case even when his ideas fly in the face of all spiritual truth as we know it. One example is his teaching that this world was not created by God. He teaches that it was dreamt by us out of our insanity, as constant, three-dimensional proof of the "reality" of separation, and as a delivery device for the punishment we unconsciously think we deserve. When you first encounter this teaching, you probably think, "Surely he can't mean this. Spiritual teachings seem to be unanimous in acknowledging that the world is the expression of God." But once the idea gets in your head, it slowly works away at you. You start to think, "You know, I've always said this is a crazy world. And yes, it has had the effect of convincing me that separation—from others, from God—is real. And, now that I think about it, it does seem to be constantly punishing me." You increasingly realize how incongruous it is to think of God creating such a place. You slowly concede that this account of the world, though initially bizarre and uninspiring, more accurately fits your experience of living in this world.

Indeed, I am constantly struck by how sober, clear-eyed, and logical the author of the Course is. I've encountered so many spiritual teachings that try to make me feel good by romanticizing the ugly realities of life. "It's all perfect." "You were doing your best." "It was meant to be." "There are no mistakes." It sometimes strikes me as so much denial. There are times when spirituality seems like a salesman whose hypnotic words can make us feel inspired about any worthless piece of junk. That is why I find the Course so refreshing. Its author looks at things without romanticizing them. He delights in plain observations and ordinary black-and-white distinctions, the kind that most spiritual seekers try to unravel with spiritual cleverness. For instance, he pokes fun at those who try to glorify the cycles of nature, pointing out that the downstroke of all these cycles is death.[14] In personal guidance to his scribes, he praised Freud's pessimistic view of the ego and criticized later theorists for trying to endow the ego with more positive, even spiritual attributes. He said, "Freud was more clear-sighted about this, because he knew a *bad* thing when he perceived it."[15]

We do not exactly expect to hear a teacher of spirituality praise Sigmund Freud for his pessimism. Yet this praise captures so much of *this* teacher's whole tenor of mind. His next comment is equally revealing: "But he failed to recognize that a bad thing cannot exist." Here we see where he is ultimately heading. With his sober, logical mind, he wants to lift us into a new vision of reality. He wants to show us a wondrous reality that is more real than the ugliness we see with our eyes. He doesn't want a spirituality that shakes free of the oppressive restraints of rationality. The problem, from his standpoint, is not rationality but *irrationality*, which he claims every one of us is mired in. He wants a spirituality in which we become fully rational; in which, rather than romantically endowing bad things with spiritual attributes, we at last reach the quiet, clear-sighted recognition that a bad thing simply cannot exist.

The net effect is that the more you read his words, the harder it becomes to write him off. You desperately want to, for there is a tug o' war going on, in which you either write him off or he pulls your mind all the way over to his side. So at first you think, "It's just hyperbole," "It's very pretty, but not very practical," or "This really applies to spiritual prodigies, not to me." But the longer you read him, the more reasonable he sounds, as if he is explaining to you in the plainest possible language how you personally can become sane and happy. Slowly, inexorably, it begins to dawn on you, "Oh my God, he really means it. He is actually for real."

This is the power of the Course's teaching—to cause us to seriously consider the unthinkable, to take our minds to radically new places. It does this like nothing I have seen. Despite the Course's popularity in certain circles, I live every day with the feeling that the world has no idea what a treasure has landed on its shores. I can only hope that this treasure will one day be discovered.

Notes

A note on reading Course references

All references are given for the Second Edition of the Course, and are listed according to the numbering in the Course, rather than according to page numbers. Each reference begins with a letter, which denotes the particular volume or section of the Course and its extensions (T = Text, W = Workbook for Students, M = Manual for Teachers, C = Clarification of Terms, P = *Psychotherapy*, and S = *Song of Prayer*). After this letter comes a series of numbers, which differ from volume to volume:

> T, P, or S-chapter.section.paragraph:sentence; e.g., T-24.VI.2:3–4
> W-part (I or II).lesson.paragraph:sentence; e.g., W-pI.182.4:1–2
> M or C-section.paragraph:sentence; e.g., C-2.5:2

Introduction

1. D. Patrick Miller, *The Complete Story of the Course: The History, the People, and the Controversies Behind 'A Course in Miracles'* (Berkeley: Fearless Books, 1997), p. 1.

2. W-pI.rI.In.6:4.

One

1. Preface, p. x.

2. T-24.VII.9:7-10:1.

3. W-pI.151.1:4.

4. W-pI.151.1:6.

5. W-pI.151.2:1-6.

6. T-14.IV.8:4-5.

Notes

7. M-20.2:2-5.

8. T-18.VI.1:5-6.

9. T-13.I.3:4.

10. T-25.I.7:1.

11. T-21.I.8:1-6.

12. T-1.II.2:1. This passage is about revelation, which could be defined as the experience of reality.

13. See *The Gifts of God*, p. 126.

14. S-1.I.4:7-8.

15. M-25.3:7.

16. T-1.V.3:2-3.

17. T-11.VI.5:6-7.

18. T-4.VII.6:2-3.

19. T-14.IV.3:2.

20. T-29.I.1:5.

21. W-pI.169.5:4-7.

22. He at least does not create animals, plants, and humans as we know them. We will see later that He creates transcendental minds, minds that are currently dreaming they are animals, plants, and humans.

23. W-pI.132.12:3-4.

24. T-11.IV.7:4-5.

25. W-pI.132.12:4.

26. M-23.4:2.

27. T-21.I.9:6.

28. T-26.IV.3:5.

29. S-1.In.1:2-3.

30. W-pI.64.3:4.

31. W-pII.11.1:1.

32. T-13.VIII.5:3.

33. W-pII.11.4:1.

34. T-28.IV.9:1.

35. W-pI.95.12:2.

36. T-8.VI.5:7.

37. T-24.VII.7:3.

38. W-pI.105.4:4.

39. T-7.I.7:10.

40. T-7.VI.13:1.

41. T-14.IV.3:9.

42. W-pI.107.2:1-5.

43. W-pI.107.3:1.

44. *The Gifts of God*, p. 127.

45. S-3.IV.7:2.

46. T-21.I.8:4.

47. T-22.In.2:8.

48. W-pI.182.1:1-6.

49. T-12.IV.5:1-2.

50. T-21.I.Heading.

51. T-21.I.6:1-3; 7:5..

Two

1. T-27.VIII.6:2.

2. T-27.VIII.6:3.

3. T-26.V.8:4.

4. T-26.V.13:1.

5. T-26.V.13:1.

6. C-2.2:5.

7. This point is based on paragraphs 1-3 of "The Ego and False Autonomy" (T-4.II), as seen in light of the original wording of the dictation. This original wording pointed out that Helen Schucman had a genuine propensity for experiencing revelation, but when she threw that experience away, it was as if she never had it. This material can be found in Ken Wapnick's *Absence from Felicity*, pp. 280-281.

8. T-4.II.3:4.

9. T-4.II.1:3.

10. C-In.4:4-5.

11. C-In.1:5.

12. C-In.2:4. When I say that the Course steers clear of purely theological issues, I mean to say

that it only touches on theological issues that it considers to have practical implications.

13. T-13.III.10:2.

14. T-16.V.4:1.

15. I am indebted to my first wife, Susan, for suggesting this answer.

16. T-10.V.4:3.

17. T-3.VI.8:9.

18. T-3.VI.7:2.

19. T-2.VIII.2:5. I am claiming that this quotation says that the initial process of separating took millions of years. However, one might read it as saying that the history of the separation, from the beginning up until now, has been millions of years. That, however, is not how it reads, which we can see from looking at the larger passage in which the quote occurs: "Judgment is not an attribute of God. It was brought into being only after the separation, when it became one of the many learning devices to be built into the overall plan. Just as the separation occurred over millions of years, the Last Judgment will extend over a similarly long period, and perhaps an even longer one" (T-2.VIII.2:3-5). We can construct a time line from this passage that will tell us what we need to know. First, "the separation occurred." The separation is talked about in the past tense as a past event. It does not say, "the separation *has been occurring* over millions of years." Second, "after the separation," an overall plan was designed for healing the separation, a plan that included the faculty of judgment. We know from elsewhere in the Course that this is the plan of the Atonement, which was designed so immediately after the separation that the two could almost be said to be simultaneous. Thus, the separation that *preceded* this plan must have been the *initial* separation. Third, once the plan of the Atonement has led us to the end of time, the final healing process will occur. This is called the Last Judgment, the very end of the journey, the final phase of our return. It is to be immediately followed by the final step, in which God lifts us home. In this passage, the Last Judgment is paralleled with the separation: Both are said to take millions of years. Since the Last Judgment is the very end of the separated condition, the separation which it

parallels must have been the very beginning of the separated condition. From several angles, then, we can see that the separation being discussed here is not the entire history of the separation, but the *initial process of separating*.

20. W-pI.132.13:1.

21. W-pII.12.2:2.

22. T-25.I.5:5.

23. W-pII.12.1:1.

24. T-4.II.8:4.

25. T-18.VI.7:5.

26. T-20.VI.11:2.

27. T-28.III.7:4-5.

28. T-18.I.5:6-6:2.

29. T-3.V.7:7.

30. T-11.V.13:5; 15:2-3.

31. T-28.V.6:2.

32. T-24.V.2:3.

33. M-14.5:1, 3, 5.

34. T-26.V.10:7.

35. T-29.VIII.6:4-6.

36. Many Course students believe that we did not make the world itself, but made only our perception of the world. Yet according to the Course, what shows that we, not God, made the world is the fact that it *changes*, the fact that things in it pass away. And change is a fundamental feature of this world. Before there were any *human* perceivers, the world was changing. "The world you see is an illusion of a world. God did not create it, for what He creates must be eternal as Himself. Yet there is nothing in the world you see that will endure forever" (C-4.1:1-3).

37. T-17.II.4:1, 6:3.

38. T-9.I.2:5.

39. W-pI.152.6:1-7.

40. W-pI.152.7:1-2.

41. T-4.II.7:5.

42. T-4.II.8:8.

43. W-pI.13.2:4.

44. T-18.VIII.3:6.

45. T-29.I.9:5-6.

46. T-19.III.7:3.

47. C-2.2:3.

48. T-21.V.2:5.

49. T-27.VII.8:7.

50. The much-respected Course teacher Ken Wapnick holds that we made the world in order to hide from God's punishment. I disagree with this view, as I have not been able to find any support for it in the Course. On the other hand, I have found the theory I have presented here (that we made it as reinforcement or proof of separateness) to be sprinkled all over the Course. In fact, the passage I have most often seen quoted in support of the theory of hiding from God's punishment is actually a support for the theory I present here. It says, "The world was made as an attack on God. It symbolizes fear. And what is fear except love's absence? Thus the world was meant to be a place where God could enter not, and where His Son could be apart from Him" (W-pII.3.2:1-4). Does this say we made the world to escape God's wrath or God's Love? It is clearly the latter. Notice that God's absence from the world ("a place where God could enter not") is the same idea as "love's absence" in the previous sentence. In light of that, we could rephrase this passage in this way: "The world was made to be the diametric opposite of God. That is why it is ruled by fear, for fear is the opposite of God's Nature of Love. In other words, the world was made to be a place where God and His Love are totally absent. By living in such a place, we seem to be apart from God." Living in an unloving world seems to prove that God is absent from us and we are apart from God. The world is apparent proof of separateness from God.

51. T-26.V.13:1.

Three

1. W-pII.4.3:4.

2. T-19.III.8:2-3.

3. T-27.III.1:5-6, 8-9.

4. T-6.II.10:7.

5. W-pI.99.6:8.

6. W-pI.156.6:4-5.

7. T-27.VIII.6:5.

8. T-22.V.4:3. In the Course, the term "universe" refers not to the physical universe, but to the universe that God created, the Sonship. "And this universe, being of God, is far beyond the petty sum of all the separate bodies you perceive. For all its parts are joined in God through Christ" (T-15.VIII.4:5-6).

9. T-22.V.4:4-5.

10. W-pI.rIV.In.4:3.

11. W-pI.156.3:3.

12. T-27.VIII.9:1. This passage depicts the Holy Spirit (Whom we have not yet discussed), not God, laughing at the separation. Yet the Course throughout portrays the most intimate continuity between God and the Holy Spirit. The Course calls the Holy Spirit God's Voice, suggesting thereby that God is the One Who speaks; the Holy Spirit the Voice spoken through. See this passage, for instance, "Listen, and hear your Father speak to you through His appointed Voice" (W-pI.106.2:1). Therefore, we can also hear God laugh through the laughter of His appointed Voice.

13. T-27.VIII.8:4.

14. T-4.II.3:4.

15. T-18.II.

16. T-18.II.1:1-4.

17. T-18.II.2:2.

18. T-18.II.2:3-5.

19. T-18.II.5:1-5.

20. T-18.II.5:8-10.

21. T-18.II.5:11-15.

22. W-pI.132.6:2-3.

23. T-16.III.6:1.

24. W-pI.96.1:4-5.

25. W-pI.64.3:4.

Notes

26. T-6.IV.6:1-7.

27. W-pII.10.5:1-3.

28. Allen Watson and Robert Perry, *A Workbook Companion, Vol. I: Commentaries on the Workbook for Students from 'A Course in Miracles,'* 2d ed. (Sedona, Ariz.: Circle Publishing, 2005), p. 218-219.

29. T-25.In.1:3.

30. T-10.I.2:1.

31. T-13.VII.17:6-7.

32. T-6.II.6:2-4.

33. W-pII.326.1:3-4.

34. This idea of God being lonely is confusing to Course students. Certainly He is not lonely in any human sense. The clue as to what this loneliness is lies in the passage itself. God knows His channels are not communicating fully with Him. He experiences this "in His Own Being and in its experience of His Son's experience." The loneliness, I would suggest, is simply this experience of the vacuum left by His Son's sleep.

35. T-4.VII.6:4-7.

36. T-6.V.1:5, 8.

37. T-26.V.3:5.

38. T-26.V.3:5.

39. See W-pI.169.9:3. One theory is that there are two scripts, one written by the ego and the other by the Holy Spirit. There are only two references, however, to the script of our passage through time and space (the other is W-pI.158.4:3). (The script references in Chapter 30 of the Text refer to a very different script, this one being not what actually transpires in our lives, but what we consciously hope and plan for—hopes and plans that are constantly dashed as the events of our lives unfold.) Both of these script references speak of a single script, which one passage clearly says is written by the Holy Spirit. My best explanation for the fact that we clearly contribute to this script is that the script is a *composite*. We give the Holy Spirit some very dark story material, which He then works into His bright script with its wonderful, happy ending.

40. T-26.V.3:6-7.

41. T-26.V.4:5.

42. W-pI.158.4:5.

43. T-26.V.5:6.

44. See T-26.V.5:7.

45. W-pI.158.4:3.

46. See T-1.II.6.

47. It does so especially in the important paragraph of T-26.V.13.

48. T-26.V.11:2.

49. T-26.V.13:3.

50. T-26.VII.16:5.

51. T-26.V.13:1.

52. T-26.V.5:3-4.

53. T-26.V.6:6-10.

54. W-pI.169.10:4.

55. W-pI.182.12:2-4.

Four

1. T-8.VI.4:1-2.

2. *The Gifts of God*, p. 126. I alluded to this same passage and its four symbols for God in Chapter 1 (key idea 1.3).

3. W-pII.222.1:2. I regard the final three references to air, food, and water to be metaphor, referring not to the sustaining of the body, but of "the life within" (as the previous phrase says). Their real meaning would then be something like this: "God is the true (spiritual) air which the real me (not my body) breathes, the true (spiritual) food which sustains the real me, the true (spiritual) water which renews and cleanses the real me."

4. T-21.V.2:4.

5. T-22.I.1:6.

6. T-1.VI.2:1.

7. T-19.II.2:2-3.

8. T-16.VII.1:3.

9. W-pII.359.1:7.

10. T-19.II.2:6-7.

11. T-27.VII.7:4.

12. T-13.II.2:3-4.

13. T-5.V.7:5.

14. T-11.V.9:1.

15. T-31.V.6:5.

16. T-13.II.3:1.

17. W-pI.101.5:3.

18. T-7.VII.1:5.

19. T-23.III.1:5-8.

20. T-30.V.2:4.

21. W-pI.101.2:1.

22. W-pI.101.3:4.

23. W-pI.167.2:6.

24. S-3.II.5:1.

25. W-pI.182.12:3-4.

26. W-pI.153.7:3.

27. M-17.5:8-9.

28. M-17.6:1-11.

29. M-27.2:3. This image may sound extreme, but it appears to be a reference to the famous 1741 sermon by American theologian Jonathan Edwards, "Sinners in the Hands of an Angry God."

30. W-pI.101.2:5.

31. T-25.VIII.6:4.

32. T-22.I.3:11.

33. T-26.VIII.6:8-7:1, 9.

34. T-9.I.8:4-5.

35. T-5.V.3:6.

36. T-13.V.5:4.

37. T-5.In.2:3.

38. T-11.V.9:1.

39. T-11.V.8:3, 5.

40. W-pI.182.3:7.

41. W-pI.163.3:1.

42. W-pII.298.1:4.

43. T-11.V.10:1-2.

Five

1. W-pII.325.1:1-3.

2. T-25.III.1:6.

3. T-31.V.12:5.

4. *Absence from Felicity*, p. 232.

5. T-24.V.2:2.

6. T-18.II.5:4-6.

7. W-pI.rIII.In.3:3-4.

8. W-pI.136.4:3.

9. W-pI.161.8:1-4.

10. T-13.II.1:1.

11. T-27.VIII.3:3-4:1.

12. T-27.VII.7:9.

13. T-21.V.2:5-6.

14. T-27.VII.8:4-7.

15. T-26.X.3:2-4.

16. T-7.VII.8:2-5; 9:2, 4-5.

17. T-13.In.2:2.

18. *DSM-III-R: Diagnostic and Statistical Manual of Mental Disorders* (Washington, DC: American Psychiatric Association, 1987), p. 396-397.

19. T-13.In.1:7.

20. T-13.In.2:3.

21. T-13.In.2:4-10.

22. T-13.In.2:11.

23. T-27.VII.1:3-4, 6.

24. M-15.3:1.

25. W-pI.195.9:3.

26. T-31.V.3:4.

27. W-pI.153.4:3-5:2.

28. T-27.VIII.5:4-5.

Six

1. We may say that we are happy. However, what we normally call happy is nothing compared to the bliss in which our true Self exists. Further, our so-called happiness is usually based on a precarious set of conditions in which our particular house of cards is arranged just right—at least for the time being. Lastly, this happiness also depends on denying all the anger, guilt, and fear we carry around just below the surface.

2. W-pI.71.2:1-3:1. To complete the last thought of this passage, our role is to decide *what* has to change, to ascertain *how* it should be changed, and then to go about *getting it* to change.

3. T-31.V.2:7-4:1.

4. The underlying commonality of our self-images, as well as our world-images, and of how we see our *relationship* with the world, has substantial implications for the various personality theories produced by modern psychology. Instead of offering *many* personality types, the Course is emphasizing the common content they all share.

5. M-15.3:1.

6. W-pI.135.1:4.

7. W-pI.135.14:4.

8. W-pI.135.15:1-2.

9. My colleague Allen Watson has written an e-book about this concept entitled *A Healed Mind Does Not Plan*. It is available on the Circle of Atonement's website, www.circleof-a.org.

10. W-pI.135.2:1-5.

11. S-1.III.6:1.

12. W-pI.50.1:3.

13. *The Gifts of God*, p. 120.

14. T-27.VIII.2:4.

15. S-1.III.6:1; W-pI.50.1:3.

16. M-13.2:6; W-pI.50.1:3.

17. W-pI.50.1:3.

18. *The Gifts of God*, p. 120.

19. M-13.2:6.

20. M-13.2:6; T-29.VIII.8:8.

21. S-1.III.6:1.

22. T-13.VII.1:3; T-27.VIII.2.

23. W-pI.50.1:3.

24. M-13.2:6.

25. T-27.VIII.2:4.

26. W-pI.50.1:3.

27. T-29.VIII.8:8.

28. T-27.I.6:9.

29. T-29.VIII.1:9.

30. T-29.VIII.8:8.

31. *The Gifts of God*, p. 120.

32. T-29.VIII.1:9.

33. T-29.VIII.1:9.

34. T-13.VII.1:3; W-pI.50.1:3.

35. T-27.II.13:5-6.

36. T-24.I.4:7.

37. T-24.VII.2:6-7.

38. T-24.VII.1:1-6.

39. T-27.VIII.1:1; 1:3-2:7.

40. T-24.VII.4:6.

41. T-18.VII.1:2.

42. T-16.V.3:1.

43. T-16.IV.3:1.

44. T-26.X.4:3, 7-8.

45. W-pI.76.8:3.

46. T-16.V.7:5-8:3.

Seven

1. T-31.V.2:4-6.

2. T-31.V.4:2-4.

3. T-31.V.5:3.

4. T-29.IV.3:1.

5. T-29.IV.4:1.

6. W-pI.21.2:5.

7. T-31.V.6:1-4.

8. W-pI.68.5:3-4.

9. T-25.VIII.3:2.

10. T-23.II.

11. T-23.II.11:3.

12. T-23.II.11:2.

13. T-23.II.12:5.

14. T-23.II.12:9.

15. T-23.II.10:1.

16. W-pI.71.2:1-2.

17. T-4.II.6:5.

18. W-pI.105.1:4; 2:1-2.

19. T-15.VII.

20. T-15.VII.6:1.

21. T-15.VII.6:2.

22. T-15.VII.6:3-4.

23. T-15.VII.6:5-6.

24. T-15.VII.7:2, 6.

25. T-15.VII.7:8.

26. S-2.II.5:2.

27. T-16.V.1:1-5.

28. T-27.I.3:1-2.

29. T-27.I.4:3, 6.

30. T-16.VII.2:1.

31. T-16.VII.5:1-2.

32. T-13.V.2:1-2.

33. T-17.III.2:5.

34. T-13.V.3:1-4.

35. T-16.VII.1:1-5.

Eight

1. T-11.In.3:5-4:8.

2. T-27.VII.12:1-2.

3. T-27.VII.12:3, 5-6.

4. T-3.VII.5:1.

5. T-6.In.1:2.

6. T-6.II.3:5-6.

7. W-pI.153.2:2.

8. The Course is saying that this device is used by us unconsciously. Yet there are those who have used it consciously. Governments, for instance, have been known to manufacture attacks on themselves in order to justify a war that they wanted to wage. No one wants to be seen as attacking without provocation, and so if the provocation isn't there, why not just manufacture it?

9. T-26.VII.4:7 and six other occurrences.

10. T-24.IV.3:5.

11. T-13.I.11:1.

12. T-15.VII.4:1-6.

13. T-15.VII.10:4.

14. T-15.VII.3:4.

15. W-pI.153.2:3-3:3.

16. T-29.VII.4:5-6.

17. T-29.VII.4:2.

18. T-29.VII.3:1-2.

19. T-27.VI.1:1, 4-5.

20. T-19.IV(B).12:1, 4.

21. T-19.IV(B).13:7-8.

22. T-17.IV.6:1-7.

23. T-17.IV.7:4.

24. T-17.IV.7:6.

25. This is actually the real meaning of the famous, but almost universally misunderstood, phrase in the Course, "all defenses *do* what they would defend" (T-17.IV.7:1). This phrase, in fact, begins the very paragraph I am com-

menting on here. It has been taken to mean that defenses do what they would defend *against*. In other words, if I defend myself against attack, then my very defense will do what I am defending against—it will attack me. While this is true, it is not what the phrase says. Defenses, in this case, do not do what they defend *against*, but what they *defend*. Meaning: a defense of the ego gives you a dose of the ego. It contains a miniature version of the ego. It does what the ego does. The full import of this phrase will become clear in the following paragraphs. The special relationship is not a haven from the ego. Being a defense of the ego, it *expresses* the ego, it *"does"* the ego.

26. T-17.IV.5:8.

27. T-17.IV.8:1-4.

28. T-17.IV.9:1-2, 10-11.

29. T-16.VII.1:3.

30. Several of the sentences in these last few paragraphs are borrowed from a book of mine entitled *Relationships as a Spiritual Journey*.

31. T-12.IV.1:3-5.

32. T-23.I.1:7.

33. T-4.V.6:2.

34. T-16.V.1:5-2:1.

35. T-13.III.10:3.

36. T-16.V.10:6.

37. T-16.V.12:4.

38. T-16.V.11:4-8.

39. T-17.IV.3:3.

40. The Course does not intend to damn all human love as a sinister attempt to attack and replace God. In fact, in its discussion of holy relationships (which we will explore in Chapter 14), it exalts human relationships as the best way, and ultimately the only way, to approach God. It tells us that relationships are our salvation, not our doom (T-20 VI.11:9). It says that "It is only in relationships that salvation can be found" (P-2.In.4:3). The description we have expounded refers to our search for salvation with one special person, as opposed to divine love which embraces all humanity, all of God's creation, and God Himself. Special love is real-

ly nothing more than a very subtle but very powerful belief that separation, not union, is salvation (T-15.V.3:3).

41. T-22.I.4:7-9.

42. T-5.V.3:7.

43. T-12.VII.13:2, 4-6.

44. T-15.I.4:6.

45. T-15.I.4:13-14.

46. T-19.IV(C).4:7.

47. W-pI.160.3:2.

48. W-pI.196.10:1-11:5.

Nine

1. W-pI.135.18:4.

2. M-24.5:3.

3. T-8.VII.2:2.

4. T-17.II.5:2.

5. T-5.I.4:6.

6. C-6.3:4.

7. T-14.VIII.2:15-16.

8. T-6.IV.12:5.

9. S-1.I.2:8-9; 3:3; 4:7-8.

10. T-5.II.8:3.

11. T-15.VIII.5:4-5.

12. W-pII.232.1:3.

13. T-27.VI.6:6.

14. T-30.II.3:3.

15. W-pI.106.2:1.

16. W-pI.125.4:1-2.

17. In fact, whenever God is speaking in the Course, He is speaking *through* the Holy Spirit. His longest speeches are found in the post-Course scribings of Helen Schucman. For instance, *The Song of Prayer* closes with a speech from God that is five paragraphs long. Helen's final authentic scribing, *The Gifts of God*, closes with a two-paragraph communica-

tion from God. This speech is particularly important. It is introduced by a statement about opening the "secret place of peace" within us, to "let the Voice within it [the Holy Spirit] speak of Him [God] whose love shines out and in and in-between." In other words, let the Holy Spirit speak about God. Yet in the very next line (in the original dictation, that is; in the printed version four paragraphs from another dictation have been inserted at this point), God starts speaking to us *as Himself*. We can only conclude that these two things—the Holy Spirit speaking about God and God speaking as Himself—are actually one and the same thing.

18. C-6.4:5-6.

19. W-pI.132.6:2.

20. It is a core teaching of Ken Wapnick that "the Holy Spirit does not work in the world," and for many students this has become axiomatic. The Course itself, however, never says this nor anything remotely resembling this. On the contrary, again and again the Course openly depicts the Holy Spirit as acting in the world. A few examples can be found in the endnotes which follow.

21. M-2.1:1.

22. W-pI.135.18:1.

23. T-13.VII.12-13.

24. P-3.III.1, 4-7.

25. T-20.IV.8:4-8.

26. T-10.I.2:1.

27. T-27.VII.13:3-4.

28. *The Gifts of God*, p. 120.

29. T-31.VIII.8:3.

30. T-5.I.6:1-4.

31. C-6.3:2-3.

32. T-13.XI.8:1.

33. T-9.VII.6:1-4.

34. T-14.VI.4:2.

35. T-14.VII.1:6.

36. M-In.4:7.

37. W-pI.99.5:4-5.

38. T-5.III.10:1-3.

39. T-7.IV.3:3.

40. T-6.V(A).5:5.

41. T-28.I.5:2.

42. T-28.I.4:3.

43. T-16.V.2:3.

44. T-20.VIII.6:9.

45. T-25.VI.4:1-2.

46. M-21.1:7.

47. M-21.5:9.

48. T-14.VI.5:1-6.

49. T-5.III.11:1.

50. T-6.II.10:1-2.

51. T-21.III.6:5-6.

52. T-9.III.8:4-10.

53. T-14.VII.5:4-8.

54. T-14.VI.5:6-7.

55. T-21.III.5:5.

56. T-25.VI.7:4-5.

57. T-21.III.6:1-3.

58. T-25.VII.1:1.

59. This same list is found twice in the Workbook, in Lesson 71 (paragraph 9) and in Lesson 275 (paragraph 2).

60. This, in fact, is a principal theme of the section entitled "Development of Trust" in the Manual (M-4.I(A)). There, it says that we go through six stages in learning how to trust the Holy Spirit completely to decide for us what stays in our lives and what goes.

61. T-18.IV.7:4; M-9.2:4.

62. T-14.XI.6:3-6.

63. T-14.XI.5:2.

64. T-14.XI.6:7-9.

65. T-14.XI.6:10-11.

66. T-31.V.17:2-5.

67. T-31.V.17:6-7. I have laid each part of this

practice out on a separate line to enhance the appreciation of it.

68. Luke 23:34.

69. There is an excellent discussion of this idea using this language in Workbook Lesson 35, paragraphs 1-2.

70. T-31.V.17:8-9.

71. T-25.II.1:1-3:3.

72. T-2.III.3:5-6.

Ten

1. T-31.V.5:3.

2. T-15.I.7:7.

3. T-31.V.6:5.

4. W-pI.101.5:3.

5. T-17.VIII.4:5.

6. W-pI.152.9:4.

7. T-13.III.6:1, 4-6.

8. T-13.III.8:1-2.

9. W-pI.166.11:3.

10. W-pII.230.2:1-4.

11. W-pI.93.7:1-6.

12. W-pI.94.4:1.

13. W-pI.158.9:4-6.

14. C-5.4:1-2.

15. W-pI.93.4:1.

16. Taken from an article in the *Washington Post*, February 20, 1997.

17. W-pI.162.1:3.

18. T-6.II.10:7.

19. T-8.VI.9:6-7.

20. T-6.II.11:1.

21. T-In.1:7.

22. T-16.IV.6:1.

23. T-29.IV.3:4.

24. M-13.4:1-4.

25. T-13.VII.9:7.

26. M-24.6:1.

27. W-pI.196.4:3-5.

28. T-18.VII.6:8; 7:3.

29. W-pI.97.3:2.

30. T-22.II.12:1.

31. T-16.VII.7:1-2. These sentences discuss bringing illusions into the holy instant and so hindering your full awareness of it.

32. T-18.VI.12. This paragraph mentions joining with "a sound, a sight, a thought, a memory, and even a general idea without specific reference."

33. My colleague Allen Watson has done a book treatment of this section, entitled *I Need Do Nothing: Finding the Quiet Center*. It is available as an e-book on the Circle of Atonement's website.

34. T-18.IV.5:4.

35. T-18.VII.4:6-9.

36. T-18.VII.4:10-11.

37. T-18.VII.4:4.

38. T-18.VII.5:1.

39. W-pI.109.5:4.

40. This image is drawn from Helen Schucman's subway experience, which is recorded in Ken Wapnick's *Absence from Felicity*, p. 52-55.

41. W-pII.317.2:5.

42. T-31.I.12:1.

43. T-18.VII.1:2; 2:1.

44. T-18.VII.5:7.

45. T-18.III.3:4.

46. T-1.II.6:1-3, 5-7.

47. I think we can see evidence of this. When someone does have a life-changing spiritual experience, they will often, in a short space of time, have a new life. Old characters and sets will drop away and new ones will appear, as

their lives scramble to adjust to the new place in the movie to which they have fast-forwarded.

48. W-pI.79.5:1-2.

49. T-21.V.3:4.

50. M-25.2:6.

51. T-1.I.1:1-3.

52. T-26.II.3:4.

53. W-pI.77.Heading.

54. T-26.II.8:5.

Eleven

1. T-11.VI.2:5-6.

2. C-In.1:1-2.

3. The end of this sentence is based on this line from the Workbook: "He [the Son of God, ourselves] belongs to You, beloved and loving, in the safety of Your Fatherly embrace" (W-pII.244.1:3).

4. T-21.In.1:7.

5. T-21.II.2:1.

6. T-13.V.3:5; T-21.In.1:1.

7. W-pII.304.1:3-4.

8. M-8.3-4.

9. M-8.1:2.

10. M-8.3:1-5.

11. M-8.3:6-7.

12. This image of hunting dog and master is taken from "The Obstacles to Peace," the subsection entitled "The Attraction of Guilt" (T-19.IV(A).11-13).

13. M-8.3:8-11.

14. M-8.4:1-8.

15. M-8.2:8.

16. See especially T-19.IV(A).11-13.

17. I think one can discern at least four levels of projection in the making of our current experience. 1) We projected the thought of separation onto the oneness of Heaven, producing the illu-

sion of Heaven shattering into different pieces. "That was the first projection of error outward" (T-18.I.6:1). 2) We projected the world itself, the illusion of time, space, matter, and energy, including all the laws of physics, chemistry, and biology. 3) We project our life events, the particular things that happen to us (see T-21.II.2). 4) Finally, we project our interpretation onto those events—our interpretation of what is worth looking at and what that "worthwhile" sense data means.

18. T-11.VI.1:1.

19. There is an excellent discussion of this cycle of perception in "Waking to Redemption" (T-11.VI.1-4). The cycle is that our *beliefs* guide our *interpretations* which become our *perceptions* which produce our *experience* which loops back around and reinforces our *beliefs*.

20. M-17.4:2.

21. W-pI.193.13:1.

22. Martin Luther King, Jr., *Strength to Love* (originally published 1963), quoted in Lucinda Varley, ed., *God in All Worlds: An Anthology of Contemporary Spiritual Writing* (New York: Pantheon Books, 1995), p. 355.

23. See "The Message of the Crucifixion" (T-6.I).

24. W-pI.23.5:1-2.

25. W-pI.31.3:3.

26. T-11.In.4:2.

27. W-pI.10.4:6.

28. T-23.IV.5:1.

29. T-23.IV.9:5.

30. P-2.IV.10:7-9.

31. T-31.V.5:3.

32. T-14.VII.6:1-4, 8-10.

33. W-pI.5.Heading.

34. T-11.VIII.4:6.

35. W-pI.198.Heading.

36. W-pI.34.6:2.

37. T-30.I.8:2; 9:2; 11:4; 12:3-4. These lines are specifically aimed at dispelling one's fear of

asking the Holy Spirit's help in making decisions (hence the reference to "asking" in the final line), but they can also be applied to other kinds of fear or upset.

38. W-pI.138.10:3.

39. T-30.VI.1:1.

40. T-25.VIII.2:4-8.

41. T-25.VIII.5:10.

42. T-18.V.2:5.

43. T-25.VIII.1:5-6.

44. T-16.VI.12:3-5.

45. T-18.IV.2:1-3. This passage is a favorite among students, but is often misunderstood. In its context it means: "Don't try to make yourself worthy of the holy instant by working up good intentions. Your 'good' intentions are simply not good enough. They are tainted with ego. What will bring the holy instant instead is your willingness to let it come. Rely on this, and do not be disturbed that it is surrounded by shadowy intentions, by tainted intentions. The holy instant will come and give you truly good intentions, holy intentions. That is *its* purpose, not yours."

46. T-25.VIII.12:4.

47. T-14.III.16:1.

48. W-pI.23.5:3-6.

49. T-29.IV.5:6.

50. T-1.I.37:1-3.

51. This is a discussion in itself. Suffice it to say that the Course never once says that the miracle is a shift in perception. But it does say several times that the miracle "entails" or "induces" or "introduces" a shift in perception. Here are some passages, with the relevant portions italicized by me: "*Miracles rearrange perception* and place all levels in true perspective. This is healing because sickness comes from confusing the levels" (T-1.I.23:1-2). "However, the *miracle entails a sudden shift from horizontal to vertical perception*" (T-1.II.6:3). "The level-adjustment power of *the miracle induces the right perception* for healing" (T-2.V(A).15:1). "This alteration of the time sequence should be quite familiar,

because it is very similar to *the shift in the perception* of time that *the miracle introduces*" (T-5.II.1:3). "These are *the happy dreams the miracle exchanges for your own*" (T-28.II.5:7). "*A miracle inverts perception* which was upside down before, and thus it ends the strange distortions that were manifest" (W-pII.13.2:3). "Father, I wake today with *miracles correcting my perception* of all things" (W-pII.346.1:1).

52. T-4.IV.11:7-8. This passage is actually a reference to Helen Schucman and Bill Thetford, the scribes of the Course. In personal guidance to the two of them, Jesus frequently described Bill as having inappropriately detached himself and therefore made himself weak and "dis-spirited." Helen, on the other hand, he described as constantly swinging between the two poles of higher awareness and rage, and thus "unstable." This passage, then, is a promise to the two of them that Jesus could heal the primary imbalance in their respective personalities.

53. This sentence is a reworking of a sentence from the Course: "You may feel that at this point it would take a miracle to enable you to do this [to guard your thoughts], which is perfectly true" (T-2.VII.1:8).

54. T-20.VIII.11:1.

Twelve

1. W-pI.162.2:4-6.

2. W-pI.121.Heading-1:4.

3. W-pI.169.12:1.

4. W-pI.122.Heading.

5. W-pI.122.4:3; 6:1; 7:1.

6. W-pI.169.12:1.

7. M-20.5:7-10.

8. P-2.II.1:1-2.

9. S-2.In.1:1.

10. M-14.3:10.

11. M-4.X.2:9.

12. M-1.4:1.

13. T-14.V.6:1.

14. T-14.V.2:2.

15. T-14.V.6:5.

16. T-14.V.2:1.

17. M-1.3:5.

18. P-2.II.3:3-5.

19. C-6.2:2.

20. W-pI.101.2:1.

21. T-9.IV.4:7.

22. W-pI.134.3:2.

23. W-pI.126.4:1; 5:2.

24. S-2.I.2:1 and six other references.

25. T-27.II.2:8.

26. S-2.II.3:3.

27. S-2.II.4:5.

28. S-2.II.5:2.

29. S-2.II.6:2.

30. W-pI.134.6:1.

31. W-pII.359.1:7. This is italicized because it comes from one of the prayers in the Workbook, all of which are italicized.

32. W-pI.134.3:1.

33. T-24.In.2:1.

34. In the last chapter (key idea 11.1) we quoted the Manual saying that the Course is not concerned with philosophical speculation but only with the correction of perception. Since forgiveness is how perception is corrected, the Course is concerned only with those ideas that support forgiveness.

35. T-23.IV.6:1.

36. Based on T-5.IV.4:4.

37. T-30.III.8:4.

38. T-30.III.10:2-3.

39. Based on T-26.X.3:2-3.

40. For a great example, see W-pI.190.5.

41. T-27.VIII.10:1-4.

42. Based on T-30.VI.2:7.

43. T-31.I.10:4.

44. T-31.II.9:2.

45. T-31.I.11:3-5.

46. T-31.I.10:3.

47. Based on T-28.IV.2-3.

48. P-3.I.4:8.

49. W-pI.161.9:3.

50. Based on T-30.VI.2:8-9.

51. T-25.VIII.14:1.

52. T-30.VI.4:7.

53. W-pII.289.Heading.

54. Based on T-31.III.1:5.

55. T-31.III.1:2-4.

56. T-31.III.1:5.

57. Based on T-17.III.1:5.

58. W-pII.1.1:1.

59. T-30.VI.2:4-5.

60. T-17.III.1:5.

61. W-pII.300.1:2.

62. W-pI.162.1:5. "These words" refers to the statement "I am as God created me," yet this idea is extremely closely related to "forgive the Son of God for what he did not do." Both ideas say, "Nothing you did apart from God has stained your innocence."

Thirteen

1. T-28.II.12:7.

2. T-13.X.2:9.

3. T-4.IV.1:5.

4. W-pI.25.2:1.

5. W-pI.25.3:1.

6. P-2.In.3:6.

7. T-14.I.4:5.

8. T-In.1:7.

9. T-15.XI.7:6.

10. Matt 5:39-41. The translation is the Scholar's Version from Robert W. Funk, Roy W. Hoover, and the Jesus Seminar, *The Five Gospels: The Search for the Authentic Words of Jesus* (New York: Macmillan, 1993).

11. The term "earthly extension" is not found in the Course, but comes from combining two Course passages. If, "Forgiveness is an earthly form of love" (W-pI.186.14:2), and, "Love is extension" (T-24.I.1:1), then forgiveness is an earthly form of extension.

12. T-16.I.2:5.

13. P-3.II.4:10-11.

14. W-pI.30.2:4.

15. Note T-27.II.13:1, where it says that "every thought extends because that is its purpose, being what it really is."

16. W-pI.rII.82.2:2.

17. P-2.VII.3:1.

18. S-2.III.5:1-3.

19. T-8.VII.12:7-8.

20. T-24.VII.4:6.

21. M-12.3:5-6.

22. W-pII.5.4:3-5.

23. M-12.4:1-2.

24. T-2.V.3:5.

25. T-2.V.5:1.

26. M-22.1:9.

27. T-12.II.1:6-7.

28. T-26.VII.16:1.

29. S-3.I.3:1.

30. P-2.IV.2:6.

31. John 5:8.

32. To provide the evidence of this I would need to go through the nearly six hundred references to "miracle" and "miracles," which I cannot do here. In lieu of that I will simply report that I have studied those references in order to answer the following question: When the Course uses the word "miracle" does the context imply an internal miracle or an inter-personal miracle? In cases where one or the other is implied, the overwhelming majority fall on the side of the interpersonal miracle. This also holds true of instances in which the Course says "a miracle is" or "miracles are."

33. For the phrase "miracle receiver" see T-1.VII.3:10 and T-2.V.3:2.

34. T-1.I.8:1; T-1.I.9:1, 3; T-1.I.18:1-3; T-1.I.21:2.

35. For the value placed on the experience of revelation in the Course, see Workbook Lesson 157, especially paragraph 7.

36. T-1.II.1:4-6; 2:3-5.

37. See, for instance, Lessons 35, 40, 67, 93, 94, 95, 97, 110, 124, 162, 164, 167, 191, and 199, along with many of the lessons in Part II of the Workbook.

38. W-pII.357.1:1-2.

39. S-2.I.4:1-6.

40. T-6.III.1:2.

41. T-12.VII.2:2-3, 5.

42. W-pI.28.5:2.

43. T-29.III.1:8. See also W-pI.187.1:2.

44. T-13.VI.9:2.

45. T-9.VI.1:1-4.

46. Of course, a person to whom we give love will often display neither gratitude nor change. The Course, however, assures us that our gift was *received*, even if not consciously *accepted* (M-6.2). As a result, "In his mind there is a part that joins with yours in thanking you" (W-pI.197.4:2). And through true forgiveness we can look on this part of his mind now (T-26.VIII.6:4). Further, this part will eventually rise and reveal itself in tangible transformation and gratitude. And in the meantime, there will be many others who *will* visibly return our gift and reflect back our holiness.

47. T-14.II.4:4.

48. T-16.III.7:4.

49. T-13.VI.10:5-7.

50. T-29.III.3:1-5; 5:2, 6.

51. T-25.IX.10:6; T-26.I.3:6; W-pI.108.6:1; W-pI.121.9:1; W-pII.225.1:1; M-2.5:5.

52. W-pI.126.1:1. See also W-pI.105.3:1.

53. M-4.VII.1:6-7.

54. The Course is referring to a nearly identical discussion early in the Text. See T-5.I.1-2.

55. W-pI.187.2:2-4.

56. M-In.3:3-8.

57. W-pII.297.1:1-3.

58. See W-pI.154.7:2; 8:6: "The messengers of God perform their part by their *acceptance* [step 1] of His messages as for themselves, and show they understand the messages by *giving* [step 2] them away....No one can receive and *understand he has received* [step 3] until he gives" [italics mine].

59. T-6.III.4:9.

60. W-pI.95.12:2.

61. T-8.VII.16:8.

62. M-In.2:8.

63. T-1.I.15:1.

64. T-25.VI.3:6.

65. T-25.VI.4:1-2.

66. T-25.VII.7:3.

67. W-pI.154.2:2.

68. Psychotherapist and theologian are mentioned in T-9.V.

69. M-2.1:1.

70. M-3.1:7.

71. M-16.1:7.

72. For instance, see M-21.4-5.

73. For instance, see T-14.III.9-19.

74. T-13.VII.10-13.

75. P-3.III.1, 4-6.

76. T-20.IV.8:5-8.

77. C-2.9:1.

78. T-20.IV.8:4, italics mine.

79. P-3.I.1:7.

80. W-pI.62.Heading.

81. T-31.VIII.1:5.

82. W-pI.191.10:7-11:8.

Fourteen

1. W-pI.79.6:2.

2. M-8.2:8.

3. T-31.VIII.6:3.

4. T-26.VII.9:1-2.

5. T-25.VI.5:1-2.

6. T-29.III.5:6.

7. T-20.VIII.4:4.

8. T-26.IX.2:2.

9. T-26.IV.6:1.

10. T-26.IV.2:4-5.

11. T-13.VI.5:1-3.

12. T-31.II.10:3-4. The last part of the quoted passage is the Course's *only* acknowledgment in twelve hundred pages of the vast field of individual differences. From its standpoint, all of our differences with another boil down to the idea that the one need for God's Love "takes, perhaps, a different form in him."

13. T-22.In.1:5-6.

14. T-26.II.2:5.

15. T-24.I.6:1-2.

16. T-28.V.1:1-2.

17. W-pI.159.2:3.

18. All three of these examples are drawn from M-3.2:2-5.

19. P-2.VII.8:4.

20. *Absence from Felicity*, p. 93-94.

21. T-13.IV.7:7.

22. Actually, since I wrote those lines, I have switched neighborhoods, though not for the reason of avoiding the neighbors' squabbles.

23. T-22.In.2:5-8.

24. T-20.VI.8:3-5.

25. T-17.IV.2:3.

26. T-15.V.5:3.

27. In my book *Relationships as a Spiritual Journey* (published by Circle Publishing), I recount the following ten points in support of the mutuality of the holy relationship:

1. The Course always speaks of the holy relationship as involving two people.
2. The Course never once says that a holy relationship takes only one.
3. The Course makes two-ness inherent to the meaning and significance of the holy relationship and to every stage in its progression.
4. The Course says what happens when only one person does his or her part. (A teacher of God, not a holy relationship, is born.)
5. The mutuality of the holy relationship goes beyond the Text discussions and so is not simply an artifact of Helen and Bill's relationship.
6. The Course discussions of the holy relationship are grounded in specific examples in which the two-ness is totally unambiguous.
7. The idea of salvation depending on a mutual joining is not in conflict with the Course's basic thought system.
8. Thinking it takes two does not necessarily result in people abdicating responsibility for their own salvation.
9. The idea that we cannot find a partner who will join with us is not supported by the Course.
10. The idea that we cannot rely on a partner to do his or her part is not supported by the Course.

28. T-13.X.2:9.

29. S-1.V.3:9.

30. T-17.V.2:4.

31. T-17.V.5:3.

32. M-2.5:4.

33. T-23.IV.7:4.

34. T-22.III.9:7.

35. T-6.V(A).5:9.

36. T-5.I.1:10-11.

37. P-2.II.6:5-7.

38. M-1.4:1.

39. M-2.5:7.

40. P-2.In.4:1.

41. P-2.In.3:3.

42. P-2.In.4:2-3.

43. M-3.2:6-8. It is common wisdom in the Course community that all relationships start out as special. While it is certainly true that most do, the passage referenced here makes it clear that some relationships start out as holy. Sometimes when two people first meet they see past separate interests and thus allow salvation to enter the relationship. They will still need to go through a process of that salvation rising up and replacing all specialness patterns. Yet just because specialness patterns remain does not mean that, in the Course's terminology, it is a special relationship.

44. T-22.I.9:5-8.

45. W-pI.184.1:1-5.

46. T-18.I.11:1-4.

47. T-22.I.11:1, 4.

48. The Course uses this imagery of uprooting the belief in sin, which was the relationship's foundation. See T-19.III.8:4-8 and T-19.IV(A).7.

49. T-18.IX.9:4.

50. T-18.IX.13:1-2.

51. T-19.IV.2:2; see also 1:6.

52. T-19.IV.

53. T-20.VII.2:1.

54. T-17.V.3:3, 7.

55. T-17.V.11:9.

56. This, in different language, is Ken Wapnick's assessment in *Absence from Felicity*, pp. 369-381.

57. We see the same thing that Helen and Bill experienced reflected in the Manual's account

of lifelong teacher-pupil relationships. In many such relationships the two will "be quite hostile to each other for some time, and perhaps for life" (M-3.5:5).

58. T-17.V.7:1-4.

59. T-17.VII.8:1-4.

60. T-20.IV.5:3.

61. T-26.II.6:5-6.

62. W-pI.105.3:2.

63. M-2.5:5.

64. T-22.IV.5:1-2, First Edition.

65. In Text Chapters 17-22, most of the time the word "brother" is used, it refers to your holy relationship partner (though much of the time the ideas given can be applied to all your brothers).

66. T-22.VI.7:1. The emphasis on the word "anywhere" is from the original dictation of the Course. This word is not emphasized in the published edition.

67. T-22.In.4:5-7.

68. T-20.IV.6:6.

69. T-18.V.5:5.

70. T-26.IX.6:1.

71. T-20.IV.6:5.

72. T-20.V.2:1-4.

73. T-22.VI.14:2.

74. M-2.5:6.

75. T-18.VII.5:3.

76. T-18.VII.6:4.

77. T-20.VIII.6:9.

78. W-pI.100.1:2-3.

79. P-2.II.8:3-5.

80. This idea is found specifically in this passage from *Psychotherapy*: "God does not know of separation. What He knows is only that He has one Son. His knowledge [of the oneness of His Son] is reflected in the ideal patient-therapist relationship" (P-2.VII.1:11-13). In other words, God's knowledge that His Son is one is reflected in the union of patient and therapist.

81. The section in the Manual entitled "Can God Be Reached Directly?" (M-26), though it does describe where the Course diverges from the traditional mystical quest, also lapses into high praise of the world's great mystics and what their achievements mean for our salvation. See paragraphs 2 and 3 in particular.

82. T-14.X.10:1, 7.

83. P-2.In.4:3.

84. M-3.1:7.

85. T-17.V.9:4.

86. T-18.III.2:2.

87. T-17.V.9:5.

88. T-14.IX.5:1.

89. T-20.IV.8:3.

90. P-2.II.1:5.

91. M-3.4:6.

Fifteen

1. T-6.III.4:9.

2. T-22.III.6:1.

3. T-22.III.5:3, 7; 6:5-6.

4. T-22.I.2:5.

5. W-pI.30.4:1.

6. Note, for instance, this passage from the Text: "Reason's goal is to make plain, and therefore obvious. You can *see* reason. This is not a play on words, for here is the beginning of a vision that has meaning. Vision is sense, quite literally" (T-22.III.1:3-6). Vision is a different kind of seeing, in which what you see is reason itself. What you are sensing is not forms but sense itself (as when something "makes sense"). With your eyes you can see only meaningless forms. With your mind you can see meaning. And the seeing of meaning, of sense, this passage implies, is the only seeing worth having.

7. W-pI.30.2:1-4.

8. T-22.I.5:4-6.

9. C-5.2:1.

10. W-pI.124.11:2.

11. W-pI.158.7:1-5.

12. T-13.VII.1:1-7. This paragraph, by the way, subtly identifies the real world with the biblical New Jerusalem. The Christian Bible culminates in an ecstatic vision of reconciliation with God in the form of a heavenly city, the New Jerusalem. It is a city in which "night shall be no more; they need no light of lamp or sun, for the Lord God will be their light" (Rev 22:5).

Sound familiar? The passage I just quoted from the Course is also about a city (the scene of stores, streets, buildings, and streetlights is clearly a city scene), and it also speaks of a realm that has no night and needs no artificial light or sunlight, for it too is lit by a constant spiritual light. "It is not lit with artificial light, and night comes not upon it. There is no day that brightens and grows dim....Nothing is there but shines and shines forever."

The point of this parallelism with the New Jerusalem seems to be that the real world, like the New Jerusalem, is the end of the road. Yet unlike the New Jerusalem, the real world is not a visible city that descends from Heaven. It is an invisible realm of God's light that is right here, right now, if we are willing to see past the visible city in front of us.

13. T-30.VII.7:1.

14. W-pI.151.9:6.

15. M-8.6:5.

16. W-pI.151.11:1.

17. T-9.VI.6:2; T-12.VII.4:1-4; T-27.V.3:1-2.

18. T-14.X.7:1.

19. T-14.VI.7:2.

20. W-pII.4.2:7.

21. T-19.IV(A).14:3-4.

22. W-pII.315.1.

23. T-11.VIII.10:1-2.

24. T-30.VII.1:4.

25. T-30.V.1:1.

26. W-pI.25.1:1.

27. W-pI.159.5:3.

28. T-31.VII.3:3.

29. T-31.VIII.8:4.

30. T-17.II.2:6.

31. W-pI.60.3:4-5.

32. T-21.In.2:4.

33. W-pI.189.1:7.

34. T-9.II.5:8-9.

35. It is almost universally believed by Course students that our brothers are our saviors because they push our ego's buttons and so flush our ego to the surface, giving us an opportunity to let it go. And there is a reference to this concept in the Course (see W-pI.192.9:4-6). Yet that is only *one* reference, and there are over a hundred references to the word "savior" in the Course. All of the other references refer to a different notion of "savior." In this notion someone saves us not because his ego attacks us and provokes our ego, but because his holiness extends to us and reveals our holiness. He saves us, in other words, not because there is ego in him, but because there is something of God in him: "Your savior...lives in God, and it is this that makes him savior unto you, and only this" (T-29.II.10:4-5). The three main ways in which our brother acts as our savior, so far as I can see, are these:

1. Our brother has been healed by our forgiveness, and so he sees something holy in us. He therefore returns our gift in the form of gratitude, extending to us his perception that we are holy. This awakens us to our holiness—it saves us.

2. Our brother extends this vision to us first, rather than extending it to us in gratitude for our gift. In the previous point, our saviors are those whom we are helping, who will often be less spiritually advanced than we are. In this point, however, our saviors are those who are helping us, and who will therefore often be *more* spiritually advanced than we are

3. Our brother doesn't consciously

extend to us at all. We see past his exterior to the Christ in him, where we see the Christ in him blessing us and causing us to realize that we are holy. This is the sense of "savior" I am talking about in this chapter.

36. S-3.II.2:3.

37. T-13.VII.6:1.

38. T-18.III.3:4.

39. T-17.II.1:1-6.

40. Robert W. Funk, "The Incredible Creed" *The Fourth R*, vol. 10, no. 3/4 (May-August 1997), p. 19.

41. T-23.IV.8:2-6.

42. T-23.IV.8:7-9.

43. T-17.II.6:1.

44. M-20.5:7.

45. W-pI.75.5:2.

46. T-14.X.1:7.

47. C-3.4:8-10.

48. See, for instance, W-pI.97.3:2.

49. T-24.VI.7:2.

50. T-11.IV.4:5.

51. T-22.IV.1-2.

52. T-6.V(A).6:6-7.

53. T-22.IV.1:8.

54. T-22.IV.2:1.

55. T-1.I.24:1.

56. W-pI.157.5:2.

57. T-1.I.45:2.

58. T-14.IX.7:2-4.

59. M-4.I(A).6:11.

60. W-pI.rV.In.9:6.

61. W-pI.199.6:4.

62. This list is drawn from a line in Lesson 136: "The body's health is fully guaranteed, because it is not limited by time, by weather and fatigue, by food and drink, or any laws you made it serve before" (W-pI.136.18:3).

63. T-12.VII.3:2-3.

64. T-14.IV.6:2.

65. W-pI.109.5:1.

66. T-6.II.10:7.

67. T-8.VI.9:7.

68. T-10.I.2:1.

69. W-pI.157.3:2.

70. T-1.II.2:7.

71. W-pI.157.7:1.

72. Incidentally, I think that all of the levels will fade away together. What I mean is that I don't think we will first completely peel away the face of innocence, then totally undo the victim, then get rid of the ego, etc. The levels are an integrated system that has one cause: the ego. If the ego stays, the entire multileveled system stays. If the ego goes, all of the levels go with it. Therefore, *as* the ego gradually goes, all of the levels gradually disappear with it. The whole structure slowly fades, all of its levels fading simultaneously.

73. T-17.IV.16:9.

74. W-pI.122.1:1-2:1.

75. W-pI.122.3:1-2; 8:4-5.

Sixteen

1. T-8.VI.4:1.

2. T-27.VIII.6:2.

3. T-23.I.11:2-4.

4. T-28.III.7:4.

5. W-pI.101.5:3.

6. M-24.5:7.

7. W-pI.166.6:1.

8. W-pI.166.4:3-4; 5:4-5.

9. T-8.III.5:3.

10. W-pI.182.3:3.

11. T-13.VII.3:1-3.

Notes

12. Ps 13:1, RSV.

13. Ps 89:46, RSV.

14. W-pII.4.5:1-8.

15. T-26.V.3:5.

16. W-pI.153.13:1-3.

17. See W-pII.265.1:1: "I have indeed misunderstood the world, because I laid my sins on it and saw them looking back at me."

18. T-8.VI.4:1-4.

19. W-pI.193.11:2-3.

20. T-1.V.4:1.

21. W-pI.153.14:1.

22. W-pI.153.12:1-2, 5.

23. T-28.IV.9:4.

24. T-9.IV.9:4.

25. T-4.IV.10:2.

26. W-pII.9.1:3.

27. T-1.I.1:1.

28. W-pII.9.2:1.

29. S-3.IV.9:1-3.

30. T-19.IV(C).5:1.

31. W-pI.163.2:2.

32. S-3.II.1:11.

33. See *Absence from Felicity*, by Kenneth Wapnick, p. 398-399. Here Jesus gives personal guidance to Helen Schucman about his resurrection. In essence, he says that the real resurrection was the raising of the mind from the tomb of the body. Therefore, the real resurrection was signified by getting the body out of the way ("and that is what 'rolling the stone away' means")—by the *disappearance* of his body, not by its *reappearance*.

34. T-26.IX.3:1.

35. W-pII.2.4:4-5.

36. W-pI.109.6:1.

37. M-14.5:1-8.

38. W-pII.9.3:1.

39. T-2.VIII.3:3.

40. W-pII.10.3:1.

41. See T-6.V(C).1:4.

42. T-2.VIII.4:5.

43. T-5.V.2:2.

44. T-2.VIII.2:5.

45. T-2.VIII.2:8.

46. T-17.II.5:2-3.

47. W-pI.rV.In.7:5.

48. T-26.III.4:3.

49. T-18.VIII.13:1.

50. W-pI.194.1:3.

51. S-1.V.4:3-5.

52. M-19.2:5-7.

53. T-5.I.7:6.

54. T-6.V(B).9:2.

55. W-pI.93.1:3.

56. M-25.1:5.

57. W-pI.110.9:4.

58. W-187.10:2.

59. M-28.4:1.

60. M-28.6:9.

61. T-13.VIII.3:2.

62. T-17.II.4:4-5.

63. W-pI.168.3:2-6.

64. This is a reference to the memory of God (as was the line from the previous passage about the restoration of "all memories the sleeping mind forgot"), a familiar concept to most Course students. The remembering of God is what occurs in God's final step. When we remember something it comes back into awareness from a submerged place in our minds. When we remember God He comes back into full awareness from the submerged depths of our minds. In this sense, to remember God is not to think about Him. It is to awaken to total union with Him beyond time and space.

65. C-4.7:2-4, 7.

66. T-17.II.4:1.

67. T-13.I.3:5.

68. M-14.2:11-12.

69. W-pI.183.11:1-3.

70. W-pI.182.5:4.

71. T-26.V.5:4.

72. T-24.II.4:5.

Conclusion

1. T-8.VII.5:1.

2. W-pI.186.10:4.

3. T-11.V.9:1.

4. P-2.In.3:6.

5. T-9.VII.4:5-6.

6. The actual passage, which comes from the Urtext, the original typescript of the Course, reads this way: "After all, Lucifer fell, but he was still an angel. He is thus the symbol for man. Atonement is the knowledge that the belief that angels can fall is false."

7. M-13.4:4.

8. T-12.III.4:1.

9. T-13.X.11:1.

10. T-12.V.9:1.

11. T-12.V.8:6.

12. S-1.I.2:4.

13. T-13.III.12:1.

14. M-27.1.

15. This quote (along with the quote in the next paragraph) is from the Urtext, the original typescript of the Course.

Index

405

www.circlepublishing.org

Circle Publishing is a division of the
Circle of Atonement Teaching and Healing Center.

The Circle of Atonement offers a wide range of teaching materials
designed to help the student walk the transformative path of
A Course in Miracles. It offers a vision of the Course that is both
faithful to it and practical for the student. Visit the Circle's website
at www.circleofa.org for a wealth of free materials, including
articles by Robert Perry, Daily Lesson Commentaries by Allen
Watson, and Course Q&A's by Greg Mackie. You may also sign
up to receive the Circle's free e-newsletter, *A Better Way*, or to
receive Allen's Lesson Commentaries or Robert's weekly class
notes by e-mail.

Contact:
The Circle of Atonement
P.O. Box 4238
West Sedona, AZ 86340
Phone: (928) 282 0790
E-mail: info@circleofa.org
www.circleofa.org

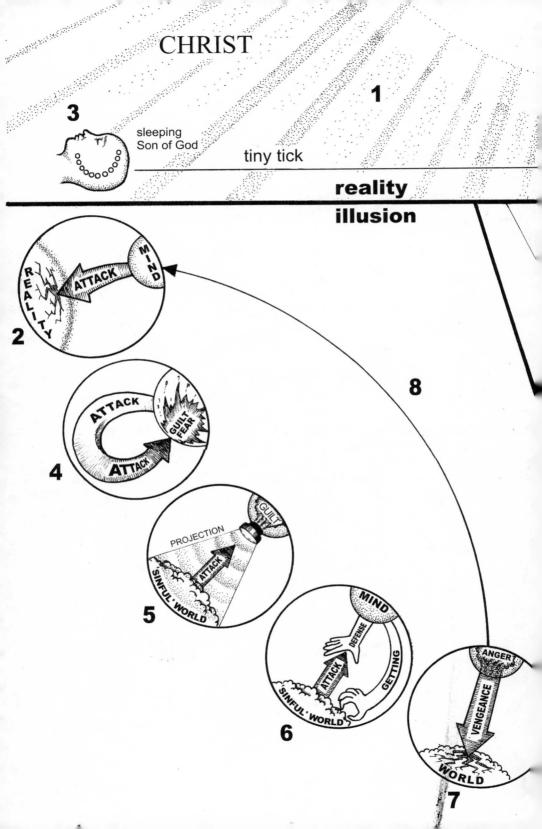